Europe, 1890–1945

Forthcoming from Oxford University Press

The Ancient Mediterranean World
Robin W. Winks and Susan Mattern-Parks

Medieval Europe and the World: From Late Antiquity to
Modernity, 400–1500
Robin W. Winks and Teofilo Ruiz

Europe in a Wider World, 1350–1650
Robin W. Winks and Lee Palmer Wandel

Europe, 1648–1815: From the Old Regime to the Age of
Revolution
Robin W. Winks and Thomas Kaiser

Europe, 1815–1914
Robin W. Winks and Joan Neuberger

Europe, 1945 to the Present: A Global Perspective
Robin W. Winks and John E. Talbott

Europe
1890–1945
Crisis and Conflict

Robin W. Winks
Yale University

R. J. Q. Adams
Texas A&M University

New York   Oxford
OXFORD UNIVERSITY PRESS
2003

Oxford University Press

Oxford   New York
Auckland   Bangkok   Buenos Aires   Cape Town   Chennai
Dar es Salaam   Delhi   Hong Kong   Istanbul   Karachi   Kolkata
Kuala Lumpur   Madrid   Melbourne   Mexico City   Mumbai
Nairobi   São Paulo   Shanghai   Taipei   Tokyo   Toronto

Published by Oxford University Press, Inc.
198 Madison Avenue, New York, New York, 10016
http://www.oup-usa.org

Oxford is a registered trademark of Oxford University Press

Library of Congress Cataloging-in-Publication Data
Winks, Robin W.
    Europe, 1890–1945 : crisis and conflict/Robin W. Winks, R. J. Q. Adams.
    p. cm.
    Includes bibliographical references.
    ISBN 978-0-19-515449-8 —ISBN 978-0-19-515450-4 (pbk.)
    1. Europe—History—1870–1918. 2. Europe—History—1918–1945. 3.
Europe—Intellectual life—19th century. 4. Europe—Intellectual life—20th century. 5.
World War, 1914–1918. 6. World War, 1939–1945. I. Adams, R. J. Q. (Ralph James Q.),
1943–   II. Title.

D395 .W48 2003
940.2—dc21   2002074865

Contents

Maps

Preface

The Value of History

History is a series of arguments to be debated, not a body of data to be recorded or a set of facts to be memorized. Thus controversy in historical interpretation—over what an event actually means, over what really happened at an occurrence called "an event," over how best to generalize about the event—is at the heart of its value. Of course history teaches us about ourselves. Of course it teaches us to understand and to entertain a proper respect for our collective past. Of course it transmits to us specific skills—how to ask questions; how to seek out answers; how to think logically, cogently, lucidly, purposefully. Of course it is, or ought to be, a pleasure. But we also discover something fundamental about a people in what they choose to argue over in their past. When a society suppresses portions of its past record, that society (or its leadership) tells us something about itself. When a society seeks to alter how the record is presented, well-proven facts notwithstanding, we learn how history can be distorted to political ends.

Who controls history, and how it is written, controls the past, and who controls the past controls the present. Those who would close off historical controversy with the argument either that we know all that we need to know about a subject, or that what we know is so irrefutably correct that anyone who attacks the conventional wisdom about the subject must have destructive purposes in mind, are in the end intent upon destroying the very value of history itself—that value being that history teaches us to argue productively with each other.

Obviously, then, history is a social necessity. It gives us our identity. It helps us to find our bearings in an ever more complex present, providing us with a navigator's chart by which we may to some degree orient ourselves. When we ask who we are, and how it is that we are so, we learn skepticism and acquire the beginnings of critical judgment. Along with a sense of narrative, history also provides us with tools for explanation and analysis. It helps us to find the particular example, to see the uniqueness in a past age or past event, while also helping us to see how the particular and the unique contribute to the general. History thus shows us humanity at work and play, in society, changing through time. By letting us experience other lifestyles, history shows us the values of both subjectivity and objectivity—those twin conditions of our individual view of the world in which we live, conditions between which we constantly, and usually almost without knowing it, move.

Thus, history is both a form of truth and a matter of opinion, and the close study of history should help us to distinguish between the two. It is important to make such distinctions, for as Sir Walter Raleigh wrote, "it is not truth but opinion that can travel the world without a passport." Far too often what we read, see, hear, and believe to be the truth—in our newspapers, on our television sets, from our friends—is opinion, not fact.

History is an activity. That activity asks specific questions as a means of arriving at general questions. A textbook such as this is concerned overwhelmingly with general questions, even though at times it must ask specific questions or present specific facts as a means of stalking the general. The great philosopher Karl Jaspers once remarked, "Who I am and where I belong, I first learned to know from the mirror of history." It is this mirror that any honest book must reflect.

To speak of "civilization" (of which this book is a history) is at once to plunge into controversy, so that our very first words illustrate why some people are so fearful of the study of history. To speak of "Western civilization" is even more restrictive, too limited in the eyes of some historians. Yet if we are to understand history as a process, we must approach it through a sense of place: our continuity, our standards, our process. Still, we must recognize an inherent bias in such a term as "Western civilization," indeed, two inherent biases: first, that we know what it means to be "civilized" and have attained that stature; and second, that the West as a whole is a single unitary civilization. This second bias is made plain when we recognize that most scholars and virtually all college courses refer not to "Eastern civilization" but to "the civilizations of the East"—a terminology that suggests that while the West is a unity, the East is not. These are conventional phrases, buried in Western perception of reality, just as our common geographical references show a Western bias. The Near East or the Far East are, after all, "near" or "far" only in reference to a geographical location focused on western Europe. The Japanese do not refer to London as being in the far West, or Los Angeles as being in the far East, although both references would be correct, if they saw the world as though they stood at its center. Although this text will accept these conventional phrases, precisely because they are traditionally embedded in our Western languages, one of the uses of history—and of the writing of a book such as this one—is to alert us to the biases buried in our language, even when necessity requires that we continue to use its conventional forms of shorthand.

But if we are to speak of civilization, we must have, at the outset, some definition of what we mean by "being civilized." Hundreds of books have been written on this subject. The average person often means only that others, the "noncivilized," speak a different language and practice alien customs. The Chinese customarily referred to all foreigners as barbarians, and the ancient Greeks spoke of those who could not communicate in Greek as *bar-bar*—those who do not speak our tongue. Yet today the ability to communicate in more than one language is one hallmark of a "civilized" person. Thus definitions of civilization, at least as used by those who think little about the meaning of their words, obviously change.

For our purposes, however, we must have a somewhat more exacting definition of the term, since it guides and shapes any book that attempts to cover the entire sweep of Western history. Anthropologists, sociologists, historians, and others may reasonably differ as to whether, for example, there is a separate American civilization that stands apart from, say, a British or Italian civilization, or whether these civilizations are simply particular variants on one larger entity, with only that larger entity—the West—entitled to be called "a civilization." Such an argument is of no major importance here, although it is instructive that it should occur. Rather, what is needed is a definition sufficiently clear to be used throughout the narrative and analysis to follow. This working definition, therefore, will hold that "civilization" involves the presence of several (although not necessarily all) of the following conditions within a society or group of interdependent societies:

1. There will be some form of government by which people administer to their political needs and responsibilities.
2. There will be some development of urban society, that is, of city life, so that the culture is not nomadic, dispersed, and thus unable to leave significant and surviving physical remnants of its presence.
3. Human beings will have become toolmakers, able through the use of metals to transform, however modestly, their physical environment, and thus their social and economic environment as well.
4. Some degree of specialization of function will have begun, usually at the workplace, so that pride, place, and purpose work together as cohesive elements in the society.
5. Social classes will have emerged, whether antagonistic to or sustaining of one another.
6. A form of literacy will have developed, so that group may communicate with group, and more important, generation with generation in writing.
7. There will be a concept of leisure time—that life is not solely for the workplace, or for the assigned class function or specialization—so that, for example, art may develop beyond (although not excluding) mere decoration and sports beyond mere competition.
8. There will be a concept of a higher being, although not necessarily through organized religion, by which a people may take themselves outside themselves to explain events and find purpose.
9. There will be a concept of time, by which the society links itself to a past and to the presumption of a future.
10. There will have developed a faculty for criticism. This faculty need not be the rationalism of the West, or intuition, or any specific religious or political mechanism, but it must exist, so that the society may contemplate change from within, rather than awaiting attack (and possible destruction) from without.

A common Western bias is to measure "progress" through technological change and to suggest that societies that show (at least until quite recently in historical time) little dramatic technological change are not civilized. In truth, neither a written record nor dramatic technological changes are essential to being civilized, although both are no doubt present in societies we would call civilized. Perhaps, as we study history, we ought to remember all three of the elements inherent in historical action as recorded by the English critic John Ruskin, "Great nations write their autobiographies in three manuscripts, the book of their deeds, the book of their words, and the book of their art."

The issue here is not whether we "learn from the past." Most often we do not, at least at the simple-minded level; we do not, as a nation, decide upon a course of action in diplomacy, for example, simply because a somewhat similar course in the past worked. We are wise enough to know that circumstances alter cases and that new knowledge brings new duties. Of course individuals "learn from the past"; the victim of a mugging takes precautions in the future. To dignify such an experience as "a lesson of history," however, is to turn mere individual growth from child into adult into history when, at most, such growth is a personal experience in biography.

We also sometimes learn the "wrong lessons" from history. Virtually anyone who wishes to argue passionately for a specific course of future action can find a lesson from the past that will convince the gullible that history repeats itself and therefore that the past is a map to the future. No serious historian argues this, however. General patterns may, and sometimes do, repeat themselves, but specific chains of events do not. Unlike those subjects that operate at the very highest level of generalization (political science, theology, science), history simply does not believe in ironclad laws. But history is not solely a series of unrelated events. There are general patterns, clusters of causes, intermediate levels of generalization that prove true. Thus, history works at a level uncomfortable to many: above the specific, below the absolute.

If complex problems never present themselves twice in the same or even in recognizably similar form—if, to borrow a frequent image from the military world, generals always prepare for the last war instead of the next one—then does the study of history offer society any help in solving its problems? The answer surely is yes—but only in a limited way. History offers a rich collection of clinical reports on human behavior in various situations—individual and collective, political, economic, military, social, cultural—that tell us in detail how the human race has conducted its affairs and that suggest ways of handling similar problems in the present. President Harry S. Truman's secretary of state, a former chief of staff, General George Marshall, once remarked that nobody could think about the problems of the 1950s who had not reflected upon the fall of Athens in the fifth century B.C. He was referring to the extraordinary history of the war between Athens and Sparta written just after it was over by Thucydides, an Athenian who fought in the war. There were no nuclear weapons, no telecommunications, no guns or gunpowder in the fifth century B.C., and the logistics of war were altogether primitive; yet twenty-three hundred years later one of the most distinguished leaders of American military and political affairs found Thucydides indispensable to his thinking.

History, then, can only approximate the range of human behavior, with some indication of its extremes and averages. It can, although not perfectly, show how and within what limits human behavior changes. This last point is especially important for the social scientist, the economist, the sociologist, the executive, the journalist, or the diplomat. History provides materials that even an inspiring leader—a prophet, a reformer, a politician—would do well to master before seeking to lead us into new ways. For it can tell us something about what human material can and cannot stand, just as science and technology can tell engineers what stresses metals can tolerate. History can provide an awareness of the depth of time and space that should check the optimism and the overconfidence of the reformer. For example, we may wish to protect the environment in which we live—to eliminate acid rain, to cleanse our rivers, to protect our wildlife, to preserve our majestic natural scenery. History may show us that most peoples have failed to do so, and it may provide us with some guidance on how to avoid the mistakes of the past. But history will also show that there are substantial differences of public and private opinion over how best to protect our environment, that there are many people who do not believe such protection is necessary, or that there are people who accept the need for protection but are equally convinced that lower levels of protection must be traded off for higher levels of productivity from our natural resources. History can provide the setting by which we may understand differing opinions, but recourse to history will not get the legislation passed, make the angry happy, make the future clean and safe. History will not define river pollution, although it can provide us with statistics from the past for comparative measurement. The definition will arise from the politics of today and our judgements about tomorrow. History is for the long and at times for the intermediate run, but seldom for the short run.

So, if we are willing to accept a "relevance" that is more difficult to see at first than the immediate applicability of science and more remote than direct action, we will have to admit that history is "relevant." It may not actually build the highway or clear the slum, but it can give enormous help to those who wish to do so. And failure to take it into account may lead to failure in the sphere of action.

But history is also fun, at least for those who enjoy giving their curiosity free reign. Whether it is historical gossip we prefer (how many lovers did Catherine the Great of Russia actually take in a given year, and how much political influence did their activity in the imperial bedroom give them?), the details of historical investigation (how does it happen that the actual treasures found in a buried Viking ship correspond to those described in an Anglo-Saxon poetic account of a ship-burial?), more complex questions of cause-and-effect (how influential have the writings of revolutionary intellectuals been upon the course of actual revolutions?), the relationships between politics and economics (how far does the rise and decline of Spanish power in modern times depend upon the supply of gold and silver from New World colonies?), or cultural problems (why did western Europe choose to revive classical Greek and Roman art and literature instead of turning to some altogether new experiment?), those who enjoy history will read almost greedily to discover what they want to know. Having discovered it, they may want to know how we know what we have learned, and may want to turn to those sources closest in time to the persons and questions concerned—to the original words of the participants. To read about Socrates, Columbus, or Churchill is fun; to read their own words, to visit with them as it were, is even more so. To see them in context is important; to see how we have taken their thoughts and woven them to purposes of our own is at least equally important. Readers will find the path across the mine-studded fields of history helped just a little by extracts from these voices—voices of the past but also of the present. They can also be helped by chronologies, bibliographies, pictures, maps—devices through which historians share their sense of fun and immediacy with a reader.

In the end, to know the past is to know ourselves—not entirely, not enough, but a little better. History can help us to achieve some grace and elegance of action, some cogency and completion of thought, some harmony and tolerance in human relationships. Most of all, history can give us a sense of excitement, a personal zest for watching and perhaps participating in the events around us that will, one day, be history too.

History is a narrative, a story; history is concerned foremost with major themes, even as it recognizes the significance of many fascinating digressions. Because history is largely about how and why people behave as they do, it is also about patterns of thought and belief. Ultimately, history is about what people believe to be true. To this extent, virtually all history is intellectual history, for the perceived meaning of a specific treaty, battle, or scientific discovery lies in what those involved in it and those who came after thought was most significant about it. History makes it clear that we may die, as we may live, as a result of what someone believed to be quite true in the relatively remote past.

We cannot each be our own historian. In everyday life we may reconstruct our personal past, acting as detectives for our motivations and attitudes. But formal history is a much more rigorous study. History may give us some very small capacity to predict the future. More certainly, it should help us arrange the causes for given events into meaningful patterns. History also should help us to be tolerant of the historical views of others, even as it helps to shape our own convictions. History must help us sort out the important from the less important, the relevant from the irrelevant, so that we do not fall prey to those who propose simple-minded solutions to vastly complex human problems. We must not yield to the temptation to blame one group or individual for our problems, and yet we must not fail to defend our convictions with vigor.

To recognize, indeed to celebrate, the value of all civilizations is essential to the civilized life itself. To understand that we see all civilizations through the prism of our specific historical past—for which we feel affection, in which we may feel comfortable and secure, and by which we interpret all else that we encounter—is simply to recognize that we too are the products of history. That is why we must study history and ask our own questions in our own way. For if we ask no questions of our past, there may be no questions to ask of our future.

Acknowledgments

The authors are pleased to record their thanks for the helpful advice during the writing of this book of Professor William C. Lubenow, Richard Stockton College; and Professor Sara Alpern, Professor Arnold P. Krammer, and Professor Roger R. Reese, all of Texas A&M University. For their careful reading and helpful critiques of the manuscript we are pleased to record our gratitude to Professor Thomas Kennedy, University of Arkansas; Professor Peter Fritzche, University of Illinois at Urbana-Champaign, and Professor Guillaume de Syon, Albright College. Unremarkable though it is to say so, it is true all the same that we are responsible for any errors of fact or interpretation.

Robin W. Winks
Yale University

R. J. Q. Adams
Texas A&M Universtiy

ONE

The New Age

∞

At least since the early church divided the notation of time based on what it calculated to be the birth of Jesus, the turn of each century has been an event of great moment. The advent of the twentieth century was certainly treated in just that fashion. The old world was passing away, and the twentieth century—with what were certain to be marvelous wonders—had arrived. The hoopla that accompanied that earlier turn of a calendar page cannot, perhaps, have equaled the celebration of the turn of the millennium on December 31, 1999. Yet it was certainly the best that the age could muster. For some at the time, the optimists, it was reasonable to look with satisfaction at a present that was a gigantic improvement on a past blighted by slavery, plague, and ignorance and a future that held the promise of conquering mankind's other curses of disease, hunger, and war. For others, pessimists all, the present was blighted by the slow but irreversible creep toward egalitarianism— a decline in the rule by "men of quality," and to them, the growth of participatory government was responsible. The civilized world was deviled by threats of international conflict, materialism, and agnosticism, and the future pointed to the ultimate victory of the wrong values, embodied by the wrong peoples.

Those of strong conviction who envisioned the best and others who feared the worst (as well as many who gave it little thought) could agree on one notion. They anticipated a new century that was to be like no other before it. In this they were both absolutely correct.

European Peoples

It surprises no one now living that the twentieth century was an age of change, and what has long been commonly called the West was the engine of that transformation. When people used this term they meant Europe, that is, Great Britain, France, the Low Countries, Italy, the Iberian Peninsula, Germany, Switzerland, and Scandinavia. Also included were the sprawling empires of Austria-Hungary and Russia, the largest nation in the world (as much Asian as European), and frequently those extensions of European culture in North America, Australia, and New Zealand.

Remarkable growth of population over the previous two centuries ensured that the European continent accounted for a quarter of the world's people on the eve of World War I. Between 1860 and 1910, the population of Great Britain (including Ireland, then a part of the United Kingdom) had grown from about 29 million to 45 million; Austria-Hungary from 33 to 51 million; Germany from 36 to 65 million. There are no comparable reliable figures for Russia, although its population in 1900 exceeded 125 million, and there seems little doubt that its growth rate in this period was at least comparable. Only France among the Great Powers lagged behind, with growth from 37 to 39 million. Growth in the United States in the period was nothing less than breathtaking, with the population increasing from 31 to 92 million.

The reasons were several: The birth rate had, with few exceptions, been steady and upward, and western migration across the continent had gathered more people in the West. Modern health practices had reduced the mortality rate through advanced medical practice and improved hygiene—people enjoyed both a better chance of surviving infancy and of living longer. The introduction of antisepsis and an increased understanding of germ-borne disease had led to broad and successful attacks on the infectious illnesses that plagued mankind. Similarly, improvements in agricultural practice led to increased food production and a healthier diet. As the actuarial tables began to predict longer life, so did they indicate that increasingly, Europe was becoming urbanized.

In 1800 only one European city, London, had a population of more than 1 million. A century later there were five more—Paris, Vienna, Berlin, Moscow, and St. Petersburg—and by mid-century another five. As significant as that was the fact that while in Europe in 1800 there were twenty-two cities whose populations exceeded 100,000, a century later there were eighty—and the trend showed no signs of abating. This growth, of course, reflected the aforementioned improvements in health and hygiene, both more evident in urban environments than in the countryside—after all, the town was where the better-trained doctors and the better-equipped hospitals usually were. Beginning in the mid-nineteenth century, movements first in Britain and Germany, and later in the century elsewhere, called for national and local government to take up the cause of public health in crowded urban environments and led to the creation of local health authorities to regulate the purity of water, food, and pharmaceuticals and to set standards for more sanitary housing. By the end of the century, social reformers in Britain had driven the state to accept responsibility for the provision of publicly built housing for the urban poor. Once begun, this trend spread among the nations and has not slackened.

More germane to the question of the stunning increase of the urban population, of course, was the trend toward migration within Europe, as thousands and then millions abandoned the farm for the city. The city offered the economic opportunity; the charms of variety, culture, and entertainment; and the anonymity that the countryside could not. Above all it seemed to hold out a possibility of freedom from the ancient tyranny of class, clan, and poverty that governed peasant existence. For many it offered a new start because lives on the farm either had become unliveable or were simply too limited for the desperate, the adventurous, or the ambitious. For some city life led to loneliness, alienation, poverty, and exploitation—to slums and to wage slavery—while for others it meant opportunity, achievement, and reward. One could not know which until one tried.

Although no one could have known it at the time, this trend of rapid population growth in the West was to be reversed by the eve of World War I, not simply because of age-old interventions of plague, famine, or war, but in large part through choice: Family size in the increasingly prosperous West began to grow smaller. Contraceptive devices such as the condom and the diaphragm would become both more effective and more widely available and, despite disapproval by various moral authorities and many years of convention, much more widely used. For those who could not or would not afford such luxuries, there had always been *coitus interruptus*, delayed marriage, or the desperate and dangerous step of abortion—severely punishable under law, although far from unknown, throughout the West for centuries.

The devastating effects of repeated childbirth on the health of women motivated several pioneers to found the modern birth control movement. What was almost certainly the first medical practice devoted to women's health and to birth control was begun in Amsterdam in the 1880s by Holland's first female physician, Aletta Jacobs Gerritson (1854–1929), a champion also both of social reform and international pacifism. The cause was to be furthered even more by the organizing efforts of indefatigable campaigners for contraception such as the socialist visionary Annie Besant (1847–1933) in Britain and, in the United States, Margaret Sanger (1879–1966)—the founder of what became the modern Planned Parenthood organization.

The impact of this demographic change is clearly demonstrated in the birth rates of European nations. To illustrate, Britain recorded 33.4 births per 1,000 population in 1850; by 1900 the number had declined to 28.7, and by 1914 to 26.1; by 1930 it was 19.6. Germany's statistics are similar: 38.5 in 1870, 35.6 in 1900, 26.8 in 1914, and 17.6 in 1930. France recorded a birth rate of 26.8 in 1850, 21.3 in 1900, 18.1 in 1914, and 18.0 in 1930. Italy's birth rate in 1862 (no figures are available for 1850) was 39.4, 33.0 in 1900, 31.0 in 1914, and 26.7 in 1930. Other European nations generally followed this trend.

For many, however, the limitation of family size was not only an issue of the health of women, and this helps to explain its impact across class and national lines: The combination of capitalism, general prosperity, and the technical wonders of industrialism and mass production had made possible a more prosperous life for many. Ambitions for a more comfortable existence for men and women had a greater chance of coming true in smaller families with fewer mouths to feed. It is also true that as agriculture became more mechanized in the West, the need for labor on the family farm decreased. Hence, in the eyes of many Westerners, what had for centuries been a practical consideration on the farm—large family size—as well as a sign of prosperity, naturalness, and even godliness, came, as the twentieth century continued, to be the exception rather than the rule.

Another reason for the relative stabilization of populations in Europe was that a great period of transnational migration of peoples, worthy of comparison with those of the Middle Ages, was at its peak in these years. By 1880, about a half million emigrants per year were leaving Europe, mainly for the United States and Canada, but also for Latin America, the Antipodes, and elsewhere. Thirty years later, this number had nearly tripled. Also, over time, the kinds of people making such journeys changed. The majority in the earlier period had largely been from the British Isles or the more westerly parts of Europe. By the latter nineteenth century the combination of cheaper transatlantic fares, aggressive recruitment by recipient nations, and the lure of a better future were drawing millions of Italians, Russians, Poles, Croats, Czechs, and Jews to the New World in search of economic opportunity, but also freedom from oppressive regimes and from religious, cultural, ethnic, and racial discrimination. Migrants learned quickly that the streets they found were not paved with gold, and many discovered in their new lands distrust and suspicion of their foreignness. They did not, however, find forced conscription, a landed aristocracy, or state religions. Above all, they found no pogroms. More than 60 million people left Europe in the century that preceded 1930, and several millions found disappointment and returned to the old country. Most, however, remained, and many—so very many—set about enriching their new homelands.

The Creative Passion

Painting

It is no exaggeration to suggest that at the turn of the twentieth century most men and women in the West continued to view and experience their world much as their grandparents had done. In these years, however, assumptions and values of all kinds were to be subjected to challenges of tremendous vitality and force, and alternatives were championed with equal energy. This phenomenon came to be called *modernism,* and while the term eventually came to be applied to everything from morals and fashion to theology, in no sphere was this more stunningly so than in the arts. A powerful and entrenched establishment ruled the "official" world of the arts—it decreed that pictures and statues of people and things must look like people and things, that is, as people and things were expected to look by the observer. They should be beautiful in that they gave pleasure to the largest number of viewers and that they followed established patterns of arrangement, perspective, color, and the like. A generation earlier, the French impressionists had abandoned the studio to go out and paint not merely to produce images of what *was*, in some conventional sense, but rather to paint the world around them as they themselves chose to see it. What they saw was the effect—the impression—of light on their subjects. The impressionists, however, remained more or less realist painters, and their pictures remained recognizable as a kind of objective reality.

By the end of the nineteenth century a group came after them called simply post-impressionists, and they went further. Arguing that the development of photography rendered irrelevant the ancient duty of the artist to record events, they painted their own subjective realities: what they, rather than others, saw in the nature of their subjects. Paul Cézanne (1839–1906) abandoned the prettiness of impressionism and sought to reveal in portraits and still-lifes the geometric shapes that lay behind all things: "to make Impressionism something solid and durable." To reveal that art must be based upon an identifiable system and seek order and permanence, the short-lived Georges Seurrat (1859–1899) painted the Paris he knew by painstakingly covering his huge canvases with innumerable tiny dots of color. Others such as the tragic Dutchman Vincent van Gogh (1853–1890) and his friend Paul Gauguin (1848–1903) sought other directions and painted as much from internal visions as from what they encountered in life. Their work abandoned all of the disciplines of established art, and they shared a sense that their "civilized" culture was spiritually damaged: van Gogh's pictures often depicted the darkness and decadence he saw around him; Gauguin finally abandoned "civilization" altogether to live on the Pacific island of Tahiti in order to paint in an increasingly primitive style the people and land he thought unspoiled and thus spiritually purer and better than the Europe he had fled.

Another Frenchman, Henri Matisse (1869–1954), led a group that went further still. Called by disapproving critics *fauves*, or wild beasts, Matisse and his colleagues rejected any attempt to create a sense of three-dimensional representation. To express what they saw, the fauves reduced their subjects to what were for them only the necessary elements. They splashed their canvases with bright colors and sought to reveal their sense of what they saw without regard for the accepted rules of composition or perspective.

A generation younger than most of these artists was a Spaniard whose impact on the world of art surpassed theirs: Pablo Picasso (1881–1973). Working and studying as a young man in Paris, the center of the art world, Picasso experimented with various techniques and styles and first drew attention to himself with his development of cubism, a kind of development of Cezanne's desire to reduce the visual image to its geometric basics. His 1907 masterpiece *Les Demoiselles d'Avignon* depicted five female nudes with shockingly distorted faces and bodies reduced to angular abstractions—a critic of the time suggested the canvas "resembled a field of broken glass." Yet even those who hated it sensed its power. Other similar paintings followed, and Picasso's long development as the dominant painter of his century was launched.

The art world was soon to discover that even cubism was not the furthest extent to which the new modernism could go. The fauves and Picasso and those influenced by them offered their own intensely internalized views of reality, but painters like Vassily Kandinsky (1866–1944), a Russian working in Germany as part of a group calling themselves the Blue Horsemen (*Der Blaue Reiter*), struck off in yet another direction with the founding of abstract expressionism. This style entirely abandoned representation and sought to reveal spiritual truths in the bright colors of the Fauves but without reference to any

Madame Matisse *(1905) by Henri Matisse. This portrait conveys the force and perplexity of the Fauvist school of painters, led by Matisse. Primitive and uncompromising by the established rules of portraiture of the time, the picture seeks to show what the husband saw in his wife's face, not what the uncareful onlooker or the camera might have seen. To many established authorities it was crude, even ugly; to the painter and his admirers it was true to the vision of the artist: what "was" rather than what merely "seemed."   (The Barnes Foundation, Merion, Pennsylvania, USA/Bridgeman Art Library: © 2003 Succession H. Matisse, Paris/Artists Rights Society (ARS), New York.)*

recognizable shapes of the evident world. When the great academies of art in the various European capitals rejected such works year after year, two significant exhibitions—the first in London in December 1910 organized by the critic and painter Roger Fry (1866–1934), and another in 1913 at the 69th Regiment Armory in New York—brought enormous attention to these new movements in painting. Not surprisingly, the established critics almost uniformly condemned the pictures and styles. Regardless of the disapproval of the critics and virtually the entire international art establishment, it could not be denied that by the time of World War I painting had been changed forever.

Architecture

Architecture in the West witnessed similar attacks on the old forms. In the United States, Louis Sullivan (1856–1924) perfected the characteristic shape of the modern skyscraper, while Frank Lloyd Wright (1867–1959) refined his own vision by building horizontal and angular prairie houses for wealthy clients and later larger structures that reflected his almost cubist style. After World War I, Wright's influence could be seen in the development of the "International Style" of huge spare block buildings, dedicated to the theme of "form follows function." The *Bauhaus* art school and workshops at Dessau, designed by the German Walter Gropius (1883–1969), were the early emblem of the movement. This trend was taken further by the Swiss-born Le Corbusier (Charles Édouard Jeanneret, 1887–1965), whose geometrically severe glass and steel skyscrapers would become models for urban commercial architecture for the remainder of the century. At about the same time, the Spaniard Antonio Gaudi (1852–1926) designed huge apartment blocks and churches in a completely opposite style, creating structures that looked as though they were made not of stone but of pastry dough. All of these buildings—so very different from one another   were attempts by their designers to accomplish what the fauves or cubists strove for in painting: to free themselves from the rules of the past and create a purer form and an improved reality. As the painters sought to portray what people "were," rather than simply what they appeared to be to the casual observer, the architects sought to design not merely buildings that sheltered people but environments that interacted with them. To their critics, such structures defied form and therefore were unworthy and unlovely; but by mid-century, it became clear that these architects had created alternative schools of design that rivaled the old standards. Great commercial and public buildings no longer necessarily resembled Greek temples or English manor houses.

Music

Music, too, became a battleground of the new and the old. At the turn of the century the reigning genius of a new musical form was the Frenchman Claude Debussy (1862–1918), who sought goals in music similar to those of impressionist painters a generation earlier. He composed works, particularly for the piano, meant to capture in sound impressions of the world he witnessed, and he did so with an originality and brilliance that broke new ground. His sensuous *Afternoon of a Faun* (1892) sought beauty without regard for the old rules of composition and became a kind of declaration of the founding of modern music and a challenge to other composers.

A thoroughly different strain of new music was pioneered by the Russian Igor Stravinsky (1882–1971), who was already well known as a composer of

Gropius House, Lincoln, Massachusetts, 1937. Walter Gropius was a leader of the architectural movement away from decoration and classicism and toward a spare functionalism that reflected the industrial age. Driven from Germany by the Nazis, who declared his ideas "decadent," Gropius came to America and designed this house while teaching at Harvard University. (Library of Congress)

ballet music when he debuted a cycle of works based upon themes derived from folk tales. *The Firebird* (1910) and more importantly *The Rites of Spring* (1913) shocked and even outraged the public—the first night's performance of the latter erupted in a near riot among an audience who shouted down his discordant composition and shrieked their disapproval of the crude costumes and the awkward and primitive movements of the dancers. Such excess, it should be noted, generated a climate of intense curiosity that kept patrons—disapproving or not—coming to see the program and made it something of a success.

Perhaps the most original approach among these composers was taken by Arnold Schönberg (1874–1951), a Viennese who had earned his living as a young man composing and conducting cabaret music. Dissatisfied with the formal constraints of serious music, Schönberg experimented with many alternatives and finally came to reject traditional tonality itself—which shocked the ear accustomed to established forms. The opening night performance of his *First Chamber Symphony* (1907) exploded in riot when furious members of the audience rushed the stage and others hurled insults at the orchestra and composer/conductor. Be that as it may, it is undeniably true that Schönberg, who in later years would immigrate to America to become an influential teacher, was founding a school of composition that later in the century would become synonymous in the popular mind with the term "modern" music.

Literature

In these first years of the new century the reaction among writers against the dominant schools of realism and naturalism, against clarity and precision, was overpowering. The movement begun in France late in the nineteenth century called *symbolism* and led by the poet Stéphane Mallarmé (1842–1898) was carried on by the master's followers well into the twentieth century. The symbolists ignored the extant rules of poetry—for them there was no precise term, no particular best word for any particular thing. Words existed for experiment, for combination and division and connection and separation. In the spirit of the expressionist painters, the object of these writers was not the edification of the reader but the satisfaction of the poet through the sheer joy of expression. The result could be great beauty, but there was almost always obfuscation and obscurity. Any movement predicated on such values was bound to attract writers, and it spread throughout Europe. Symbolism produced its geniuses—the poets Stefan George (1868–1933) in Germany or Rainer Maria Rilke (1875–1926) in Austria, and in Ireland William Butler Yeats (1865–1939) among them—but in its day it earned only the disapproval of critics and expressions of confusion from an uncomprehending reading public.

A similar trend is apparent in prose writing, with the movement away from the starkness of Zola or Tolstoy and the naturalists who dominated the last generation of the previous century. Young novelists like the Irishman James Joyce (1882–1941) and the Briton Virginia Woolf (1882–1941) began to experiment with what came to be called stream-of-consciousness writing, which concentrated on the inner life of characters rather than on traditional plot, story, and character development. These writers would find their voices only in the years after World War I, but their development—and much of the direction of the modern novel—was being laid in these decades.

Certainly there were alternatives, and some quite comprehensible to the reader: John Galsworthy (1867–1933) in Britain brilliantly continued the tradition of the novel of social criticism with *A Man of Property* (1906), the first novel of several in an extended tale of a prosperous English family, which eventually would carry the saga of the Forsyte clan through three generations. Without grandiloquence or vulgar moralizing, Galsworthy questioned the comfortable Victorian values of the British middle classes. In Germany, Thomas Mann (1875–1955) also established a brilliant reputation early with the publication at twenty-five of *Buddenbrooks*, the first of many works that would examine the roles and interaction in Germany of materialism, family, society and the burdens of the artist. With such writers as these, serious literature and the equally serious questions it raised continued to be a part of the culture and experience of ordinary people.

The New Sciences

Educated men and women of the mid-nineteenth century, while they might have known little of its origins or verifications, had little trouble accepting the

*The Irish-born James Joyce, after abortive attempts at careers in medicine and music, found
his place in English literature. His writings, particularly his controversial stream-of-
consciousness novels Ulysses (1922) and Finnegans Wake (1937), paid little attention to
conventions of time and plot—for Joyce, character and consciousness were all. Ultimately he
was hailed as a genius and pioneer of the modern novel.   (Beinecke Rare Book and Manuscript
Library, Yale University)*

Newtonian explanations of the universe. Despite the stunning brilliance of
the founding genius, the final product as received by the popular mind was
mechanistic and logical and seemed allied, rather than contradictory, to common sense. It was not at all difficult to understand why generations
embraced the tale of Newton being struck on the head by an apple and
thereby inspired to conceive an explanation of the cosmos. As the eighteenth-
century poet Alexander Pope indicated, it appeared that God had in fact said:
"Let Newton be, and all was light." As the nineteenth century passed into the
twentieth, however, science was to undergo another massive upheaval, and
of all that this brought about nothing is as evident as the fact that the gulf of
understanding between the scientist and the common citizen was to grow to
unbreachable proportions. In the day-to-day work of modern science, quan-
tification surpasses the abilities of sense perception to understand: Things are
measured and calculated that are too small, too large, too fast, and too distant
to grasp when one relies on the common sense that gets us through the day.
And it is even more remarkable when one contemplates how quickly this
change in affairs came about.

The nineteenth century had witnessed the enshrinement of the atomic theory of matter— all things, it postulated, were made up of small particles called atoms. This seemed comfortably to suit the Newtonian ideal, and that apparently was that. Late in the century, however, Antoine Bercquerel (1852–1908) established in his experiments with uranium the existence of radioactivity and posited the existence of subatomic particles. Also in France, the collaboration of Pierre (1859–1906) and Marie (1867–1934) Curie resulted in the discovery of two further radioactive elements, polonium and radium. The three shared the Nobel Prize for Physics in 1903 (the first woman to receive the honor, Mme. Curie would in 1911 become the first person to receive a second), and their work provided irresistible evidence to support the conclusion reached in Britain by J. J. Thompson (1856–1940) and the New Zealand–born Ernest Rutherford (1871–1937) that the atom was not the smallest building block of matter.

As there was brilliant work in the laboratories, so were there equally brilliant proposals to explain a new conception of the world from the theoretical physicists. In Germany, Max Planck (1858–1947) revealed an idea in 1900 that chipped away at the elegant simplicity of Newtonian physics: His quantum theory posited that radiant energy took place not in a constant stream but in abrupt installments he termed quanta. More stunning—and, when laymen tried to understand it, even less comprehensible—were the theories of an obscure Jewish patent office clerk in Switzerland, Albert Einstein (1879–1955). A curious and awkward boy, impatient with subjects that failed to challenge him, Einstein had not been a particularly successful student, although at university he had displayed stubborn genius. He failed in his quest for a university teaching appointment and settled into a seemingly dull life of examining applications in the patent office in Bern. His undemanding post left him plenty of time to continue his interest in mathematical physics, and in a thirty-page paper published in 1905 he offered up his first pronouncement of an entirely new conception of the universe. His *special theory of relativity* held that time and space were not as they appeared, constant and unchangeable, but rather were relative to the observer, for only the speed of light was constant.

While Newtonian concepts continued to be useful, "true enough," for every day purposes in a world in which we see and touch only slow-moving ordinary things, they no longer could be useful or "true" for ultimate realities. Difficult to grasp and virtually impossible to illustrate, the work of scientists like Planck and Einstein could not help but drive deeper the wedge between the scientist and the layman. The "truth of ultimates"—of speed, mass, and time itself—had become too difficult to understand, and even most highly educated nonscientists finally were given no choice but to accept. In deciphering more of the secrets of the universe, this brilliant generation of theoretical physicists made it in many ways more confusing, more mysterious, and perhaps more frightening to their contemporaries—and to those who came after. And of course, although it may be a cliché, it is nonetheless true that neither these scientists and technicians nor the laymen who struggled to understand their theories could foresee to what it would all lead—to jet propulsion, space travel, and the atom bomb.

New Visions of Society

In their passion to make their own way apart from the previous century, some thinkers after 1900 posed what they considered to be new answers to old questions about the nature of man, the best life, and the ideal organization of society. Most of these new solutions, not surprisingly, sought change, and many did so at the expense of the morally or materially comfortable.

The Growth of Social Darwinism

Some alternative visions had been around for a while and in the new century reached a kind of intellectual critical mass; several of these were downright dangerous. Although trained in Britain as an engineer, Herbert Spencer (1820–1903) was drawn to both science and philosophy. A decade before his death he completed his masterwork, the *System of Synthetic Philosophy*, which to its many admirers seemed to bring the power and insight of Charles Darwin's great work in biology to questions of human nature and society. In a blow to what was seen then as modern and practical, Spencer's social Darwinism declared that human history was a long and rather brutal tale of the survival of the fittest. Nature was cruel in the jungle at the moment in order to be kind in the long run: The controlling force was the survival and improvement of the species. So it was, the social Darwinists said, in society: The breaking of the feeble, the stupid, and the damaged in the greater scheme of things strengthened the human race as the strong, the clever, and the capable thrived. How plausible this all seemed, particularly to those who saw themselves among Spencer's elect.

The protests of prominent biologists that this new movement was a vulgarization that exploited the language of Darwin without understanding its substance were not strong enough to counter its attraction to many, particularly of the middle classes in the West, who saw in all of this endorsement of their own successes. Here was scientific validation of the middle-class conviction that the universe was designed to reward hard work, attention to duty, thrift, intelligence, and self-help and to punish laziness, waste, stupidity, sexual promiscuity, and reliance on charity. Above all, Darwin seemed to vindicate the notions that the poor were poor because they were unfit, badly prepared by nature for living a competitive life, and that efforts by private charity or state action to take from the well-to-do and give to the poor were useless attempts to reverse the course of evolution. Spencer summed up this view:

> Of man, as of all inferior creatures, the law by conformity to which the species is preserved, is that among adults the individuals best adapted to the conditions of their existence shall prosper most, and that individuals least adapted to the conditions of their existence shall prosper least. . . . The ultimate result of shielding men from folly is to fill the world with fools.*

---

*Herbert Spencer, *Principles of Ethics* (1879) (New York: D. Appleton, 1900), II, p. 17; Spencer, *Autobiography* (London: Williams and Norgate, 1904), II, p. 100.

Spencer later tempered some of what appeared to be the harshest aspects of his philosophy, and, while he never condoned "shielding men from their folly," he decided that the emotions promoted by religion—kindness, compassion, love—were also in accord with the intentions of the laws of the universe as summed up in evolution. Mutual extermination might be the law for tigers, but not for human beings. Indeed, Spencer and many other social Darwinists held that the altruistic sentiments that impel one toward acts of charity were the highest achievement of the evolutionary process.

The social Darwinists were, then, faced with this primary difficulty: Darwin seemed to have shown that the struggle for life within a given species and among rival species was the law of the universe; but human history and human feelings showed that humanity could not look on suffering with indifference. One way out of this dilemma was to humanize and ease the struggle, so that incompetents were shelved but not destroyed. Many who held this view turned to eugenics, or selective breeding. Since, according to strict Darwinian theory, acquired characteristics were not transmitted by heredity, no amount of manipulation of the social environment, no amount of wise planning of institutions, would alter human beings. Many who turned to this solution became convinced that the "better" elements of society—the leaders, the successful—despite all of their qualities might not continue to thrive if the "degenerate" elements of the population—the rapidly breeding social and economic lower orders, the feeble-minded, the insane, criminals— pushed them aside by the weight of sheer numbers. Therefore, the only way to secure permanent improvement of the race was by deliberate mating of the fit with the fit and discouragement (and perhaps even prevention) of breeding among the "degenerates." Eugenics societies grew up in most European countries and in America in the early years of the century to foster just such a solution.

The eugenicists, however, immediately ran up against the fact that in choosing a mate the individual human being is influenced by many motives, and no master breeder can decide who shall mate with whom. In any state with even the most rudimentary system of civil liberties and in which any one of the world's major religions was influential, such experimentation on any broad scale was unthinkable. Hence, eugenics enthusiasts were restricted to exhortation and to propaganda programs to make their case, and they were not without their successes as even such liberal-minded nations as the United States and Britain and her Empire restricted the receipt of immigrants on the basis of race and "desirability." The movement continued to gain influence and legitimacy through early years of the century, not reaching its peak until the 1920s but declining to insignificance when the horrors of Nazi-inspired experiments in Germany and elsewhere became known.

"Race Patriots," Anti-Semitism, and the Birth of Zionism

By far the commonest way out of the dilemma facing the social Darwinists lay in the notion that the struggle for existence really goes on among human

beings organized in groups—as tribes, races, or national states. This struggle
was thus lifted from the biology of the individual to the politics of communities. Accordingly, a group that defeated another group in war had thereby
shown itself to be fitter than the beaten group; it had a right—indeed, in evolutionary terms, a duty—to eliminate the beaten group, seize its lands, and
people these lands with its own fitter human beings. The British imperialist
Cecil John Rhodes (1853–1902) once held that a world wholly and exclusively
peopled with Anglo-Saxons would be the best possible world. This view
came to be called racialism, or in today's terminology racism, and held that
inherent differences among the various races determined cultural and individual achievement, so that one race might be considered superior to another
in a given context. While widely recognized for the evil it is in our time, such
a view seemed early in the century to be an obvious answer demanded by the
sciences of genetics and biology. European believers in racialism looked at
the rest of the world and convinced themselves that their own superiority
was verified by the commonsense evidence of their own eyes.

"Race patriots" (as they were often called by their admirers) believed that
Homo Sapiens had already evolved into what were really separate species. A
black skin, for instance, was for them a sign of innate inferiority; and blacks
(or Native Americans in the United States) would have to go the way of the
dinosaurs. Intermarriage between the races was forbidden by custom or by
law as contrary to God's intention and because it would degrade the "higher
race." As yet few dared preach genocide, the wholesale extermination of those
held to be of inferior race; most racists wished to see the "inferiors" duly subjected to their "superiors," "kept in their own place," or living "among their
own kind."

Of the major industrial powers in this period, only the United States
included a sizeable nonwhite minority. While the last of the self-proclaimed
"civilized" nations to end legal race slavery, and despite the passage as a
result of the Civil War and the Emancipation Proclamation of the Thirteenth,
Fourteenth, and Fifteenth Amendments to the Constitution, which outlawed
racial discrimination, the great republic of the new world had not succeeded
after its prolonged civil war in finding a suitable accommodation between
the former master and slave races. By the early 1880s in the United States, not
only the states of the old Confederacy but also most of the border states and
much of the Midwest had passed what were termed "Jim Crow" laws—the
name apparently was taken from a popular folk song of pre–Civil War days.
The laws constituted a code of social regulation that ensured the separation
of the races in employment, housing, transportation, and education, and with
it came an equally binding but informal system of separation in social interaction. Schools, housing, hospitals, parks, trains, buses, and even such trivi-
alities of everyday life as public telephones and water fountains became
racially segregated in much of the country. On the eve of the new century the
final test of the "Jim Crow" system came in the *Plessy v. Ferguson* decision by
the United States Supreme Court (1896), which enshrined the fiction of "separate but equal" in the provision of services by the state of its citizens, black

and white. It would be more than a half-century before the obvious truth was accepted that separate was by definition unequal.

Although Darwinism and these offshoots that claimed to be its social counterparts could be misread as the basis for a new doctrine of progress, and although they supported the industrial societies in their expectations of unlimited growth, essentially Darwinism and much of racism were intensely pessimistic. Darwin had emphasized accident, not order, as the nature of causation. In contrast to the more ebullient of the social Darwinists, many commentators believed that the "lower races" would eventually triumph, for brute strength would overtake sensitivity. The "lower races" were breeding faster and less selectively, democratic egalitarianism was leveling down the best while encouraging the worst; consequently, evolution was sliding downward rather than heading upward.

From the mid-nineteenth century, many of these despondent thinkers had looked to the work of Joseph Arthur, Count de Gobineau (1816–1882), titled provocatively *Essay on the Inequality of the Human Races* (1853–1855). This French diplomat and writer had concluded that there was a clear hierarchy of races, with the "pure" Germans—for him, not necessarily the inhabitants of modern Germany, but the fair-skinned, blue-eyed populations of Scandinavia, England, northern France, and Belgium—at the top of the racial pyramid. The racial elements of this argument were carried forward by the curious figure of Houston Stewart Chamberlain (1855–1927), the son of a British admiral, nephew of two famous generals, and son-in-law of the German composer Richard Wagner. Chamberlain turned his back on his own country and went to live in Germany, among the people he considered the most highly developed and naturally superior in the world. His most famous work (published in German in 1899 and in English in 1911), *Foundations of the Nineteenth Century,* argued that European civilization was endangered by what he saw as lower and mongrelized races: Asians, Africans, the Mediterranean Europeans, and, not at all least, the Jews. This unlovely trend of thought at this point merged with (and lent a sort of pseudoscientific legitimacy to) an ancient form of intolerance: anti-Semitism.

Jews had gained political emancipation in western Europe over the course of the nineteenth century, but the specter of anti-Semitism lingered. By the outset of the new century, in the more democratic Britain, France, and the United States, for example, it could be found in a most polite form: Britain had already had a prime minister, Benjamin Disraeli, who was a Christian of Jewish parentage, and the United States would by 1916 have a Jewish Supreme Court justice, Louis D. Brandeis. The legislatures of these and other nations had Jewish members (and in the British House of Lords, Jewish peers), most of Vienna's newspapers were owned by Jews, and there were many Jews in the learned professions (particularly medicine and university teaching) and among the owners of major banks, utilities, and the world's first international wire service. It is impossible to conceive of the fine arts or letters of the period without the contributions of Jewish composers, painters, and writers. Yet there existed anti-Semitism just below the surface of polite society, as Jews in Catholic-dominated societies remained stigmatized as "killers of Christ" and, in Protestant cultures at the very least, unsaved souls ripe for conversion. There was a sense of "otherness" that prevented complete acceptance of a people who themselves had many reasons to be suspicious of complete assimilation. Hence within legal systems that guaranteed them complete civil liberties, Jews were informally barred from country clubs, universities, and military regiments. As we shall see in the next chapter, the Dreyfus affair in France, which spanned the last years of the nineteenth and the early years of the twentieth centuries, revealed that even in Europe's greatest republic anti-Semitism was an ugly fact of life.

It could be far uglier. The pogrom—state-tolerated and even state-sanctioned violence against Jews—was still known in the Russian Empire. In 1897 in Vienna an extremely popular and virulently anti-Semitic mayor, Karl Lueger (1844–1910), was elected—so vulgar and violent was his hatred for the Jews that the Emperor Francis Joseph refused for several years to ratify his election—and it was in Lueger's Vienna that Hitler lived as a young man and developed the intellectual framework of Nazi racial doctrine.

Many European Jews, and particularly those in Eastern Europe where anti-Semitism was at its worst and most violent, had since the latter nineteenth century responded if possible by emigration. Some turned to political radicalism, hoping in socialism to find an answer to a better and more tolerant secular state. Still others, particularly in the democratic West, saw the future of their people in assimilation—retaining their religious identity but blending their culture into that of their own countries. Yet there was another answer that was destined to become a major and controversial force in the twentieth century. A Jewish physician in Russian Poland, Leon Pinsker (1821–1891), published in Germany in 1882 a portentously titled booklet called *Auto-Emancipation*. After witnessing anti-Semitic violence against Jews in the Russia of 1891, Pinsker abandoned his previous conviction that guaranteed civil liberties within the European nations were the answer to anti-Semitism. From this point he advised that the only hope for the Jewish people was political independence based upon a Jewish national consciousness: Jews must make their own homeland.

Much moved by Pinsker's arguments was a Viennese journalist, playwright, and publicist, Theodor Herzl (1860–1904), who concluded that the evidence of the pogroms and the Dreyfus case rendered assimilation fruitless. The Jews were one people spread thinly through many lands—a permanent and forever defenseless minority—and for Herzl they would remain so unless they came together and restored to greatness a Jewish nation-state. This he argued in an influential book titled *The Jewish State* (1896), and in *Old New Land* (1902) he described his idealized restored state of Israel. His efforts led to the creation of the Zionist movement.

In 1897, Herzl convened the First Zionist Congress in Basle, Switzerland, which declared the goal of Zionism as the establishment of "a home for the Jewish people in Palestine secured under public law." While he captured the imagination of Jews throughout the world, he was not without his critics among his coreligionists. Jews, particularly in the democracies, were not all prepared to abandon assimilation as the response to anti-Semitism. Although Herzl died in 1904, Zionism continued to flourish and eventually triumph among religious and secularized Jews alike. The Great Powers would come to endorse Herzl's dream, although in these years before World War I none could anticipate the horror that would befall European Jewry only a genera-tion later.

Other Responses: Positivism and Elitism

There were other answers to the challenges of the new century—answers apart from social Darwinism, racialism, and separatism. Like some of these others, certain thinkers were coming to reject the nineteenth century's gener-ally optimistic positivism, with its conviction that mankind acted according to rational and discoverable principles. His own times had convinced William James (1842–1910), the American physician, philosopher, and early champion of the infant discipline of psychology, that people did not act according to principles at all but rather reacted pragmatically (thereby enshrining the word in the modern vocabulary) to stimuli they encountered. He went further, attacking long-held notions of consciousness itself, coining the famous aphorism: "We do not weep because we are sad, but we are sad because we weep." Metaphysical systems for James were bunk: Principles do not work because they are true—they work and therefore become true.

Much admired by James was the French philosopher Henri Bergson (1859–1941), another antagonist of both the positivists and the social Dar-winists. Bergson insisted that the will to believe was primary: Not natural selection, he continued, but the creative urge—the *élan vital*—was at the heart of human progress. Like James, he concluded that in mankind passions always governed reason.

Another direction, and a dangerous one, was taken by thinkers who were closer to the social Darwinists than to James or Bergson—but who sometimes drew strength from the arguments of these latter. These were the elitists who viewed the spread of the franchise, of capitalism, even of public education with alarm. No positivist optimism rang true for them, for the West stood at a dangerous crossroads: Would it decline because of the bastardization of leadership, aesthetics, and nobility by mongrelized mass democracy? The elitists' answer was that hope lay with the "best" people, based not simply on race or ethnicity but on quality, ability, and virtue.

In Italy, the work of the conservative legal scholar and later senator Gae-tano Mosca (1858–1941) led to his conclusion that all systems of government, regardless of the differences, led to the natural gravitation of power into the hands of ruling elites. From the other end of the political spectrum, the social-ist Robert Michel (1876–1936), a German-born and -trained social scientist whose outspoken criticism of the regimes of his own country led him to take refuge in universities in Italy and Switzerland, published his most important work in 1911, *Political Parties*. He theorized an "iron law of oligarchies," postulating that political organizations, even those with the most impeccably democratic agendas, inevitably evolved into oligarchies with power and influence concentrated into the hands of the few. For him, like Mosca, grand conceptions like "popular sovereignty" and the philosophies that justified them in an age when mass politics were a reality were eventually destined to become mere tools in the hands of elites, traditional or revolutionary.

Undoubtedly the most difficult of the philosophers of elitism to categorize was the German Friedrich Nietzsche (1844–1900). Although his life ended with the nineteenth century, his impact had only begun to be felt. A brilliant student, he accepted a prestigious professorial chair at the University of Basle in Switzerland at the age of twenty-five, although he held it only ten years before his health began to fail. For the next ten years he lived in near-isolation, and in 1889 suffered a complete mental breakdown. Now completely insane, he lived in seclusion under the care of a sister who worshiped him and worked indefatigably to popularize his views.

Although he began as a disciple of the German philosopher Arthur Schopenhauer (1788–1860), Nietzsche abandoned most of the teachings of that pessimist and developed his own even more perplexing worldview. He turned against all elements of political democracy and praised in his greatest work, *Thus Spake Zarathustra* (1883–1885, which began to appear in translation only in 1909), a natural leadership of the *übermensch* (in popular usage, the superman), the life-affirming warrior-aristocrat, a member of a master-caste that exhibited the ultimate life force, the will to power (a concept he retained from Schopenhauer), and used it to seize control and lead the nation to glory and to truth.

Although deeply devout as a young man, Nietzsche turned against the dominant Western religions, declaring Judaism and Christianity—with their emphases on obedience, charity, and sacrifice—to be "slave mentalities." Sympathy for one's fellow man he considered as contemptible as these religious systems—and so were materialism, capitalism, democracy, and, of course, all forms of socialism. At the same time, he loathed both militarism and anti-Semitism—the first as vainglorious and stupid, the latter as an ideology of self-justification and envy.

Nietzsche was never aware of his appeal outside of a small segment of the intelligentsia, for his works were not well known until he had already begun his slide into madness, and only after his death were they widely translated and read. Even then, understanding them was far from easy. His reasoning was complicated, erratic, and murky. He wrote not in the usual prose of the philosopher but in a kind of blank verse; and, rather than in closely developed essays, he employed epigrams and maxims to capture the attention of the reader. Of belief he wrote: "Nothing is true; everything is allowed"; of suffering and progress, "Almost everything we call higher culture is based upon the spiritualizing and intensifying of cruelty." Of religion he declared: "God is dead. We have killed him", and, hence, man stood alone, dependent upon his own will: "You shall become who you are."

The price of such powerful but esoteric prose is the age-old burden of all such prophets: to be interpreted and appropriated by those who read their prophecies. Nietzsche certainly never anticipated the rabid nationalists, racists, and fascists who came "to glory," in his words—and there is no doubt that he would have held them in utter contempt. Although he excited, enraged, and even inspired many, it was to be the ultimate fate of his thought and his memory to be twisted and hijacked by a barbarous Nazi regime.

Freud and the Science of Mind

Of all the thinkers and doers discussed in this book, perhaps none is more identified in the common mind with modern times than Sigmund Freud (1856–1939). This may well be absolutely appropriate, for who can we say has a greater claim on the foundation of a modern "science of the mind"? Whose work in such esoteric and learned areas has become more a part of everyday thought and language than his? Born in a small town in what was then Austrian Moravia, his family was forced to flee by anti-Semitic violence when Freud was a small boy, and he grew to manhood in Vienna. There he remained until driven out by the Nazis a year before his death. Drawn to science from an early age, Freud took a degree in medicine in 1881, and his interest gravitated to neuropathology and the study of mental disorders. He collaborated with more senior practitioners who relied upon hypnosis to bring their patients to reveal their anxieties. But, ultimately dissatisfied with the limitations of this "cathartic" methodology, after a decade of research, collaboration, and finally private practice, Freud developed an alternative method of treatment.

To this in 1896 he gave the name psychoanalysis—the "talking cure"—through which the patient was brought through careful interrogation and "free association" of subjects to reveal the experiences of the past that had caused his disorder. Yet Freud was convinced that like physical illness, it was in the discovery of the causes that healing lay, and the causes of personality disorders were to be found in the patient's past experiences—revealing and neutralizing them would return the sufferer to mental health. Memories of these damaging experiences lay buried in the personal unconscious, he was certain; and to explain how they remained hidden and therefore dangerous to the patient's recovery, Freud developed his theories of repression and resistance. Repression was the protective mental device through which painful or damaging experiences were cloaked from the conscious mind, while resistance was the defense that made the patient unaware that repressed memories existed. The answer to unlocking these damaging experiences lay in gaining access to the unconscious, and Freud concluded first that one path of access lay through the study of that window of the unconscious available to most people—dreams. His psychoanalytic method was developed in this period: the dimly lit room, the couch, the relaxed atmosphere, and the analyst seated outside of the scope of vision of the patient.

In his first important book, *The Interpretation of Dreams* (1900), Freud began to reveal his theory. This was followed by *The Psychopathology of Everyday Life* (1904), which argued that evidence of the unconscious and of the workings of repression and resistance were just below the surface of the conscious life.

Hence, revealing slips of the tongue ultimately became "Freudian slips," and such common elements of life as forgetfulness or sleeplessness were suggested as possible examples of his system. However, in these and other works, and in his lectures and papers no portion of his analysis was more controversial than his conclusion that no force played as great a role in human development as sexuality. This was a subject that only the most daring would have considered discussing in public in those days, and it was this emphasis that made him not merely an innovator but a controversialist and even a revolutionary. In 1905, he published *Three Essays on the Theory of Sexuality*, the most shocking portion to his contemporaries being his theory that all human beings experience sexual feeling and desire, including young children. He revealed his belief in the Oedipus complex—the desire of the male child (Electra complex, in the case of females) to possess his mother and replace his father—and in the concept of penis envy, the damaging sense of sexual inferiority begun in the childhood of females. He explained his belief, as well, that it was in the burial of these and other sexual disorders through the devices of repression and resistance that many neuroses were begun. In a world emerging from Victorian certainties, it was almost too much, but there was more.

Like the expressionist painter Kandinsky, the poet Mallarmé, or the prophet Nietzsche, for Freud answers lay in the unconscious—the secret, the inner life. His cartography of the mind led him eventually to postulate that the personality is formed of three principal elements: the *ego*, the *superego*, and the *id*. The first of these, the *ego*, was the part of the self in which reason was centered—the faculty that made civilization itself possible. The *superego* was in essence the human conscience, the repository of morality. These two forces were pitted in each human being against the *id*: the drive toward the irrational, toward the satisfaction of appetites, regardless of what they might be. In most men and women, the only available method of participation in a society that did not exist for our own pleasure was to depend upon the ego and superego to act as censors, to restrain and crush the unacceptable drives of the id. In this conflict, this internal war, the human psyche became a seed bed for neurosis.

Despite the obvious fact that his writings were outraging many of his medical colleagues, Freud was appointed to a post at the University of Vienna in 1902—due more to the intervention of an admiring and influential patient than to official approval of his work—and he began to teach his theories in a systematic way. Within a few years he had gathered around him a brilliant international circle of professionals who learned and practiced and in their own time spread the psychoanalytic method. By 1910, this local Viennese circle had become the International Psychoanalytical Association. Two would eventually break with the master—both disturbed by what they considered the overemphasis on sexuality—to found schools of analysis of their own. The Austrian Alfred Adler (1870–1937) left Freud's circle in 1911 to pursue investigations of the psychology of the individual. The Swiss Carl Jung (1875–1961), once Freud's closest collaborator, withdrew in 1913 to found a rival school of analysis drawn to his work on the "collective unconscious." Yet it must be said that most remained in Vienna with Freud or returned to their own countries to found practices or teach Freudian principles.

Freud would go on to examine culture and religion, to found psychobiography, to comment on literature and politics. Without false modesty he compared himself and his findings to those of Copernicus, for he was certain he had corrected the view of the human universe. While some of his theories continue to perplex and even irritate professionals and lay persons alike, it should not be denied that he offered an entirely new approach to understanding the makeup and functions of the human mind. He laid the foundations for a new subset of medical practice and pioneered an equally original technique of therapeutic treatment. Although the methods and even certain assumptions among practitioners today vary, the essence of Freud's revolution has become an accepted part of the medical disciplines. If we seek proof, all we need do is look at any telephone directory in almost any city in the world under "physicians" and then let our eyes stray down the page until we come to "psychiatrists."

New Women

Moving Toward Equality

The values that in the West dominated polite society in the nineteenth century, with their stress on order and their near worship of respectability, had carefully defined a place for women. While it is shallow and exaggerated to see women as slaves in this period, it is very true that the notion of essentially separate spheres of life, based on different notions of participation in human relationships, were presumed to be natural and reinforced not only by law but by divine, historical, and physiological necessities. In this view, women bore society's ultimately greatest responsibility—procreation—and it had been decided by their very nature that this was to be their primary contribution to human history. They were "obviously" physically more delicate than men, and therefore their psychological makeup was assumed to be correspondingly more fragile. They were more sensitive, more emotional, incapable of the hardening necessary for business, public life, or war. They were as innocent of strong sexuality as were children. In all, they were, if not closer to God (there were of course no women clergy within the orthodox faiths), then closer to the angels. All of this was believed in the sense that to challenge it was to put oneself among the revolutionaries; yet there could have been few men or women who did not with their own eyes witness its utter falsity every day of their lives. Such is the power of social conventions.

Most meaningful to our time, when the personal and the political are so often intermixed, was the fact that in the West—where civil liberties and the protection of political rights under law were stronger than elsewhere in the world—this fact was undeniable: There was in every nation fundamental and legally enshrined inequality based upon gender.

By the first decade of the twentieth century the legal status of adult females in virtually the entire West reflected much change over the preceding century, as women were granted control over their own property and increased rights to education—including, if reluctantly, the universities. Divorce laws as they pertained to the sexes were made more equal and liberalized (although divorce remained an almost crippling social taboo outside of the United States, where it was more common but was still socially undesirable), and the learned professions (in addition to the accepted "female professions" of teaching and nursing) began the slow process of opening up to women. The "New Woman" seemed in the eyes of anxious critics of both sexes to be everywhere: dressed in daring fashions—perhaps wearing the baggy trousers called "bloomers" as she raced along on her "safety bicycle"—engaging in strenuous pursuits like tennis or golf, or quoting the emancipating works of Freud or the British physician Henry Havelock Ellis (1859–1936), both of whom demanded the acceptance of the idea that women, despite the dictates of previous generations, experienced sexuality on a level equal with men. What came to be called *feminism* was certainly not born in the twentieth century, but in that century it came of age; and it became dangerous to those old ideas with which it could not and would not coexist. It is ironic to note in our own time, an age in which the use of tobacco has once again been relegated to the scrap heap of social and health taboos, that early radical feminists were said to have cheered when in 1896 the rather bohemian Duchesse de Clermont-Tonnerre scandalized London society by openly lighting a cigarette in that playground of the rich and the elegant, the Savoy Hotel.

The Fight for the Vote

The primary battle in the struggle to achieve legal parity between the sexes involved the question of the franchise. The nineteenth century had been the climacteric for men in the movement toward popular political participation, as the United States, Britain, France, Germany, and much of the West witnessed the massive broadening of the enfranchised male population. It is not difficult to understand that women and the growing number of men who championed their cause would look to electoral enfranchisement as both a symbol and an effective tool at least of political equality. This certainly seemed logical to many who valued change in a generation when ideas of change seemed to be in the air. The franchise appeared to be the key to all change in a time when legislatures seemed capable at last of beginning to pass laws to make reform real. For suffragists, as believers in the cause came to be called, the vote was enough—an end in itself. Others believed that if the franchise could be secured for women, then all other inequities would soon fall: Millions of women voters in the democracies would make such progress impossible to prevent.

Organizations dedicated to enfranchisement grew up in all Western nations, with the largest and most vociferous in the English-speaking world. In the United States Elizabeth Cady Stanton (1815–1902) and Susan B.

Anthony (1820–1906), sober New Englanders who had supported the causes of abolition and temperance, founded what eventually became the National American Suffrage Association—an organization with thousands of members in the years before World War I. In Britain, Millicent Garrett Fawcett (1847–1929) led the National Union of Women's Suffrage Societies (NUWSS), and Emmeline Pankhurst (1858–1928) founded the competing and more militant Women's Social and Political Union (WSPU). In the United States a similar story was told, with the debate over militancy between the majority National American Woman Suffrage Association and a more impatient organization, the Woman's Party, in this same period.

The movement, however, was not without its successes: As early as 1867 women won the right to vote in New South Wales in Australia, in 1869 in Wyoming Territory in the United States (and eleven other states by 1914), and in 1886 in New Zealand. In 1894 British women were granted the vote in local elections, but in Europe only in Finland (1906) and Norway (1913) did women gain the vote in national elections.

In the United States and Britain, where the issue was most keenly debated, the movement for women's suffrage followed a path that would become common in the century to come for groups seeking recognition and political change. Women's suffragists took their demands into the public forum at every opportunity, organizing local and national associations, raising funds, and initiating publicity campaigns, mass meetings, and marches of the faithful. Predictably, they made converts; equally predictably, they often encountered resistance and sometimes rejection and abuse. The difficulty of achieving their desires combined with the power of the opposition to the cause presented a dilemma: Were women, despite their political disadvantages, to continue to play the game by the rules, or would they turn to harsher methods? Was it to be peaceful protest or militancy?

The question of whether the activist campaigns of the British WSPU or their American sisters hastened or, by creating a strong reaction, delayed the ultimate achievement of the vote is unanswerable. The question of how to bring about change—change for which great resistance is likely—in a free country in modern times seems typically to raise this debate, and it will be confronted again in other contexts in this volume. In this way, these women were pioneers in more ways than one.

SUMMARY

After many decades of steady population growth, by 1900 birth rates in Europe had declined, but improved health, sanitary, and dietary practices had lowered infant mortality and raised life expectancy statistics. It was also true that these factors as well as internal migration were turning Europe into an increasingly urban culture. During the same period, massive emigration, much of it to the Americas, also accounted for surplus population.

The new century witnessed powerful new movements in the arts, as *modernism* became a powerful force in the visual arts, and rebels against the old academic style painted the reality they rather than others saw. A solid basis for a truly modern art was laid. It is worth noting, however, that popular acceptance of the "new arts" was not rapid in developing—a fact that did not concern these artists.

Similarly, in architecture bold innovators established new styles that substituted their own visions for the long-established rules of classicism. Much the same can be said of music, as composition was forever altered by pioneers demonstrating their rebellious creative efforts before often uncomprehending audiences. Again, popular acceptance came slowly.

In literature the old rules also suffered at the hands of experimental writers who used language in new and sometimes startling ways. Poets and novelists sought to show the world as they perceived it and paid little attention to the desires or, for that matter, to the understanding of the reader.

In the very different world of the sciences stunning change was also sprung on an unprepared world. By the early years of the century, science's understanding of the nature of matter and energy followed an extended and revolutionary path. The existence of radioactivity and of subatomic particles was demonstrated, and the quantum theory of light was theorized. Physics was forever changed, and the elegant model of the Newtonian universe shattered. In 1905, perhaps the greatest of this generation of geniuses, Einstein, published his *special theory of relativity,* which demolished forever the commonsense view that space and time were simply as they appeared. As such ideas filtered down to the level of the layman, it was clear that in future the truth of ultimates—of speed, mass, and time—would no longer be truly comprehensible to the nonscientist.

The early twentieth century also witnessed new visions of the social order. Spencer's suggestion that society mimicked the order of nature as explained by biology came to be called social Darwinism and asserted that the inexorable morality of the survival of the fittest also held among people and communities. Some interpreted this to explain that the various races were naturally divided among superior and inferior strains. Hence, racism for them was a natural, even a beneficial system. It is easy to see how among some Europeans, such a morality could justify the worst excesses of imperialism. In America it provided a rationalization for the institutionalized racism of the "Jim Crow" system.

An ancient form of racism was anti-Semitism, common throughout Europe and particularly virulent in the Russian Empire. In response, the Zionist movement was founded by European Jews who rejected assimilation and called for the establishment of a Jewish national state in Palestine.

Other challenges to the social order emanated from other thinkers, and many shared a reverence for force and authority. Not the least of these was proposed by Nietzsche, whose views of a society ruled by a master-caste, above ordinary morality and freed of all limitations imposed by Christianity, democracy, and capitalism, remained strangely influential well into the new century.

Personality itself was to be reinterpreted by Freud, the effect of whose theories of the unconscious life, sexuality, and individual development can hardly be exaggerated. Despite determined opposition, psychoanalysis as a healing practice was established in due course as an orthodox field of medicine.

Movements for women's suffrage became active before the First World War and achieved their first successes during the war. The Scandinavian states of Finland and Norway became the first in Europe to accord women the franchise. The major democracies did not follow suit, however, and this important issue remained unsettled until after the war.

TWO

The Modernization
of Nations

∞

In recent years historians have often asked whether the best unit for study is a society or a nation, since many questions relating broadly to demography and society cannot be properly addressed within a single nation's borders. Certainly a cross-national approach was appropriate to the discussion in the last chapter of this book. But because nationalism was triumphant in western Europe in the nineteenth century, the nation as a unit of study appears to be indispensable to gaining any understanding of the politics of the twentieth century. As humanity sought to define a sense of security with a particular nation, church, ideology, economic doctrine, or tribe, both *cooperation*—that is, a bringing together of once-diverse groups into ever larger and self-consciously identified groups—and *competition* among these groups became more intense.

Meliorism, the term for the belief that the world could be improved by human effort, gave a special dynamism to the modern political "isms"—nationalism, imperialism, conservatism, liberalism, socialism, communism, fascism—and to democracy itself. At the same time, movements and dangers (such as famine) that once affected only a relatively specific place became generalized, in the sense that falling cash crop prices in West Africa, depletion of oil production in the Middle East, or major technological innovations in Japan could have rapid repercussions in Europe and North America. Technology in the nineteenth and twentieth centuries would alter the world radically, so that within a decade a person might experience more change than an earlier civilization had seen in a century. Hence the Great Powers in this period, the largest and most powerful political entities of modern times, lived within themselves—with their own languages, their varieties of Christianity, their systems of political organization, and not least of all their ambitions and self-images—while at the same time conscious of being a part of a greater whole, the West. Not surprisingly, the history of twentieth-century politics is often a story of the conflict of those two powerful forces: national self-interest and international cooperation. It would be useful first to consider very briefly these ideologies and then the nations in which they uneasily coexisted.

Political Ideas

In the West, the twentieth century created no really new political ideologies, but contented itself with refining those that had been inherited from an earlier time. Political ideology is a complicated business, but the following will serve as working discussions and general definitions.

To the European conservative, the past was the guide, the measure of things in the world. The best system of governance was monarchy, the best system of religion was the age-old faith of the nation, validated over the centuries, and it was best if joined by bonds of loyalty and law and perhaps blood to the state. The conservative "understood" the need for a class system that provided a "place" for all members of society and insisted that with privilege went responsibility. Above all, the conservative rejected the confidence and even faith of liberals in the all-conquering power of human reason.

While all this was so, the trials of the nineteenth century had separated conservatism from simple reaction (the belief that change was inherently for the worse and always to be opposed). Conservatives in western Europe had fashioned modern arguments to counter opposing ideologies: By the early twentieth century conservative parties in Britain, the United States, and elsewhere had embraced programs of economic and social reform. Almost everywhere they laid claim to nationalism—originally a revolutionary or liberal belief—and some on the Continent were drawn to varieties of social Darwinism, elitism, and racialism.

The traditional rival of conservatism in the West was liberalism. This was a peculiarly nineteenth-century body of belief, and its adherents were the Newtonians of politics: They had great faith in human wisdom, reason, and the ability of mankind to solve the problems of society—and they saw solvable problems everywhere. To the liberal, man was a "perfectable" creature, capable of learning and of improvement. If men and women pursued their own "enlightened self-interest," with respect for their fellows, society would eventually reach the goal of becoming the truly humane organism of which it was capable. Therefore, progress was a fact for the liberal, and history was evidence of it: After all, had slavery not been abolished? Was famine not all but forgotten in the West? Was science not making the world more knowable and liveable every day?

Unlike conservatism, liberalism had from the outset been bound to a specific economic perspective, for liberalism was capitalist to its very core. British liberals congratulated themselves on providing a paradigm for the best form of state: one that pursued a policy of peace, retrenchment, reform, and free trade. The nation that existed with regard for its neighbors, with the most financially restrained administration, with a constant eye on the improvement of society, and all within a system in which the government interfered as little as possible with trade—such a nation was the highest form of state.

While the conservative passion for orderliness might appeal to peasant or peer, liberalism was always closest to the heart of the bourgeoisie, with its reverence for capitalism. While it may seem to our eyes at first glance that this reformist doctrine might have special appeal to those seeking a better chance than life had dealt them at birth, there was another ideology that often successfully directed its message to the masses of the working classes. That, of course, was socialism.

As we shall see, there were many socialisms, some shading off past Marxism and in the direction of anarchism at one end of the spectrum, and orderly, reformist, and politely constitutional parties at the other. But, reformist or revolutionary, they all shared certain common beliefs. First, socialism as it emerged into the twentieth century rejected the confidence of its rivals that society was somehow "naturally" headed in the proper direction, be it the conservative notion that society should move forward with an eye on the rear view mirror or the liberal confidence in capitalism and the inevitability of progress.

Socialists may have claimed that their inspiration was the *New Testament*, or Marx's *Communist Manifesto;* they may have been committed to achieving power through a democratic political party and parliamentary elections, or through violent revolution, but they shared a commitment to their vision of social justice—to the achievement of a world in which capitalist competition and an economically reinformed class structure no longer divided the world into haves and have-nots.

Socialists of all stripes agreed that the capitalist system had to be jettisoned completely, or at least much revised, and replaced with one under which the "means of production"—the economic infrastructure—was controlled in the name of all by the representatives of the vast majority, the workers themselves.

By 1914, labor unions throughout Europe had come to a greater or lesser degree, depending upon the nation and the trade, under the influence of socialist thought. Every state that could remotely be called democratic had some form of socialist movement contending for the votes of an enfranchised working class—Germany had perhaps the strongest, and the United States the weakest. Socialism had been the anathema of every European government in the previous century, and now all had accepted that, in one way or another, it was there to stay.

Britain: Toward Democracy and Crisis

At the outset of the twentieth century Great Britain was, as it remains, a monarchy—reigned over by the great figure of Queen Victoria (r. 1837–1901), then more than fifty years on the throne. Even so formidable a sovereign, although she possessed great influence, enjoyed little actual power, for final political authority lay with Parliament. The most popular British monarch since the days of the Tudors, Victoria may well have been the focus of the patriotic attentions of her subjects, and also the grandmother of European royalty through the marriages of her many children and grandchildren, but the affairs of government were directed in the name of the constitutional monarch by her cabinet, who ruled with the authority of the Parliament.

This legislature, the oldest among the Great Powers, consisted of two houses: the House of Commons (elected on the basis of near-universal manhood suffrage) and the House of Lords (consisting of an unelected hereditary peerage). The two houses were in theory equal in power, but enfranchisement of working-class men, plus the ancient precedent that the lower house controlled public finance, ensured that in the twentieth century—if controversy erupted—the elected Commons took precedence. This was finally clarified in law in 1911 when a Parliament Act reduced the power of the Lords over Commons legislation to a mere delaying or suspensive veto. Heredity peers would continue to sit in the Lords for the remainder of the century, but by 2001, what remained of the hereditary principle had virtually been abolished in the upper house and replaced (except for a small contingent of "hereditaries") with appointed life peerages—that is, those that lasted only for the peer's lifetime.

Unlike other European nations, Britain had developed and remained generally wedded to an electoral system with two great competing political parties, although not to the exclusion of one or more so-called lesser third parties. This system seemed to thrive best in English-speaking lands (Britain, her Dominions, and the United States), for on the Continent, a multiparty or coalition system usually prevailed—not only in France, Italy, and Germany but also in the smaller democracies of Scandinavia, Switzerland, Holland, and Belgium, as well as in Spain, which had established a bicameral legislature in 1876. A two-party democracy had the clear advantages of promoting clarity of debate and choice and a sense of security. In the century that lay ahead, however, it is also true that neither the two-party system nor parliamentary governments proved ultimately to be the norm for newly independent and modernizing states.

At the turn of the twentieth century, contending for votes—and power—in Britain were the Conservatives and Liberals. The former claimed their origins dated at least to the time of the seventeenth century Restoration of the monarchy. They had strong appeal to the land-owning classes, the military, devoted adherents of the established church, and agricultural workers, and by our period they often claimed the support of tradespeople, some of the urban working class, and patriots, enthusiastic imperialists and adherents of the resurrected theory of protecting the British internal market from unfair international trade practices through tariffs.

The Liberals, whose political ancestors were the Whigs of earlier times, found supporters among businessmen, religious nonconformists, white-collar radicals, and the more politically conscious workers. While some Conservatives were willing to consider the highly explosive notion of erecting trade tariff barriers, the Liberals were committed to the core idea of nineteenth-century

Four generations of British monarchs: the elderly Queen Victoria flanked on the left by her grandson, the future George V, and her son, who would succeed her as Edward VII. She is holding Prince George's son, who would reign briefly as Edward VIII. (Hulton Archive/Getty Images)

classical economics: free trade. Still, as we shall see, the Liberal party had since the 1880s embraced a different controversial idea in Irish Home Rule.

By the latter nineteenth century, the prosperity, sense of confidence, and general air of political and social innovation associated with Victorian Britain were on the wane. There was an undeniable economic depression in agriculture, and rates of growth of commerce and industrial output were disappointing. In the eyes of some, an unfortunate move from duty toward frivolity seemed to mark the Edwardian period, named after Victoria's successor, the pleasure-loving but philanthropic King Edward VII (r. 1901–1910). There were other troubles: the political status of Ireland, a small but troublesome war in South Africa (1899–1902) with the *Boers,* the white Dutch-speaking

Emmeline Pankhurst (center) and her daughter and chief lieutenant, Christabel (third from left), led the Women's Social and Political Union in Britain on a militant campaign for women's suffrage in the years preceding the First World War. Shown with a group of followers, Mrs. Pankhurst rejected compromise and favored the "argument of the broken window pane." (Hulton Archive/Getty Images)

minority, over the question of who would control the strategically important Cape territory; and a worrisome and expensive naval armaments race with Germany in a time when the recently enfranchised workers demanded social reforms—all this confronted the British people at the same time.

Under such conditions, many Britons came to doubt the wisdom of the free-trade policies that had prevailed since mid-century. The Germans and others were not only underselling the British abroad; they were invading the British home market! Why not protect that market by a tariff system, as was done by all other industrial powers? Few in Britain believed that the home islands, already too densely populated to constitute a self-sufficient economy, could surround themselves with a simple tariff wall. But their Empire was worldwide, with abundant agricultural resources. Within it the classical eighteenth-century mercantilist interchange of manufactures for raw materials could still (in theory) provide a balanced economic system.

Joseph Chamberlain (1836–1914), a reform leader from Birmingham who had broken with the Liberal party and allied with the Conservatives over the issue of Irish Home Rule, became a leading protectionist, giving special importance to the establishment of a system of imperial preference through which the whole complex of lands under the Crown would work together in a tariff union. Many Conservatives, particularly those who burned with a passion for imperial unity in a world order that looked more threatening every day, welcomed the issue. Chamberlain's new program, which he called Tariff Reform and Imperial Preference, launched in 1903, proposed moderate tariffs on foreign raw materials and manufactured goods, but also the far more controversial step of duties on imported foodstuffs. These were to be combined with remissions on tariffs for goods traded within the Empire. The new Conservative prime minister, Arthur James Balfour (1848–1930), was sympathetic to many elements of Chamberlain's plan and his goal but dreaded his impetuosity. If Liberals hated tariffs as an article of faith, many loyal Conservatives had grave reservations about facing the voters with a plan that would end the fifty-year reign of free trade and almost certainly lead to a rise in the cost of living. The prime minister could not endorse the "whole hog" tariff plan, and, Chamberlain—with Balfour's cooperation—left the Cabinet in 1903 to stump the country for tariff reform. Balfour, who had been prime minister only a year, was left trying to hold together a party and cabinet increasingly riven by dissension, with some supporting and others opposing with equal ardor the tariff reform program. Finally, by December 1905, the divided government fell. The Liberals won an enormous electoral victory in the next month, winning 400 seats to only 157 for Balfour's followers and 113 for third parties, and formed their first long-lived government in twenty years.

The Liberals moved in another direction, toward the welfare state—old-age pensions, social security through compulsory insurance managed by the state and in part financed by public revenue; minimum wage laws; extended compulsory free public education; and a variety of public works and services. While once associated with a rigid concept of the minimalist state combined with mild reform, the "New Liberalism" now took on the new cause of active interventionism in the name of the people.

In 1909, the Chancellor of the Exchequer, David Lloyd George (1863–1945), introduced the "People's Budget." This plan extended the traditional British practice—Britain had, after all, perfected the modern graduated income tax in the nineteenth century—that those who enjoyed a comfortable income paid the lion's share of direct taxes. It proposed making the rich finance the new welfare measures through increased progressive taxation on incomes and inheritances; but it went beyond this, authorizing a reassessment of all land in the nation in pursuit of taxing the "unearned increment"—the seemingly natural "fact" that land increased in value over time without any effort on the part of an owner who had inherited it. This was nothing less than a proposal for altering the social and economic structure of the nation. The bill passed through the Commons and was rejected by the Lords—an obviously provocative action. After two elections, in January and December 1910, the Liberals lost their majority, winning almost exactly the same number of Commons seats as the Conservatives (272 each), although the Conservative majority in the Lords did agree to the budget. To keep their government in power, the Liberals appealed for the support of a third party, the Irish Nationalists, a single-issue party dedicated to gaining Irish Home Rule. The Irish supported the Liberals and in 1911 joined them in passing the Parliament Act, which clarified that the upper house had no power over money bills and left the

Lords with no more than a suspensory veto of two years over any bill passed in three successive sessions by the Commons. The new King George V (r. 1910–1936) reluctantly gave his pledge that, if the Lords would not pass the Parliament Bill, he would create enough peers to make a new majority. The Lords surrendered and passed the bill, sacrificing their own political power. From this point, the Liberal social reform program was safe.

In the generation after 1880 there was a major change in the political orientation of British parties. Many Liberals, who had believed that the government that governed least (and least expensively) governed best, had come to believe that the state must interfere to some degree in domestic life to help the underdog and had adopted Lloyd George's plan for redistributing the national wealth by social insurance financed by taxation. Meanwhile, many Conservatives, members of a party that had stood in the mid-nineteenth century for factory acts and mild forms of the welfare state, came to embrace a laissez faire or anti-interventionist attitude opposing government interference in the economy—a program much like that of the Liberals of 1850.

One factor in this reversal had been the growth of the political wing of the labor movement, which in 1906 won thirty seats in the Commons (and approximately another twenty, if the so-called Lib-Labs, Labourites campaigning under Liberal colors, are counted). In this year they began to call themselves the Labour party. Labourites sought a welfare state, and many of them also wanted a socialist state in which at least the major industries would be nationalized. The new party had the backing of many upper- and middle-class voters who sympathized with the quest for social reorientation. From their ranks came intellectuals like George Bernard Shaw (1856–1950), H. G. Wells (1866–1946), G. D. H. Cole (1889–1959), and Sydney and Beatrice Webb (1858–1947 and 1858–1943, respectively), who in the 1880s formed the influential Fabian Society. The Fabians preached the "inevitability of gradualness," the attainment of social democracy not through revolution but by the peaceful parliamentary strategy of advancing one step at a time. They took their name from the Roman general Fabius Cunctator, "who waited," and wore down the Carthaginians in the third century B.C.

By the early 1900s Fabianism seemed to be working. The Liberals, who depended in part on Labour votes to maintain a majority, put through much important legislation in the interest of the worker: acceptance of peaceful picketing, the sanctity of labor union funds, and employers' liability to compensate for accidents (all in 1906); modest state-financed old age pensions (1908); health and unemployment insurance (1911); and minimum wage regulations (1912). Part of the motivation for Liberal social legislation was a desire to forestall Labour initiatives. But over the long run the vast majority of working-class voters gravitated to the Labour party. The Liberal party was beginning a long decline that would be hastened by the effects of World War I and would drive its right wing to Toryism and its left to Labour.

The imperialist wing of the Liberal party, led originally by Chamberlain until his defection to the other side of politics, remained unreconciled to this trend, and in 1901 a union between the Fabians and disaffected Liberals began to hint that a new national party was needed to make national effi-

---

The Written Record

BEATRICE WEBB ON "WHY I BECAME A SOCIALIST"

One of the leading intellectuals in the socialist movement in Britain was Beatrice
Potter, who became the wife of the Fabian socialist and administrator Sidney Webb.
In *My Apprenticeship* she addressed the question, "Why I Became a Socialist."

Can I describe in a few sentences the successive steps in my progress towards
Socialism?

My studies in [London's] East End life had revealed the physical misery and
moral debasement following in the track of the rack-renting landlord and capitalist profit-maker in the swarming populations of the great centres of nineteenth-century commerce and industry. It is true that some of these evils—for
instance, the low wages, long hours and insanitary conditions of the sweated
industries, and the chronic under-employment at the docks, could, I thought,
be mitigated, perhaps altogether prevented by appropriate legislative enact-
ment and Trade Union pressure. By these methods it might be possible to
secure to the manual workers, so long as they were actually at work, what
might be regarded from the physiological standpoint as a sufficient livelihood.
Thus, the first stage in the journey—in itself a considerable departure from
early Victorian individualism—was an all-pervading control, in the interest of
the community, of the economic activities of the landlord and the capitalist.

But however ubiquitous and skillful this State regulation and Trade Union
intervention might become, I could see no way out of the recurrent periods of
inflation and depression—meaning, for the vast majority of the nation, alter-
nate spells of overwork and unemployment—intensified, if not actually
brought about by the speculative finance, manufacture and trading that was
inspired by the mad rush to secure the maximum profit for the minority who
owned the instruments of production. Moreover, "Man does not live by bread
alone"; and without some "socialism"—for instance, public education and public health, public parks and public provision for the aged and infirm, open to all
and paid for out of rates and taxes, with the addition of some form of "work or
maintenance" for the involuntarily unemployed—even capitalist governments
were reluctantly recognising, though hardly fast enough to prevent race-dete-
rioration, and the régime of private property could not withstand revolution.
This "national minimum" of civilised existence, to be legally ensured for every
citizen, was the second stage in my progress toward socialism.

Beatrice Webb, *My Apprenticeship* (Hammondsworth: Penguin Books, 1938), II, pp.
439–40. Copyright by the London School of Economics and Political Science.

---

ciency its goal. As the Liberal party fragmented, declined, and sought to hold
on to its followers against the rise of Labour, it became more of a coalition
than a functioning whole within a two-party system. On one subject (and
with certain colorful exceptions) it remained reasonably united, however: the

significance of the British Empire. As one member of Parliament (and one of the founders of the study of geopolitics), Halford John Mackinder (1861–1947) argued, free trade would protect imperialism. He maintained that Britain must become a nation of "organizers," of workers whose patriotism led them to realize that they existed primarily to serve the national ends of the state.

In a controversial work first published in the 1930s, the historian George Dangerfield described Britain in the last years before the First World War as caught up in a time of "unrest" that extended both deeper and further than politics alone and threatened the very social fabric of the nation. Although ordinary people were at the time far less sophisticated in their knowledge about economics than in our own time, all who earned their livings could not avoid firsthand knowledge of the effects of changes in the value of money. In these years, as Britain's industrial mastery was slipping away, it was clear that income was not going as far as it once did: hence, the national standard of living seemed to be endangered. Not surprisingly, wage workers at the lower levels of the income ladder felt the most threatened. In a nation with a well-established system of trade unions (which in the latter nineteenth century had added millions of women and unskilled men to a movement once made up almost entirely of the skilled) this led to higher compensation demands and to widespread strikes across the industrial spectrum. When the "labor unrest" ended with the coming of war, more worker-hours had been lost to industrial disputes than in any comparable period in British history. Victorian complacency among both labor and management was shattered; organized workers were more conscious of the power latent in organization; large trade unions formed partnerships to cooperate in future actions; union leaders thought by workers to be complacent were challenged by the rank and file. Perhaps the most important by-product of this difficult period was the raising of what socialists called "class consciousness." When Britain experienced the nation's only General Strike in 1926, the great industrial action—a failure, as it turned out—owed much to the memory of the labor unrest of 1910–1914.

As noted in the last chapter, Britain also experienced in these years a great campaign for women's suffrage. Although the goal of securing votes for women in national elections was not new in the years before 1914, there was a distinct change evident among both the campaigners and the methods they used. Frustrated at what she considered the glacial progress of the movement under the established suffrage organizations, beginning in 1912 Mrs. Pankhurst led the upper- and middle-class ladies of her own Women's Social and Political Union on a campaign of increasing violent protest that they called "direct action." They slashed pictures in the National Gallery, broke up political meetings, assaulted politicians, smashed windows in London's elegant shops, and chained themselves to railings while they cried out "Votes for Women!" Nor surprisingly, the government of the day—a Liberal cabinet, by the way, with a majority of moderate suffragists—reacted strongly to the lawbreaking and saw that the militant "suffragettes" (as they called themselves) were arrested. Once tried and imprisoned, they turned to hunger striking, leading to their release by the embarrassed authorities and a repetition of the process. The WSPU was small, certainly never more than a few thousand, with only a handful taking part in "the argument of the broken window pane." Yet they gained attention and publicity for the cause to a degree that the more moderate suffragists could not rival. Equally interesting is the fact that Mrs. Pankhurst and her followers not only excluded all men from their society but also divorced themselves from what might be considered their natural allies: socialists and the temperance and pacifist movements.

It is impossible to establish a firm causal link between the labor and the suffrage movements, much less between their organizations or leaders. It is undeniable, however, that both unpredictable campaigns fed the tension, drama, and anxiety of the time. There is another point worth mentioning: Although the goal of the radical WSPU was not achieved in the prewar years—and many argue that their extremist methods impeded rather than hastened women's suffrage—it is hard to deny them their part in the movement to raise the consciousness of women and encourage them to seek and even demand a fuller, more complete life in the new twentieth century. It is not difficult to argue toward a similar conclusion regarding many among the working classes.

A third area of contention challenged the internal cohesion of Great Britain in the years leading up to the Great War. It cut across class, gender, and economic barriers and touched on such fundamental issues as race, religion, and the political unity of the United Kingdom: This was Britain's "Irish Problem."

The "Irish Problem": The Struggle for Home Rule

As in eastern Europe, Britain was faced with a nationality problem that grew more acute near the end of the nineteenth century. Within the overwhelmingly Celtic and Roman Catholic population of Ireland, by ancient conquest, settlement, or purchase, there existed a privileged Protestant minority—frequently landowning, often absentee, and usually segregated from their Irish neighbors. In most of the island, despite their political and economic significance, they were a tiny minority. Only in six of the counties of Ulster in the northeast, where the settlement of devoted Protestants usually of Scottish descent had been a concerted policy of British governments of the sixteenth and seventeenth centuries, did they claim a majority. Although there were also native Irish among the ruling classes, many of them had been Anglicized and had embraced Protestantism.

For three centuries religious, political, and economic problems in Ireland had remained unsolved. Over the course of the nineteenth century the nation had been joined to Britain as an integral part of the United Kingdom (1801), a solution rejected from the outset by many Irish. Although the granting of full political rights to Irish Catholics in 1829 led to the application to Ireland of the reformist measures of the nineteenth century, these measures did not satisfy those Irish who wished for separation. This dissatisfaction became hatred for many after the national catastrophe of the potato famine of the mid-1840s. More than a million Irish died of starvation or related disease, and they blamed the London government for taking insufficient steps to ameliorate the disaster. An additional million emigrated, taking their anger with them to the Americas, Australia, or New Zealand.

Further reforms followed in due course, but none dimmed the longing among many for some degree of self-rule. The longing remained just that—punctuated by periodic outbreaks of insurrectionist violence followed by retaliatory coercion by the state—without organizing leadership. This need was met in a Protestant landlord of Anglo-American stock, Charles Stewart Parnell (1846–1891), who made the Irish cause his own. He organized the Irish National Party and in the 1880s truly became the "Uncrowned King of Ireland."

In 1886, the Liberal leader William Ewart Gladstone (1809–1898) responded to Irish wishes and brought in a bill to grant the Irish limited self-government. This drove Chamberlain and his imperialist followers out of the Liberal party forever. It failed to pass through Parliament and resulted in a Conservative election victory. Gladstone, in his eighty-fourth year, returned to power in 1893 for a fourth time and brought in a second Home Rule Bill, this time getting it through the Commons but failing in the Lords. Two years later the Conservatives scored an electoral triumph, turning this time to "killing home rule with kindness," a policy of economic and political reforms in the island. However, from this point nothing but self-governance, inside or outside the United Kingdom, would please Irish nationalists.

The sense of Irish nationhood was nourished by a remarkable literary revival in English and Gaelic by writers like the poet W. B. Yeats (1865–1939), the dramatist John Millington Synge (1871–1909), and Lady Augusta Gregory (1859–1932), cofounder of Dublin's Abbey Theatre, which staged plays with deeply Irish themes. Irish men and women everywhere—particularly Irish Americans—came eventually to conclude that nothing would satisfy them but an independent Irish state.

As noted earlier, the British Liberal government found that after the two elections of 1910 they needed the votes of the Irish Nationalists in the Commons to carry out their plan to destroy the power of the House of Lords. The deal was struck between the two parties: home rule in return for support for the Parliament Act of 1911. The act passed, and the Liberals brought in their Home Rule Bill in 1912—which the Lords could now delay but not stop. The crisis over home rule became more intense—with Conservatives and other supporters of the union between Britain and Ireland, as well as the militant Ulster Protestants, determined to defeat home rule or, if this was not possible, at least to prevent the subjugation of Ulster to a Catholic Irish majority. Pro–home rulers were equally adamant. As Europe drew closer to war in 1914—the year the Home Rule Bill was scheduled to become law under the provisions of the Parliament Act—Irishmen of both sides drilled openly in the streets of Irish cities in private sectarian armies. Men and women spoke of the possibility of civil war, and some suggested that the British army would mutiny rather than march to enforce home rule in Ulster. The outbreak of war in 1914 placed the Irish question in abeyance for the duration, but when the killing stopped on the western front in 1918, it began in the streets of Dublin and Cork. When settlement came in 1921, home rule—that is, autonomy within the United Kingdom—was no longer enough to satisfy Irish nationalists, and the only solution seemed to be to divide the island in two: the majority of the island became a largely Catholic self-governing Dominion (the Irish Free State, which declared itself independent in 1937 and finally a republic in 1948), while a Protestant-dominated province in the six counties of the northeast remained and remains a part of the United Kingdom of Great Britain and Northern Ireland. The division set the stage for a ferocious civil war, remembered as "the Troubles," in the Free State between supporters and opponents of the 1921 settlement and, years later, for violent controversy over the status of Northern Ireland in our own time.

France: The Third Republic, 1890–1914

Born in the chaos and humiliation of 1870, when France was defeated in the Franco-Prussian War and the political authority of the Second Empire of Napoleon III collapsed with its military ineptitude, the Third Republic (the ordinal making reference to the two revolutionary republics of the eighteenth and nineteenth centuries) evolved by necessity when there was no other system to run the country. The new republic would establish a bicameral National Assembly—the lower house, or Chamber of Deputies, elected by universal manhood suffrage, and the upper, the Senate, by nomination by regional elected officials. The head of state was the president, whose powers were so limited that the true chief executive was the premier, who depended upon the support not of the president but of a majority in the Chamber.

After two Napoleons and several would-be autocrats had come and gone, the Third Republic purposely would be structured to make the path to power difficult for any future aspiring military dictator, a so-called man on horseback. As late as 1889, the dashing General George Boulanger (1837–1891), a popular military hero supported by a curious coalition of monarchists, radicals, and nationalists who sought a war of revenge against Germany, seemed on the verge of attempting a military coup. In the end, he lost his nerve, fled the country, and eventually took his own life. But he was not forgotten by any side, either opponents or supporters of the republic.

Political consensus itself was difficult to achieve in the new system: The nation remained divided for a generation over whether to restore some form of limited monarchy or to embrace the republic. Monarchist political parties—both legitimist (favoring the Bourbon heir) and Orléanist (supporting the heir of France's last king, Louis Philippe)—quarreled with each other while at the same time bitterly opposing supporters of the republic. Catholics and anticlericalists divided over relations between church and state, and the commitment of the republic to freedom of religion did little to reconcile the devout to a form of government that refused a special status to the religion of the overwhelming majority. So, on the right, many in the church, the army, and among the wealthy still hoped for government by a single strong man. The political left was also divided, between pro- and anti-Marxist socialists, anarchists, and syndicalists.

This atmosphere of dissension was not improved by a series of scandals in the last years of the nineteenth century—the president's son-in-law was implicated in the selling of the nation's most distinguished award for national service, the Legion of Honor; then the company organized to construct a canal through the Isthmus of Panama collapsed in failure and financial scandal. Ferdinand Vicomte de Lesseps (1805–1894), toast of the world when in 1869 he had successfully completed the Suez Canal, saw his reputation destroyed. Ministers and deputies had accepted bribes for backing the shaky canal–building enterprise, and anti-Semitic propagandists were able to make much of the fact that several Jewish financiers were implicated. Bad as it was, these scandals were to pale before the Dreyfus affair, in which the force of modern anti-Semitism first attained worldwide attention.

Captain Alfred Dreyfus (1859–1935), a Jew from a wealthy family that had fled to France when Alsace was lost to Germany, was the almost accidental victim of an espionage intrigue and of the anti-Semitism then prevalent in France. Accused of selling military secrets to the Germans, he was railroaded to trial as a scapegoat, largely because he was the first Jew to serve on the French general staff. He was convicted of treason in 1894 and sentenced to life imprisonment on Devil's Island, off the coast of South America. In 1896 an intelligence officer, Colonel Georges Picquart (1854–1914), became convinced that the document on which Dreyfus had been convicted was a forgery and that the real traitor was a disreputable adventurer, Major Ferdinand Esterhazy (1849–1923). Picquart was quietly shipped off to Africa by his superiors, but the Dreyfus family, by independent investigation, arrived at the conclusion that Esterhazy was the traitor and sought to reopen the case. Esterhazy was tried and acquitted, but the affair was now too public for silencing. In 1898, the famous novelist Emile Zola (1840–1902) brought matters to a crisis by publishing in the press an open letter, *J'Accuse*. Zola accused the military leaders, one by one, of deliberately sacrificing an innocent man to save the reputation of the army.

France was now divided into Dreyfusards and anti-Dreyfusards. Dreyfus was retried in the midst of a frenzied campaign in the press. The military court, faced with new evidence brought out by the suicide of the forger of the most incriminating of the original documents used to convict Dreyfus, nonetheless again found Dreyfus guilty of treason. However, Dreyfus was then pardoned by the president of the republic, and in 1906, after tensions had abated, he was acquitted by a civilian court and restored to the army with the rank of major.

Bitterly divisive though the Dreyfus affair was, the years of debate brought radicals, socialists, liberals, republicans, anticlericals, and intellectuals—all suspicious of the army, of the church, and of anti-Semitism—into a loose alliance. Many on both sides of the question worked themselves into a mass hysteria in which the question of Dreyfus' guilt was wholly submerged in the confrontation between the "two Frances"—the France of the republic, heir to the great revolution and the principles of 1789, and the France of the monarchy, of throne and altar, and of the army, which had never reconciled itself to the principles of the great revolution.

With the victory of the Dreyfusards, the republic punished the church for supporting the army and the anti-Dreyfusards. In a series of measures between 1901 and 1905 the triumphant republicans destroyed the Concordat of 1801 between Napoleon I and the pope that had established the Roman Catholic church in a privileged position in the French state. Catholic teaching orders were forced to dissolve, and some twelve thousand Catholic schools were closed. The state would no longer pay the clergy, and private corporations organized among the faithful would take over the expenses of worship and the ownership and maintenance of the churches. But Catholicism was not outlawed. Catholic education, while severely handicapped, was not formally persecuted. Indeed, the separation did not radically alter the fundamental social position of the church in France. The upper classes and the peasantry of the north, northeast, and west remained for the most part loyal Catholics; many of the urban middle and working classes and many peasants in parts of the south, southwest, and center remained either indifferent Catholics or determined socialists.

The Third Republic had become more republican without moving noticeably toward becoming a welfare state. This was hardly surprising in a country that remained essentially a land of small farm-owning peasants, conservative in their agricultural methods, and of relatively small family-controlled industries, conservative in their business methods. French business owners preferred internal financing because they wished to maintain their independence, either because the firm was part of family property or because they preferred substantial emergency reserves to meet sudden drops in the market or unexpected technological changes, mostly from outside France.

For many in France, life improved during this period, although at the cost of vast dislocations for others. In the growing cities a wandering population, sometimes turning to crime or to organized violence, contended with the migration of the law-abiding poor, who sought greater security in areas of new industrial growth or in the new labor organizations. The transportation system could not always cope with these shifts in population, so that resources were scarce in various regions at different times, enhancing a common sense of social identity among the activist and the angry. Increasingly, women became part of the urban work force, sharing in its grievances and its growth, although usually the only jobs open to them were those that demanded the least skills and were therefore the lowest paid. By the end of the nineteenth century women would be found in metal foundries, bleaching mills, potteries, and brickyards and at the mouths of coal pits and stone quarries. However, most women working outside of agriculture were in the textile or garment industries or in domestic service.

French women and girls lagged behind their British and American sisters in another field of social welfare: public education. While girls had been permitted admission to the state secondary education system in 1880, they were denied a curriculum leading to higher education. The handful of French women at university in these years, therefore, remained smaller than in these other nations. It is also true, however, that the number of female students in public and private secondary schools, as well as the universities, increased steadily until the coming of the First World War. In this environment it is not surprising that the agitation for increased political rights for women was not on the scale of that in the English–speaking nations—and, in fact, French women would not receive the franchise until after the Second World War.

The upper and middle classes ate and lived well, although the petty bourgeois found that inflation often forced economies on them, as wives became increasingly expert at specialized shopping and cooking. "Second-hand" foods became commonplace—foods that had been prepared and served to one family, with the remainder, often decayed, sold to a poorer family. There was an especially brisk trade in Paris in such leftovers, as population growth moved too rapidly for economic adjustments to provide, or transport to supply, sufficient staples. Throughout the nineteenth century the policing of food and water supplies was a subject of middle-class concern. The women working in a textile factory—exposed to dangerous machinery, laboring fifteen to eighteen hours without sanitary facilities (there were seldom public or workplace toilets), subjected to chemicals and fibers that brought on brown lung and early death—could hope for little more than food that was, at least, "ripe." And yet French men and women remained devoted to the fatherland, *la Patrie.* Their growing sense of nationalism led to an increasing assumption that public authorities must deal with such matters as health, transport, and safety.

Italy: Unity and Frustration

Traditionally divided into possessions of larger countries, small independent states, and free cities since the Middle Ages, Italy was a nation but not a state until after 1861. The unification of a new Kingdom of Italy—the *Risorgimento*—under Victor Emmanuel II of the House of Savoy, king of Piedmont-Sardinia, came principally through the efforts of the romantic nationalist adventurer Giuseppi Garibaldi (1807–1882) and his private army of "Red Shirts" and of Victor Emmanuel's own chief minister, Count Camilo Cavour (1810–1861). The new kingdom encompassed almost the entire peninsula and the surrounding islands and established its capital in Florence. The population of the former papal territories, those lands whose traditional overlord had long been the pope, had chosen to join the new state, ensuring that the papacy remained hostile to the kingdom for another sixty years. The city of Rome, the last vestige of secular authority of the pope, was garrisoned by the troops of its self-appointed protector, Napoleon III. When the French emperor recalled his soldiers to fight the Prussians in 1870, Rome fell to the new kingdom. Thereafter it inevitably became the capital, and for the next half-century, disapproving popes declared themselves "prisoners" within the Vatican.

The kingdom of Italy was not without its problems: The disapproval of the papacy meant that, like France, Italy suffered from deep division between pro-clericals and anticlericals. Ardent Catholics resented the loss of the Papal States without papal consent. Italy, while now accorded the status of Great Power, was much the poorest in that exclusive fraternity. She lacked natural resources, particularly coal and iron, the benchmarks of industrialism and modernity. Much of the mountainous central portion and the south of Italy was marginally productive, with a poverty-stricken, illiterate peasantry and a small but tenacious feudal aristocracy. The economy was based on agricul-ture, and most farming was done using age-old methods on vast inefficient estates, the *latifundia,* owned by a small number of great families. Neapolitans and Sicilians resented the new political preponderance of northerners in the unified kingdom. At least half of Italy lacked experience in self-government in a land of deep-seated class antagonisms, characterized by profound mis-trust of governments, and where fervent local loyalty often took precedence over national consciousness.

Not surprisingly, Italy moved slowly toward democratization. The lower house of the national legislature, the Chamber of Deputies, enjoyed consid-erable authority, but it was initially elected on a severely limited franchise. After 1881 the property qualification for voting was reduced to the payment of a relatively modest direct tax, but it was not until 1912 that something close to universal suffrage was introduced.

As Rome remained the eternal city and the Vatican the nerve center of the church for the world's many millions of Catholics, after the *Risorgimento* popes refused to recognize the Italian kingdom and forbade believers—largely unsuccessfully—to participate in politics and urged a boycott of the state. The "Roman Question" remained unsettled until 1929, when Benito Mussolini and Pope Pius XI agreed to recognize the papal monarchy of Vati-can City as a tiny sovereign state of only 108 acres.

The new kingdom did make appreciable economic progress, however. Railroads built and managed by the state pushed rapidly into the undevel-oped south. A new merchant marine and an army and navy gave Italy some standing as a power. Even national finances seemed for a time to be sound. In politics, however, the workings of the new national state were burdened with persistent political corruption and unashamed political opportunism. Meanwhile, the industrial proletariat remained small, labor poorly orga-nized, and democratic socialists both too few and too divided to be an effec-tive instrument of opposition and reform. Moreover, the economic progress of the north, while the south remained impoverished, exploited, and neg-lected, increased regional antagonism and harmed sincere efforts at a shared national progress.

As the twentieth century grew near, under the leadership of the last of the great *Risorgimento* figures, Francesco Crispi (1819–1901), Italy developed imperial aspirations. Since Great Britain and France had empires, and since a true Great Power had to have a "place in the sun," such reasoning decreed that some way of territorial expansion had to found, if Italy was to be taken

seriously as a Great Power. Such logic was dangerously flawed: Italy had little economic need of colonies; compared to her neighbors, she had modest
strength with which to take them; she did have an expanding surplus population difficult for her economy to absorb, but they had little trouble finding
destinations of migration. It appears true that Crispi was concerned about
discontent in some nationalist circles over the fact that thousands of Italians
had been left out of the new kingdom and remained within the lands of
Italy's formidable neighbor, Austria-Hungary. Imperial expansion elsewhere
might turn the minds of the ambitious away from this *Italia irredenta* (unre-
deemed Italy). Crispi might have thought this way, but Italian imperialists
did not: Their dreams of imperial expansion were grounded in the sheer
desire to possess colonies—Great Powers were supposed to have them. Perhaps the view of that supreme skeptic, the German Prince Bismarck, summed
it up accurately, if unkindly: Italy had a "great appetite, but such bad teeth."
Her only successes came with the acquisition of two of the poorer parts of
Africa in the late nineteenth century: Eritrea on the Red Sea and Somaliland
on the horn of Africa where the Red Sea meets the Indian Ocean.

Italy overreached herself in attempting to add the only independent
monarchy in Africa, Abyssinia (now called Ethiopia). In 1896, Italian troops
moved against Abyssinia and, to the shock of the world, were soundly
defeated by the Emperor Menelik II (r. 1889–1913) at Adowa. The national
humiliation cast a shadow over Italy comparable to that of the Dreyfus affair
in France, and this was deepened by a bank scandal and the severe economic
depression that followed. Severe bread riots broke out in Milan in May 1898,
and in 1900 King Humbert I, who had succeeded Victor Emmanuel II in 1878,
was assassinated by an anarchist. The new king, Victor Emmanuel III (r.
1900–1946), who was believed to have liberal leanings, gave heart to many,
and the years just before the First World War were a time of comparative
quiet, prosperity, and partial reconciliation with the church. Also, in
1890–1914 vast emigration to North and South America absorbed much of
the surplus population, easing short-term economic pressures.

Yet frustrated Italian imperialism was still seeking an outlet. Denied
Tunisia by French occupation in 1881 and then forced from Abyssinia, Italy
finally got from the Great Powers a free hand in poor and parched Tripoli, a
fragment of the old Ottoman Empire, today called Libya. In 1911 Italy fought
the Tripolitanian War with Turkey for the territory and this time was successful. Of Italy's fragmentary north African empire, Bismarck was said to
have remarked that it seemed that Italy would go along with "whomever
promised her the most sand."

The industrial growth of Europe, which had begun in Britain, spread to the
Continent after 1880, but Italy presented a pattern of substantial industrialization in some areas and continued sluggishness in others. Italy remained on
the margin of the industrializing process that was so rapidly transforming
Germany, partly because of a growing preoccupation with winning an overseas empire. The gap widened between the northern industrial triangle of
Genoa, Milan, and Turin and the south. By 1900 the south of Italy accounted

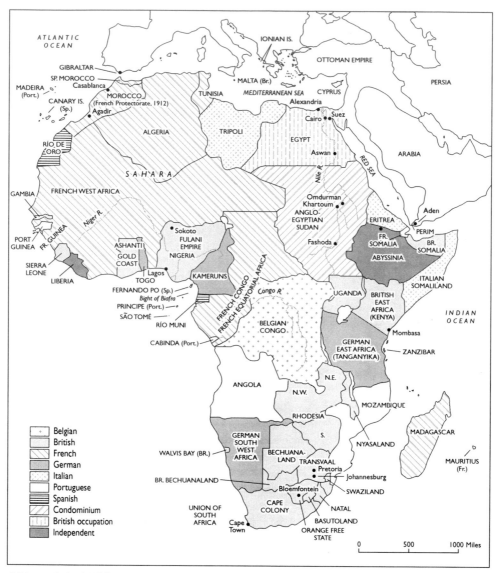

Africa and the Middle East, 1910

Emperor Menelik II, King of Kings, Conquering Lion of Judah, Emperor of Ethiopia, and, in his defeat of the Italians at Adowa in 1896, the first non-European to defeat a modern European army. (*Hulton Archive/Getty Images*)

for 42 percent of the land and 26 percent of the population of the nation; yet it had but 17 percent of the industrial work force and only 12 percent of the taxable property. The south was unable to supply a market for northern Italian goods, while the north could not find work for all its surplus labor. The result was a widespread emigration exceeded in Europe only by the Irish.

Demographic and economic factors left Italy divided internally along geographic and class lines. The political left advocated further social reforms to achieve social justice and political equality, but accomplished relatively little because of internal dissension. The remnants of the left wing of the *Risorgimento* split into largely non-Marxist factions, and no successful reform party emerged from the middle class. Italian parliamentary government remained weak. Italian class structure militated against the development of effective multiple parties, and political debate increasingly appeared to be shaped by intellectuals who purported to speak either for a ruling elite or for the Italian masses.

Germany: The Nation-State

There was no German nation-state until 1871, and it was largely the creation of Prince Otto von Bismarck (1815–1898). Brilliant, unscrupulous, ruthless, a genius at maneuvering and at concealing his real intentions, he towered over his native Prussia after 1862 and, as chancellor, over the new Germany he created, until his abrupt dismissal by the newly crowned Kaiser William II (r.

1888–1918) in 1890. The young monarch was only twenty-nine when he came to the throne, after the three-month reign of his mortally ill father, Frederick III. The new kaiser was intelligent, ambitious, and strong-willed; he was also a passionate nationalist, an admirer of German militarist traditions, and adamantly opposed to the more liberal sentiments of his parents. More important, he was an impulsive arrogant man who had no intention of playing a quiescent second fiddle to the titanic figure of his chancellor.

Bismarck believed politics to be the "art of the possible." Since further conflict in the future was inevitable, wisdom dictated moderation toward defeated enemies, for they might be needed one day as allies. Since life threw into conflict a shifting kaleidoscope of social classes, political parties, special-interest groups, sectional loyalties, intemperate individuals who had attained positions of power, and entire nations and states, one could not expect to predict with accuracy a nation's future needs in terms of alliances. Therefore, a nation's leaders must always have an alternative course of action ready, a course not too brutally contradicted by any firmer alliance, so that the middle ground might be credibly taken. After Bismarck, Germany appeared to lose sight of these principles.

Upon his accession, William II proclaimed his sympathy for the working classes. When Bismarck's antisocialist law, meant to allow the state powers to single out and control the parliamentary Social Democrats as well as more radical political groups, came up for renewal, the kaiser insisted on softening the coercive powers of the act. Bismarck objected, as he did over an international workers' conference, over relations with Russia, and over the kaiser's insistence that he be allowed to meet individual ministers without the customary presence of the chancellor. Finally, in 1890, William commanded Bismarck to resign.

The young emperor was intelligent and patriotic but also unsteady, neurotic, menacing, and without the intention or courage to back up his threats. William was ill suited to govern any country, much less the militaristic, highly industrialized imperial Germany, with its social tensions and its lack of political balance. Tendencies already present under Bismarck became more apparent. The Prussian army, and especially the reserve officers, came increasingly to exercise great influence on William II. Party structure reflected the strains in German society. The Liberals, a party of big business, usually had little strength in the Reichstag, the lower house of the national legislature. The Liberals were also divided by local and regional rivalries. The great landowners banded together in protest against a reduction in import duties on agricultural goods. In 1894 they organized the Agrarian League, which spearheaded conservative measures. In 1902 they forced a return to protection.

In Germany, unlike France and Britain, women were generally given little role to play in the reform movement. Denied the right to vote, they were usually barred from membership in political organizations and labor unions. Whereas in France women had traditionally been leaders in the arts, in Germany they were denied access to professional training; and while the first public secondary schools for girls were established in the 1890s, they were not comparable to the excellent *Gymnasia*, the rigorous institutions for boys. Women were admitted to universities after the turn of the century, but it remained difficult for them to achieve higher degrees. The goal set for women was to provide their husbands and families with "a proper domestic atmosphere."

Those few women who were openly politically active usually joined pacifist and socialist associations, since the socialists advocated equal pay for equal work. By 1900 there were over 850 associations working for women's rights in Germany, but during the Empire few of their stated goals were achieved. Although the Progressive party endorsed the principle of suffrage for women in 1912, it did little to achieve that end. Many women worked in the textile industry, and in 1878 women were admitted to the German civil service—a move prompted not so much by feminist effort as by the need for people who could operate the telegraph, telephone, and typewriter. Women of the middle classes were thus brought into the work force, although they were paid less than men.

Women were assigned, or accepted, roles in childhood nurturing that in time led to careers in teaching, especially in the kindergarten movement, which had its origins in Germany. Although suppressed in Prussia, in part because kindergartens were viewed as too progressive, the movement took root elsewhere in western Europe and later in Germany once again. The feminist movement in Germany embraced child care as a profession, held that the sacred role of women was to be mothers of the nation, and argued that women must take the lead in agitating for legislation by which the state would recognize its obligation to care for women and children, protecting them from abusive husbands and fathers and from homelessness. Germany prepared a uniform civil code that, in 1896, permitted women to become guardians over children, and motherhood was seen as a career. Women also led the way in the campaign against infant mortality, initiated widespread debates about reproductive rights and the concept of population quality, and launched the new profession of social work. One leader, Frieda Duensign (1864–1933), studied law in Switzerland, entered the field of child welfare service, and helped to put female workers at the heart of Germany's growing juvenile court system.

Meanwhile, issues of military, colonial, and foreign policy began to complicate the tense internal politics of Germany. After Admiral Alfred von Tirpitz (1849–1930) became minister of the navy in 1897, he convinced the emperor of the need to build a high seas fleet to replace the limited navy designed only for coastal and commercial defense. This suited William II perfectly, for he had long felt a curious love-hate relationship with Britain, long the world's greatest naval power. The mother of the young kaiser was a daughter of Britain's Queen Victoria, and William II loved his grandmother, whom he thought regal and strong, as much as he distrusted his mother, who was tainted in his eyes with liberal sentiments—he also hated his maternal uncle, King Edward VII, whom he thought debauched, unmanly, and unworthy of his place. William respected and envied the British Empire and, above all, admired the Grand Fleet. He loved to dress in the British uniforms given him by his uncle, and the desire for a great fleet of his own—a worthy challenge to a Britain whose best days were past her—was irresistible.

But an army and navy were only the most obvious weapons of world power. The Colonial Society, founded to support the case for overseas expansion, grew rapidly in membership as Germany acquired territories in the Far East and in Africa, despite the drain on the national budget (for these colonies were never profitable). Pan-Germans planned a great Berlin-Bagdad railway to the Near East and cried for more adventure and more conquest. It is impossible not to see a boastful and irrational nationalist excitement in all of this similar to that which moved some of the Italian imperialists. The terrifying difference was that imperial Germany had a great appetite and very good teeth, indeed.

William's naval and colonial policies predictably embittered Germany's relations with Great Britain, traditionally the world's greatest naval and imperial power. Germany had long been thought of as a traditional friend to Britain. As long as Bismarck was in control, the British could reasonably hope that Germany would confine her ambitions to altering the existing order in Europe: After 1890 it seemed that Germany also intended to alter the world balance of power, and the British felt their interests directly threatened. The Germans could, for example, give no suitable answer to the question: Against whom might a great new fleet be employed?

Foreign policy in both nations was shaped by a complex mixture of social, economic, political, and ideological factors ranging from religious and cultural connections through the changing attitudes of parties, the press, pressure groups, and the bureaucracies. Leaders in business and politics in both countries worked for a harmonious relationship between the nations, but in the end they failed.

Britain had other than diplomatic and military reasons to be apprehensive of German power. By the eve of the First World War, Germany had overtaken Britain in heavy industrial production and was her rival in many of the major export trades. This surging development of Germany made its militarism possible, while its militarism in turn fed industrialism. Beginning later and with fewer advantages than England, Germany recognized that it lagged behind commercially and made an early commitment to sophisticated technology. As in Britain, railroads provided the first surge of activity, followed by the industrial development of the Ruhr Valley. Germany soon forged ahead in steel, organic chemistry, and electricity.

Economic issues were always close to the surface in all German political debate. When the Ruhr proved to be rich in coal and transportation costs were moderate, a mixture of private initiative and state assistance industrialized the region almost before political debate could take shape. Similarly, modern methods of scientific forestry began to be adopted and agriculture similarly became more efficient. Assisted by an active cooperative movement and by state-supported agricultural schools and experimental stations, German grain growers exported food until 1873. Thereafter, as cheap grain from eastern Europe began to enter Germany, economic policy turned toward protectionism. National efficiency—whether in the growth of larger and larger factories, firms, and cartels or in more productive agriculture—became a goal on which nearly all parties could agree. By 1914 Germany was largely self-sufficient in many significant areas of industry.

Austria-Hungary: Dividing Humanity into Nations

In a sense, nationalism was a doctrine invented in Europe in the nineteenth century to account for social, economic, and political changes that required a single descriptive term. The concept of nationhood easily led to the assumption that humanity was divided—by divine intent, nature, or the material force of history—into nations, and that therefore the course of history was toward the self-determination of those peoples. The American Declaration of Independence had asserted such a principle, and the French Revolution and the decades that followed had brilliantly illustrated its power. By the mid-nineteenth century most people in western Europe assumed that the only legitimate type of government in the West was that which carried a society toward independence.

Most commentators on nationalism argue that certain common characteristics can be identified, so that a "nation" can be objectively defined. These characteristics include a shared language, a common object of veneration (usually called the homeland), a shared life in a common territory under similar influences of nature and common outside political pressures, and the creation of a state of mind that strives toward a sense of homogeneity within the group. This sense of common identity is fostered by holding to common symbols, rituals, and social conventions through a common language (or variant of it), religion, and sense of mutual interdependence. Usually the positive aspects of such a sense of group identity will be strengthened by a negative emphasis on those who lack such characteristics.

Nationalism may be fed by what the historian Hans Kohn termed "vital lies"—beliefs held to be true and so central to a sense of identity that to question them at all is to be disloyal. These certain historical ideas may be untrue—even lies consciously fostered—but because of widespread belief in them, they have the vitality and thus the function of truth. Most modern societies think of their way of life as superior to others. Most peoples believe themselves chosen—whether by God or by history.

During the course of the twentieth century such assumptions about national identity and the nation as the source of group and individual security and stability have become commonplace. But what now seems natural was, in fact, unfamiliar or still emerging as part of the process of modernization in the nineteenth century. This was especially so among the many language groups of the Habsburg Empire of Austria-Hungary. For what was known after 1867 as the Dual Monarchy, "modernization" did not mean unification. It meant fragmentation and a trend toward representative government only in relation to divisive nationalisms, not toward new national issues. The empire was a living anachronism, decentralized and lacking all of the unifying principles of the modern nation-state. Yet this enormous medieval remnant was accepted as a matter of course by the other European powers because, with its huge and diverse population and sizeable economic presence, its collapse would have destabilized the delicate balance among the Great Powers.

After a generation of "Germanization" and the failure of autocratic centralized rule from the imperial capital of Vienna, in the *Ausgleich,* or compromise, of 1867 the Empire was reorganized into a kind of partnership, with administrative power vested in Austria and Hungary, and the Crown serving as the unifying instrument. Each half of the Dual Monarchy had its own parliament and administration, with foreign policy, military affairs, and finance in the hands of three joint ministers appointed by the emperor. A customs union, subject to renewal every ten years, united them. Every ten years the quota of common expenditure to be borne by each partner was to be renegotiated. A unique body, the "delegations," made up of sixty members from each parliament, which met alternately in Vienna and Budapest to decide upon a common budget—then passed on to both parliaments—and supervised the activities of the three common ministers. In practice the delegations seldom met and were almost never consulted on questions of policy. The system favored Hungary, which had 40 percent of the population and never paid more than a third of the Empire's expenditures. Every ten years, therefore, when the quota of expenses and the customs union needed joint consideration, a new crisis arose. The common bond meant to hold the system together was the person of the monarch, who was at once king of Hungary and emperor of Austria. The figure on whose shoulders this responsibility rested in this period was Francis Joseph (r. 1848–1916), whose long reign exceeded that of any other monarch of modern times.

The Nationality Question in the Empire

One overwhelming problem remained common to both halves of the monarchy: that of national minorities who had not received their autonomy. Some of these minorities (Czechs, Poles, Ruthenes) were largely in Austria; others (Slovaks, Romanians) were largely in Hungary; the rest (Croats, Serbs, Slovenes) could be found in both. These nationalities were at different stages of national consciousness. Some were subject to pressures and manipulation from fellow nationals living outside the Dual Monarchy. All had some leaders who urged compromise and conciliation with the dominant Germans in Austria and Magyars in Hungary, as well as others who advocated resistance and even revolution. The result was a chronic and often unpredictable instability in the Dual Monarchy.

After years of turmoil, compromise seemed finally to have been reached at the turn of the century when a new law demonstrated the abandonment of one of the most controversial elements of the old policy of Germanization and required that all civil servants in Bohemia, the largely Czech-populated part of the Empire (who previously were required to know only German), be bilingual after 1901. The violent reaction of the Germans in the Vienna parliament brought down the ministry, while Czech extremists began to talk ominously about a future showdown between the German Austrians and Russian-led Slavs. No Austrian parliament could stay in session, and government had to be conducted by decree in the name of the emperor.

Under the stress of this prolonged agitation and influenced by the apparent triumph of constitutionalism in Russia, Francis Joseph finally decided to reform the franchise. In 1907 all citizens in Austrian lands were enfranchised and could vote for deputies in the new parliament, 233 of whom would be German and 107 Czech, a figure nearly proportional to the census figures, since Czechs constituted 23 percent of the Austrian population. Yet in 1913 the Bohemian provincial legislature, or Diet, was dissolved and in 1914, as Europe moved close to a major war, Czech members of the Austrian parliament refused to allow national business to proceed. When World War I began, both the Bohemian and Austrian parliaments were in dissolution and the emperor and his ministers ruled alone. Perhaps chief among the many causes for this general parliamentary breakdown was the failure to give the Czech provinces the full internal self-government already enjoyed by the Magyars, which they had sought since the 1867 *Ausgleich*.

Czech nationalism had not been killed either by coercion or by half-hearted compromise. It was fostered by an active Czech-language press, by patriotic societies, by Czech schools, and by the *sokols* (hawks), a physical-training society with strong nationalist leanings. At the ancient Prague University, Czech scholars supported the idea of a separate national identity. Perhaps the most influential of them was Thomas Masaryk (1850–1937), professor of philosophy and student of Slavic culture, who deeply influenced generations of students and upheld democratic ideals in politics. He inspired poets and novelists to write of a glorified national past for a popular audience, and from 1907 he formally led the Czech independence party. In 1918 Masaryk would become president of the new nation of Czechoslovakia.

Of all the minority nationalities in the Empire, the Czechs were in the best position to exercise independence. Substantial in population, with a high percentage of artisans skilled in the armaments, porcelain, glassware, lace, brewing, and sugar beet industries and with a thriving tourist trade that gave them access to the broader world, the Czechs also were at the center of growing heavy industry.

Of all the minorities in Austria, the Poles (18 percent of the population) were the least overtly discontented. Most of them lived in Galicia, where they formed the landlord class. Like the Czechs, the Galician Poles asked for provincial self-government on the Magyar model and were denied. But they had their own schools, and Polish was the language of regional administration and the courts. The Poles enjoyed favorable financial arrangements, and after 1871 there was a special ministry for Galicia in Vienna.

The contrast between this relatively nondiscriminatory treatment of Poles in Austria and the brutality suffered by Poles living in Prussian and Russian

Poland led Poles everywhere to look to Polish Galicia as the center of Polish national life and culture. Polish exiles took refuge in the cities of Kraków and Lemberg (later Lvov). Here were splendid Polish universities and opportunities to serve the Habsburg Crown in the provincial administration. The universities trained generations of Poles who would be available later for service in independent Poland. Polish literature and the study of Polish history flourished. Slowly, industrialization began, and a promising petroleum industry was launched. Only the Ruthenes (Ukrainians) and the Jews continued to suffer systematic discrimination and hardship.

The other minorities in Austria were far less numerous: In 1910 less than 3 percent of the population was Italian, about 4.5 percent was Slovene, and less than 3 percent was Serb and Croat. The Italians of the south Tyrol and Istria were far more important than their numbers suggest, however. Of all the Austrian minorities, the Italians proved to be the most anxious to get out of the Habsburg monarchy altogether. Both Serbs and Croats in Austria were divided; some preferred autonomy within the Empire, and others hoped one day to join a south Slav state.

Minorities in Hungary

In Hungary minority problems were even more acute. The Slovaks, the Romanians, and the Serbs and Croats living in Hungary were the worst victims of a deliberate policy of Magyarization. The Magyar aim was to destroy the national identity of the minorities and to transform them into Magyars; the weapon was language.

The Magyars, who made up only 55 percent of the population of their own country (exclusive of Croatia), had an intense devotion to their own language—an Asian tongue quite unrelated to the German, Slavic, or Romanian languages of the minorities. They tried to force it upon the subject peoples, particularly in education. All state-supported schools, from kindergartens to universities, wherever located, had to give instruction in Magyar, and the state postal, telegraph, and railroad services used only Magyar.

The Slovaks, numbering about 11 percent of the population of Hungary, were perhaps the most Magyarized. Poor peasants for the most part, the more ambitious of them often became Magyars simply by adopting the Magyar language as their own. As time passed, a few Slovaks came to feel a sense of unity with the closely related Czechs across the border in Austria. The pro-Czechs among the Slovaks were usually liberals and Protestants, while Catholic and conservative Slovaks advocated Slovak autonomy.

The Romanians, who lived in Transylvania, amounted in 1910 to about 17 percent of the population of Hungary and were a majority in Transylvania itself. For centuries they had fought constantly to achieve recognition of their Greek Orthodox religion. Despite laws designed to eliminate the use of their language, the Romanians fiercely resisted assimilation. Some hoped that Transylvania might again be made autonomous, as it had been in the past. Many pressed for the enforcement of a liberal—and ignored—Hungarian nationalities law of 1868. But when in 1892 they petitioned Vienna on these

Nationalities in Central Europe and Eastern Europe, about 1914

points, their petition was returned unopened and unread, and when they circulated the petition widely abroad, their leaders were tried and jailed.

Under Magyar rule, some Serbs and Croats lived in Hungary proper, where they had been ruled by the Magyars since shortly after the *Ausgleich*. Discontented with the Hungarian administration, they hoped to be united with the independent kingdom of Serbia to the South. The majority of Croats in the monarchy lived in Croatia itself, where they had become strongly nationalistic under the impact of the Napoleonic occupation a century earlier. The province enjoyed a limited autonomy under the Magyars: There was in the Hungarian administration a minister for Croatian affairs, responsible for financial and security matters. A local parliament in the Croatian capital of Zagreb sent representatives to the Budapest legislature when Croatian affairs were under discussion, and Croatians formed part of the regular Hungarian imperial "delegation." The Croatian language was spoken by Croat representatives at the sessions of any body they attended and was the language of command in the Croatian territorial army. The Croats exercised considerable control over their own educational system, courts, and police; however, control over tax assessment and collection remained in Budapest.

By the first decades of the twentieth century this system was under great pressure. Nationalists of the Croat party of the Right sought complete autonomy and looked with disdain on Serbs and any non-Catholic south Slavs. Croatian Catholics themselves discriminated in matters of religion against the Croatian-speaking Serb minority among them, who were Greek Orthodox by faith. By this point, the governor of the province, appointed by Budapest, enjoyed the cooperation only of the Magyarized Croats who made up the landowning classes or served in the imperial government. From 1907, the government in Budapest required that all employees of the state railways speak Magyar; the Croats, considering this an insult against their language and culture, began to boycott Hungarian-made goods. By 1909, an already tense atmosphere became more so with the show trials of some fifty Croats charged by the state with plotting to unite the provinces of Croatia and Bosnia with Serbia. Although convicted on slim evidence, the Croat nationalist defendants' sentences were soon reversed by a higher court. Worst of all, nationalism soon found expression in terrorism, and in 1912, 1913, and again in 1914, Bosnian nationalist students attempted to assassinate the Hungarian governor.

The districts of Bosnia and Herzegovina had a special status in the Dual Monarchy. Although technically still possessions of the Ottoman Empire, occupation and administration of the two provinces had been granted to Austria-Hungary at the Congress of Berlin in 1878. Although solidly south Slavic, the population included both Muslim and Roman Catholic minorities. Most Orthodox Christians were peasants, working on the estates of Muslim landlords.

These provinces perpetually threatened to create an explosion. Many observers in Vienna pressed for some sort of all-south-Slav solution that would join Dalmatia (the narrow Croat-occupied region along the Adriatic coast), Croatia, and Bosnia-Herzegovina into one kingdom under Francis Joseph, with the same status as Hungary—creating a triple, rather than a dual, monarchy. Advocates of such a three-part empire came to be known therefore as "Trialists" and met with violent Magyar opposition.

Then in 1908 a revolution in Turkey led by young army officers afforded the Austrian foreign minister, Alois Graf von Aehrenthal (1854–1912), a chance to act. Fortified by a prior secret agreement with Russia (which he violated by acting without first seeking Russia's agreement to his taking action), he annexed the two troublesome provinces in October and announced that they would be given a Diet of their own. This move precipitated a major European crisis, which threatened to cause a war—tensions eventually subsided as the offended Russians (recently defeated in the Russo-Japanese War in 1904–1905) were unready for a conflict. This left the Serbs bitterly disappointed and the Balkan peoples in turmoil.

Society and Politics in Austria and Hungary

In the latter nineteenth century, two new political movements gathered momentum among the Germans of Austria: Pan-Germanism and Christian Socialism. In the early 1880s, moderate Austrian Germans had wanted to hand over the Slavic lands they governed to the Magyars to rule, and then unite Austria economically with Germany. The Pan-Germanists were more radical. They demanded that overwhelmingly Catholic Austria become Protestant and agitated for political union with Germany. The Christian Socialists, however, became the most important Austrian political party. Devoted to the church in a nation that was 90 percent Catholic and outspokenly loyal to the Habsburgs, they appealed to both the peasant and the small business owner by favoring social legislation and by opposing big business. The most famous Christian Socialist leader was the mayor of Vienna, Karl Lueger (1844–1910). Although an outspoken anti-Semite, he built a reputation as Austria's leading social reformer, sponsoring public ownership of city utilities, parks, and playgrounds; free milk for schoolchildren; and other welcome services while catering to his followers' hatred of Jews, Marxists, and Magyars.

To Pan-Germans and Christian Socialists, the Austrian Social Democrats, founded in 1888, responded with a Marxist program calling for government ownership of the means of production and for political action organized by class rather than by nationality. But the Austrian Social Democrats were not revolutionaries, and they set as their immediate goals such political and social gains as universal suffrage, fully secular education, and the eight-hour working day. They were usually led by intellectuals, many of them Jewish, but they were followed by an ever-increasing number of workers. On the nationality question, Social Democratic leaders strongly urged democratic federalism. Each nationality should have control of its own affairs in its own territory; in mixed territories, minorities should be protected; and a central parliament should decide matters of common interest.

Through it all, Emperor Francis Joseph thought of himself as the last "monarch of the old school." Immensely conscientious, he worked hard reading and signing state papers for hours every day. He was without imagination, inflexibly old-fashioned, and extremely conservative. He was intensely pious, and his mere longevity inspired loyalty. His decisions usually came too late and conceded too little, and his responsibility for the course of events is large.

The aging monarch faced bitter personal loss time and again. His son Rudolf committed suicide in 1889 after a scandalous love affair; his empress, Elizabeth, was murdered by an anarchist at Geneva in 1898; and the assassination of his nephew and heir, Francis Ferdinand, in Sarajevo in 1914 would trigger a world war. Still, he reigned with determination far longer than any other European monarch, loyal to the Habsburg ideal to the end.

Despite imperial tragedy and divisive politics, Vienna was one of the great cities of Europe and the world. Its cosmopolitan air, its rapid growth, its mixture of frivolity and high seriousness were remarkable. Here was a city that boasted a cultural and intellectual life as rich as its history, its architectural beauty, and its legendary cuisine. With its pious emperor and beautiful churches, Vienna was obviously a very Catholic city, yet it also was home to a large and influential Jewish community. The city could boast of being one of the European capitals of "official culture"—of painting, opera, and literature—and intellectual orthodoxy. Yet its cafés and cheap lodging houses proved to be magnets for artists and intellectuals from across the Empire dedicated to revolt against the old norms.

In Hungary the situation was rather different. The great landed nobility, owning half of Hungary in estates of hundreds of thousands of acres each and loyal to the dynasty, was a small class numerically. Hungary had a much larger class of country gentlemen whose holdings were far smaller and whose social position was lower, but whose political influence as a group was greater. Since the mid-nineteenth century, many members of this gentry class had entered the civil service or the professions. Throughout the century the towns had become steadily more Magyar, as members of the gentry and peasantry moved into them. At the bottom of the social pyramid was a class of industrial workers in the cities, mostly in the textile and flour-milling industries.

The Jewish population also grew rapidly, mostly by immigration. Many Jews were converted and assimilated and became strongly Magyar in sentiment; but, as in Austria, they remained the object of discrimination, especially among the poorer city population and in the countryside, where they were associated with money lending and tavern keeping, two professions that kept peasants in their debt. Nonetheless, anti-Semitism in Hungary never became as important a political movement as in Austria.

The Catholic church was immensely powerful and rich, but it was the faith of only about 60 percent of the population. Some magnate families and many of the gentry had never returned to Catholicism after the Reformation, remaining Calvinists. Several hundred thousand Germans, chiefly in Transylvania, were Lutheran, and there also were Magyar Unitarians. Clericalism could never have become the dominant force in Hungary that it was in Austria.

Thus, because of its differing social and religious structure, Hungary did not produce strong parties like the Austrian Social Democrats and Christian Socialists. Hungary never effectively changed its law of 1874 by which only about 6 percent of the population could vote. The only real source of Magyar political differences was the question of Hungary's position in the Dual Monarchy. Some, followers of the mid-century revolutionary nationalist Louis Kossuth (1802–1894), favored complete independence; others, called the Tigers, wished to improve the position of Hungary within the monarchy by securing Hungarian control over its own army, diplomatic service, and finances—and by limiting the tie with Austria only to the person of the monarch. While the Tigers were generally victorious, the Kossuthites were able to disrupt the government in 1902, and in 1905 they won a majority in the Budapest parliament. When Francis Joseph refused to meet the demands of the new majority and appointed a loyal general as premier of Hungary, the Kossuthites urged patriots not to pay taxes or perform military service, and until 1910 they kept parliament in constant convulsion. It was in this utterly unstable atmosphere that Hungary received the news on June 28, 1914, that Archduke Francis Ferdinand, heir to the throne of the Dual Monarchy, had been assassinated.

Imperial Russia: The Struggle for Modernity

In Russia the process of modernization took far longer than in western Europe, and with good reason: Serfdom had been abolished only in 1861, and Russia entered the twentieth century with neither a national legislature nor a constitution. When reform came, it seemed to come only as a result of military defeat—after the Crimean War (1854–1856) in the mid-nineteenth century and in the period following the humiliation of the Russo-Japanese war (1904–1905). During most of the period up to the First World War, Russian czars claimed for themselves the autocratic rights that Peter the Great had exercised.

From 1894 the czar was Nicholas II (r. 1894–1917). Handsome and regal in appearance, as well as an exemplary husband and father, Nicholas in his public life displayed perhaps the worst attributes possible for one thrust by fate into his position. He was poorly educated and hopelessly xenophobic and possessed an almost mystical faith in the character of his huge population and a deep devotion to the Orthodox church. He proved to be a weak man with hopelessly limited imagination, and like many other such rulers in other times and places, he hid his indecision and confusion behind an unremitting commitment to political and social reaction. His nation was to him "Holy Russia," and he was its "little father," and the Russia of his imagination was that of Crown, altar, and aristocracy—held together with strict bonds of obedience and in an atmosphere of isolation from modernity.

*The Russian royal family among Cossacks early in the First World War. On Czar Nicholas'
right is the Czarina and to his left the crown prince; they are flanked by three of the royal
princesses.   (Beinecke Rare Book and Manuscript Library, Yale University)*

Like his father Alexander III (r. 1883–1894), Nicholas hated and distrusted
all appeals for liberal reforms on the Western model. These reactionary monarchs, relying always upon a large and entrenched bureaucracy, limited the
already modest franchise for the elected regional councils, or *zemstvos,* and
city assemblies created in the 1860s (the electorate of St. Petersburg was less
than 1 percent of the city population) and pursued a vigorous persecution of
minority nationalities and particularly of Jews, a policy called Russification.
In 1891, twenty thousand Jews were expelled from Moscow to the Pale of Settlement, an area roughly identical to Byelorussia and Ukraine. Official
pogroms were directed against them, especially in Kiev. A quota was applied
to Jews, limiting their entry into high schools and universities. One result was
massive emigration; more than a fifth of Russia's 5 million Jews left, many for
America. Another result was that many disaffected Jewish intellectuals were
driven to join the various revolutionary movements that had sprung up to
oppose the policy of reaction.

When compared to the Western powers, the organization of Russian society appeared to be nearly medieval. The aristocratic caste, a minuscule percentage of the population, owned the vast majority of arable land; a small
urban middle class managed business life and monopolized the civil service
and the coming of industrialization in the latter nineteenth century. The overwhelming majority, the peasantry, was tied by ignorance and economic
necessity to the villages of the vast countryside. There was no legislature or
independent judiciary, and civil liberties as known in the West hardly existed.

Although large numbers of schools for both boys and girls had been established since the mid-nineteenth century, they remained insufficient for the needs of an enormous population with the highest rate of illiteracy among the Great Powers. The privileged, with their great wealth, could enjoy a life of incredible luxury, as the vast majority struggled to survive.

Yet these years were also notable for steady growth in other spheres. In 1892 Count Sergei Witte (1849–1915) came to the ministry of finance. Witte began the Trans-Siberian Railroad, put Russia on the gold standard, attracted much-needed investment capital (especially from France), and balanced the budget, in part through a government monopoly on the sale of vodka. The state-owned railroad network doubled in length between 1894 and 1904, and the need for rails stimulated the steel industry. Correspondingly, the number of urban workers multiplied, and strikes in protest against wretched working conditions became common. In 1897, the working day was fixed by the state at eleven hours for adults, and other provisions were adopted to improve and regularize conditions. These laws, however, proved difficult to enforce, and actual improvements in industry were minimal.

Under the circumstances, many of the young generation of would-be revolutionaries now turned to Marxist "scientific" socialism, embracing beliefs in the inevitability of the class struggle and predicting the downfall of capitalism. A small clandestine group of the intelligentsia—intellectuals, students, professors, and other educated opponents of the extant system formed in 1894–1895 at St. Petersburg—proposed to overthrow the regime, working with all opponents of the class system. The foremost member of the group was Vladimir Ilyich Lenin (1870–1924), a young middle-class lawyer who had just completed an intensive five-year study of the works of Marx and was a fervent convert to the movement. His new activities gained him the attention of the secret police and led to a three-year internal punitive exile in Siberia. After being released, his underground group joined with others to form the Social Democratic party in 1898, and within a few years most of its members were in exile in the West.

Within the new party, dissension soon arose over the question of organization. Should the new party operate under a strongly centralized authority, or should each local group of Social Democrats be free to agitate for its own ends? Lenin insisted on a small, tightly knit group of directors, ruling from the center. At the party congresses of Brussels and London in 1903, the majority voted with him. Lenin's faction thereafter was called by the name *Bolsheviki*, meaning majority, as against the *Mensheviki*, or minority, which favored a loose, democratic system of organization. The Mensheviks held to the ideas of another exile, George Plekhanov (1857–1918), who felt that Russia would be ripe for socialism only after capitalism and industrialism had progressed sufficiently to fulfill the needs of a Marxist class structure. Both groups remained Social Democrats, or SDs as they were often called.

Meanwhile, in 1901, non-Marxist revolutionaries also organized a political party, the Socialist Revolutionaries, or SRs. Whereas the SDs as Marxists were initially interested almost exclusively in the urban workers, the SRs were populists, and chiefly concerned with the peasantry. Their aim was the redistribution of the land, and, frustrated and marginalized by the czarist system, they turned to terrorism and assassinated several cabinet ministers between 1902 and 1907. Rejecting any gestures of moderate change offered by the government, they demanded a complete reordering of Russian society under the slogan: "We don't want reforms. We want reform!"

The moderates and liberals were a third political grouping—intellectuals indignant over government repression who favored nothing more radical than compulsory free private education and agrarian reform. The regime stubbornly made no distinction between them and the terrorists and revolutionary Marxists. Thus the moderates also were forced to organize. In 1905 they took the name Constitutional Democrat party and were thereafter usually referred to as *Kadets*, from the Russian initials KD.

The Russo-Japanese War

The plan to build the Trans-Siberian Railroad made it desirable for the Russians to obtain a right-of-way across Chinese territory in Manchuria. St. Petersburg took the diplomatic initiative in preventing Japan from establishing itself on the Chinese mainland after Japan crushed China in war in 1895; in exchange, Russia then required the Chinese to allow the building of the new railroad. In 1897 Russia seized Port Arthur, the very port it had earlier kept out of Japanese hands. Further friction with the Japanese took place in Korea, in which both Japan and Russia were interested. Then, after the Boxer Rebellion of 1900—when the European powers and the United States sent armed forces into China to put down an anti-Western uprising—the Russians kept their troops in Manchuria when the other major powers withdrew theirs. After it became apparent that the war party had won control in Russia, the Japanese, without warning, attacked units of the Russian fleet anchored at Port Arthur in February 1904. The Russo-Japanese war had begun.

The main Russian fleet, which had steamed all the way around Europe and across the Indian Ocean into the Pacific, was decisively defeated by the Japanese in the battle of Tsushima Strait (May 27, 1904). This came as a stunning surprise to many who had dismissed Japanese power on racialist grounds and anticipated a victory by the European power. To the Russian people, the war was a mysterious, distant political adventure of which they wanted no part and by which they had now been humiliated. Many intellectuals opposed it, and the SRs and SDs openly hoped for a Russian defeat, which they expected would shake the very foundations of the czardom. Faced with growing unrest at home and military defeat in the war, the Russian government was persuaded by the American president Theodore Roosevelt (1858–1919, president 1901–1909)—himself concerned about the possibility of Japan radically disrupting the Asian political and economic balance of power—to accept his mediation. The Japanese also actively wished settlement, and the result was the Treaty of Portsmouth, New Hampshire (1905).

Witte, who had opposed the war from the outset, was sent to Portsmouth as Russian representative at the peace conference. Here he not only secured excellent terms for Russia but also won a favorable verdict from American public opinion, which had thought of Russians as either brutal autocrats or bomb-throwing revolutionaries. By the 1905 treaty, Russia officially recognized the de facto Japanese protectorate over Korea; ceded Port Arthur and the southern half of Sakhalin Island to Japan, together with fishing rights in the North Pacific; and agreed to evacuate Manchuria. Russian prestige as a Far Eastern power was not deeply wounded or permanently impaired by the defeat. Yet the effect of the reverse in Asia was to transfer Russian attention back to Europe, where a world crisis had already begun.

The Revolution of 1905

Immediately after the war the future Kadets held banquets throughout Russia to adopt a series of resolutions for presentation to a kind of national congress of zemstvo representatives. Although the congress was not officially allowed to meet, its program—a national constitution, guarantees of civil liberties, class and minority equality, and extension of zemstvo responsibilities—became widely known and approved. Nicholas II dimmed hopes for change by issuing a vague statement and taking measures to limit free discussion.

Ironically, it was a police informer who struck the fatal spark. A popular priest, Father George Gapon, had been planted by the government to combat SD efforts at organizing St. Petersburg workers and to substitute his own union. He organized a parade of workers to demonstrate peacefully and to petition the czar directly for an eight-hour day, a national assembly, civil liberties, the right to strike, and other moderate demands. When the workers tried to deliver the petition to the monarch at his great winter palace, Nicholas left town. Troops panicked and fired on the unarmed demonstrators, many of whom were carrying portraits of the czar to confirm their loyalty. Hundreds of workers were killed on the infamous "Bloody Sunday" (January 22, 1905).* The massacre made revolutionaries of the urban workers, and the increasingly desperate moderate opposition joined with the radicals.

Amid mounting excitement, the government at first seemed to favor the calling of a *zemski sobor*, consultative rather than legislative, but still a national assembly of sorts. But while the czar hesitated—indecisive as always—demonstrations occurred throughout the summer of 1905. In October the printers struck. No newspapers appeared, and the printers, with SD aid, formed the first *soviet*, or workers' council. When the railroad workers joined the strike, communications were cut off between Moscow and St. Petersburg. Soviets multiplied and relations between the czar and his subjects collapsed.

The Bolsheviks saw the soviet as an instrument for the establishment of a provisional government, for the proclamation of a democratic republic, and for the summoning of a constituent assembly. This program differed relatively little from that of the moderate liberals, who originally had hoped to

---

*All dates in this text use the Western (adopted in Russia only after the 1917 Bolshevik Revolution), rather than the old Russian, calendar.

keep the monarchy and obtain their ends by pressure rather than by violence. At the time, the Bolsheviks, like other Marxists, assumed that it was necessary for Russia to pass through a stage of bourgeois democracy before the time for the proletarian revolution could come. They were therefore eager to help along the bourgeois revolution.

Nicholas was faced, as Witte (now the czar's first minister) told him, with the alternatives of either imposing a military dictatorship or summoning a legislative assembly. The czar seemed to chose the latter course, and in October 1905 he issued a manifesto that promised full civil liberties at once and the creation of a legislative assembly, the *duma*. A supplementary manifesto in December pledged that the duma would be chosen by universal manhood suffrage. In theory, this October Manifesto ended the autocracy, since the duma was to be superior to the czar in legislation.

Yet the October Manifesto did not meet with universal approval. On the right, a government-sponsored party called the Union of the Russian People demonstrated against it, proclaiming their undying loyalty to the czar, and organized their own storm troops, the Black Hundreds, which killed more than three thousand Jews in the first week after issuance of the manifesto. On the left, the Bolsheviks and SRs made several attempts to launch their violent revolution but failed, and the government was able to arrest their leaders and to end their uprising after several days of street fighting in Moscow in December 1905. In the center, one group of propertied liberals, pleased with the manifesto, urged that it be used as a rallying point for a moderate program; they were the Octobrists, so called after the month in which the manifesto had been issued. The other moderate group, the Kadets, wished to continue to agitate by legal means for further immediate reforms. But the fires of revolution burned out by early 1906 as Witte used the army, strengthened by troops returned from the Far East, to put down any new disturbances.

The Dumas, 1906–1914

Under the newly developed electoral system to choose the duma, male suffrage was universal but indirect. Voters chose an electoral college, which then selected 412 deputies. The SRs and SDs boycotted the election, and the Kadets emerged as the largest party in the duma. Before the new legislature met, however, Witte acted to neutralize many of its more alarming aspects: A list of "fundamental laws" were declared beyond the duma's legislative competence; large loans were secured to put the government beyond the ability of the duma to coerce the regime financially; and the Crown was declared to have total control of foreign affairs and of matters related to peace and war. The finance ministry was to have full power over loans and currency. The czar's royal council was transformed into a two-hundred-member Council of the Empire appointed by the monarch, made virtually coequal with the duma in legislative power, and given the authority to submit an annual budget, apart from that passed by the duma. The czar was thus left the discretionary power to choose a budget that best suited him. Finally, the czar could dissolve the duma at will, provided he set a date for new elections; when it was not in session he could legislate by himself, and the duma could overrule the monarch only if it acted within the first two months of the next legislative session.

The first duma, remembered as the "Duma of Popular Indignation," met between May and July 1906 and addressed a list of grievances to the czar. Their program included radical land reform to redistribute state and church land (as well as some large private holdings) to the peasants. This was flatly refused, and the duma was promptly dissolved. Maintaining that such a dissolution was illegal, the Kadet deputies crossed the border into Finland (which had gained administrative autonomy as a result of the 1905 reforms) and there issued a manifesto of their own, urging the Russian people not to pay taxes or report for military service unless the duma was recalled. Its authors were tried in absentia and declared ineligible for office, thus depriving future dumas of the services of these capable moderates.

With the May dissolution, Witte was retired, and among the new ministers was the brilliant reactionary Prince Peter Stolypin (1862–1911), who took the powerful post of minister of the interior. Stolypin engineered a series of agricultural reforms that freed the peasants from the local rural villages or communes to which they were bound following the end of serfdom. Peasants thereafter could to a degree detach themselves economically from the commune by requesting that they be granted a single unitary tract. More than 9 million peasant households emancipated themselves from the communes between 1906 and 1917, and this success earned the deep suspicions of Lenin and other revolutionaries who knew full well that no revolution could succeed in Russia without the peasants.

At the same time that his agrarian program was going into effect, Stolypin carried on an unremitting war against terrorists and revolutionaries. He did all that he could to interfere with elections to the Second Duma, but the SRs and SDs were well represented, so that the duma (March–June 1907) would not work with the government. It was dissolved because it refused to suspend the parliamentary immunity of the SD deputies, whom Stolypin wanted to arrest.

After the dissolution of the Second Duma, the government illegally altered the election laws, cutting the number of delegates from the peasants and national minorities and increasing the number from the gentry. By this means the government won a majority, and the Third Duma (1907–1912) and the Fourth (1912–1917) lived out their constitutional terms of five years apiece. Although unrepresentative and limited in their powers, they were still national assemblies. The dumas improved the conditions of peasant and worker and helped strengthen national defense. Their commissions, working with individual ministers, proved extremely useful in increasing the efficiency of government departments. The period of the Third Duma, however, was also notable for the continuation of the policy of Russification.

Under the Fourth Duma, the government tended even more toward reaction. The leftists organized for another revolution, working in unions, coop-

eratives, evening classes for workers, and a network of other labor organizations. A vast web of police spies challenged them at every turn. Meanwhile,
the imperial family drifted into a dangerous situation as the deeply devout
and autocratic Czarina Alexandra fell under the influence of a charismatic,
half-mad, and power-hungry, self-anointed holy man. This rather notorious
rogue, Gregory Rasputin (1872–1916), was said to have the mysterious ability—which may in reality have been a gift for hypnosis—to stop the bleeding
attacks of the young crown prince, who suffered from hemophilia. Since the
empress had enormous influence over her beloved husband, Nicholas II, and
Rasputin had her complete confidence, scandalous rumors circulated that the
disreputable monk was the true ruler of Russia. This horrified loyal supporters of the Crown and supplied a useful weapon to those in the capital who
knew how to manipulate rumor. Thus, when the First World War began, Russia was in the throes of a major crisis precipitated by the government's reactionary policies, the scandal of Rasputin's influence, and the indignation of
the loyal duma.

The Autocratic Monarchies in 1914

By 1914 in Russia, the Habsburg Empire, and Germany, modern political parties had coalesced around certain principles. What each party stood for was
determined largely by the peculiar circumstances of the country that gave it
birth. Certain parallels among these monarchies reached across national
boundaries. No group in either Germany or Austria-Hungary was comparable to the Russian populists (Social Revolutionaries), but the German Liberals, Austrian Liberals, and Russian Kadets or Octobrists had similar views. So
had the ultra-nationalistic Pan-Germans and the Pan-Slavs. The Social
Democrats were Marxist in all three countries, but becoming less revolutionary in Germany and Austria-Hungary, and more so in Russia.

During this period all of the European powers experienced economic
boom and occasional depression; the industrial revolution hit central and
eastern Europe late, but with terrific impact. By the start of the twentieth century, Germany had made such advances that its steel production surpassed
that of Britain and was second in the world only to that of the United States.
Although far behind Germany both in resources and in technology, Austria-
Hungary, too, was rapidly becoming industrialized. In Russia transport and
industry boomed. Yet in these three countries, the landed nobility continued
to exercise political influence quite out of proportion to their numbers.
Everywhere the existence of a new and underprivileged class of urban workers stimulated intellectual leaders to form Marxist political groups, to preach
the class struggle, and, except in Russia, to strive for immediate improvements in conditions rather than for violent overthrow of the regime.

Russia emancipated its serfs in 1861; the most rapidly modernizing nation
of the nineteenth century, the United States freed its slaves two years later.
The United States had stood aloof from developments in Europe, opening
and exploiting its own vast frontier regions. By the end of the century, it, too,

was moving onto the world scene. Its modernization was extraordinarily rapid, and while its political system bore marked comparisons to that of Britain, and its industrialization to that of Germany, it demonstrated that its path to modernization was in many significant ways unique.

The United States: The Emerging Great Power

Although thousands of miles from the European land mass and more than a century of independence from Great Britain, the United States, in culture, language, and political tradition, was unquestionably to be considered with the European Great Powers. In other terms she also deserved mention with these great nation-states: Her population, size, and enormous potential power were self-evident. Perhaps even more stunning was the fact that the nation had developed from infancy to greatness in little more than a century. Two sets of statistics will suffice to illustrate: In 1790 the United States comprised 892,000 square miles; in 1910, 3,754,000 miles. Even more important, the population of the United States was 3,929,000 in 1790, and 91,972,000 in 1910—a total far greater than either of the most powerful European states, Germany and Great Britain, and second only to that of Russia. Still more important, the exploitable natural resources and the combined industrial and agricultural capacities of America were greater than those of any other single country. She produced more coal, iron ore, and steel—the bases of industrialism—than any rival. With a stable political system on a continent protected by two oceans that she dominated, it was hard to deny the young republic membership among the Great Powers.

Born in the desires of Britons to find a better future in a new world, these immigrants to America brought with them the English language, experience of political organization, and dedication to the idea of civil liberties. The new nation benefitted from the influx of other immigrants and from the wealth of resources on an unexploited continent, and they showed little patience for (and often much cruelty to) the thinly distributed indigenous people whom they found. By the mid-nineteenth century, a horrific civil conflict severely tested the young republic and in the bloodiest possible way settled issues of sectionalism and slavery for all time. By the dawn of the new century, the United States of America was both conditioned and able to assume her place as a Great Power—although it was far from clear that her people were ready for such a role on the world stage.

Free Enterprise and Government, 1890–1917

At the time of the Civil War, the American economy was still in some respects "colonial"; that is, it produced mainly foods and other raw materials, to be exchanged abroad for manufactured goods. In financial terms the United States was dependent on foreign money markets. But within a half-century the nation was transformed into an industrial power. This could not have occurred without an abundant work force—aided by massive waves of new immigration in the 1890s from eastern and southern Europe. The traditions

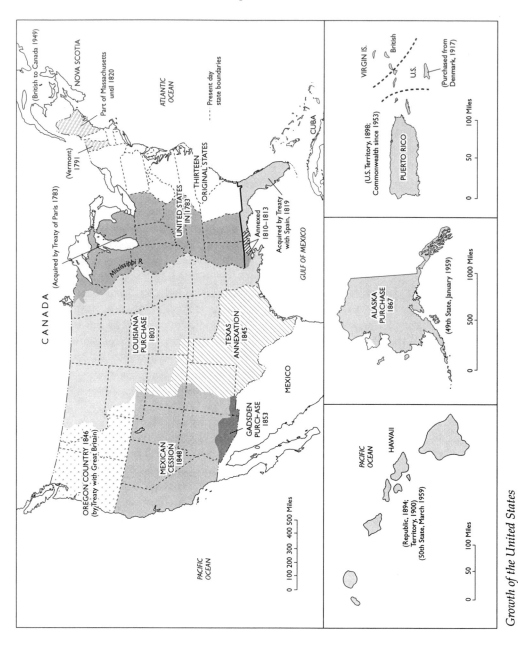

Growth of the United States

of initiative and freedom of enterprise were a basis for a national sense of aggressive and buoyant optimism, as the indigenous population, the American Indians, were systematically pushed aside in the name of progress.

The great expansion in national wealth was achieved in a climate of opinion that overwhelmingly supported the view that the federal government should not interfere directly with business enterprise beyond maintaining public order, enforcing contracts, exercising control over the coinage of money, and, for much of this time, maintaining a protective tariff. Nor were the individual states expected to go beyond these limits, although at times some did.

Many of the same forces that produced reform in Britain gradually brought to the United States minimum wage acts, limitation of child and female labor, sanitary regulation, control of hours of labor, and workmen's compensation. By the early twentieth century public opinion was ready for increased participation by the national government in the regulation of economic life.

Republican president Theodore Roosevelt promised to give labor a "square deal" and to proceed vigorously with "trust busting"—attacks on great trusts or combinations that had come to monopolize important sectors of the American economy. Although Roosevelt did not fulfill all his promises, his administration did take action against the trusts in railroads and tobacco and pressed for regulation of the great corporations by the federal government. John D. Rockefeller's (1839–1937) powerful Standard Oil Company, which controlled much of the petrochemical industry in America, was broken up in 1911, but only after the government's case reached the Supreme Court. The work of the social legislators and of the muckrakers, writers who produced exposés of questionable business practices, was not in vain. American big business was to grow much bigger in the century after "TR," but it was also more aware of the need to court public opinion.

During the first administration of the Democrat Woodrow Wilson (1856–1929, president 1912–1921), the process of regulation gained momentum. The Federal Reserve Act of 1913, for example, gave federal officials greater control over banking, credit, and currency. Meanwhile, the Sixteenth Amendment, legalizing an income tax, and the Seventeenth, providing for direct election of senators, made the federal republic more democratic in practice. While to some outsiders American political life—like all other things American—sometimes seemed to be one great brawl, with Americans disagreeing loudly and widely over everything in the national life, this apparently chaotic society achieved extraordinary material growth and political stability that required the tacit agreement of millions of men and women holding a generally common goal of modernization.

Despite general public distrust, government in the United States came to play a larger and larger part in the lives of all. Although this was also true of local and state government, it was especially so for the federal government. The increasing importance of the national government and the decreasing initiative of state government were as clear in this period as was the material growth and increased nationalism of the United States.

The Written Record

THE INFLUENCE OF SEA POWER

The new "navalism," which already had assertive advocates in Britain and Germany, derived many of its doctrines from the writings of an American officer, Captain Alfred T. Mahan (1840–1914). Mahan's book *The Influence of Sea Power upon History* (1890) and his later works assigned navies a place of preeminent importance in determining power status and found an influential audience at home and abroad, especially in Germany, Britain, and Japan.

It has been said that, in our present state of unpreparedness, a trans-isthmian canal will be a military disaster to the United States, and especially to the Pacific coast. When the canal is finished the Atlantic seaboard will be neither more nor less exposed than it now is it will merely share with the country at large the increased danger of foreign complications with inadequate means to meet them. The danger of the Pacific coast will be greater by so much as the way between it and Europe is shortened through a passage which the stronger maritime power can control. The danger lies not merely in the greater facility for dispatching a hostile squadron from Europe, but also in the fact that a more powerful fleet than formerly can be maintained on that coast by a European power, because it can be so much more promptly called home in case of need. The greatest weakness of the Pacific ports, however, if wisely met by our government, will go far to insure our naval superiority there. The two chief centres. San Francisco and Puget Sound, owing to the width and the great depth of the entrances, cannot be effectively protected by torpedoes; and consequently, as fleets can always pass batteries through an unobstructed channel, they cannot obtain perfect security by means of fortifications only. Valuable as such works will be to them, they must be further garrisoned by coast-defense ships, whose part in repelling an enemy will be coordinated with that of the batteries. The sphere of action of such ships should not be permitted to extend far beyond the port to which they are allotted, and on whose defense they form an essential part; but within that sweep they will always be a powerful reinforcement to the seagoing navy when the strategic conditions of a war cause hostilities to center around their port. By sacrificing power to go long distances, the coast-defense ship gains proportionate weight of armor and guns; that is, of defensive and offensive strength. It therefore adds an element of unique value to the fleet with which it for a time acts. No foreign states, except Great Britain, have ports so near our Pacific coast as to bring it within the radius of action of their coast-defense ships. . . .

The military needs of the Pacific States, as well as their supreme importance to the whole country, are yet a matter of the future, but of a future so near that provision should immediately begin.

A. T. Mahan, "The Influences of Sea Power upon History," *Atlantic Monthly*, LXVI (December 1890), pp. 22–24.

The United States Becomes a World Power

Quite as clear, although still the subject of complex debate among Americans, was the emergence of the United States as a great international power. From its first days the new republic had a Department of State concerned with foreign affairs and a traditional apparatus of ministers, consuls, and, later, ambassadors. By the Monroe Doctrine of the 1820s it took the firm position that European powers were not to extend further their existing territories in the Western Hemisphere. This was an active expression of American claims to a far wider sphere of influence than the continental United States. Although Americans took no part in the nineteenth-century balance-of-power politics in Europe, they showed an increasing concern with the balance of power in the Far East, where they had long traded and wanted an "Open Door" to commerce. As a result of a brief war in 1898 with Spain that broke out in Cuba, the United States annexed the Philippine Islands and Puerto Rico from Spain, and the newly "independent" Cuba became a veiled American protectorate. As a result of the machinations of Americans resident in the island kingdom of Hawaii, in 1898 it too became a territory of the United States.

Theodore Roosevelt, who owed his rapid political rise partly to his military exploits in the Spanish-American War, was a vigorous expansionist. He pressed the building of the Panama Canal, which opened in 1914; stretched the Monroe Doctrine to justify American military intervention in Latin America; upheld the Far Eastern interests of the United States; and advocated a larger navy. Roosevelt wanted to see his country play an active part in world affairs, as exemplified by his arbitrating the peace settlement between Russia and Japan in 1905.

After over a century of expanding wealth and trade, the United States had come to take full part in international commercial relations. Except when the federal government was blockading the Confederacy during the Civil War, it had stood firmly for rights to trade. This fact alone might have brought the United States into the First World War of 1914–1918, as it had brought it previously into the world war of 1792–1815. But by 1917 America was an active participant in the world state system, even though it had avoided any formal, permanent, entangling alliances. The great themes of modern European history—industrialism, modernization, national unity and nationalism, imperialism, intellectual ferment—were all so evident that Americans could not question that they were part of the broad stream of history.

SUMMARY

By the turn of the twentieth century three major ideologies claimed the allegiance of most men and women interested in politics in the West. Conservatism stressed history, morality, community, and order. Liberalism, the traditional alternative, placed much faith in human reason, opportunity, progress, and capitalism coupled with materialism. The newest ideology to emerge from the nineteenth century, socialism, rejected the capitalist ethic and called for "social justice"—that is, the redistribution of wealth through the intervention of the state, with some socialists espousing revolution and others democracy.

By 1900, Britain was a monarchial parliamentary democracy. Early in the century the Liberals replaced the Conservatives as the ruling party, bringing their agenda of nonsocialist interventionist reform. As the world neared the brink of world war, British politics became deadlocked in a struggle over the Irish Question, the matter of whether to grant Ireland political autonomy within the United Kingdom. This issue dominated domestic politics until 1914, as a realigned British foreign policy solidified a new partnership with former adversaries France and Russia.

The French Third Republic, born in defeat after the Franco-Prussian War in 1870, had struggled to establish a stable political system out of the mutual antipathy of monarchists and republicans. By 1900 a multiparty democracy functioned, although the sought-after stability was difficult to achieve. Further challenges were posed by severe economic inequity, rapid social change, and rivalry with a traditional enemy, a Germany growing stronger by the day. This was somewhat balanced by the rapprochement with Great Britain.

Italy had been united only since 1860, and the kingdom entered the twentieth century as an unstable multiparty constitutional monarchy. With grave maldistribution of population, resources, industrialization, and wealth, all largely definable in regional terms, Italy was a Great Power in name only, and her attempts to recapture Roman glories in a North African Empire did nothing to alleviate her problems.

Formed only in 1871 after the Prussian defeat of France, Germany presented a remarkable picture of success and vitality. Industrialization had come late but successfully, and her monarchy and political system appeared to be stable, if authoritarian. Kaiser William II was young, impulsive, and ambitious and ruled a nation that aspired to be the greatest in Europe.

Problems, however, existed: The emperor was much under the influence of the military, and the political parties reflected the strains of a class and regionalism that simmered below the orderly surface. Extremely dangerous was the fact that both the emperor and the most zealously patriotic Germans were determined to have a navy second to none—to complement what was already the best army in Europe. This put the Empire on a collision course with Britain, a traditional friend who was rapidly coming to distrust Germany.

Austria-Hungary was a multinational empire held together largely by the ties of its component regions to the Habsburg dynasty. Many languages, religions, and nationalities were ruled in the west by Austrians and in the east by Magyars, and the greatest threat to the Empire's survival lay in the dissatisfaction of many of the subject peoples. After years of repression, by 1914 some efforts at accommodation of the minorities, most belatedly in the east, were in place, but they proved to be too little and too late.

Like Austria-Hungary, Russia too encompassed many different peoples. The political system was premodern, without constitution or parliament, ruled after 1894 by the suspicious and reactionary Czar Nicholas II. Defeat in the Russo-Japanese war sparked the revolution in 1905 and the ostensible declaration of constitutional laws and a parliament, the duma. Change was more apparent than real, however. The old order continued to have its way, and the violent revolutionary movement that had long threatened the Czarist system continued. This maelstrom gave birth to Lenin's Bolsheviks, ultimately the successful instrument of revolution.

Through the nineteenth century the United States expanded to continental size, and her wealth and population (spurred by massive immigration) increased proportionally. In a successful two-party democracy, the American people were unsure at the turn of the century whether they wished to be a Great Power or not. Those in favor seemed to carry the day, as in 1898 a short and victorious war was waged against Spain, and for the first time a New World nation defeated one of the old colonial powers. However, below the surface problems of social reform and of political reality remained unsolved.

THREE

Great War,
Great Revolution

∽

On June 28, 1914, the Habsburg archduke Francis Ferdinand, heir to the throne of Austria-Hungary, and his wife, Sophie Chotek, were assassinated in the streets of Sarajevo, capital of the province of Bosnia, which had been occupied by Austria-Hungary since 1878. The assassin, Gavrilo Princip (1895–1918), was a Serbian nationalist. The Austro-Hungarian government, alarmed by the ambitions of Serbian nationalists, took the occasion of the assassination to issue a severe ultimatum to Serbia. The Serbian government's refusal to accept the ultimatum in its entirety led to an Austrian declaration of war on Serbia on July 28. Within the week, the great states of Europe were engaged in a general war—the Central Powers (Austria-Hungary and Germany, joined by Turkey and, later, Bulgaria) against the Allies (Serbia, Russia, France, and Britain, eventually supported by eighteen other nations).

Princip's bullet would eventually cost 36 million casualties in killed, missing, and wounded. After the war, and particularly after the failure of the peace settlement and the widespread disillusionment with leaders who apparently had so naively fought a "war to end all wars," much public debate took place about where the greatest responsibility for the war lay. This debate over the *causes* of the war became confused with the moral issue of *responsibility* for the war.

Causes of the War

One factor that made war more likely was the unification of Germany and of Italy. The creation of these two new major states altered the balance of power in the European state system; the efforts of statesmen during the next forty years to adjust the system ultimately proved unsuccessful. The older established powers were unwilling to give up their own claims, and after 1850, with the principle of national sovereignty well established, smaller western European states were no longer open to annexation by the great powers.

Thus there was little territory available in Europe for making adjustments. In the late nineteenth century only the Balkan lands of the weakening Turkish Empire remained as possible territorial pickings for ambitious powers. Even there, the growth of national feeling in Romania, Serbia, Bulgaria, and Greece made formal annexation difficult.

Meantime, influenced by their rivalries in Europe and abroad, the great powers were choosing sides in a series of alliances and agreements. By the early years of the twentieth century two increasingly armed camps existed: the Triple Alliance (Germany, Austria-Hungary, and Italy) and the Triple Entente (France, Britain, and Russia). After 1900 almost any crisis might lead to war.

Shifting National Self-Images

Nationalism and the accompanying shifts in the balance of power both influenced and were profoundly influenced by public opinion, often shaped by the public press. Throughout western Europe and in the United States a jingoistic press, often intent on increasing circulation, competed for "news," and not all papers were careful to separate the verifiable from the rumor, the emotional atrocity story (even when true) from the background account that would explain the context for the emotion.

Technology made printing far cheaper than it had ever been. In 1711 the highly influential English paper *The Spectator* sold two thousand copies a day, and there was only a handful of effective competitors; in 1916 a Paris-based newspaper sold over 2 million copies a day, and there were hundreds of other newspapers. This revolution in communicating the printed word had taken place in the nineteenth century. *The Times* of London began to use steam presses in 1814, producing copies four times as fast as before. In Britain and France and later in central Europe, the railway made a national press possible—the papers of Paris could be read anywhere in France the next day. After the 1840s the invention of the telegraph encouraged the creation of news services and the use of foreign correspondents; the same story thus might appear throughout the nation, although in different papers.

When Richard Hoe (1812–1886), a New Yorker, invented a rotary press in 1847 that could produce twenty thousand sheets an hour, the modern newspaper was born. Linotype and, from the 1880s, monotype machines were also used to set books, and by 1914 there had been a massive leap in the sale of all reading matter. This in turn gave rise to greater censorship in some societies, and everywhere to an awareness that the printed word could be manipulated to political purposes.

The printed word was supplemented by illustrations. The battle map was introduced to the public in the American Civil War. After 1839 daguerreotypes began to replace painting as a means of conveying reality. In the 1880s, mass-produced cameras became available. A simple box camera, the Kodak, was invented in 1888, and with the concurrent commercialization of the halftone screen, newspaper pictures became commonplace.

Police in Sarajevo arrest a man after a failed assassination attempt on the life of the Habs-
burg archduke Francis Ferdinand, heir to the throne of Austria-Hungary. The arrested man
in the photograph was long identified as Gavrilo Princip, who succeeded in killing the arch-
duke on the same day. It is now thought to be Nedeljko Cabrinovic, one of Princip's six
coconspirators.   (Illustrated London News/Hulton Archive/Getty Images)

Newspapers became more important in political life. In Britain Alfred
Harmsworth (1865–1922), in France Charles Dupuy (1844–1919), and in the
United States two competitors, Joseph Pulitzer (1847–1911) and William Ran-
dolph Hearst (1863–1951), brought all the elements together to create mass
journalism. The two Americans worked to promote war with Spain in 1898,
and all these papers supported the establishment and jingoist views.

The introduction of universal peacetime conscription by the Continental
powers further stimulated the introduction of compulsory universal elementary education, and later of universal manhood suffrage. These led to a further growth in the number of readers, to greater political content in the press,
and to the quest for technological innovation in rapid typesetting. One could,
by 1900, genuinely speak of "public opinion" as a force in world affairs.

Thus the outbreak of war in 1914 saw in each belligerent nation broad public support of the government. Men marched off to war convinced that war
was necessary. Even the socialists supported the war. Yet, public opinion
might as easily have been led against war, had an increasingly complex
alliance system not cut off national options and individual leaders not cho-

sen the course they did. For example, in the hectic five weeks after the assassination at Sarajevo, the German kaiser, William II, belatedly tried to avoid a general war. But in the decisive years between 1888 and 1914 he had been an aggressive leader of patriotic expansion, encouraging German youth to believe that while their enemies were numerically superior, Germany's spiritual qualities would more than compensate for brute strength.

German ambitions and German fears had produced an intense hatred of Britain. At first few English returned this hate, but as the expensive race between Britain and Germany in naval armaments continued and as German wares progressively undersold British wares in Europe, in North and South America, and in Asia, the British began to worry about their prosperity and leadership. The British were worried about their obsolescent industrial plants and their apparent inability to produce goods as efficiently as the Germans; they were critical of their commercial failures abroad; and some feared their increasingly stodgy self-satisfaction. There was, in effect, a crisis of imperialism in British domestic politics.

In France prewar opinions on international politics ran the gamut. A large socialist left was committed to pacifism and to an international general strike of workers at the threat of actual war. However, an embittered group of patriots wanted *revanche*, or revenge, for the defeat of 1870. The revanchists organized patriotic societies and edited patriotic journals. The French, like the British, had supported movements for international peace—the Red Cross, conferences at the Hague in 1899 and 1907, and various abortive initiatives by the international labor movement. But French diplomats continued to preserve and strengthen the system of alliances against Germany, and in July 1914 it was clear that France was ready for war.

Triple Alliance and Triple Entente, 1879–1918

After 1871 Bismarck sought to isolate France diplomatically by building a series of alliances from which it was excluded. He sought to keep on good terms with both Austria and Russia and, what was more difficult, to keep both these powers on good terms with each other. Since both wanted to dominate the Balkans, Bismarck's task was formidable.

Bismarck laid the cornerstone of his diplomatic system by a defensive alliance with Austria-Hungary in 1879, an alliance that held until 1918, and by the League of the Three Emperors (1872–1878, 1881–1889), which bound Germany, Russia, and Austria together. The three powers agreed to act in common when dealing with Turkey and to maintain friendly neutrality should any one of them be at war with a power other than Turkey. Next, Bismarck secured an alliance among Germany, Austria-Hungary, and Italy directed chiefly against France—the Triple Alliance of 1882, often renewed, which still existed on paper in 1914.

Bismarck maintained a precarious balance on this series of tightropes through the 1880s. Uppermost in his mind was the danger that the Russians, fearful of Austrian designs upon the Balkans, would desert him and ally themselves with France, always anxious to escape from the isolation that Bismarck had designed for it. In 1887 Russia did refuse to renew the League of the Three Emperors, but Bismarck was able to repair the breach by a secret Russo-German agreement known as the Reinsurance Treaty. The two promised each other neutrality in case either was involved in a war against a third power; but this neutrality was not to hold if Germany made an "aggressive" war against France or if Russia made an "aggressive" war against Austria. Since Russian nationalist agitation continued against both Austria and Germany, Bismarck in 1888 made public the terms of the Austro-German alliance and allowed the main terms of the Triple Alliance to be known informally as a warning to Russia.

Then in 1890 William II dismissed Bismarck. The emperor's advisers persuaded him not to renew the Reinsurance Treaty with Russia, as it was incompatible with the Dual Alliance (the 1879 alliance with Austria-Hungary), and shortly afterward what Bismarck had worked so hard to prevent came about. After lengthy secret negotiations, Russia and France in 1894 made public an alliance that ended French isolation. It was a defensive agreement by which each was to come to the other's aid in the event that Germany or Austria made "aggressive" war against either ally.

Great Britain still remained technically uninvolved by a formal alliance with a European ally. The next development was to align Great Britain against the Triple Alliance by informal agreement. Britain sought first to come to an understanding with Germany; when rebuffed, the British then concluded a formal alliance with Japan (1902) and informal "understandings" (*ententes*) with traditional rivals France (1904) and Russia (1907). What chiefly drove Britain to these actions was the financially burdensome naval race with Germany and the rapid alienation of British public opinion. Fear of Russia rather than fear of Germany inspired Britain's alliance with Japan; in the Entente Cordiale France gave England a free hand in Egypt and England gave France a free hand in Morocco. More important, the base was laid for further collaboration, particularly in advance planning for military and naval cooperation in case of war.

The final stage in aligning the two camps came in 1907 when Russia came to an understanding with Great Britain. Both countries made concessions in regions where they had been imperialist rivals—Persia, Afghanistan, Tibet— and the British at last made some concessions to Russia's desire to open up the Bosporus and Dardanelles to its warships. The agreement was informal and left Britain less than fully committed to any binding Continental alliance system; nevertheless, it rounded out the Triple Entente against the Triple Alliance.

As the Entente took shape, a succession of military and diplomatic crises inflamed public opinion and further circumscribed the room to maneuver. First came a deliberately theatrical gesture by the kaiser, when in 1905 he made a ceremonial visit to Tangier in Morocco as a signal that the Germans would not recognize the Anglo-French assignment of Morocco to France. The British then indicated clearly to the French that they would support them.

Moreover, the British and the French now began informal military and naval conferences, which the French, at least, believed committed Britain to armed support if the Germans attacked.

At an international conference on the question of the independence and territorial integrity of Morocco, held at Algeciras in Spain (1906), Germany was outvoted, although it had called for the conference; France pursued plans for a protectorate in Morocco, dividing the country with Spain. The Algeciras conference also marked the beginnings of participation by the United States in the European system, although very tentatively. In 1904 a person thought to be a naturalized American citizen had been seized by a Moroccan chief, and Theodore Roosevelt had sent a truculent cable. Two years earlier, at the urging of Jewish citizens in the United States, the State Department had protested against Romanian persecution of Jews. Given this protest over a domestic Romanian matter, the State Department could not readily refrain from action where an American citizen was thought to be concerned. Roosevelt sent two representatives to Algeciras, who helped conciliate differences between the two camps.

A decisive turn came in 1908, when Austria formally proclaimed its annexation of the Turkish provinces of Bosnia-Herzegovina, already occupied for thirty years. Austria's actions infuriated the Serbs, who hoped to annex Bosnia. It also infuriated the Russians, who did not know that their foreign minister had informally agreed with his Austrian counterpart to permit the annexation in exchange for Austria's services in opening the Straits to the Russian fleet. But Russia gained nothing, for Britain would not permit the Straits to be opened.

What directly prompted the Austrian annexation of Bosnia-Herzegovina was the successful rising against the Ottoman sultan in the summer of 1908 by the Young Turks. A Pan-Turanian movement was instigated largely by Turks from central Asia (and named for their nomadic Turanian ancestors), whose independent principalities had been conquered by Russia during the reign of Alexander II and who were now undergoing forced Russification; they sought to group the Turkish peoples of central Asia with the Ottoman Turks and Magyars of Hungary. Austria was determined that Serbia and Croatia would remain under its rule.

A second Moroccan crisis in 1911 heightened tensions in western Europe. The kaiser sent a German gunboat, the *Panther*, to the Moroccan port of Agadir as a protest against French occupation of the old city of Fez. In ensuing negotiations, well publicized in the press, the Germans agreed to give the French a free hand in Morocco, but only at a price the French considered blackmail: Part of the French Congo was ceded to Germany. French opposition to this bargain was so intense that the government fell, and thereafter no French ministry dared make concessions to the Germans.

Events followed with bewildering and interlocking impact. In 1911 Italy seized upon the Agadir crisis to demand Tripoli from Turkey. In the yearlong Turco-Italian war that followed, Italian nationalists, led by the romantic poet and adventurer Gabriele d'Annunzio (1863–1938), at last saw the chance for

*In Treue Fest (In Unwavering Allegiance), a photo montage of Germany's emperor William
II and Austria-Hungary's Francis Joseph, emperor of Austria and king of Hungary, on a
propaganda postcard at the beginning of World War I. The mass distribution of material of
this kind was meant to mobilize popular support for the war effort in both countries.
(Österreichische Gesellschaft für Zeitgeschichte, Photoarchiv, Vienna)*

substantial imperial gains. Italy annexed Tripoli, bombarded the Syrian coast, and occupied Rhodes and the other Dodecanese islands. By the Treaty of Lausanne in October 1912, Italy confirmed its new possessions.

In the meantime, the war over Tripoli (Libya) had proved a prelude to the Balkan Wars of 1912–1913, as the Balkan states struck at a preoccupied Turkey. In the first of these wars, Montenegro declared war on Turkey, as did Bulgaria, Serbia, and Greece ten days later. The war went against the Turks, but Russia warned the advancing Bulgarians not to occupy Constantinople or the Russian fleet would be used against them. The Serbs reached the Adriatic by overrunning Albania; intent on preventing Serbian access to the sea, the Austrians declared for an independent Albania. Russia supported Serbia, and in November 1912 Austria and Russia began to mobilize. The Russians, belatedly realizing that they were not prepared for war, abandoned the Serbs, who, with Bulgaria, came to terms with Turkey. By a treaty of May 30, Turkey ceded substantial territory in Europe, abandoned its claims to Crete (which was annexed to Greece), and left the status of Albania and the Aegean islands to the powers.

One month later the second Balkan War erupted when the Bulgarian military commander attacked Serbia and Greece without informing his government. Both nations counterattacked, Romania and Turkey entered the war on their side, and in six weeks, by the Treaty of Bucharest, Bulgaria was stripped of much that it had gained. In a separate treaty with Turkey, Bulgaria was forced to give back Adrianople. During the negotiations Serbia invaded Albania and only withdrew in the face of an Austrian ultimatum.

During this time, the Anglo-German naval race had continued unabated. In February 1912 Lord Haldane (1856–1928), British secretary for war, went to Berlin to suggest that Britain would support German expansion in Africa in exchange for a freeze on the size of the German fleet. Germany refused.

Britain now faced a major dilemma. In 1897 its fleet had been the greatest in the world; with the introduction of its massive and expensive *Dreadnought* in 1905, a new standard in armor and armament had been attained. But the Germans had matched it, and escalation on both sides had continued. In 1911 Winston Churchill (1874–1965), who was committed to a fully modernized navy, became Britain's first lord of the admiralty. In 1912 a new naval law made it clear that Germany intended to match the British. The British concluded that they could halt rising naval expenditures only through a naval agreement with France by which France would control the Mediterranean and Britain would focus on the North Sea, the Straits, and the Near East.

The Final Crisis, July–August 1914

The diplomats and statesmen were drawn into war because they believed that a diplomatic defeat or loss of face for their nation was worse than war. Wishing to end once and for all Serbian agitation among south Slavs in the Habsburg lands, Austria-Hungary accused the Serbian government of complicity in Gavrilo Princip's assassination of Francis Ferdinand on June 28,

1914, and made stiff demands on Serbia. Although the plot was carried out by a terrorist organization, the Black Hand, which included officers in the Serbian army, there is no evidence to indicate that the Serbian government was involved. Before acting, Austria-Hungary consulted Germany, which promised to support whatever policy Austria might adopt toward Serbia— the equivalent of a diplomatic "blank check."

Encouraged, the Austrian government on July 23 sent Serbia an ultimatum to be answered within forty-eight hours. The ultimatum may have been designed to be unacceptable. It required that publications hostile to Austria be suppressed, anti-Austrian patriotic organizations be dissolved, teachings that smacked of propaganda be barred from the schools, officials known for conducting anti-Austrian campaigns be dismissed, Serbian officials believed to be involved in the assassination plot be arrested, and a formal apology be made. These demands the Serbs might have accepted, but two others they could not: that Austrian officials work with the Serbians in investigating the plot and that judicial action be taken against any found guilty by this joint investigation. While accepting most points, the Serbian reply was evasive on the most important ones, and the Serbs had begun mobilization before delivering it. Serbia apparently hoped this stratagem would allow time for further negotiations, but the Austrian minister immediately left Belgrade, and Austria began to call up its troops. Austria declared war on July 28.

Germany supported Austria in this decision, but the German diplomats still equivocated, putting pressure on Vienna to act against Serbia while trying to find out whether Britain would remain neutral in a general war—a constant German goal. If war were to come, the Germans wished to place the guilt on Russia. Since Russia was beginning the full mobilization of its armies, the kaiser, on July 29, told Czar Nicholas II in a personal telegram about German attempts to get the Austrians to compromise. Apparently this telegram caused full Russian mobilization to be modified into partial mobilization against Austria and caused the Austro-Russian talks to be resumed on July 30. If German Chancellor Theobald von Bethmann-Hollweg (1856–1921) could make it appear that a full-scale European war was the fault of the Russians, then he still had some hope of Britain's neutrality.

But mobilization was not easy in Russia, a country of vast distances and poor communications. The Russian military feared that their enemies would get the lead on them, so the Russian government decided to renew general mobilization. Germany at once insisted that all Russian mobilization cease, and, when it continued, ordered its own at 4:00 P.M. on August 1. Germany declared war on Russia three hours later.

France, meantime, had determined to stand by its Russian ally and mobilized at 3:55 P.M. on August 1. Having failed to get Britain to guarantee French neutrality, and apparently convinced that France would come to Russia's support, Germany invaded Luxembourg on August 2 and demanded from Belgium permission to cross its territory, in exchange for Belgian neutrality. Belgium refused, and on August 3 Germany declared war on France and invaded Belgium to seize the ports on the English Channel and bear down upon Paris from the west.

Britain had been wavering. Although her entente with France did not legally bind the two nations together, it had led to close coordination of defense plans by the French and British military and naval staffs, and so perhaps Britain would have come into the war anyway. What made entry certain was German violation of the neutrality of Belgium. Sir Edward Grey seized firmly upon the German invasion of Belgium as grounds for taking action, which he supported for political reasons. On August 4 Britain declared war on Germany. Bethmann-Hollweg, informed of this action, let slip the phrase that Britain had gone to war just for a "scrap of paper"—the treaty of 1839 that established Belgian neutrality. This unhappy phrase not only solidified British opinion in favor of the war but was primarily responsible for the later charge of war guilt that was laid against Germany.

The Entry of Other Powers

By August 6, when Austria declared war on Russia, all the members of the Triple Alliance and the Triple Entente had entered the war, with the exception of Italy, which declared neutrality. The Central Powers of Germany and Austria-Hungary stood against the Allies—Russia, France, Britain, and Serbia. Japan came in on the side of the Allies late in August. Turkey joined the Austro-German side in November. After receiving competing territorial offers from both Allies and Central Powers, Italy joined the Allies in May 1915, as did Portugal and Romania in 1916. In time much of the world joined in; there were fifty-six declarations of war before the end of 1918.

Americans had hoped to avoid entanglement in the European conflict, and for a time public opinion was deeply divided. While many Americans sided with Britain and France because they felt these two powers were fighting to assure that democratic government would survive in Europe, many others continued to think of Britain as the traditional enemy. Americans still thought of themselves as upholding a tradition of isolation from wars that originated in Europe. To a considerable extent this was true, for no overseas invader had set foot on American soil since 1815. The American government committed itself quickly to a policy of neutrality.

As the war raged in Europe, however, public sympathies increasingly turned against the Central Powers, and against Germany in particular. Americans read of the war through British dispatches, heard atrocity stories that were directed against the Germans, and viewed the Habsburgs as attempting to suppress legitimate aspirations for the self-determination of peoples. Furthermore, the European war helped the United States economically, for Britain and France bought enormous quantities of goods from the United States. Within a year after the beginning of the war, the economies of the United States and the Allied powers were closely intertwined.

Still, the American business community had no reason to see the United States actively enter the war, for neutrality paid handsomely. President Woodrow Wilson (1856–1924) campaigned in 1916 on a pledge to keep the United States out of the conflict if possible. But he suspected that if German desperation over the flow of American foodstuffs to Britain were to continue,

avoiding war would be very difficult. This proved to be so. American definitions of neutral shipping seemed to the Germans to openly favor the British.
Germany felt obliged to use its most powerful maritime weapon, the submarine, and in 1915 it proclaimed the waters around the British Isles to be a war
zone in which enemy merchant ships would be sunk on sight. Neutral vessels entering the zone did so at their own risk. Americans insisted on exercising their rights on the high seas, including traveling on passenger vessels
of combatants. On May 7, 1915, the British transatlantic steamer *Lusitania* was
sunk by a German submarine; 1,198 people died, including 124 Americans.

The United States protested in the strongest terms. Throughout the remainder of 1915 German submarines complied, limiting their attacks to freighters.
Nonetheless, further incidents followed, and in 1916 Germany formally
agreed to abandon unlimited submarine warfare. Late that year Germany initiated peace efforts, but the Allies rebuffed these attempts. Early in 1917 German military leaders gained the upper hand, and on February 1 submarine
attacks on all neutral and belligerent shipping became official policy. Three
days later an American naval vessel was sunk after warning, and Wilson
asked Congress to sever diplomatic relations with Germany. Six more ships
were sunk in the next month. In the meantime, on March 12 a new democratic
government was set up in Russia, effectively knocking Russia out of the war
and potentially releasing German troops from the eastern front to the western. Wilson attacked the German submarine policy as "warfare against
humanity," and on April 6 the United States declared war on Germany. Even
so, Americans were careful to maintain their separate status, not joining the
Allies formally.

German resumption of submarine warfare was the immediate cause of
American entry into the war, but there were, of course, other causes.
Although neutrality had paid well, interest groups in the United States
assumed that war would bring even higher profits. So much had been lent to
the Allied nations that American creditors could not afford to see them
defeated. Public opinion was outraged by the German submarine policy.
Many Americans feared that their nation's security would be hurt if Germany were victorious; at the least, the world order would be reorganized.
Perhaps above all, more Americans simply felt emotionally closer to Britain
than to the Germans, and they were unprepared to see Europe unified under
German domination. Wilson no doubt did not believe that he was embarking
on a war to "make the world safe for democracy," but he did believe that
democracy would not be safe if the Central Powers were victorious.

Nationalism

Why did war begin precisely where and as it did? Need all the nations that
were drawn into it have participated? Which nation was primarily responsible for causing the war? Within that nation, which groups, which leaders?
Given war, need it have taken the form that it did? In part because the victor
writes the history, the majority of historians have blamed Germany or the tot-

A poster from World War I reminds good Frenchmen and women to contribute their wealth generously to the war effort, as soldiers generously contributed their blood. Poster art, already well developed in the nineteenth century, became a powerful weapon of political propaganda during the war. (Library of Congress)

tering Austro-Hungarian Empire for the war. However, most historians do agree on certain matters concerning the outbreak of the war.

Nationalism was the root cause of World War I. The heir to the Austro-Hungarian Empire was assassinated by a Serbian nationalist, and the empire determined to stamp out Serbian nationalism by extracting humiliating concessions from the Serbs. Since Russia was the defender of the Serbs and a supporter of Serbian nationalism, Russia was drawn into the circle of war; because Germany was the protector of Austria, it, too, saw no choice but aggressive action. Because Russia was in alliance with France, that nation was drawn in. All sides used the rhetoric of defense, all took the actions of offense. No one could have guessed how destructive the war would be, or some nations might well have elected not to honor their treaty commitments. In a sense, the war was caused by a series of miscalculations as to the intentions of the enemy, the enemy's strengths, and where national self-interest lay.

Still, war between these nations alone need not have engulfed the world had other nations not feared one or more of the prospective combatants. Britain was convinced that the Germans were intent on asserting world power; the German invasion of Belgium appeared to confirm the German bid for, at the least, European dominance. The Ottoman Empire feared the Russians and distrusted French and British intentions in the Near and Middle East. Italy and Japan were determined not to be left out in any postwar realignment of power. The United States did not wish to see a German victory or the emergence on the European Continent of a military dictatorship that would threaten American growth and institutions. In the end the war became a world war because the belligerents either had or wished to have overseas colonies, and their colonial dependencies, or the lands that they coveted, were swept into the conflict.

The Course of the War

Nearly everyone involved—leaders, soldiers, and ordinary citizens—presumed that the war would be brief and decisive, like the Franco-Prussian conflict of 1870. They could not have been more wrong: World War I took the lives of 8 million soldiers, and caused far more deaths through malnutrition and war-spawned diseases, and created birth deficits through economic dislocation and the loss of those in the age group most likely to beget children. The collapse of the Russian economy, followed by widespread famine and epidemic, meant that, despite staggering military losses, northwestern Europe emerged from the war in a dominant position once again.

Resources of the Belligerents

Even before the American entry, the Allies had an overwhelming superiority in total population and resources. The Central Powers had in their own Continental lands not more than 150 million people; Britain, France, Russia, and Italy in their own Continental lands had at least 125 million more people than their enemies. Moreover, in their overseas possessions, which included the 315 million people of India, the Allies had many millions more. As for material resources, the Central Powers had, especially in Germany, admirably organized industries and enough coal and iron to fight a long war, but here, too, the statistics were overwhelmingly in favor of the Allies. Moreover, although German submarines and surface raiders seriously interfered with Allied lines of communication, on the whole the Allies were still able to get food and other supplies from their overseas sources.

In the long run, the side with the most men and materials wore down its enemies and won the war, but it was by no means an uneven struggle. The Central Powers won many battles and seemed at critical moments close to final victory. Germany and Austria adjoined one another and had interior lines of communication, which enabled them to transfer troops rapidly from one threatened front to another, and had for years been firmly allied. Most important of all, Germany was ready for war, with an efficiently organized military machine and a good stock of munitions. The German people were united in support of the war, and they enjoyed the great psychological advantage of being on the offensive, of carrying the war to the enemy.

By contrast, geography and language separated the western Allies from Russia. German control of the Baltic and Turkish control of the Straits proved a serious obstacle to communication between Russia and its allies, which had to take roundabout and difficult routes. For the Allies, transfer of troops between eastern and western fronts was militarily almost impossible, even had it been politically possible.

Russia, Britain, and France had only recently come together, and then not as close allies. Each had many sources of conflict with the others. They had no experience of mutual cooperation, no common language. France and Britain were democracies, and although the peoples of both supported the war, Britain, in particular, was unused to centralized military and political control. Unified military planning and administration were never achieved between Russia and the western Allies. Even among Britain, France, and the United States on the western front, unification was not achieved until the French general Ferdinand Foch (1851–1929) was appointed commander in chief in 1918.

Finally, of the three great Allied powers in 1914, only France was ready, and France, with only 39 million people against Germany's 65 million, was the weakest of the Allies in manpower. Britain was well prepared on the sea, but the navy could not be of direct use against the German army. The situation in Ireland remained tense. Russia had universal military service and a huge army, but it had vast distances to overcome, an inadequate railway system, a less-developed heavy industry, and a military and political organization that was riddled with inefficiency and corruption.

Military Campaigns, 1914–1918

The Western Front. The German attack through Belgium was the first stage in the plan prepared by Alfred Graf von Schlieffen (1833–1913), chief of the general staff from 1891 to 1906. The strong right wing was to take Paris and fall on the rear of the French, who would be pinned down by the left wing. With France quickly eliminated, the Germans would then unite their forces and attack the Russians, who would still be in the throes of mobilization. Britain, an island nation, would be held off and attacked if necessary.

The German plan failed for two reasons. First, the German chief of staff, Helmuth von Moltke (1848–1916), who succeeded Schlieffen, had weakened the right wing to send divisions to the east. When the right wing neared Paris, it had too few divisions to take the capital and then turn on the French army as planned. Second, the French, although at first preparing an offensive eastward, shifted their armies northward and westward in time to meet the invading Germans. With the help of a small British force, the French exploited a gap that opened between the German armies, who lost their first great test, known as the first battle of the Marne (September 5–12, 1914).

The opposing forces then engaged in what came to be called the "Race to the Sea," with the Germans trying to outflank the Allies and reach the Channel ports first, thus shutting the short sea passage to future British reinforcements. But they failed here, too, and throughout the war the ports of Calais and Boulogne and the southwestern corner of Belgium were to remain in Allied hands.

By the autumn of 1914 this western front was stabilized. Between the Channel and the Swiss border of Alsace near Basel, hundreds of thousands of soldiers faced each other in a continuous line. Both sides dug in and made rough fortifications, the central feature of which was a series of parallel trenches deep enough to conceal a man standing upright. As time went on these trenches were supplied with parapets, machine-gun nests, and an elaborate network of approach trenches and strong points, until the entire front became one immense fortification. Thousands of local actions in the four years of trench warfare shifted the lines here and there, and a series of partial breakthroughs occurred on both sides. But on the whole the lines held, and the actual fighting in the West was confined to an extraordinarily narrow, although very long, field in which changing weaponry gave the defense increasing advantages over the offense.

The Eastern Front.   The eastern front, where the Russians faced both the Germans and the Austrians, was crucial to Allied tenacity in the West. Millions of men were involved on both sides, and had the Russians not held out until the end of 1917, the Allies in the West could hardly have withstood the reinforcements that the Germans and Austrians would have been able to send to France and Italy. Although the war in the East was more fluid than the war in the West, even in the East there were long periods of stalemate.

The Russians began well. They took the Galician capital of Lemberg, now Lvov, and by the end of September 1914 they had reached the northern ends of the passes leading into Hungary through the Carpathian Mountains. On August 19–20, 1914, the Russians won the battle of Gumbinnen. The alarmed Germans reorganized their eastern command. The brilliant general Erich Ludendorff (1865–1937), under the nominal command of Paul von Hindenburg (1847–1934) and aided by the exceptional staff officer Max von Hoffman (1869–1927), moved successfully against the two Russian armies. Late in August at Tannenberg, the Germans decisively defeated a Russian army, taking 100,000 prisoners. Early in September the Germans again won decisively at the Masurian Lakes, taking another 125,000 prisoners.

The Germans' hard-pressed Austrian allies to the south were by now clamoring for help, and the western front was still demanding men. Hindenburg

Trench warfare in World War I, 1917. The war on the western front was generally one of position and was fought out in murderous battles of attack and defense over four years—all ending essentially where it began in 1914. At Cambrai in November 1917, pictured here, the first massed tank assault in history was carried out by the British army. Although successful initially, the attack bogged down, and in the end no territory was gained. As was characteristic of this war, each side sustained more than forty thousand casualties. (Imperial War Museum, London)

and his aides had to do their best with what they had. In a series of hard-fought battles in Poland, they relieved the pressure on the Austrians. The end of 1914 found the Austrians hanging on in Galicia and the Germans in a good position to push eastward from East Prussian and Polish bases. In two great joint offensives in May and July 1915 the Central Powers won substantial successes, inflicting on the underequipped Russians severe losses from which they never really recovered.

In 1916 the Russians, with a new commander, General Aleksei Brusilov (1853–1926), undertook a major new offensive against the Austrians in the south. The Brusilov offensive was begun without adequate preparation. It scored a striking success at first, in places driving the Austrians back some eighty miles, and taking 200,000 prisoners. Once more the Germans came to the rescue; with fresh troops transferred from the West, they halted Brusilov, costing him a million men and exhausting his supplies.

It was in the backlash of this defeat that the Russian Revolution, which began early in March 1917, was born. During the moderate early phase of that uprising, before the Bolshevik revolution of November 1917, Brusilov undertook one last desperate offensive. But he was soon checked, and the Russian army began to disintegrate; the way was open for the Bolsheviks to carry out their promise to make peace. By the end of 1917 Russia was out of the war. It was forced by the Central Powers to sign the punitive Peace of Brest-Litovsk (March 1918), by which Russia lost its Polish territories, its Baltic provinces, the entire Ukraine, Finland, and some lands in the Caucasus. The last went to Turkey; most of the others came under what proved to be the temporary domination of Austria and Germany.

The Italian Front.   In the meantime, in April 1915, as her price for joining the war on the side of the Allies, Italy had concluded with Britain, France, and Russia the secret Treaty of London, which promised the Italians Trent and Trieste plus other lands at Austro-Hungarian and Turkish expense. In May the Italians formally declared war on Austria-Hungary, and a new front was added along the Austro-Italian frontier at the head of the Adriatic. Since much of this front was mountainous, action was largely confined to some sixty miles along the Isonzo River, where for two years there was a series of bloody but indecisive engagements that pinned down several hundred thousand Austrian troops. Then in the late autumn of 1917, with Russia already beaten, came a blow that very nearly knocked Italy out. The Germans and Austrians broke through at Caporetto and sent the Italians into retreat across the Venetian plains. French and British reinforcements were hastily rushed across the Alps, but what did most to stop the Austro-Germans was the grave difficulty of supplying their armies in such a rapid advance. The Italians were finally able to hold along the line of the Piave River.

The Dardanelles and the Balkans.   Ultimately more significant was the Dardanelles campaign of 1915. With the entry of Turkey into the war on the side of the Central Powers in November 1914, and with the French able to hold the western front against the Germans, a group of British leaders decided that British strength should be put into amphibious operations in the Aegean area, where a strong drive could knock Turkey out of the war by the capture of Constantinople. The great exponent of this eastern plan was Winston Churchill, first lord of the admiralty. The point of attack chosen was the Dardanelles, the more southwesterly of the two straits that separate the Black Sea from the Aegean. The action is known as the Gallipoli campaign for the long, narrow peninsula on the European side of the Dardanelles that was a key to the action.

The British and French fleets tried to force the Straits in March 1915, but they abandoned the attempt when several ships struck mines. Later landings of British, Australian, New Zealand, and French troops at various points on both the Asian and European shores of the Dardanelles were poorly coordinated and badly backed up. They met fierce and effective resistance from the Turks, and in the end they had to withdraw without taking the Straits. The cost of this campaign was enormous: 500,000 casualties. The Anzac (Australian and New Zealand) troops felt they had been led into senseless slaughter by British officers, and a sense of a separate Australian nationalism was clearly expressed for the first time.

Serbia's part in the crisis that had produced the war meant that from the start there would be a Balkan front. In the end all Balkan states became involved. The Austrians failed here also, and although they managed to take the Serbian capital, Belgrade (December 1914), they were driven out again. Bulgaria, wooed by both sides, finally came in with the Central Powers in the autumn of 1915. The Germans sent troops and a general, August von Mackensen (1849–1938), under whom the Serbs were finally beaten.

To counter this blow in the Balkans, the British and French had already landed a few divisions in the Greek city of Salonika and had established a front in Macedonia. The Greeks themselves were divided into two groups. One was headed by King Constantine (1868–1923), who sympathized with the Central Powers but who for the moment was seeking only to maintain Greek neutrality. The other was a pro-Ally group headed by the charismatic prime minister Eleutherios Venizelos (1864–1936), who had secretly agreed to the Allied landing at Salonika. Venizelos did not get firmly into the saddle until June 1917, when Allied pressure compelled King Constantine to abdicate in favor of his second son, Alexander (1893–1920). Greece then declared war on the Central Powers.

Meanwhile Romania, which the Russians had been trying to lure into the war, yielded to promises of great territorial gains at the expense of Austria-Hungary; Romania came in on the Allied side in August 1916. The Central Powers swept through Romania and by January 1917 held most of the country. When the Russians made the separate Peace of Brest-Litovsk with the Germans in March 1918, the Romanians were obliged to yield some territory to Bulgaria and to grant a lease of oil lands to Germany.

The Macedonian front remained in a stalemate until the summer of 1918. Then, with American troops pouring rapidly into France, the Allied military leaders decided they could afford to build up their forces in Salonika. The investment paid well, for under the leadership of the French general Franchet d'Esperey (1856–1942), the Allied armies on this front were the first to break the enemy completely. The French, British, Serbs, and Greeks began a great advance in September all along a line from the Adriatic to the Bulgarian frontier. They forced the Bulgarians to conclude an armistice on September 30, and by early November they had crossed the Danube in several places. The armistice in the West on November 11 found the tricolor of France, with the flags of many allies, well on its way to Vienna.

The Near East and the Colonies. This truly worldwide war, fought in the Near East, Africa, and the Far East, as well as in every ocean, made it clear that non-Continental events were no longer mere sideshows. The war in the Near East, in particular, would unleash nationalisms that continue to the present day. The Turks, trained and officered by German experts, had often resisted effectively. In April 1916 they forced the surrender of the British forces at Kut in Mesopotamia (modern Iraq) and marched up the Tigris-Euphrates Valley.

The following year the British marched north again and took Baghdad, effectively ending Turkish authority in Mesopotamia.

In 1894 the Armenians had revolted and been brutally suppressed, leading Britain and France to pressure Turkey into promising reforms. The reforms were not put into operation, however, and the Armenian revolt continued. In 1895–1897 eight thousand Armenians were killed. The remaining Armenians in Turkey had bided their time; now they felt that the World War provided them with their opportunity. When the Russians launched an offensive near Lake Van, the Armenians nearby took over the Turkish fortress and turned it over to the Russians. Declaring that Armenians everywhere were helping the Russians, the Turkish government ordered the removal of all non-Muslims from military areas or lines of communication. In the forced removal thousands of Armenians died of exposure in the desert; Armenian men were massacred, the women raped, and survivors forcibly converted to Islam. The Armenians were reduced to a remnant at the end of the war, an estimated 1 million having died.

Elsewhere the British exploited Arab dislike for the Turks, with the particular assistance of the romantic colonel T. E. Lawrence (1888–1935), who knew the Arabs intimately and helped coordinate an Arab revolt with a British expedition from Egypt under General Sir Edmund Allenby (1861–1936). By the end of 1917 the British held Jerusalem. In September 1918 a great British offensive in Syria was so successful that on October 30 the Turks concluded an armistice and left the war.

From these campaigns there later emerged not only the independent Arab states but also the Jewish national state of Israel. In November 1917, in the Balfour Declaration, named for the British foreign secretary and former premier Arthur James Balfour, the British promised "the establishment in Palestine of a national home for the Jewish people." This promise bore fruit in the mandate of 1922 from the League of Nations, by which such a home was set up under British protection.

In their overseas colonies the Germans, although cut off from the homeland by the British navy, fought with great skill. In East Africa they managed to hold out in a series of campaigns, so that they still had forces in the field on Armistice Day, November 11, 1918, and their commander did not surrender until November 23. But elsewhere the Germans fought from inadequate bases and with inadequate forces, so that by the end of 1914 the British, Australians, New Zealanders, South Africans, French, and Japanese had pretty well taken over the German overseas possessions.

Allied Victory

The War at Sea.   In the long run British sea power and American supplies proved decisive. The Allied command of the sea made it possible to draw on the resources of the rest of the world, and in particular to transfer large numbers of British and later American troops to the crucial western front. Sea power also enabled the Allies to shut Germany and its allies off from overseas resources. The Allied blockade slowly constricted Germany, limiting not merely military supplies for the armies but also food supplies for the civilian population. At the end of the war many Germans were suffering from malnutrition, and the death rate among children and old people was soaring, important factors in German surrender. Furthermore, it had been the doctrine of the freedom of the seas that had brought the United States into the war. In this sense Germany lost the war at sea doubly, because the submarine had made obsolete the traditional rules of war on blockade, stop-and-search before attack, and provision for the safety of passengers and crews. The United States had insisted on their observance, and yet they could not be observed if the submarine was to exploit its main strategy: remaining beneath the surface.

Nevertheless, when the Germans launched their unrestricted submarine warfare, they made serious inroads against the merchant ships that were essential to Britain. By the end of 1917 some 8 million tons of shipping had been sunk by the Germans, most of it by submarines. The submarine menace was only slowly overcome by extensive use of convoys, depth bombs, antisubmarine patrols, and the development of small, fast subchasers and destroyers.

The navy of surface vessels that the Germans had built up since the 1890s never played a decisive part in the war itself. German surface raiders caused severe damage in the first year, but in January 1915 British battle cruisers defeated the Germans in the battle of the Dogger Bank, and for the remainder of the year the Germans limited themselves to minelaying and to concentrating on their *Unterseeboot* (submarine) warfare. In 1916 a new commander sought to use the German high seas fleet more effectively; destroyer groups conducted raids, battle cruisers bombarded the English coast, and in May the Germans tried to trap part of the British grand fleet in harbor. Forewarned, British Admiral Sir John Jellicoe (1859–1935) put to sea, and in the running battle of Jutland, fought in the North Sea May 31–June 1, 1916, the British forced the Germans to run for port, although British losses were much heavier. The German surface navy never again seriously threatened Britain's command of the sea in European waters.

New Weapons. This war also saw the beginnings of air warfare. German dirigibles (known as *Zeppelins*) raided London many times in 1916 and 1917, and both sides made airplane bombing raids on nearby towns. But the total damage was relatively light and did not affect the final result. The airplane was more important for scouting. The fighter plane was greatly improved during the war, and a base was laid for the development of the modern air force.

Although the invention of the airplane did not alter traditional warfare, an intensified type of trench warfare was developed, especially on the western front. The machine gun, the repeating rifle, and fast-firing artillery, with the guidance of spotter planes, could pour in upon an attacking force such deadly fire that it was almost impossible for either side to break through the opposing trench systems on a wide front. Because of the new technology and trench warfare, both sides suffered losses of a magnitude never known before.

Two new weapons almost broke the deadlock. One was poison gas, first used by the Germans in shells in October 1914, with disappointing results. Then in April 1915 the Germans used chlorine gas discharged from cylinders. The overwhelmed French broke in a wave five miles wide, leaving the line completely undefended. But the Germans were not prepared to follow through, and the gap was closed once the gas had dispersed. Military technicians developed a simple countermeasure, the gas mask, which became part of the equipment of every soldier on both sides.

The second new weapon came much nearer to producing decisive success. This was the tank, a British invention. The tank acquired its name when early models were shipped under tarpaulins, which the curious were told covered water tanks. But the new weapon was used too soon, in inadequate numbers, and before sufficient mechanical tests had been made, in the British Somme offensive of 1916. With substantial modifications, tanks were used again at the battle of Cambrai late in 1917, when three hundred tanks broke through the German lines. Failure to follow up quickly gave the Germans a chance to drive the British back, but the battle had clearly shown what tanks could achieve when well used.

The Entry of the United States.   Both sides knew that the entry of the United States, with its fresh forces and vast industrial capacity, would be telling, were the war to last another year. But the Central Powers anticipated victory before American forces could be in the field. The French were crumbling, the burden of fighting had fallen increasingly on the British during 1917, and the Allies attempted "the one big push" on the western front while they still could, in the spring of 1917. The British were successful at Arras, the Canadians at Vimy Ridge, but the French were denied the easy victory promised them by their generals in the ravines of the Aisne, and their exhausted troops mutinied. To contain the Germans, the British general, Sir Douglas Haig (1861–1928), threw his troops into nine successive attacks in waterlogged terrain at the third Battle of Ypres from July 31 to November 15. Except for the Canadian capture of Passchendaele, the British line gained only nine thousand yards at the cost of nearly half a million casualties. Allied morale was low as the death rate soared and British military leadership proved inept. The establishment of a Supreme War Council in late November to unify Allied strategy did little to bring order to a chaotic and increasingly divisive situation.

Thus early in 1918 Germany decided to throw everything it had against the Allies on the western front before the American troops arrived in force. Germany now had troops released from the eastern front. General Ludendorff turned to massive application of the barrage, in which a long discharge of artillery would flatten out a section of enemy defenses and the no-man's land in front of the troops, forcing the enemy to retire to rear trenches. The initial barrage would include gas shells to knock out enemy observation posts and guns. A rolling barrage would ensue, advancing one kilometer an hour, with infantry following behind. Used on the Somme in combination with dense fog, this tactic had helped the Germans to pierce the British line along a 41-mile front, capture 80,000 prisoners, inflict 200,000 casualties, and approach Amiens, a major communications link. In the midst of this crisis General Foch, instructed to coordinate the Allied armies, became commander in chief.

Slowly the tide turned. The Germans sustained heavy losses as they advanced, and they lacked reserves. The French and British held the Germans after an advance on the Lys River. Ludendorff secretly shifted his troops and pressed on the Marne to within forty miles of Paris, where American and French troops held the south bank of the Marne at Chateau-Thierry on June 1–4. Ludendorff attacked along the Marne again in July, but by then he had lost 800,000 men, and British, French, and American troops drove the Germans back. On August 8 a surprise attack by the British, using 450 tanks, broke through the German lines near Amiens, and German units refused orders. Then, from September 26 to November 11, a Franco-British attack on the West and a Franco-American attack on the South nearly closed the Germans in a pincers in the Argonne forest and along the River Meuse. Ludendorff's troops were in slow and generally orderly retreat, but suffering from low morale and without supplies, and he was determined that Germany itself should not be invaded. On September 29 he called on the government to request an armistice; the German chancellor resigned the following day, and his successor appealed directly to President Wilson to call a peace conference on the basis of Wilson's Fourteen Points. The Allies were reluctant to accept these conditions, and Wilson hinted that the Americans would conclude a separate peace. On October 27 the Austro-Hungarian Empire, which was breaking up, also asked for an armistice. On November 3 mutiny in the German fleet at Kiel and in much of northwest Germany, and on November 7 revolution in Bavaria, made it impossible to continue. Ludendorff had been dismissed, and William II abdicated on November 9 and fled to Holland. Negotiations that had begun on November 8 were concluded at 5:00 A.M. on November 11, when the armistice was signed. All was, at last, quiet on the western front.

The Home Fronts

In World War I soldiers and sailors were, for the most part, civilians, unused to military ways. Behind the front—subject to rationing and regimentation in daily living—families, too, were part of this great "total war." They, too, bore up under it, although in France in 1917, after the bloody failure of the "one big push," civilian and military discontent almost broke French morale. And in Germany the armistice was the result, in part, of a psychological collapse under intolerable spiritual and material pressures.

The Germans were slow to organize for total war. They failed notably to ensure the proper and equitable distribution of food supplies, so that as 1918 wore on, whole sectors of the urban population began to suffer from

The Written Record

WAR IN THE TRENCHES

The war in the trenches was unremitting tedium punctuated by moments of intense action. Long after the war a distinguished British historian, Charles Carrington (1897–1981), who was a young man on the Somme, wrote of his experience:

After a battle you buried your comrades and saw to it that their graves were marked with a wooden cross and a name. If you had time, and if it was not too dangerous, you did as much for other British dead. The enemy came last in priority, and more than once I have cleared a trench of its defunct tenants by throwing them over the parapet, where someone might or might not find and bury them when the battle was over. There were so many live inhabitants in the landscape as I saw it at Contalmaison in November 1916 that corpses had been cleared off everyone's premises, unless you went up to the new front where it was too dangerous for burial-parties to work. But in rolling forward the armies left desert areas behind, where no one had either need or inclination to go, in winter dreary beyond description, inhabited only by giant rats, fattened on corpse-flesh, in summer strangely beautiful with carpets of wild flowers and loud with skylarks. Clumps of scarlet poppies sprang up wherever the chalky subsoil had been disturbed by digging or by shell-fire. Long afterwards you could find corpses in nooks and corners of this wilderness . . .

The killed and wounded were all lost by harassing fire, mostly on their way up or down the line. Once in position at Le Sars you could not show a finger by daylight, and by night every path by which you might be supposed to move was raked by machine-guns which had been trained on it by day. The entrance to the village, that is the gap in the ruins where the Bapaume Road passed through, the only way, by which you must pass, was under continuous shell-fire. If you could reach your funk-hole, and crouch in it, there was a fair chance of your coming out of it alive next day to run the gauntlet of the Bapaume Road again. In your funk-hole, with no room to move, no hot food, and no chance of getting any, there was nothing worse to suffer than a steady drizzle of wintry rain and a temperature just above freezing-point. A little colder and the mud would have been more manageable. Life was entirely numbed; you could do nothing. There could be no fighting since the combatants could not get at one another, no improvement of the trenches since any new work would instantly be demolished by a storm of shell-fire.

From *Soldiers from the Wars Returning* by Charles Carrington. Copyright © 1965 by C. E. Carrington. Reprinted by permission of David McKay Company, a division of Random House, Inc.

malnutrition. Nor were their finances and war production managed as efficiently as industrial production before the war had led everyone to expect.

Sooner or later, all countries engaged in the war felt obliged to introduce drastic wartime economic planning. In Britain a series of Defense of the Realm Acts clamped down severely on the right to say and do what one liked. In May 1915, the first of the Munitions of War Acts were passed, which gave to the state in this liberal democracy control not only over all necessary factories and raw materials but also management, labor, and profits in those industries. Beginning in 1915, the "men of push and go," mostly businessmen and academics, temporarily entered government service to aid in running the newly enlarged state. When the United States entered the war in 1917, a similar path was followed by the so-called dollar-a-year men. Like their British opposite numbers, these outsiders from business and the universities helped to build up an enormous new central government that regulated the economy as it had never been regulated before. And of course all the belligerents engaged in a war of propaganda or, as it came to be called later, psychological warfare.

The Allies won the battle of the production lines, in which the United States played a major part. In the end, government control in the democracies (following the model of the British Ministry of Munitions formed in 1915) proved to be more effective than in the autocratic states. Allied production was slow in getting started and suffered from mistakes, bottlenecks, and hasty experiments. In the beginning the Allies were often at cross-purposes in production as well as in military strategy. Nevertheless, the Allies eventually fully exploited their potential superiority over the Central Powers in material resources.

The Allies also won the most critical phase of the war of propaganda. They sought to convince the neutral world, especially the United States, Latin America and the Swiss, Dutch, Scandinavians, and Spaniards, that the Allies were fighting for the right and the Central Powers for the wrong. Most of the neutral West was early convinced that the cause of the Allies was just, or would at least prove victorious—a conviction strengthened by the public perception of the traditional liberalism of France and Britain, in contrast with the traditional autocracy of the German and Austrian empires.

Allied propaganda was certainly anything but balanced in its message, most notably in its successful efforts to dramatize what it presented as frightful atrocities in Belgium committed by the bestial "Hun." The new state-sponsored allied propaganda machine emphasized and exaggerated the brutality of the German occupation forces in Belgium, although German treatment of civilians was extremely harsh. A small amount of evidence, once demonstrated, served to prepare the public to believe far worse. Allied propaganda also stressed that it was Germany who had marched first and had invaded a small neutral nation, whose integrity she had once guaranteed by treaty, and Austria-Hungary, which had invaded Serbia, another small country. This made it possible to ignore the complex web of various national ambitions that underlay the coming of war. These undeniable military facts, however, would serve to condemn the Central Powers in the eyes of much of the world when the peace was made in 1919.

In Russia, the four years of war saw no major changes in political structure. The Central Powers retained their incompletely responsible parliamentary governments, and the parliaments on the whole were reasonably submissive. Despite the strengthening of the executive in wartime, France, Britain, and the United States carried on their democratic institutions. In Britain the skillful but indecisive Liberal leader Herbert Asquith (1852–1928) was succeeded in December 1915 by David Lloyd George, who had proved himself an admirable organizer of war production. Clemenceau—the Tiger, as he was known to his friends and enemies alike—came to power at the end of 1917, at a time when defeatism threatened both the military and the civilian strength of France. He took firm command of the war effort and disposed summarily of the disaffected politicians.

The war brought substantial changes to social life on the home front. An entire generation of young men, potential leaders in industry and politics, was destroyed in Britain and France. In both countries and in the United States women were employed in factories, on streetcars, at the lower levels of politics, and just behind the lines as nurses in military hospitals. At the end of the war, when demobilized men expected to return to their jobs, women who had acquired skills were thrown out of work, and many turned to socialism.

Moral codes concerning sexual propriety also changed, for the men felt they might never return from the front, and the old practices requiring a slow courtship were often cast aside. While the double standard in sexual conduct was intensified—soldiers could violate the conventions of marriage without blame, while women were expected to remain faithful to their departed men—there were many who began to question these conventions. Sexual promiscuity and "social diseases" became more prevalent, as all societies began to challenge the authority of the family, the church, or the school over moral conduct.

The Peace Settlements

The warring powers met at Versailles to settle with the Germans and at other châteaux around Paris to settle with the rest. Peace congresses never meet in a world that is really at peace, for there is always an aftermath of local war, crises, and disturbances; in 1918–1919 these were so numerous and acute that they conditioned the work of the peace congresses. In addition, throughout 1918–1919 an influenza epidemic more devastating than any disease since the Black Death swept across the world, taking 20 million lives and disrupting families and work everywhere.

Postwar Instability

The most worrisome crises were in Russia. No sooner had the Germans been forced to withdraw from the regions they had gained at Brest-Litovsk than the Allies sent detachments to various points along the perimeter of Russia—on the Black Sea, on the White Sea in the far north, and on the Pacific. The Allies' dread of final Bolshevik success and of the possible spread of Bolshevism westward added to the tensions at Versailles.

Bolshevism was clearly spreading westward. While the German revolution of November 1918 had been carried out under socialist auspices, through the winter of 1918–1919 there were communist riots and uprisings, and in Bavaria in April a soviet republic was proclaimed. The new republican government of Germany put these communist movements down, but, ominously for the future, only by an appeal to the remnants of the old army and to officers thoroughly hostile to any type of republic. After the breakup of the Austro-Hungarian monarchy in the autumn of 1918, the successor states—Czechoslovakia, Austria, Hungary, Yugoslavia, Romania—were disturbed by deep social and economic upheaval. In Hungary Béla Kun (c. 1886–c. 1940), who had worked with Lenin in Moscow, won power through a socialist-communist coalition and then set up a Bolshevik dictatorship. In August 1919 a Romanian army forced Kun to flee. Finally, groups of German ex-soldiers—*Freikorps* (Free Corps) made up of embittered officers and recruits who could not adjust to civilian life, and joined by university students—were clamoring for the return of the monarchy and were attacking communists. Two major communist theoreticians, Karl Liebknecht (1871–1919), founder of the Sparticist Party, which mounted the 1919 revolt, and Rosa Luxemburg (1870–1919), who had helped found the Communist party in Germany, were killed by soldiers while being taken to prison.

In the Near East the Allies had even greater instability to contend with. Greece was now up in arms against the Turks. Its nationalists had revived the hope of a restored Byzantine Empire. Greek armies landed at Smyrna in Asia Minor in the spring of 1919. The French and British, to whom control over different parts of the former Turkish Empire had been assigned, began at once having trouble with Arab leaders, while Jews were pressing for a national home in Palestine in accordance with the Balfour Declaration, to which the Arabs were bitterly opposed.

In India the aftermath of war was particularly disastrous as the epidemic of influenza swept the subcontinent. Indians had fought well as professional soldiers on the Allied side during the war; educated Indians thought their country was ripe for much more self-rule. Widespread disorders culminated in the Amritsar massacre in April 1919, in which a British general ordered his soldiers to fire on an unarmed crowd, killing or wounding some sixteen hundred people.

The situation in China was even less stable. There a revolution in 1911–1912 had ended the rule of the Manchu dynasty and inaugurated a precarious republic. The internal distractions of the Chinese and the weakening of Russia led the Japanese to renew their ambitious plans in north China. The presence of American troops in occupation of Archangel and Murmansk in north Russia, and within the port at Vladivostok, would color future relations with the Soviet Union.

The world was in turmoil when the Allies assembled to make peace. The problems that faced the peacemakers were worldwide, complex, and often insoluble, in the sense that no decision on a given problem could possibly satisfy all the groups concerned. Yet the world expected more from them than from any previous settlement. In the minds of many, this war had been a war to "make the world safe for democracy," a war to end war.

In 1918 many of these hopes were embodied in Woodrow Wilson's Fourteen Points. Wilson's primary concerns were to secure the freedom of the seas and to create a League of Nations to organize peace thereafter. He and his advisers had formulated the language of the Fourteen Points to make them useful in case of complete victory, a stalemate, or even defeat, for they were put forward as negotiating points. At the peace conference, however, they became rigid demands. These points were:

1. Open covenants of peace must be openly arrived at.
2. Absolute freedom of the seas must be guaranteed.
3. Economic barriers must be removed to establish equality of trade conditions among nations.
4. Guarantees must be given to reduce national armaments.
5. Colonial claims must be adjusted impartially, with the interests of the colonial populations given equal weight.
6. Russian territory must be evacuated.
7. Belgium must be restored.
8. All French territory should be freed, and Alsace-Lorraine restored to France.
9. The frontiers of Italy should be adjusted in accordance with "nationality."
10. The peoples of Austria-Hungary should be assured of autonomous development.
11. Romania, Serbia, and Montenegro should be evacuated and Serbia given access to the sea.
12. Turkey should be assured its sovereignty, but the nationalities under Turkish rule should be given an opportunity for autonomous development, and the Dardanelles should be opened to free passage.
13. An independent Polish state should be created with secure access to the sea.
14. A general association of nations must be formed to afford mutual guarantees "to great and small states alike."

Other hopes and promises that contradicted the Fourteen Points were not embodied in a single document. There were three categories: the previous diplomatic commitments made by the Allies; the widespread popular hopes fanned by Allied propaganda and promised at the end of the war by some Allied leaders; and the long-established habits and traditions that had become part of the dominant policies and trends of each nation.

In the first category, the most difficult of the diplomatic commitments was the contradictory set of promises made to Italy and Serbia by the original

Entente, including Russia, about the disposal of Habsburg lands. In the second category were the promises, widely believed by the British and French peoples, that Germany would be made to pay the whole cost of the war in reparations, its war criminals would be punished, and it would be forever rendered incapable of aggression. In the third category were the deeply rooted drives of the various nations—French desires for revenge against Germany, for hegemony in Europe, and for security; British longing for Victorian serenity and economic leadership, safe from German commercial competition; and the nationalist aspirations of the new states of central Europe. Important, too, was the American wish to be free from European alliances and entanglements as soon as possible.

The question of German war guilt seemed to be confirmed by the peace settlements, but in the years to come the issue would be much debated, and by the 1930s, a resurgent German nationalism would have renounced both the guilt and the settlements. Historians have debated the question of war guilt, or primary responsibility for the war, or more simply the exact nature of the chain of cause and effect, and have arrived at often differing conclusions. Following a second World War, some German scholars in particular argued that blame for the first World War should not have been laid at Germany's door. Questions of war guilt are vexations, but it seems irreduceably true that Bosnia and Serbia bore much of the responsibility for putting a match to the powder keg. Yet, two small and undeveloped nations can hardly be held responsible for a war that engulfed the world, and specific decisions made by specific leaders in all the participating nations must also be taken into account. Still, when one asks which nation finally disturbed the status quo in Europe sufficiently to bring on the war, it is difficult to answer with any other name than Germany.

Peacemaking and Territorial Settlements, 1918–1923

The peace conference first met formally on January 18, 1919. Nearly thirty nations involved in the war against the Central Powers sent delegates. Russia was not represented. The defeated nations took no part in the deliberations; the Germans, in particular, were given little chance to comment on or criticize the terms offered them. German anger over this failure of the Allies to accept their new republic was to play a large part in the ultimate rise of Adolf Hitler.

The conference got off to a good start. Wilson's Fourteen Points already seemed to guarantee peace; it was believed that the proposed association of nations, working together in the freedom of parliamentary discussion, would eliminate the costly burdens of armament. However, the conference took on a familiar pattern. The small nations were excluded from the real negotiations; the business of the conference was carried on in private among the political chiefs of the victorious great powers—the Big Four of Wilson, Lloyd George, Clemenceau, and Italian premier Vittorio Orlando (1860–1952). Decisions were made with only indirect consultation of public opinion and with all the pressures, intrigue, compromises, and bargaining common to earlier peace conferences.

The professional diplomats of the smaller states had probably never expected that they would be treated on equal terms, but the completeness of their exclusion from the work of the conference annoyed them and angered their peoples. More important, all the major powers had large staffs of experts—economists, political scientists, historians, specialists in many fields—who were confident that they would do the real work and make the real decisions. They drew up report after report, but they did not make policy. The most celebrated of these experts was an economist, John Maynard Keynes (1883–1946), who represented the British Treasury at Versailles until he quit in disgust and wrote a highly critical and influential analysis, *The Economic Consequences of the Peace.*

Keynes would become the most famous economist of the twentieth century. His work was both theoretical and practical. In *The Economic Consequences* he attacked the negotiators at Versailles, and especially Wilson and Lloyd George, skillfully arguing that the treaty was unworkable as well as immoral and that it would lead to economic ruin throughout Europe. Those who came sooner or later to agree that the Treaty of Versailles needed to be revised to lessen the harsh punitive elements came to be called "revisionists," a movement largely confined to the English-speaking nations that had been Germany's enemies but had not suffered invasion. The reception of Keynes' work drove a wedge between the British, French, and Americans. In time Keynes would produce his *General Theory of Employment, Interest, and Money,* published in 1936, which would tackle the Great Depression that he had predicted, arguing that the usual government policy—cutting spending in the face of inflation—was wrong, and that governments should spend in order to pull the economy out of depression. This argument paved the way for deficit financing with its many short-range benefits and long-range problems.

Wilson and his experts were gradually persuaded to accept harsher peace terms. The reparations bill against Germany was lengthened; Poland, Italy, and Japan made claims to lands that could not be justified on the basis of self-determination by the peoples concerned. Wilson compromised on a dozen points, but he would not let the Italians have Fiume, though Italy might have neighboring Trieste and the coveted Trentino. Yet Fiume was Italian-speaking and historically was linked with Venice. The Italian delegation left the conference in anger, but Wilson was immovable.

The covenant of the League of Nations was an integral part of the Treaty of Versailles. The League was no supranational body but a kind of permanent consultative system initially composed of the victors and a few neutrals. The way was left open for the Germans and the Russians to join the League, as they later did. The League had an assembly in which each member state had one vote, and a council in which five great powers (Britain, France, Italy, the United States, and Japan) had permanent seats, and to which four other member states were chosen by the assembly for specific terms. A permanent secretariat, to be located at Geneva, was charged with administering the affairs of the League. The League never fulfilled the hopes it had aroused. It did not achieve disarmament, nor did its peacemaking machinery prevent aggression. The great powers simply went their usual ways, using the League only as their policy makers saw fit.

More relevant to the work in Paris was the problem of territorial changes. The peacemakers were confronted not merely with the claims of the victorious Allies but also with those of the new nations that had sprung up from the disintegrating Austrian, Russian, and Turkish empires. They had to try to satisfy diverse land hungers without too obviously violating the principle of "self-determination of peoples." This principle was hard to apply in much of central Europe, where peoples of different language and national consciousness were mixed together in a mosaic of minorities. The result was to multiply the number of sovereign nations.

France regained Alsace-Lorraine, siezed by the Germans in the Franco-Prussian War. The Saar Basin was to be separated from Germany for fifteen years as an international ward supervised by the League of Nations. During that period its coal output would go to France, and at its close a plebiscite would determine its political future. The Rhineland remained part of the German Republic, although it was to be demilitarized and occupied for a time by Allied soldiers. Belgium was given some small towns on the German border. After a plebiscite provided for in the Treaty of Versailles, Denmark recovered the northern part of Schleswig, which the Danish Crown had lost to Prussia in 1864. Poland, erased from the map as an independent state in 1795, was restored and given lands that it had possessed before the partitions of the eighteenth century but that contained large German and other minorities.

The old Habsburg Empire was completely dismembered. Charles I (1887–1922) had come to the Habsburg throne in 1916 and had sought separate peace negotiations. But the empire broke up under him as ice breaks in a spring river: On October 15, 1918, Poland declared its independence; on October 19, Serbs, Croats, and Slovenes at Zagreb declared the sovereignty of a south-Slav government; on November 1, Charles granted Hungary independence. When Austria-Hungary signed a separate armistice on November 3, it had virtually ceased to exist. The heart of its German-speaking area was constituted as the republic of Austria, which was forbidden to join itself to Germany, and the heart of its Magyar-speaking area became a diminished kingdom of Hungary. The Czech-inhabited lands of Bohemia and Moravia were joined with Slovakia, to which were added the Ruthenian lands of the Carpatho-Ukraine frontier further east to form the "successor state" of Czechoslovakia.

Another successor state was Yugoslavia, officially the kingdom of Serbs, Croats, and Slovenes, a union between prewar Serbia and the south-Slav territories of the Habsburgs. Romania, which received the former Hungarian province of Transylvania, was also rewarded with Bessarabia, a Russian province that the Bolsheviks could not defend. Greece received Thrace at the expense of Turkey and Bulgaria. Wilson's refusal to accept the partition of Albania among Yugoslavia, Italy, and Greece saved that country from destruction.

Out of the former czarist domains (other than Poland) held at the end of the war by the Germans, the Baltic republics of Estonia, Latvia, and Lithuania were created. In time plebiscites determined other territorial adjustments, notably whether parts of East Prussia and Silesia should go to Poland or remain German. The new Polish state was granted access to the Baltic Sea through the so-called Polish Corridor, a narrow strip of German territory that had once been Polish and that terminated in the almost wholly German port of Danzig. The Poles wanted Danzig, but the Allies compromised by making it a free city and by giving the Poles free trade with it. The Polish Corridor now separated East Prussia from the rest of Germany, and Germans had to cross it in sealed trains.

Outside Europe the Near East presented the most acute problems. By the Treaty of Sèvres of October 1920, the Turks were left with only Constantinople and a small area around it in Europe, and with Anatolia in Asia. Mesopotamia and Palestine were given as mandates to Britain, while Syria and Lebanon were granted as mandates to France. The Greeks were to hold Smyrna and nearby regions in Asia Minor for five years, after which the mixed Greek and Turkish population would be entitled to a plebiscite. But the Treaty of Sèvres never went into effect, although it was signed by the sultan. A group of army officers headed by Mustafa Kemal led a popular revolt in Anatolia against the government at Constantinople and galvanized the Turkish people into a renewed nationalism. In the Greco-Turkish War of 1921–1922, the Turks drove the Greek army into the sea and set up a republic with its capital at Ankara in the heart of Anatolia. The Allies were obliged to conclude the Treaty of Lausanne with this new government in 1923; the new treaty transferred the area of Izmir (Turkish for Smyrna) and eastern Thrace from Greek to Turkish control and was much more advantageous to the Turks than the Treaty of Sèvres had been.

The Lausanne settlement included a radical innovation: a formal transfer of populations, affecting 2 million people. Greeks in Turkey, except for Istanbul (the former Constantinople), were moved to Greece, and Turks in Greece, except for western Thrace, were moved to Turkey. Each government was to take care of the transferred populations, and though much hardship resulted, on the whole the plan worked. No such exchange occurred on Cyprus, the British-controlled island in the eastern Mediterranean, where Greeks outnumbered Turks four to one and where the two peoples were so thoroughly intermingled in the towns and villages that an exchange would have been extremely difficult. Nor were measures taken to satisfy the national aspirations of two other minorities—the Muslim Kurds of eastern Anatolia and the Christian Armenians, many now dispersed from northeastern Anatolia to northern Syria.

Under the mandate system, control over a conquered territory was assigned to a power by the League of Nations, which undertook to see that

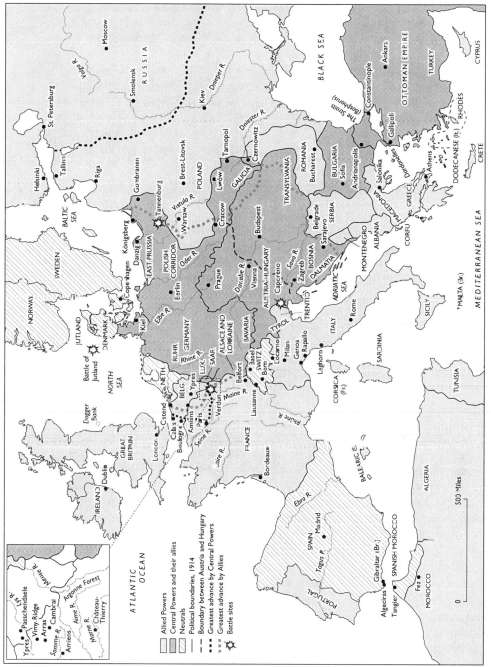

World War I, 1914–1918

Allied Powers
Central Powers and their allies
Neutrals
Political boundaries, 1914
Boundary between Austria and Hungary
Greatest advance by Central Powers
Greatest advance by Allies
Battle sites

the terms of the mandate were fulfilled. This system was designed to prepare colonial peoples for eventual independence. Under it the former German overseas territories and the non-Turkish parts of the Ottoman Empire were distributed. Of Germany's African possessions, East Africa went to Britain; Southwest Africa went to the self-governing British Dominion of the Union of South Africa; and both the Cameroons and Togoland were divided between Britain and France. In the Pacific the German portion of New Guinea went to Australia, western Samoa to New Zealand, and the Caroline, Marshall, and Mariana island groups to Japan. In the Near East France secured Syria and Lebanon, while Britain took Palestine, Transjordan, and Iraq (the new Arabic designation for Mesopotamia).

After land transfers, the most important business of the peace conferences was reparations, which were imposed on Austria, Hungary, Bulgaria, and Turkey, as well as on Germany. It was, however, the German reparations that so long disturbed the peace and the economy of the world. The Germans had to promise to pay for all the damage done to civilian property during the war, and to pay at the rate of $5 billion a year until 1921, when the final bill would be presented to them. They would then be given thirty years in which to pay the full amount. The amount was left indefinite at Versailles, for the Allies could not agree on a figure, but the totals suggested were astronomical.

The Versailles settlement also required Germany to hand over many merchant ships to the Allies and to make large deliveries of coal to France, Italy, and Belgium for ten years. The western frontier zone, extending to a line fifty kilometers east of the Rhine, was to be completely "demilitarized"—that is, to contain neither fortifications nor soldiers. In addition, the Allies could maintain armies of occupation on the left bank of the Rhine for fifteen years or longer. The treaty forbade Germany to have either submarines or military planes and severely limited the number and size of surface vessels in its navy. Finally, Article 231 of the Treaty of Versailles, the troublesome "war guilt clause," obliged Germany to admit that the Central Powers bore sole responsibility for starting the war in 1914.

The League of Nations was potentially a means by which a new generation of international administrators might mitigate the old rivalries. The reparations could be, and were, scaled down. The new successor states were based on a national consciousness that had been developing for at least a century. Although some might protest at the "Balkanization of Europe," it would have been impossible to deny national independence to the Czechs, the Poles, the Baltic peoples, and the south Slavs. Germany, although not treated generously, was not wiped off the map, as Poland had been in the eighteenth century. The new German republic retained most of the territory and population of the old monarchy and the potential once again to become the most powerful nation on the Continent. While elements of the treaty were harsh or badly managed, Versailles was in the end simply a compromise peace like many treaties before it.

The treaty, contained, however, too many compromises for the American people, who were not used to striking international bargains. The American refusal to ratify the Treaty of Versailles was the result of many forces. Domestic politics were an important part, for the Republicans had won control of Congress in the elections of November 1918. President Wilson, a Democrat, made no concessions to the Republicans, either by taking Republicans to Paris with him or by accepting modifications in the treaty that would have satisfied some of his Republican opponents. The Senate feared that the League would drag the United States into future wars. Wilson declared that Article X of the League Covenant had turned the Monroe Doctrine into a world doctrine, for it guaranteed "the territorial integrity and political independence" of all League members. But opponents argued that were the United States to sign the Covenant, the League could interfere with American tariffs and immigration laws. The Senate refused to ratify the treaty and ended the technical state of war with Germany by congressional resolution on July 2, 1921. Separate treaties were then signed with Germany, Austria, and Hungary, by which the United States gained all the rights stipulated for it by the Treaty of Versailles.

It is unlikely that even a more pliable and diplomatic president than Wilson could have won Senate ratification of a defensive alliance among France, Britain, and the United States. Without United States participation, Britain refused a mere dual alliance with France against a German attack. France, still seeking to bolster its security, thereupon patched up a series of alliances with the new nations to the east and south of Germany—Poland, and the Little Entente of Yugoslavia, Czechoslovakia, and Romania—a wholly unsatisfactory substitute for Britain and the United States as allies.

The peace left France with uneasy dominance of Europe, dependent on the continued disarmament and economic weakening of Germany, on the continued isolation of Russia, and on the uncertain support of unstable new allies. Moreover, France had been disastrously weakened by the human and material losses of the war. Germany was in fact still the strongest nation on the Continent. The Great War had checked, but not halted, its potential ability to dominate the Continent.

One most important matter was not directly touched upon by the Versailles settlement: Russia, or the Union of Soviet Socialist Republics (USSR), the formal name of the new communist state. Yet in many senses, the most important result of World War I was the emergence of this new state.

The Russian Revolution of 1917

Although Russia was shaken by domestic crisis in 1914, the country greeted the outbreak of World War I with demonstrations of national patriotism. The Duma supported the war, while the left-wing parties abstained from voting for war loans but offered to assist the national defense. Yet it was the war and the regime's failure to deal with the crises it provoked that precipitated revolution.

The Immediate Background to Revolution, 1914–1917

Russia was geographically isolated from the munitions and supplies that would otherwise have come from the Allies. Despite Russia's great resources

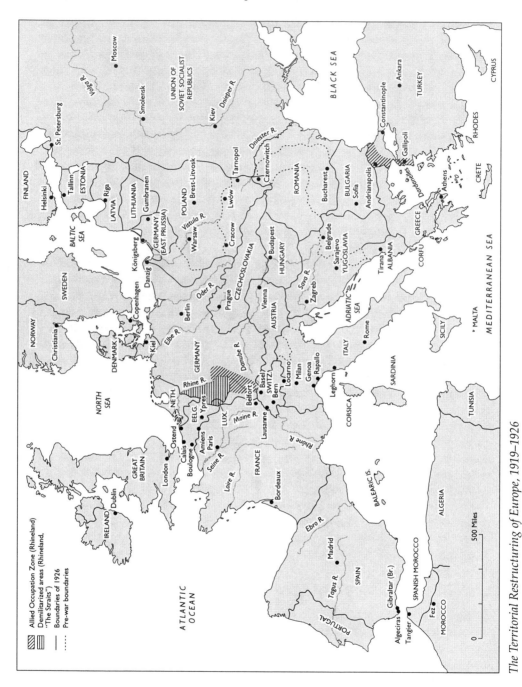

The Territorial Restructuring of Europe, 1919–1926

in agriculture and potential for industry, transportation was inadequate from the beginning, and when the trains were used to move troops, food shortages developed in the cities. Losses in battle were staggering from the first; the Russians suffered nearly 4 million casualties during the first year of war.

By mid-1915 the center and left groups in the Duma, known as the Progressive Bloc, were urging moderate reforms, such as the end of discrimination against minority nationalities and an increase in the powers of the zemstvos. In the autumn of 1915, in answer to a demand by the Progressive Bloc for a cabinet that would be responsible to it and not to the czar, Nicholas dismissed the Duma and took personal command of the armies in the field, leaving his wife in authority in St. Petersburg. She in turn left matters in the hands of her favorite, Rasputin.

With the empress and Rasputin in control, a gang of shady adventurers, blackmailers, and profiteers bought and sold offices, speculated in military supplies, put in their own puppets as ministers, and created a series of scandals. Confusion, strikes, and defeatism mounted at home during 1916, while the armies at the front, lacking transport, equipment, supplies, and medical care, slowly bled to death. The conservatives began to denounce Rasputin publicly, and in December 1916 he was murdered.

Despite repeated warnings from moderates in the Duma that the government itself was precipitating a revolution by its failure to create a responsible ministry, the czar remained apathetic. When news of Rasputin's death reached Berlin, the Germans saw a chance to knock Russia out of the war by promoting independence movements in the Ukraine, Poland, and Finland and by aiding Russian revolutionaries. Relatives of the imperial family and members of the Duma began to plot for Nicholas's abdication. In the early months of 1917 all conditions favored revolution, but the revolutionaries were not prepared.

The March Revolution.   By February only ten days' supply of flour was left in the capital, and the regional commander set up a rationing system. Long lines, closed shops, and the prospect of starvation led to disorder. In the Duma "unfit ministers" were attacked. The left-wing deputies turned to the secret organizations, which had already been working up public opinion against the government's dismissal of thousands of factory workers after a strike. The strikers demonstrated in the streets, and thousands of other workers, led by the wives of the workers, massed in a march that was broken up by mounted police. By the third day the Bolsheviks had taken charge of the continuing strikes and parades. The czar's secret police, the *Okhrana*, conducted mass arrests. But the soldiers were now refusing orders to stop the workers as they sought to march across the River Neva from the workers' quarter to the palaces, and on March 10 (February 27 in the old Russian calendar) many soldiers handed their weapons over to the crowd. The insurgents captured the arsenal with forty thousand rifles, and Petrograd (as St. Petersburg was now called) was in their hands.

The Revolution of February and March 1917, a product of despair and high emotion, remained virtually leaderless and without a program, since those who had been planning revolution were not yet fully prepared. The main Bolshevik leaders were still abroad or in exile, and the radical agrarian group (the Social Revolutionaries, SRs) and the more philosophical Marxists (the Social Democrats, SDs) were also caught by surprise. Nonetheless, by March the Romanov dynasty, which had ruled since 1613, was without hope.

A determining factor in the overthrow of the czar was the disintegrating loyalty of the garrison of Petrograd. When the czar ordered his troops to fire on the rioters, only a few obeyed, and in revulsion against the order, the troops joined the dissidents and began to hunt the police. On March 12 the Progressive Bloc in the Duma formed a provisional government to keep order until there could be a constituent assembly. By March 14, when the czar finally decided to appoint a responsible ministry, it was too late. On March 15 he abdicated in favor of his younger brother, Michael, and on March 16 Michael refused the throne.

Before that, on March 12, leftists, including many released from prison by the mobs, formed a Soviet (Council) of workers and soldiers, modeled on the 1905 Soviet. Its "Army Order No. 1," setting up a committee of soldiers within every unit of the army to control weapons, dealt a blow to military discipline and organization. The Soviet created a food-supply commission and published newspapers; its fifteen-man executive committee of SRs and Mensheviks became the policy makers of the revolution. The Soviet located its headquarters in the same building as the Duma and was soon in conflict with it. The Duma wanted to get its provisional government functioning quickly, to restore public order, and to carry on the war with efficiency for the honor of Russia. Some Duma members were monarchists; some wanted to continue the war and receive Constantinople as a reward; most felt the question of citizens' rights was secondary to these more pressing matters. The Soviet, on the other hand, knew that the great mass of Russian people did not care about Constantinople and wanted an immediate peace, as well as land and food.

The Marxists among the Soviet leaders—mainly Mensheviks—believed in the necessity of a preliminary bourgeois revolution, and they did not yet regard the Soviet itself as an organ of power. Therefore, although they would not participate in the provisional government, they offered it their limited support. Despite their widely differing political and economic aims, both the Duma and the Soviet agreed to grant political liberties immediately and to summon an assembly to establish the future form of government and give Russia a constitution. The provisional government was composed mainly of Kadets (Constitutional Democrats) and other moderates and was headed by the liberal prince Georgi Lvov (1861–1925). It also included one member of the Soviet, the moderate SR Alexander Kerensky (1881–1970), minister of justice, who was a member of the Duma.

The Provisional Government.   The provisional government—which held office between mid-March and early November 1917—was a total failure. Russian moderates had no experience of authority. They were separated by a great cultural gulf from the lower classes. Their opportunity to rule came amid a fearful war, which they felt they had to pursue while reconstructing and democratizing the enormous and unwieldy Russian Empire. Moreover, the Soviet held many of the instruments of power, yet refused to accept responsibility. Workers and soldiers in the capital supported the Soviet. In the provinces the new governors appointed by the provisional government had no weapon except persuasion to employ against the local peasant-elected soviets, which multiplied rapidly.

The two great issues facing the provisional government were agrarian discontent and the continuation of the war. The peasants wanted land, and they wanted it immediately. The provisional government, however, believed in acting with deliberation and according to law. It refused to sanction peasant seizures of land. Instead, it appointed a commission to collect material on which to base future agrarian legislation. As to the war, the provisional government still unrealistically hoped that Russia might win and thus gain the territories the Allies had promised. But the Soviet subverted discipline in the armies at the front by issuing a "declaration of the rights of soldiers," which virtually ended the authority of officers over enlisted men. Even the Bolshevik members of the Soviet, who now began to return from exile, demanded only that Russia participate in general peace negotiations, which should begin at once.

Lenin

The most important of the returning Bolshevik exiles was Lenin. He had returned to Russia from abroad for the Revolution of 1905, but he left Russia once more for exile in the West in 1908. From abroad he joined with a small group of socialists in opposing the war and urging that it be transformed into a class war. He considered the war to be the product of imperialism, itself produced by capitalism; thus, war, empires, and capitalism must all be destroyed if society was to be reformed.

Although he had for a time despaired of living to see a true socialist revolution, Lenin was anxious to get back to Russia. The German general staff thought his return would help disrupt the Russian war effort, so the German military transported Lenin and other Bolshevik leaders across Germany from Switzerland to the Baltic in a sealed railroad car. Lenin arrived at the Finland station in Petrograd on April 16, 1917, a little more than a month after the March revolution.

Most Russian Social Democrats had long regarded a bourgeois parliamentary republic as a necessary preliminary stage to an eventual socialist revolution. Therefore, they were prepared to help transform Russia into a capitalist society. They favored the creation of a democratic republic and believed that complete political freedom was absolutely essential for their own rise to power. Despite the Marxist emphasis upon the industrial laboring class as the only proper vehicle for revolution, Lenin early realized that in Russia, where the "proletariat" embraced only about 1 percent of the population, the SDs must seek other allies. During the Revolution of 1905 he had begun to preach

Doing History

SIMPLE ERRORS: THE WEST AND RUSSIAN HISTORY

The way in which certain simple matters of fact are sometimes dealt with in the West when the subject is Russia illustrates the problem of understanding the historical development of a relatively isolated nation. For example, for years some writers insisted that Lenin's first name was Nikolai or Nicholas because of his use of the initial N, not understanding Russian and communist customs concerning abbreviations and pseudonyms. This "discovery" was repeated in the American press as recently as 1983.

Many texts give different dates from those given here for certain events; virtually all disagree over the precise sequence of events and over the nature of leadership in the Duma and the first Soviet. Events that took place in March according to the Western calendar employed throughout this book are frequently referred to as taking place in February because of the different Russian calendar. The number of deaths in any specific demonstration, mutiny, or battle reveal dramatic discrepancies in different books. These inconsistencies in both Soviet and modern Western literature on the Russian Revolution are symptomatic of the degree to which Russia was cut off from the West at the time. Matters of straightforward chronology, of fact, even of names or birth and death dates were subjects of rumor or propaganda both inside and outside Russia. Later, when Soviet leadership ordered the rewriting of much of Russian history so that Russian citizens would not have access to other, and thus confusing, points of view, many aspects of Russian history fell under even greater suspicion.

Russian history clearly represents the problems of accurately recording and intelligently interpreting the past when a society has either been long ignored or cut off from alternative interpretations of its past. It also illustrates how a political leadership may attempt to make history as a discipline serve its own ends by rewriting the past to fit contemporary expectations.

the need for limited tactical alliances between the Bolsheviks and the SRs, who commanded the support of the peasantry; when that alliance had served its purpose, the SDs were to turn on their allies and destroy them. Then would come the socialist triumph. Lenin's view, however, was not adopted, even by most Bolsheviks. Together with the Mensheviks, they continued to urge that a bourgeois revolution and a parliamentary democracy were necessary first steps.

Because Lenin did not trust the masses to make a revolution (by themselves, he felt, they were capable only of trade-union consciousness), he favored a dictatorship of the Bolshevik party over the working class. Because he did not trust the rank and file of Bolshevik party workers, he favored a dictatorship of a small elite over the Bolshevik party. And in the end, because he did not trust anyone's views but his own, he favored, although never explicitly, his personal dictatorship over this elite. Another future Russian leader, the brilliant Lev Davidovich Bronstein, known as Leon Trotsky (1879–1940), early warned that Lenin's views implied one-man dictatorship.

Trotsky, for his part, argued that the Russian bourgeoisie was so weak that the working class could telescope the bourgeois and socialist revolutions into one continuous movement. After the proletariat had helped the bourgeoisie achieve its revolution, the workers could move immediately to power and could nationalize industry and collectivize agriculture. Although foreign intervention and civil war were to be expected, the Russian proletariat would soon be joined by the proletariats of other countries, who would make their own revolutions. Except for this last point, Trotsky's analysis accurately forecast the course of events.

Lenin's greatest talent was as a skillful tactician. Even before he returned to Russia in 1917, he had assessed some of the difficulties facing the provisional government and decided that the masses could take over at once. Immediately upon his arrival, therefore, he hailed the worldwide revolution, proclaiming that the end of imperialism, the last stage of capitalism, was at hand and demanding that all power immediately be given to the soviets. These doctrines were known as the April Theses.

Almost no one save Lenin felt that the loosely organized soviets could govern the country or that the war would bring down the capitalist world in chaos. Still, Lenin called not only for the abandonment of the provisional government and the establishment of a republic of soviets but also for the confiscation of estates, the nationalization of land, and the abolition of the army, government officials, and the police. He was offering land at once to the impatient peasants, peace at once to the war-weary populace. This program fit the mood of the people far better than the cautious efforts of the provisional government to bring about reform by legal means. Dogmatic, furiously impatient of compromise, and entirely convinced that he alone had the courage to speak the truth, Lenin galvanized the Bolsheviks into a truly revolutionary group waiting only for the right moment to seize power.

The November Revolution

The provisional government faced a crisis. Kerensky, now war minister, emerged as the dominant leader. He failed to realize that it was no longer possible to restore the morale of the armies. A new offensive ordered on July 1 collapsed as soldiers refused to obey orders, deserted their units, and hurried home to their villages, eager to seize the land. The soviets became gradually more and more Bolshevik in their views. Although the June congress of soviets in Petrograd was less than 10 percent Bolshevik, the Bolshevik slogans of peace, bread, and freedom won overwhelming support.

An armed outbreak by troops who had accepted the Bolshevik slogans found the Petrograd Soviet professing unwillingness to assume power. While crowds roared outside, the Soviet voted to discuss the matter two weeks later and meanwhile to keep the provisional government in power. The govern-

The Written Record

LENIN'S ADDRESS AT THE FINLAND STATION

On the day Lenin arrived at the Finland station in Petrograd, he declared that the World War must be transformed into a series of civil wars, the bourgeois revolution into a social revolution, so that a crisis of European capitalism might be precipitated. In a memorable confrontation, he instantly revealed that he would not accept the more moderate expectations of the Petrograd Soviet. The following account is drawn from the notebooks of a journalist who was on the spot:

The train was very late. . . . But at long last it arrived. A thunderous *Marseillaise* boomed forth on the platform, and shouts of welcome rang out. . . . Behind [the master of ceremonies] . . . Lenin came, or rather ran, into the room. He wore a round cap, his face looked frozen, and there was a magnificent bouquet in his hands. Running to the middle of the room, he stopped in front of [N. S.] Chkheidze [(1864–1926), the chairman of the Soviet] as though colliding with a completely unexpected obstacle. And Chkheidze, still glum, pronounced the following "speech of welcome" with not only the spirit and wording but also the tone of a sermon:

"Comrade Lenin . . . we welcome you to Russia. But—we think that the principal task of the revolutionary democracy is now the defence of the revolution from any encroachments either from within or from without. We consider that what this goal requires is not disunion, but the closing of the democratic ranks. We hope you will pursue these goals together with us." . . .

Lenin . . . stood there as though nothing taking place had the slightest connection with him . . . and then, turning away from the Ex[ecutive] Com[mittee] delegation altogether, he made this "reply":

"Dear Comrades, soldiers, sailors, and workers! I am happy to greet in your persons the victorious Russian revolution, and greet you as the vanguard of the worldwide proletarian army. . . . The piratical imperialist war is the beginning of civil war throughout Europe. . . . The hour is not far distant when at the call of our comrade, Karl Liebknecht [who was still alive at the time], the peoples will turn their arms against their own capitalist exploiters. . . . The worldwide Socialist revolution has already dawned. . . . Any day now the whole of European capitalism may crash. The Russian revolution accomplished by you has prepared the way and opened a new epoch. Long live the worldwide Socialist revolution!" . . .

To another *Marseillaise,* and to the shouts of the throng of thousands, among the red-and-gold banners illuminated by the searchlight, Lenin went out by the main entrance and was about to get into a closed car, but the crowd absolutely refused to allow this. Lenin clambered on to the bonnet of the car and had to make a speech.

N. N. Sukhanov, *The Russian Revolution, 1917,* trans. Joel Carmichael (London: Oxford University Press, 1955), pp. 272–74, quoted in M. C. Morgan, *Lenin* (London: Edward Arnold, 1971), pp. 104–6. Sukhanov (1833–1931?), while in favor of revolution, was anti-Bolshevik. Although Lenin criticized Sukhanov as a Social Democrat who did not understand the workers, he accepted his account of the revolution as factually accurate.

ment declared that Lenin was a divisive agent of Germany, and Lenin went into hiding in Finland to avoid arrest.

Kerensky became premier. General Lavr Georgyevich Kornilov (1870–1918), chosen by Kerensky as the new commander in chief of the armies, quickly became the hope of all conservative groups. In August Kornilov plotted a coup, intending to disperse the Soviet. His attitude toward the provisional government was less clear, but had he succeeded he would probably have demanded a purge of its more radical elements. Tension between Kornilov and his superior, Kerensky, mounted. The Soviet backed Kerensky, fearing Kornilov's attack. When Kornilov refused to accept his dismissal as war minister and seemed about to march against Petrograd, the Bolsheviks threw themselves into preparations for defense. Kornilov's troop movements were sabotaged, however, and by September 14 he had been arrested.

The Kornilov affair turned the army mutiny into a widespread revolt. In the countryside farms were burned, manor houses destroyed, and large landowners killed. After the great estates were gone, the peasantry attacked the smaller properties, although they allowed owners in some districts to keep a portion of their former lands through redistribution.

Amid these disorders Lenin returned to Petrograd. Warning that Kerensky was planning to surrender Petrograd to the Germans, Trotsky gained control over a Military Revolutionary Committee to help defend the city and to transform the committee into a general staff for the revolution. Beginning on November 4, he addressed huge demonstrations and mass meetings, and on November 7 (October 25 on the old Russian calendar) the insurrection broke out as Trotsky intended. The February Revolution had failed, to be replaced by the October Revolution.

In Petrograd the revolution had been well prepared and proceeded with little bloodshed. Military groups loyal to the Bolsheviks took control of key points in the city. The Bolsheviks entered the Winter Palace, where the provisional government was meeting, and arrested the ministers. Kerensky escaped and the Military Revolutionary Committee took over. A long-awaited Congress of Soviets, representing less than half of the soviets in Russia, opened on November 8. Both Lenin and Trotsky appeared. When the Mensheviks and right-wing SRs walked out, Trotsky called them garbage that would be swept into the trash cans of history. Cooperating with the left-wing SRs and adopting their land program, Lenin abolished the property rights of the church, of landlords, and of the Crown. He transferred the land thus affected to local land committees and soviets of peasant deputies, transforming at a stroke the isolated Russian villages by "legalizing" a process already begun. He also urged an immediate peace without annexations or indemnities and appealed to the workers of Germany, France, and England to support him in this demand. Finally, a new cabinet, called a Council of People's Commissars, was chosen, with Lenin as president and Trotsky as foreign *commissar*.

The Bolsheviks installed as commissar of nationalities a younger man, a Georgian named Joseph Dzhugashvili (1879–1953), who had taken the name Stalin, suggesting a steel-like hardness. Under Lenin's coaching, Stalin had become the party authority on questions relating to the many minority nationalities and had published a pamphlet on the subject in 1913.

Outside Petrograd the revolution moved more slowly. In Moscow there was a week of street fighting between Bolshevik Reds and anti-Bolshevik Whites, as those opposed to the revolution were called. Elsewhere, in factory towns the Bolsheviks usually won speedily; in nonindustrial centers it took longer. A main reason for the rapid and smooth success of the Bolsheviks was that the provincial garrisons opposed the war and willingly allied themselves with the workers. Local military revolutionary committees were created in most places and held elections for new local soviets. Most of Siberia and central Asia came over, but Tiflis, the capital of Georgia, went Menshevik and passed resolutions calling for a constituent assembly and the continuation of the war. Gradually the town of Rostov-on-Don, near the Sea of Azov, became the main center of White resistance, as Kornilov and other generals together with a number of the leading politicians of the Duma gathered there

Late in November an agreement was reached with the left-wing SRs, three of whom entered the government, and peace negotiations were begun with the Germans. The revolution proper was over and Lenin was in power. The Russian state, however, was disintegrating and decomposing socially on all sides. On November 25 the Bolsheviks held elections for a constituent assembly, the first free election in Russian history. As was to be expected, the Bolshevik vote was heaviest in the cities, especially Moscow and Petrograd, while the SR vote was largely rural.

Disregarding the fact that 62 percent of the votes had been cast for his opponents, Lenin maintained that "the most advanced" elements had voted for him. The constituent assembly met only once, in January 1918. Lenin dissolved it the next day by decree and sent guards with rifles to prevent its meeting again. The anti-Bolshevik majority was deeply indignant at this unconstitutional act of force against the popular will, but there was no public outburst and the delegates disbanded. In part this was because the Bolsheviks had already taken action on what interested the people most—peace, bread, and freedom—and in part because the Russian masses lacked a democratic parliamentary tradition.

War Communism, 1917–1920

The first period of Soviet history, which runs from the end of 1917 to the end of 1920, is usually called the period of *war communism*, or military communism. The term implies that the main features of the period were determined by military events; civil war raged, and foreign powers intervened on Russian soil. But the term is also somewhat misleading. This was a period of militant as well as military communism, symbolized early in 1918 by the change of the party's name from Bolshevik to the Russian Communist party. The cap-

Lenin addresses a crowd in Red Square Moscow in 1918, in celebration of the first anniversary of the Bolshevik Revolution. (Hulton Archive/Getty Images)

ital was shifted from Petrograd, with its exposed location on the western fringe of Russia, to the greater security of Moscow. And a newspaper, *The Communist*, began publication. The Bolsheviks firmly believed that world revolution was about to begin, probably first in Germany, then spreading to Britain and ultimately to the United States. This view led the Bolsheviks to hasten the construction of a socialist state in Russia.

By 1920 the state had taken over all enterprises employing more than ten workers. Labor was compulsory and strikes were outlawed. The state organized a system of barter, which replaced the free market. Internal trade was illegal; only the government food commissary could buy and sell. Money disappeared as the state took over distribution as well as production. It expropriated the banks and in effect wiped out savings. Church and state were separated by decree, and judges were removed from office and replaced by appointees of the local soviets. Nine opposition political parties were liquidated (among them the Kadets) or persecuted (the SRs and Mensheviks).

The government subjected the peasantry to ever more severe requisitioning. It mobilized the poorer peasants against those who were better off (called *kulaks*, from the word meaning "fist"). By calling for a union of the hungry against the better fed, the regime deliberately sowed class hatred in the villages and stimulated civil war in the countryside. A decree forming a secret police, the *Cheka* (from the initials of the words meaning "extraordinary commission"), was issued in December 1917, and terror became a weapon in the civil war.

Before the communist government could function at all, peace was necessary, as the army had virtually ceased to exist. Negotiations between the Russians and the Germans and Austro-Hungarians at Brest-Litovsk dragged on into 1918. Finally, on March 3, 1918, the Russians signed the Peace of Brest-Litovsk, which deprived them of the entire Ukraine, the Baltic provinces, Finland, and some Caucasian lands, undoing three centuries of Russian territorial expansion. The treaty cost Russia a third of its population, 80 percent of its iron, and 90 percent of its coal. Many communists resigned rather than accept the peace, and the left SRs quit the government. The Germans overran the Ukraine and the Crimea and installed a highly authoritarian regime. The Whites, with German help, put down the Reds in Finland.

Civil War, 1918–1921

During the months following Brest-Litovsk, disorder in the countryside as a result of requisitioning and class warfare was swelled by the outbreak of open civil strife. During the war a legion of Czechs resident in the country and of deserters from the Habsburg armies had been formed inside Russia. When Russia withdrew from the war, the Czech, nationalist leader, Thomas G. Masaryk (1850–1937), wanted to have the Czech corps sent to the French front. Czech, Soviet, and Allied representatives therefore decided to transport the Czech corps to Vladivostok, from which they could sail to France. As the Czechs gathered, the communists became suspicious of their intentions and ordered them to disarm. The Czechs then took control of the Siberian railroad. When the Soviet government tried to take reprisals against the Czechs, who numbered fewer than thirty-five thousand men, the Czechs seized several towns in western Siberia. The local soviets were unprepared, and the SRs were sympathetic to the Czechs. Local anti-Bolshevik armies quickly came into being. In July, in fear that the Whites would rescue the former czar and his family, then under house arrest in Ekaterinburg in the Ural Mountains, the leader of the local soviet decided that the last of the Romanovs had become expendable. Encouraged by Lenin, he arranged for the brutal murder of Nicholas II; his wife, the former Czarina Alexandra; his son and four daughters; his doctor; his servants; and his dog. Their bodies were then taken into the countryside and unceremoniously dumped down an abandoned well, where they were not found until after the collapse of the Soviet state eighty years later.

Shortly before the executions the Allies had decided to intervene in Russia on behalf of the opponents of Bolshevism. The withdrawal of Russia from the war had been a heavy blow to the Allies, and they now hoped to protect the vast amounts of war supplies still at Vladivostok and Archangel. They also wished to create a new second front against the Germans in the East.

The Czechs overthrew the local soviet in Vladivostok in June 1918, and by early August, British, French, Japanese, and American forces had landed. The Americans occupied Vladivostok to safeguard railroad communications in the rear of the Czechs. Of the Allies, only the Japanese had long-range territorial ambitions in the area. In effect, the Bolshevik regime had now been displaced in Siberia. The SRs disbanded the soviets and reestablished the zemstvos. Soon there were three anti-Red governments in three different Siberian centers. In August 1918 a small British and American force landed at Archangel. Then on August 30 an SR assassin killed the chief of the Petrograd Cheka, and Lenin, who was in Moscow, was shot twice. The Bolshevik leadership feared a general counterrevolution in which any doctor might be involved, so the seriously wounded Lenin was taken directly to his apartment rather than to a hospital. The woman who allegedly had attempted to kill him was shot without a trial, and since responsibility for her act was never proven, rumors multiplied. Blaming the bourgeoisie, the Moscow Cheka shot six hundred people. Cheka retaliation elsewhere was massive.

The regime now sped up its military preparations. As minister of war, Trotsky imposed conscription, and by a mixture of appeals to patriotism and threats of reprisals against their families secured the services of about fifty thousand czarist officers. The Red Army, which was Trotsky's creation, grew to more than 3 million strong by 1920. Its recapture of Kazan and Samara on the Volga in the autumn of 1918 temporarily turned the tide in the crisis that seemed about to engulf the Soviet state.

The German collapse on the western front in November 1918 permitted the Bolsheviks to repudiate the Treaty of Brest-Litovsk and move back into parts of the Ukraine, where they faced the opposition of local forces. Elsewhere, the opposition consisted of three main armies. An army of Whites moved from Rostov-on-Don south across the Caucasus and received French and British aid. Other forces in western Siberia overthrew the SR regime in Omsk, where their commander, Admiral Alexander Kolchak (1874–1920), became a virtual dictator. Yet another army, including many former members of the German forces, operated in the Baltic region and threatened Petrograd from the west. In the spring of 1919 the Reds defeated Kolchak, and by winter took Omsk. Although the Reds also reconquered the Ukraine, mutinies in their own forces prevented them from consolidating their victories. In the summer of 1919 the White army took Kiev and struck north, advancing to within 250 miles of Moscow itself. A second army advanced to the suburbs of Petrograd, but by the end of 1919 the Reds were able to defeat the White threat, although one White general, Baron Peter Wrangel (1878–1928), retained an army in the Crimea in 1920. Trotsky now called for the militarization of labor to reconstruct the ravaged country.

After the defeat of the Whites, the Reds had to face a new war with the Poles in 1920, led by Poland's national hero, Josef Pilsudski (1867–1935). A long-time fighter for Polish independence and organizer of the independent Polish Legion that he had led against the Russians in the World War, the indefatigable Pilsudski became the first provisional president of the new Polish republic, and was now a field marshal and commander of its armed forces. He wanted to establish the Polish frontier as it existed in 1772, the year of the first partition. His immediate objective in 1920 was to drive the Bolsheviks out of the Ukraine and associate the Ukraine with Poland in a common but federally organized state. Beyond that he intended to bring White Russia, Lithuania, and Latvia into the federation also. The effect on Soviet power in the loss of mineral resources and coastlines would have been substantial, which is why the Western powers now swung around in support of Pilsudski's enterprise.

Although after an initial retreat the Red Army nearly took Warsaw, it failed to do so. Eager to finish off the remnant of the Whites and persuaded that there was no hope for a communist regime in Poland, the Reds now concluded peace in October 1920. The Poles obtained much of White Russia and the western Ukraine. This area was not inhabited by Poles but had been controlled by Poland down to the eighteenth-century partitions. It lay far to the east of the "Curzon line," an ethnic frontier that had been proposed by the British foreign minister, Lord Curzon (1859–1925), during the Versailles negotiations and that Pilsudski had rejected. The final line, established at Riga in 1921, bisected Byelorussia and the Ukraine roughly where the Uniate (or church of Eastern rites that recognized papal authority) and Orthodox churches met. The size of the ethnic minorities transferred to Poland under this treaty, combined with their mistreatment by the government in Warsaw, was a principal factor making Poland ungovernable in the interwar years, except by military dictatorship.

The Reds now turned on Baron Wrangel, who had marched northward from the Crimea and had established a moderate regime in the territory he occupied. He was forced to evacuate, assisted by a French fleet, in November 1920. The White movement was virtually over. Many circumstances accounted for the Whites' failure and the Reds' victory. The Whites could not unite on any political program beyond the overthrow of the Reds, for they were deeply divided ideologically. Their numbers included everyone from czarists to SRs, and they disagreed so violently on the proper course for Russia to follow that they could agree only to postpone discussion of these critical problems. Their own regimes were often repressive, so that they did not build local followings, and their troops were at times undisciplined. Moreover, although their movement was located on the geographical periphery of Russia—in Siberia, the Crimea, the Ukraine, the Caucasus, and the Baltic— the Whites never reached an understanding with the non-Russian minorities who lived in these regions.

Most important, the Whites could not command the support of the peasantry. Instead of guaranteeing the results of the land division already carried out with Bolshevik approval, the Whites often restored the landlords in areas they temporarily controlled. The peasantry grew sick of both sides. Food production was curtailed, and atrocities were frequent. Moreover, the Whites simply did not command as much military strength as did the Reds, who outnumbered them and who had inherited much of the equipment manufactured for the czarist armies. Holding the central position, the Reds had a unified and skillful command, which could use the railroad network to shift troops rapidly. The Whites, moving in from the periphery, were divided into at least four main groups and were denied effective use of the railroads.

Finally, the intervention of the Allies on the side of the Whites was ineffectual and amateurish. It probably harmed the White cause, since the Reds could speak as the national defenders and could portray the Whites as the hirelings of foreigners. Without the "capitalist" and White threats on the periphery, the center might not have rallied behind Lenin.

The struggle for power in Russia in no sense ended with the civil war. Famine was raging, and class hatreds were exploited on an unparalleled scale. Industry was producing at only an eighth of its prewar output, agricultural output had fallen by 30 percent, and distribution was breaking down. The new regime was losing support. But by early 1921 all major nations in the West were undergoing intense political change as the postwar effort to absorb returning troops, to restore prewar conditions in the victorious nations, and to live with defeat in others created widespread instability.

In the nineteenth century the Russian population had grown nearly 200 percent, changing the Russian countryside from being underpopulated to being overpopulated. While emigration to Siberia had carried off 5 million people between 1870 and 1914 and another 3 million had gone to the New World, much of the surplus peasantry had been taken into the towns. Thus Russia had acquired that demographic group essential to the modern state and to its revolution: an urban proletariat. This group existed only in certain centers in Siberia or on the periphery, but it was powerful within the area where Lenin had built his authority. While the World War had cost Russia nearly 4 million dead, and 14 million more had died from disease and malnutrition during the revolution and the civil war, which produced a severe birth deficit in the 1920s, Russia continued to grow.

Having put down a serious rebellion of the naval forces at Kronstadt in March 1921, Lenin left a nation on its way toward unity, with a population that despite revolution, war, and famine had regained its prewar levels, and with the expectation of an international communist revolution. Ill from the end of 1921, the man who had reinterpreted Marx tried to prepare his successor. Lenin died in January 1924. By then much of the West was aware that the peacemaking at Versailles had not brought security to Europe and that the Russian Revolution and its aftermath had assured continued instability for much of the world. Inadvertence is always a by-product of great events, and one of the least predictable of the many unanticipated results of the catastrophic war was its role as a catalyst of the modern environmental movement.

The Environment

The concept of environmentalism, and especially of ecology—the science of the relationship between organisms and their environments—did not become a human preoccupation until the mid-twentieth century, although there was much speculation and development of informed opinion earlier. Expeditions, largely by sea, in the eighteenth and early nineteenth centuries, some accompanied by scientific observers, had opened an awareness of the differences in how people in different parts of the world lived, especially after the popularization of the concept of evolution; how species were influenced by their surroundings, including climatic changes; and how, in turn, human beings had, by choices they had made, altered their environments. Both Charles Darwin (1869–1882) and the Baron Humboldt (1769–1859), who had traveled widely and seen evidence of these changes for themselves, reflected on the nature of the forces at work in shaping and changing natural environments.

Self-conscious study of the way in which humankind had shaped nature began in Germany and Switzerland, and in the United States, in the nineteenth century. Of course there had been those who had noted connections between agricultural practices, erosion, and changed landscapes from antiquity, and leaders of state and the military were perfectly aware of how war could devastate the countryside. The development of geology as a subject of scientific inquiry had alerted scientists and others to the force of climate change across time. But on the whole leaders were not inclined to see a relationship between their short-term actions and long-term results—that is, to develop a sense of stewardship toward the land, with a view to protecting it for use by distant future generations—except when moved by religious conviction. Broadly, those who believed that all that happened in the world arose from God's will, or God's design, saw little reason to be concerned with environmental change. Even among a secular elite, including those who accepted the conclusion of Voltaire's *Candide* that it was best to cultivate one's own garden, there was a tendency to restrict one's concerns to geographically limited areas, and the Enlightenment thinkers of the eighteenth century and the nationalist advocates of the nineteenth century tended to focus, whether in western Europe or in Asia, on the problems of the emerging nation-states.

Perhaps the first person to set out in an explicit way the concepts of what, in the latter half of the twentieth century, would be called ecology (and the environmental movement) was an American, George Perkins Marsh (1801–1882). A lawyer, congressman, and diplomat, Marsh closely observed nature in his home state of Vermont, noting, for example, how the impact of the railroad age—the building of trestles, the cutting down of forests for railway ties and for fuel—altered fish spawning or the interaction between plant species. After extensive diplomatic experience as U.S. minister to Turkey and then to the kingdom of Italy, he wrote two books that in the twentieth century would be seen as the "fountainhead of the conservation movement." The first of these, *Man and Nature*, published in 1864, deeply influenced the relatively narrow circle of those who read it, and the second, *The Earth as Modified by Human Action* (1874), made clear the problems that thoughtless exploitation and modification of the environment brought.

Such concerns were, on the whole, limited to some scientists, social commentators, and naturalists until the end of World War II, however. The eighteenth century's emphasis on man and reason, the nineteenth century's scramble for imperial possessions and the creation of world markets, and the powerful sense in the emerging democracies in Europe and North America that frontier and overseas lands were manifestly destined to be possessed and transformed for the material benefits of the encroaching societies led to a triumphalism that produced little popular thought about environmental change. While here and there nations and groups set lands aside as forest reserves, established schools for the scientific study of forestry (in this Germany was a leader), or designated areas as "national parks" for the benefit of the people of the nation—Yellowstone National Park in the United States was the first such, in 1872—emphasis was on forests as a form of agriculture and commerce and parks as places of recreation and spiritual renewal, not as locations for species protection and invigoration. This initial period of limited environmental concern often is dated by historians as running from Marsh's publications in the second half of the nineteenth century to the publication of an influential post–World War II book by Rachel Carson, *Silent Spring* (1962), which reached a broad public with its warning of how chemical pesticides, then much-promoted by the agrochemical industry in the United States, Australia, and western Europe, caused female infertility and often contaminated breast milk (this at a time when breast-feeding was coming back into practice and when there was growing public alarm over the effects on public health of atomic and nuclear testing).

The debates framed by Marsh in 1874 and Carson in 1962 were active in Europe as well, where vast areas of land had been devastated by two world wars. Such debates were not yet significant in Africa, Asia, and much of Latin America, and indeed often were dismissed by emerging independence and nationalist leaders in these areas as simply arguments put forth by rich nations possessing high technology to suppress poor peoples and emerging states from enjoying prosperity based on the natural resources within and beneath their soils. In China, for example, the view of the past was that it was cyclical, turning on the birth and death of dynasties that were "the mandate of heaven," and although Western travelers and observers increasingly included China (which, by adopting the Gregorian calendar in 1911, became more explicable to those observers by increasingly seeing itself in linear time) and Japan in their broad analyses, these countries had little or no "environmental" or, indeed, conservation movement of significance.

The vast devastation of World War I—with its trench warfare across northern France, the postwar poverty of Germany, the complete breakup of the Austro-Hungarian Empire, and the utter destruction of the countryside in areas subject to shelling and to attacks (as at Gallipoli) from beachheads upon to highlands—visually informed a new generation about environmental disaster as wrought by human action. Following World War I, population resettlement and growth, often hurried and unplanned, filled up farmlands in Russia and eastern Europe, Canada, and the United States and created dramatic and evident "dust bowls" that revealed the need for education, state action, and a sense of stewardship. When young children were killed on French beaches by buried shells or bombs from wars that had been fought two decades or more earlier, there came to be a greater awareness of how actions taken in the past could reach out to shape the present of individuals as well as groups.

During this time two other changes in thought began to move concern from conservation—the practice of good management in order to conserve natural resources for future use—to the environment more broadly, including the argument that humankind had a stake in species retention and diversity. The first of these was growing knowledge about climate change across time, about the impact on species and on the landscapes inhabited by men and women of long periods of cooling and warming, of movements under the seas, and of natural "disasters," a word that indicated that a change in nature was socially judged to have impact, often with great loss of life, on the lives of individuals. The Eurocentric world, which conveniently can be dated from the expeditions of Columbus to the New World from 1492 to 1504 to 1942, when World War II truly became a worldwide conflict, no longer seemed a sufficient unit of study. More and more it was understood how rainfall, glacial movement, rising sea levels, temperature changes, water and air pollution, disease proliferation, and other long-range environmental developments must be taken into account to understand the historical record. The destruction of the urban environments of Germany, Japan, Russia, and elsewhere by World War II, and the use of the first atomic bomb on Japan by the United States in August 1945, brought home as never before the capacity of human action to destroy, reshape, indeed poison both the human and the natural environment.

The second change was less pronounced at mid-century. One element in the popularity of Rachel Carson's work was that, as a woman, she saw the environment from a more gendered point of view. Her concern with the pesticide DDT was, in part, because it contaminated human milk and was stored in fat tissue and passed through the placenta to offspring before birth, with numerous ill effects, proof of which led to the banning of DDT in America and Europe. Many factors were at work in the women's movement, of course, but one undoubtedly was a growing awareness of the gendered effects of pollution, both broadly and in the workplace. Officially perhaps a third of the world's employed were women, but unofficially about two-thirds of the work was done by women, and as women increasingly participated in political decisions issues of the environment came to the fore.

Over all these issues was another preoccupation of moralists, theologians, statesmen, scientists, feminists, and historians: population growth. Until the early nineteenth century population growth had varied but on a general upward curve; after about 1820 economic growth rapidly began to outstrip population growth, with rising per capita incomes in the West and a powerfully emergent middle class. By 1890 population growth in western Europe and the United States was relatively slow (as it was in Japan and Russia as well), although the worldwide trend was inexorably rising. In time worldwide pressures on resources—oil, water, and food supply—would become contentious and immigration would become a major human and policy issue. World population doubled between 1850 and 1930, from 1 to 2 billion; by 1975 it had doubled again, to 4 billion. Well before this many commentators had pronounced population growth and the movement and displacement of peoples to be the preeminent social, political, economic, and environmental issue of the future.

SUMMARY

The creation of a unified Italy and Germany altered the balance of power in Europe in the 1860s and 1870s. Nationalism, imperialism, great-power alliances, and public opinion—influenced by newspapers and photos—helped fuel tensions. By the early 1900s the Triple Alliance and the Triple Entente had taken shape. A naval arms race between Germany and Britain as well as diplomatic and military crises in Morocco, the Balkans, and elsewhere contributed to an uneasy peace.

The assassination of Habsburg archduke Francis Ferdinand, heir to the throne of Austria-Hungary, set off a crisis that led to war. Austria took a strong stand against Serbia, holding it responsible for the assassination. When Serbia rejected demands, Austria declared war. Germany, Russia, France, and Britain aided their respective allies. Italy declared its neutrality but later joined the Allies. Other European nations were drawn into the conflict. By 1917 repeated violations of neutral shipping brought the United States into the war.

The Schlieffen plan for German armies to eliminate France before turning to the Russian front did not succeed. German soldiers were pinned down on the western front, where a stalemate existed throughout much of the war. Millions more were tied down on the eastern front until 1917, when Russia withdrew from the war. The war was fought on other fronts in the Near East, East Africa, and the Far East, as well as on the oceans of the world. The last German offensive in the spring of 1918 could not be sustained, and by that summer the Allies were advancing on the western front. On November 11, 1918, a defeated Germany signed an armistice.

On the home fronts, wartime economic planning anticipated the regulated economies of the postwar era. Both sides waged virulent propaganda warfare. War contributed to changes in social life and in moral codes.

President Wilson's Fourteen Points embodied the hopes for peace. However, conflicting aims among the Allies over reparations, punishment of Germany, and territorial settlements soon dashed liberal hopes for peace. Russia and the Central Powers were not represented at Versailles as the Big Four—Wilson, Lloyd George, Clemenceau, and Orlando—bargained, compromised, and established new nations. An international organization, the League of Nations, was set up with a consultative assembly, but it did not fulfill the hopes of its early supporters.

In the end, the United States refused to ratify the treaty. France, weakened by the war, had its way with reparations, while Germany, still potentially the strongest nation in Europe, reluctantly accepted the treaty.

Strikes and shortages of bread as well as huge losses in the war prepared the way for revolution in Russia in 1917. From the outset, the provisional government and soviets were in conflict. When the moderate provisional government failed to meet crises at home and abroad, Lenin, who had returned to Russia from exile, called for a program that appealed to the Russian people.

In November 1917 the Bolsheviks seized power in Petrograd. The Bolshevik revolution brought great changes to Russia, although the new regime displayed much continuity with old Russia—an autocratic dictator, an elite of bureaucrats and managers, secret police, and Russian nationalism.

Of all of the unanticipated results of World War I, none seems so surprising as the role played by the conflict in spurring the development of the modern environmental movement. The destruction of large areas of their continent in warfare brought home to Europeans a heightened sensitivity to the fragile nature of their environment. This awareness would only increase in a century of massive technological progress existing side by side with devastating destruction.

FOUR

Between the Wars: A Twenty-Year Crisis

∞

The years between World War I and World War II were marked more by movements to the extreme right than by movements to the extreme left, despite the Western democracies' fear of Bolshevism. Beginning in the early 1920s a fascist regime took over in Italy and by the 1930s in Germany and Spain. Much of eastern and southeastern Europe were firmly fascist or quasi-fascist states by the late 1930s. Since these individual fascist states were the products of different societies, they came into power under different circumstances, commanded vastly different resources, and differed in other important respects. But they also had several characteristics in common. The fascist regimes in Italy and Germany in particular were products of disillusionment with the failure of democratic or even socialist policies to achieve stability and security. Economic depressions played a significant role in the rise of dictators almost everywhere. These dictators demonstrated a flair for the dramatic—war cries, special salutes, elaborate ceremonies, uniforms that set the faithful apart from the mass.

Europe's age of fascism, from roughly 1919–1945, did not envelop France, Scandinavia, Switzerland, Britain, or the United States, although they may have had vigorous fascist parties. Fascism everywhere was essentially a reaction against the devastating impact of the Great War on basically liberal nineteenth-century societies that found that victory had not brought harmony, as well as on fragmented and conservative societies that had been branded the aggressors in the war. Thus a sense of anger was basic to fascist states. Within each nation frightened peoples responded with a new nationalism in the face of an international challenge—communism—and an international disaster—universal war followed by universal depression after 1929.

In the phrase of many observers, the twentieth century became an "Age of Anxiety," especially as the European nations began to recognize that they were moving toward economic chaos and political collapse. The European nations had been bled far more deeply by World War I than they realized. Nations that were now powers of the second rank sought to continue to behave as though they were powers of the first rank, especially in aggressive foreign policies. Under such conditions renewed clashes, while not inevitable, were highly likely. Given the emotional base for most fascist movements, compromise was equally unlikely.

Fascism has become an almost meaningless term, one of those things that "everybody knows," for virtually everybody knows something of it—but seldom is this enough to understand what it was. Fascism was not a political ideology in the manner of conservatism or socialism; rather, it was an amalgam of old ideas—something from conservatism, from reaction, from liberal nationalism, from anti-Semitism, even from monarchism—and new practice that made up a different style and approach to authoritarian rule.

While all varieties of fascism were not completely alike in detail, certain elements, certain "vital lies," were universal. The first of these was the importance of the irrational in national life. In this way, it was a belief in opposition to the power of reason—an intense emotional nationalism, a deep sense of national destiny—and in the power and purity of blood, race, and war; all of these ranked high in fascist belief. All mattered more than reason, for at base the greater fascists believed that ordinary people were sheep ready to be led by the most powerful beat—the rhythm of passion. The uniforms, pageants, titles, and symbolism all exceeded that of any comparable system—it was no coincidence that Wagner, the master romantic myth-maker, was commandeered to be the preferred composer of Nazism.

Second, we must include the glorification of violence. Mussolini and Hitler, the most important fascist dictators, had both been common soldiers in World War I, their first followers were ex-soldiers, and their initial grievances and demands all addressed the recent war. Furthermore, the style and trappings of their movements all borrowed from the military, from the world of war. And they and others of their ilk mastered the art of the impassioned speech that always returned to the myth of the purification and glorification of "the people" in battle. Likewise, violence in everyday life was to be tolerated, even embraced. All fascist movements spawned private armies that knew how to deal with their enemies on the street, not with reason but with the cudgel. All, once in power, came to use terror as an everyday method of governance. Violence, especially to peoples left angry and aggrieved after the peace settlements, certainly was not without its appeal.

Another element the fascist movements shared was that of the leadership principle: Mussolini's title was prime minister, but tellingly he preferred to be called *Duce* (leader); Hitler, similarly, was the *Führer*. Fascist doctrine explained it all: Nations, especially great nations held down by wicked and destructive conspiracies, had no time for liberal-minded politicians, for elections and parliamentary majorities—what was called for was to find the Great Man provided by destiny and to trust and obey him. Unable to do everything, the Great Man delegated to the man below him, and he to the next below him, and so on, providing a pyramid of authority with leader at the top and petty officials at the base, exercising a small part of the leader's authority.

A fourth vital component was a deep belief in racism. As we have been reminded in an earlier chapter, racism was far from new, but the fascists—particularly the German followers of Nazism—took the old ideas and added to them to explain both the humiliations of the past and the needs of the future. Fascists made much of the greater significance of the community—the "people"—as opposed to the individual, and the true people were of one race who could be held down only through treachery. The Great War, for example, had been lost only because the Fatherland had been betrayed from within, and what better villain that the Jew—with his alien religion, his alien racial origins, and his simple "otherness" from the "real" German? It went farther still: Fascism blended this with a willful misinterpretation of Nietzsche and with the useful pseudoscience of Gobineau, Houston Stewart Chamberlain, and the phrenologists to prove to its satisfaction the inherent superiority of the north European—the Aryan. And the purest Aryan was, of course, the German. The other fascists did not match the Germans in this but did the best they could with what they had to work with: Mussolini made much of his people as the heirs of the Romans and Franco of Spain's glorious age of conquest.

Finally, all fascist systems embraced totalitarianism (a word coined by the Italian fascists), that is, the obliteration of the boundary between public and private life. It should be added, too, that to conduct the life of a totalitarian state, fascists learned much from the apparatus of the new Soviet dictatorship. The personal *was* political, and the state had the right and the duty to be everywhere: in government, of course, but also in education and faith, courtship and marriage, work and play, law and morals. The fundamental ideas of the fascist state were before its people at all times and places; they explained all and justified all. The population was expected to demonstrate its loyalty and acquiescence in these and all other phases of life. Fascism exonerated itself for its excesses on the basis of the absolute need to protect the interests of "the people." Only a totalitarian system, the fascists insisted, with all power directed toward the needs of the community as interpreted and expressed through the party could best meet those needs. Thus grafted to this was the importance of the party, which acted as the partner of the state—not a party like the British Conservatives, French Radicals, or German Social Democrats, which periodically contested elections. Fascist parties acted in the manner of Lenin's communists, as elite groups that excluded all other parties and whose members alone were allowed to hold power.

There were, of course, differences. The German and Italian fascists literally captured their regular armies only after they came to power; the Spanish Falange grew from the army. Certain of the east European regimes combined a fascist approach with monarchism; Hitler had no desire to resurrect the monarchy, and Mussolini compromised with and finally overshadowed his king. The Iberian and Italian fascists worked closely or at least compromised with the church; Hitler sought to supplant it. Tellingly, among the fascist states, only the Nazis created so powerful and effective a machine of repression as the Gestapo, and only the Nazis sought a "final solution to the Jewish problem." Compare all of this, for example, with international communism,

A Closer Look

COMPARING FASCISM AND COMMUNISM

Speaking at Naples in October 1922, Mussolini recognized that at the heart of fascism, as at the heart of nationalism, lay a vital lie—a belief held so strongly that it had the force of truth. He referred to this belief as a myth that, if universally accepted, would become reality:

We have created our myth. The myth is a faith, it is passion. It is not necessary that it shall be a reality. It is a reality by the fact that it is a good, a hope, a faith, that it is courage. Our myth is the Nation, our myth is the greatness of the Nation! And to this myth, to this grandeur, that we wish to translate into a complete reality, we subordinate all the rest.*

This "vital lie" illustrates one of the differences between fascism and communism: The former places far greater emphasis on the nation. But there are many other differences as well. In a 1964 article in *World Politics,* Klaus Epstein, a professor of history at Brown University, explained the differences as follows:

It is a notorious fact that fascist regimes take on many of the features of the Communist enemy they combat (for example, the use of terror, concentration camps, single-party dictatorship and destruction of man's "private sphere"). Yet it is important to keep communism and fascism sharply distinct for analytical purposes. They differ in their avowed aim, ideological content, circumstances of achieving power, and the groups to which they appeal. Fascists seek the greatness of the nation (which need not exclude a racialist internationalism); Communists, the world triumph of the working class (which need not exclude a strong Russian nationalism). Fascists stand in avowed revolt against the ideas of 1789; Communists pose as the heirs and executors of those ideas. Fascism has a miscellaneous and heterogeneous ideological content; communism prides itself upon the all-embracing logic of its [world view]. Fascism glories in an irrational world of struggle; communism aims ultimately at a rational world of peace and harmony (which does not preclude some pride in the violent methods required prior to the final achievement of utopia). Fascism has triumphed in some highly developed communities through abuse of the electoral process (e.g., Germany); communism typically achieves power through military occupation or successful use of violence in backward communities demoralized by prolonged military strains (Russia, Yugoslavia, China). Fascism has special appeal to the lower middle class and sections of the frightened upper class; communism generally finds its greatest resonance in sections of the working class, peasantry, and intelligentsia. Fascism consists, finally, of a series of national movements lacking centralized overall direction, while communism is a centralized world movement in which each member party obeys the orders emanating from a single center.**

*Quoted in Herbert Finer, *Mussolini's Italy* (New York: Universal, 1935), p. 218.

**Klaus Epstein, "A New Study of Fascism," *World Politics,* XVI (1964), in *Reappraisals of Fascism,* ed. Henry A. Turner, Jr. (New York: Franklin Watts, 1975), p. 10.

which, at the peak of its power, consisted seemingly of one great and many small Moscows, one great and many small Stalins, one great and many small KGBs. The reason for these differences, as we shall see, is that fascism was less a uniform political ideology, as Marxism-Leninism sought to be, than a series of adaptable national movements—similar but not mirroring one another.

The First Triumph of Fascism: Italy

Although Italy was one of the victorious Allies, it finished World War I with a sense of defeat. Six hundred and fifty thousand Italians had been killed and a million wounded. Italian industry slumped immediately after the war, and within a few months 10 percent of the industrial workers were unemployed. Prices rose rapidly, and wages failed to keep up. The promised pensions for wounded veterans and families of those who had been killed were long delayed. Strikes and disorders became frequent. Many young men were released from the armies with no trade but war and no job to go to; they drifted restlessly, prey for leaders with glittering promises.

Perhaps most important, the Italian government began to spread propaganda among the Italian people to the effect that their wartime allies were robbing them of the territories promised under the secret Treaty of London (1915) in exchange for Italy's entrance into the war on the side of the Allies. From Austria-Hungary they received Trieste, the Trentino, part of the Tyrol (and a quarter-million Germans), and the district of Istria, at the head of the Adriatic (containing a half-million Slavs) but were denied the half of Dalmatia that had in fact been pledged to them by Britain and France in the treaty. The United States, neutral in 1915, had never agreed to this arrangement and now would not accept it. Nor would the three nations agree to Italy's demand for the Adriatic port city of Fiume (in 1920 declared a free city, to Italy's advantage), despite the storms of protest arising from Italy. Many Italians concluded that they had shed their blood in vain.

The Rise of Mussolini

Some Italians, supporting Gabriele d'Annunzio, seized the city of Fiume, which had not been awarded to Italy by the Treaty of London. D'Annunzio ran his own government in Fiume until the end of 1920. In November 1920, when the Italian government signed the Treaty of Rapallo with Yugoslavia by which Fiume was to become a free city, Italian forces drove d'Annunzio out. But d'Annunzio's techniques of force, haranguing of mobs from a balcony, straight-arm salute, black shirts, rhythmic cries, and plans for conquest inspired Benito Mussolini (1883–1945), founder of Italian fascism.

Between 1918 and 1922 Mussolini created and brought to power a new political force in Italy. In October 1922 he was summoned to office by King Victor Emmanuel III and gradually created a totalitarian state of which he was the undisputed ruler. Suppressing all opposition at home and threatening the peace abroad, fascist Italy served in some degree as a model for the

Nazis in Germany, for the Falangists in Spain, and for totalitarian regimes in virtually all the European successor states of the Habsburg and Ottoman empires.

Mussolini was born in 1883; his father was a socialist who had begun his career as an anarchist under the influence of Bakunin. Trained as an elementary school teacher, Mussolini was a passionate socialist himself when young, and he was imprisoned for opposing the war against Turkey over Tripoli (1911). In 1912 he became editor of the most important Italian socialist newspaper, *Avanti* (Forward).

When World War I began, Mussolini opposed Italy's entry. He loathed militarism, was himself a draft dodger, and urged soldiers to desert the army. A vehement atheist, he also opposed nationalism and referred to the Italian flag as "a rag to be planted on a dunghill." But then, during 1914, Mussolini changed his mind, favoring "relative neutrality"—meaning that socialists should leave themselves free to support Italian entry if such a course seemed likely to prove favorable to them. When the Italian Socialist party refused to follow this idea, he resigned as editor of *Avanti* and founded his own newspaper, *Il Popolo d'Italia* (The People of Italy), in Milan and began to advocate an immediate Italian declaration of war on the side of the Allies. For this the Socialist party expelled him.

After his expulsion from the Socialist party, Mussolini agitated for war, speaking to groups of similarly minded young men called *fasci* (the word was drawn from the ancient term for a bundle of rods bound around an axe, an emblem of office in the Roman Republic of antiquity and much-used as a symbol by modern nations—including on United States coinage). Soon after Italy entered the war in 1915, Mussolini was drafted and sent to the front. He was wounded in 1917; when out of the hospital, he again edited his newspaper. In 1919 Mussolini founded his first *fasci de combattimento* (groups for combat), bands of discontented ex-servicemen, eventually borrowing the trappings first used by d'Annunzio for his private legion—black shirts, military discipline, and an attitude of violence and menace toward their opponents.

During 1920 and 1921 the industrialists and landowners, squeezed by taxation and inflation, became bitter. Shopkeepers and tradespeople wanted the street disorders to end and food prices to be regulated. Professionals and others with fixed incomes suffered, as prices and wages went up and salaries lagged behind. The police grew tired of suppressing local disorders; ex-servicemen, insulted by anarchists and communists for their war records, grew more patriotic.

All these groups identified those they did not like as Bolsheviks. After a series of fascist-socialist street fights and riots, these anti-Bolsheviks began to look to Mussolini's fascist bands to defend their interests. D'Annunzio's defeat left Mussolini as his natural heir. The leftist opposition to Mussolini was further weakened when the communists split off from the Socialist party in 1921. The fascists grew enormously, from 30,000 in May 1920 to 100,000 in February 1921 to more than 300,000 in October 1922. Liberal parliamentary leaders of Italy felt that the fascist bands were teaching the left a useful lesson, so they encouraged army officers to issue rifles, trucks, and gasoline to the fascists and assigned officers to command their operations. The police were encouraged to look the other way during disorders started by fascists, and local judges were urged to help by releasing arrested fascists. Mussolini's newspaper was circulated free to the soldiers in the army.

A campaign of terror now began against the socialists and Christian Democrats, as the fascist squadrons cruised around Italy in trucks, burning down labor union offices, newspaper offices, and local Socialist party headquarters and attacking labor leaders and local antifascist politicians. An estimated two thousand people—antifascist and fascist, police and bystanders—died by violence between October 1920 and October 1922. Mussolini had demonstrated that control over sources of information, rapid mobility, and the use of terror and intimidation could effectively silence opposition in a divided and frightened society.

In the elections of May 1921 Mussolini and thirty-four other fascists were elected to the Chamber of Deputies (the lower house of the Italian parliament), along with ten Nationalists, their political allies. The momentum of the fascist movement was now too great to be slowed down. Fascism became a political party in November as a necessary step in the drive for power. Too late, the government became alarmed and tried to take measures against the fascists, but the squadrons were too strong, the police too accustomed to collaborating with them, and the liberal politicians themselves as yet unaware that a tightly directed armed mob could take over the state.

In the fall of 1922 it was clear that the army would not resist a fascist coup in Rome. When a decree of martial law was presented to the king, he refused to sign it, probably influenced by his knowledge that the army would not fight the fascists and that his cousin would gladly take his crown. The cabinet resigned, and on October 29 the king telegraphed Mussolini in Milan to come to Rome and form a cabinet. Mussolini arrived by sleeping car the next morning, just ahead of thousands of followers. This was the famous "March on Rome," which was not a coup, as advertised, but the celebration of the legal assumption of office by the fascist leader.

Fascist Dictatorship and Corporative State

Mussolini gradually turned his premiership into a dictatorship. A month after coming to office he obtained dictatorial powers that were supposed to last only until the end of 1923. Although the constitution theoretically remained in force, Mussolini took over the administration. He created a fascist militia almost 200,000 strong, which owed complete allegiance to him. He enlarged the regular army and required its members to take an oath of personal loyalty to him. Before his dictatorial powers expired, he secured from parliament a new electoral law that provided that the political party that received the largest number of votes in a general election, if that amounted to at least one quarter of the vote, should automatically receive two thirds of the seats in parliament; the rest of the seats would be divided proportionately. In the election of April 1924 the fascists polled 65 percent of the votes cast; the first all-fascist cabinet was then appointed. Meanwhile, local administration was made secure by the appointment of fascist prefects and subprefects in the provinces.

Early in 1924 the leader of the opposition to Mussolini, the socialist Giacomo Matteotti (1885–1924), published *The Fascists Exposed*, in which he reviewed the outrages the fascists had committed on their way to power. It seemed probable that further revelations were in store, exposing some of Mussolini's cabinet members as corrupt. On June 10 Matteotti was murdered; the crime was traced to Mussolini's immediate circle. This scandal rocked Italy, and for a moment it seemed that Mussolini would fall. But he dismissed from office those who were involved and pledged himself to restore law and order. In protest against the murder and the failure to vigorously prosecute those who had participated, opposition deputies walked out of the Chamber. Since they were then refused readmission, they thereby played into Mussolini's hand. In effect, the murder of Matteotti marked the beginning of Mussolini's true dictatorship.

Next, a series of new laws tightened control over the press, abolished secret societies like the Freemasons (whom Mussolini had loathed since his socialist youth), and replaced all elected local officials by men appointed from Rome. Opponents of the regime were arrested and exiled to islands off the Italian coast. Early in 1926 Mussolini was empowered to govern by decree. Three attempts on his life led to a new law providing the death penalty for action against the king, the queen, or Mussolini. All opposition political parties were abolished in that same year, and the Fascist party was left as the only legal political party in Italy.

The Italian state and the Fascist party were increasingly coordinated. Mussolini was both the *duce* of the fascists and the *capo di governo* (chief of state). At one time he held eight cabinet posts simultaneously. The members of the Fascist Grand Council, about twenty of the highest party functionaries, all appointed by Mussolini, held all the significant posts in the administration that were not held by Mussolini himself. In 1928 the Grand Council was given important constitutional duties: preparing the lists of candidates for election to the Chamber, advising Mussolini, and proposing changes in the constitution or in the succession to the throne. The Grand Council thus became a kind of third house, above the other two houses of parliament, the Senate and the Chamber.

Mussolini believed that the interests of labor and capital should be made to harmonize with the overriding interests of the state, and representation should be based on economic interests organized in "syndicates." Such an idea was not new. The French syndicalist Grorges Sorel had already argued in this vein. But Sorel believed in syndicates of workers only. Mussolini believed in producers' syndicates as well as workers' syndicates.

In 1925 fascist labor unions were recognized by employers as having the sole right to negotiate labor contracts. In April 1926 the state officially recognized producers' and workers' syndicates in each of six areas—industry, agriculture, commerce, sea and air transport, land and inland waterway transport, and banking—plus a syndicate of intellectuals, making thirteen syndicates in all. Each syndicate could bargain and reach contracts and could assess dues upon everyone engaged in its economic field, irrespective of membership in the syndicate. Strikes and lockouts were forbidden.

In 1928 a new electoral law provided for a new Chamber of Deputies with 400 instead of 560 members. The national councils of the thirteen syndicates could nominate a total of 800 candidates. Each syndicate had a quota, half to be selected by the employers and half by the employees. Cultural and charitable foundations could nominate 200 more candidates. When the total list of 1,000 was completed, the Fascist Grand Council could either select 400 of them, strike out names and add names of its own, or even substitute an entirely new list. The voters would then vote in answer to the question: "Do you approve of the list of deputies selected by the Fascist Grand Council?" They could vote yes or no on the *entire* list, but they could not choose from among the candidates. If a majority voted yes, the list was elected; if not, the procedure was repeated. Universal suffrage was abolished, even for this very limited form of election. Payment of a minimum tax or dues to a syndicate was required of each voter; women could not vote.

In 1938 the impotent Chamber of Deputies replaced itself with the Chamber of Fasces and Corporations. Nothing remained of the old parliamentary constitution that had been set up by Cavour except the Senate, nominally appointed by the king but actually subservient to Mussolini. This new structure was the *corporative state* (so named because each of the seven syndicate areas had been declared a corporation). But despite much oratory by fascist sympathizers about the corporative state and its virtues, it appears that the new bodies never had much to do with running the economic or political life of Italy, which remained firmly under the direction of the fascist inner bureaucracy.

During the 1930s the fascist version of the planned economy made its appearance in Italy. A concerted effort was launched to make Italy more self-sufficient in agriculture. In 1932 official figures reported that domestic wheat production could supply 92 percent of the nation's normal needs, and the drive was enlarged to include other cereal products. The government subsidized steamship and air lines, encouraged the tourist trade, and protected Italian industries with high tariffs on foreign products. Marshes were drained and land was reclaimed. Enormous sums were spent on public works, and great strides were made in hydroelectric power. Public transportation became efficient.

The state also reached into the life of the individual at almost every point. Although Italy was overpopulated, Mussolini made emigration a crime. Beginning in 1926 he pursued a vigorous probirth policy, encouraging people to marry and have the largest possible families by reducing their taxes, extending special loans, taxing bachelors, and extending legal equality to illegitimate children. This was a concern common throughout the continent, which led to no appreciable increase in the birthrate in Italy. He hoped in this way to swell the ranks of his armies and to strengthen his claim that Italy must expand abroad. Textbooks in the schools, books in the libraries, professors in the universities, plays on the stage, and movies on the screen became vehicles of fascist propaganda. The secret police endeavored to discover and suppress all opposition movements. This was the totalitarian state in action.

In 1929 Mussolini settled the Roman question—that of the annexation of the Papal States without the pope's consent—by entering into the Lateran Pact with the papacy. This treaty recognized the independence of Vatican City, over which the pope had temporal power. Mussolini also recognized Catholicism as the state religion. He gave up the power to tax contributions to the church or the salaries of the clergy, and paid $105 million to compensate the papacy for Italian confiscation of papal territories. On its part, the church agreed not to engage in politics in its publications.

Yet although many church officials viewed the fascist movement sympathetically, difficulties arose after these agreements had been concluded. In an encyclical, Pope Pius XI (r. 1922–1939) indicated his disapproval of Mussolini's economic policies and of the corporations as "serving special political aims rather than contributing to the initiation of a better social order." Mussolini now charged that the church's Catholic Action Clubs were engaged in politics and dissolved them. The pope denied the charges and denounced the Fascist party's practice of monopolizing the time and education of the young. In 1931, however, a further agreement was reached, and the clubs were reopened.

Mussolini's wish to re-create the glories of ancient Rome plus domestic population pressures impelled him to undertake a policy of adventure in the Mediterranean, which he called *Mare Nostrum* (Our Sea) as a sign that he was the heir to the Caesars. In time he would send settlers into Libya, which he called Italy's Fourth Shore. This policy of expansion began in 1923, after five Italians working for the League of Nations were assassinated as they marked out the new frontier between Albania and Greece. Mussolini thereupon bombarded and occupied the Greek island of Corfu, just off Albania, and refused to recognize the League's right to intervene until British pressure led to a settlement of the matter.

Most important, Mussolini alienated Italy from its earlier allies, France and Britain. His policy of adventure led him eventually to military aggression in Ethiopia, in Spain, and in Albania. It drove him into an alliance—a Rome-Berlin axis—with another fascist, Adolf Hitler, and led him to voice loud claims against the French for Corsica, Tunisia, Nice, and Savoy. Mussolini's grandiose fascist ideology spurred Italy to win a larger degree of self-sufficiency, to rebuild its seaports, and to create a merchant fleet and navy.

The Italian alliance with Germany was also responsible for the official adoption of anti-Semitism in 1938. With only seventy thousand Jews, most of whom had long been resident, Italy had no "Jewish problem" of the kind Hitler was alleging existed in Germany. Italian Jews were entirely Italian in their language and sentiments and were distinguished from other Italians only by their religion. Many of them were prominent fascists; many others were antifascist. There was no widespread sympathy in Italy for the govern-ment's adoption of Hitler's racial policies, yet Hitler's dominating influence led Mussolini to expel Jews from the Fascist party and to forbid them to teach or to attend school, to intermarry with non-Jews, or to obtain new licenses to conduct business.

Opportunistic, ruthless, quick-witted, Mussolini loved power, but he also genuinely cared about Italy. Although the lives of many improved under his regime, the lives of others were brutalized. Many commentators then and since would find him simple, a man floundering beyond his depth; other commentators would find him shrewd, careful, and well aware of how his unpredictable yet emotionally exciting personality could make him attractive to many and keep him firmly in power. The policies that carried him into war in alliance with Germany in 1940 would end in his death in 1945, hanging upside down on a communist gallows, his personality still an enigma.

The Weimar Republic: Germany, 1918–1933

Two days before the armistice of November 11, 1918, the German Social Democrats proclaimed a republic. On July 31, 1919, this republic adopted a constitution drawn up by a national assembly at Weimar; it is therefore known as the Weimar Republic. The republic passed through three phases: a period of political threats from both left and right and of mounting economic chaos, from 1918 to the end of 1923; a period of political stability, fulfillment of the Versailles Treaty requirements, and relative economic prosperity, from 1924 to late 1929; and a period of economic depression and mounting right-wing power, from late 1929 to January 1933, when Hitler became chancellor.

Years of Instability, 1918–1923

Germans were shocked by their defeat in 1918. The military authorities who ran the German Empire during the last years of the war had not revealed to the public the extent of German reverses on the battlefield, and no fighting had taken place on German soil. Now the defeated and demoralized armies came home. Schooled in reverence for the military, the Germans could not grasp the fact that their armies had lost the war. Moreover, the Allies, under the leadership of Wilson, simply refused to deal with the supreme command of the German armies. Field Marshal von Hindenburg was never required to hand over his sword to Marshal Foch or to sign the armistice. Rather, it was the civilian politicians who had to bear the disgrace. Thus, the Allies unin-tentionally did the German military caste a great service.

The generals declared that the German armies had never really been defeated. A legend that Germany had been "stabbed in the back" by civil-ians—by liberals, socialists, communists, and Jews—took deep root. This leg-end was widely disseminated by politicians, especially those who had a stake in the old Prussian system—monarchists, large-scale agrarians, industrial-ists, militarists.

In retrospect, the Allies also blundered by including the "war-guilt" clause in the Treaty of Versailles. The German signatories were obliged to acknowledge what none of them believed (and what subsequent historians would disprove): that Germany alone had been responsible for the outbreak of the war. The clause made it harder for the German public to acknowledge defeat, to sweep away the militarists, and to create a republic. Instead, it led many Germans to devote their energies to denying war guilt, to attack the enemies who had saddled them with the charge, and to await a chance to show by force that the generals had been right—that Germany had been betrayed from within.

Threats to stability from the left strengthened the anti-republican forces of the right. Responsibility for launching the republic and for preventing disorder fell upon the "majority socialists," made up of Social Democrats and right-wing Independent Socialists, and led by a Social Democrat, Friedrich Ebert (1871–1925). A moderate group, the Social Democrats made no attack on agrarian property, and they allowed the Junkers to keep their estates and the social and political position that went with them. The Social Democrats concluded collective bargaining agreements with the industrialists that guaranteed an eight-hour day, rather than trying to nationalize German industry.

But the left wing of the Independent Socialists and the communist Spartacists agitated for proletarian revolution on the Russian pattern. Unable to operate effectively through soviets, the left tried to stage a revolution in the winter of 1918–1919, and Ebert called in the army to stop it. The generals used not only regular units but also the newly formed volunteer units, or Free Corps, made up mostly of former professionals who were embittered by Germany's recent military defeat and who were opposed to the new democracy. To protest the use of troops, the right wing of the Independent Socialists withdrew from the government, and as civil strife continued, the communists attempted a new coup, which the troops again put down.

The old parties of imperial Germany reappeared, often with new labels. The right wing of the old Liberals now emerged as the People's party, including the more moderate industrialists, with a platform of private property and opposition to socialism. Its leader was Gustav Stresemann (1878–1929). Former progressives and left-wing Liberals now formed the new Democratic party, a middle-class, republican, democratic group, including many of Germany's most distinguished intellectuals. The Catholic Center party reemerged with its name and program unchanged. It accepted the republic, rejected socialism, and, under pressure from its trade union members, favored social legislation; but under pressure from its right wing of aristocrats and industrialists it opposed far-reaching reform. On the right, the former Conservatives reemerged as the National People's party, or Nationalists, dominated by the Junkers as before. The Nationalists had the support of some great industrialists, most of the bureaucrats, and a substantial section of the lower middle class who did not accept the republic.

When the Germans voted for a national constituent assembly in January 1919, the parties supporting the republic won more than 75 percent of the seats, with the Social Democrats alone obtaining nearly 40 percent. The assembly met in Weimar, elected Ebert president of Germany, and formed a government that reluctantly signed the Treaty of Versailles. The assembly also adopted the new constitution. The new Germany was still a federal state, but the central government had great authority to legislate for the entire country. The president might use armed force to coerce any of the states that failed to obey the constitution or national laws. The cabinet was responsible to the lower house, or Reichstag, which was to be chosen by universal suffrage of all citizens (including women) over twenty.

The president, who was to be elected every seven years, was given considerable authority. He was empowered to make treaties, appoint and remove the cabinet, command the armed forces, appoint or remove all officers, dissolve the Reichstag, and call new elections. Furthermore, he could take any measure he deemed necessary to restore order and might temporarily suspend the civil liberties that the constitution granted. Yet the Reichstag could order such measures repealed. The chancellor was a prime minister, appointed by the president, with responsibility for planning policy. The powers of the president made dictatorship a real possibility, while proportional representation required that votes be cast for entire party lists of candidates, thus preventing independent politicians from obtaining office and encouraging small splinter parties to multiply.

In March 1920 a right-wing *putsch,* or "coup," led by the ex-bureaucrat and anti-republican Wolfgang Kapp, drove the government from Berlin for several days. The commander of the Berlin military district, supported by Ludendorff and Free Corps leaders, had hoped to bring to power an East Prussian reactionary. Ebert defeated the putsch by calling a general strike that paralyzed Germany. An immediate outgrowth of the strike was a communist revolt in the Ruhr. To suppress the communists, German troops entered the area, which had been demilitarized by the Versailles Treaty; this action led to French military intervention and a brief occupation of the Ruhr and Frankfurt.

In April 1921 the Allies presented their bill for reparations, which totaled 132 billion gold marks. The politicians of the right favored outright rejection, while the Weimar parties realistically decided that the threat of invasion made this course impossible. Again the moderates had to take responsibility for a decision that was certain to prove unpopular. The minister for reconstruction, Walter Rathenau (1867–1922), a Democrat, hoped that a policy of "fulfillment" might convince the Allies that Germany was acting in good faith and might in the long run lead to concessions. An intensely patriotic German, Rathenau was also a Jew, and he attracted the particular venom of anti-Semitic nationalist orators.

Secret terrorist groups on the right now began a campaign of assassination. In August 1921 they murdered a Catholic Center politician who had signed the armistice, a leading moderate. The assassins escaped through Bavaria, and when one of them was caught, the courts acquitted him. When the League of Nations awarded to Poland a substantial area of the rich province of Upper Silesia containing many Germans, the right grew still angrier. Rathenau was killed in June 1922 by men who believed that by murdering a

Jew they could avenge the "betrayal" of the German army. In the wake of this assassination, Stresemann's People's party moved away from the National-ists, who were viewed as tainted with murder, and worked with the Center and Democrats.

The political maneuvers to meet the increasing threat from the right were largely nullified, however, by the economic problem posed by steadily grow-ing inflation, which in 1922 and 1923 reached unprecedented extremes. Infla-tion is a complicated economic phenomenon still not well understood, but the single chief cause for the runaway inflation in Germany was probably the failure of the German government to levy taxes with which to pay the expenses of the war. The imperial regime had expected to win and to make the losers pay Germany's expenses by imposing huge indemnities. So it had paid for only about 4 percent of the war costs through taxation. As defeat neared, the government borrowed more and more money from the banks. When the loans came due, the government repaid them with paper money that was not backed by gold. Each time this happened, more paper money was put into circulation, and prices rose; each rise in prices led to a demand for a rise in wages, which were paid with more paper money. The inflation-ary spiral was underway. Instead of cutting purchasing power by imposing heavy taxes, the government permitted buyers to compete with each other for goods that were in short supply, thus causing prices to shoot up even fur-ther, and speeding up the whole process of inflation.

During these months the German government begged for a moratorium on reparations payments and for a foreign loan. But the French were unwilling. They had already spent billions to rebuild those parts of France that the Ger-mans had devastated during the war, and they wanted the Germans to pay the bill. As a guarantee, the French demanded the vitally important German industrial region of the Ruhr. Despite British opposition, the French occupied the Ruhr in January 1923, after the Germans had defaulted on their repara-tions payments. The French declared their intention to run the mines and fac-tories for their own benefit, and thus make up for the German failure to pay reparations.

The Germans could not resist with force, but they declared the occupation of the Ruhr illegal and ordered its inhabitants to embark on passive resis-tance—to refuse to work the mines and factories or to deliver goods to the French. This order the people of the Ruhr obeyed. Local tension in the occu-pied area became serious when the French took measures against German police and workers, and German Free Corps members undertook guerrilla operations against the French. But the most dramatic result of the French occupation of the Ruhr was its effect upon the already desperate German economy. Not only was the rest of Germany cut off from badly needed goods from the occupied area, but the Ruhr inhabitants were idle at the order of the German government and had to be supported at government expense. The printing presses ran off ever-increasing amounts of ever-more-worthless marks. The exchange rate went from thousands of marks to the dollar to mil-lions, to billions, and by December 1923, well up into the trillions.

Such astronomical figures become meaningful only when we realize their personal and social consequences. A student who set off one afternoon for the university with a check for a year's tuition, room, board, and entertainment found, when he arrived the next morning, that the money would only pay for the journey. Lifetime savings were rendered valueless; people were seen trundling wheelbarrows full of marks through the street to buy a loaf of bread. Those who lived on fixed incomes were utterly ruined, and the investments of the middle classes were wiped out. Real estate took on fantastic value, speculation flourished, and some speculators made fortunes.

For the German worker, inflation did not mean the liquidation of savings, because the worker usually had none. But it did mean a great drop in the purchasing power of wages, so that the worker's family suffered from hunger and cold. Since the financial position of the labor unions was destroyed, they could no longer help the workers, who deserted the unions. The great industrialists, however, gained from the inflation, in part because it crippled the labor unions, but still more because it wiped out their own indebtedness and enabled them to absorb small competitors and build giant business combines.

Politically, therefore, inflation greatly strengthened the extremists of both right and left. The middle classes, although pushed down to the economic level of the proletariat, would not support the working-class parties of Social Democrats or Communists. Disillusioned, they would not support the moderate parties that bolstered the republic—the People's party, the Center, and the Democrats. So the Nationalists, and Hitler's Nazis above all, reaped a rich harvest of the frightened and the discontented. The hardships of the working class led many workers to turn from the Social Democrats to the Communists. But Soviet Russian constraints on the leaders of the German Communist party prevented any concerted revolutionary drive until the fall of 1923, by which time poor organization and strong governmental repression had doomed their efforts.

With the country seething in crisis, Stresemann became chancellor in the fall of 1923 and proclaimed that Germany could not keep up passive resistance in the Ruhr. He ordered work to be resumed and reparations to be paid once again. Political troubles multiplied when the right refused to accept the new policy. At the height of the agitation in Bavaria, Adolf Hitler broke into a right-wing political meeting in a Munich beer hall and announced that the "national revolution" had begun. At gunpoint he tried to get other local leaders to support him in a march on Berlin. Troops broke up the demonstration with only a few casualties. Hitler was allowed to use his trial as a propaganda platform for his ideas and was sentenced to the minimum term for high treason—five years. This was a mistake he would not again make, vowing to come to power by legal means. He spent only eight months in jail, during which time he wrote large portions of *Mein Kampf* (My Battle), soon to be the bible of the Nazis.

In 1921–1922 a new element had emerged among the welter of right-wing organizations in Bavaria. This was the National Socialist Party of the German Workers (called *Nazi* as an abbreviation of the word National) led by Hitler.

Born in 1889, the son of an Austrian customs official, Hitler seems always to have felt bitter and frustrated. In 1907 he had been rejected by the Vienna Academy of Fine Arts, and he became an odd-job man, hovering on the edge of starvation. His hatred of the Jews began during these years. Because Karl Marx himself had been of Jewish origin and because many Viennese Jews were socialists, Hitler associated socialism with the Jews and saw both as responsible for his personal troubles.

Hitler drew philosophical and pseudoscientific support for his hatred from many of those pillars of anti-Semitism we discussed in chapter 1. From Gobineau he took the theory of "Nordic" and "Aryan" supremacy; from Nietzsche, the idea of the "superman"; from the master-composer of romantic opera, Richard Wagner (an avid reader of Gobineau), a glorious mythical history of the German nation; and from Wagner's son-in-law, the Englishman Houston Stewart Chamberlain, arguments against democratic government, capitalism, and the Jews—altogether a powerful mixture of racism, nationalism, and radicalism.

Hitler moved to Munich in 1913. In 1914 he enlisted in the German army, fought through the war as a corporal, and then returned to Munich. While employed as a political education officer for the troops, Hitler discovered a small political group that called itself the German Workers' party, which espoused nationalism, militarism, and radicalism. Hitler joined the party in 1919 and soon proved himself to be far abler than any of his colleagues. He urged intensive propaganda to unite all Germans in a greater Germany, to eliminate Jews from political life, to guarantee full employment, to confiscate war profits, to nationalize trusts, to encourage small business, and to grant land to the peasants.

Hitler was a charismatic orator with almost hypnotic gifts in capturing a crowd, and by 1921 he had made himself absolute leader, the *Führer* of the Nazi party. His position had been strengthened by the organization under Ernst Röhm (1881–1934) of the party's Gymnastics and Sports Division recruited from among the members of Free Corps, the dissolution of which had been demanded by the former Allied powers. By the end of the year this "club" had become the *Sturmabteilung* (SA) or "Storm Troops," in semimilitary dress with their signature brown shirts (copied from Mussolini's black shirts) and red swastika armbands; soon they were openly battling their enemies in the streets. The SA also patrolled mass meetings, provided a body guard for the *Führer*, and served as a kind of private army for their leader and party.

Hitler's closest collaborators included Herman Göring (1893–1946), a wartime flying "ace" who had shot down twenty Allied planes, who took on the job of giving the SA a military polish; Rudolf Hess (1894–1987), Hitler's secretary, who struggled with the task of coordinating the disparate parts of the party; and Alfred Rosenberg (1893–1946), a Baltic German distinguished by his fanatical hatred of Jews and Bolsheviks, the first editor of the party newspaper and later the official philosopher of Nazism. They and others worked out the basic theories of Nazism, including, as we have noted, several elements imitative of the Marxism that they so hated. The most important of these was the conviction that bourgeois politicians could not be expected to rescue the German people from their degradation because they could not unite mind and violence in one organization. This Hitler was determined to do, as he felt the Marxists had done, by uniting ideology and terror in one movement.

Economic Recovery, 1924–1929

Communist disorders and the Nazi beer hall putsch marked the last phase of the inflation period. Shortly before Hitler's move, Stresemann had given extraordinary financial powers to two tough-minded centrists, Hans Luther (1879–1962), minister of finance, and Hjalmar Schacht (1877–1970), banker and fiscal expert. All printing of the old currency was stopped. A new bank was opened to issue new marks, which were assigned the value of the prewar mark. The new currency was backed not by gold but by an imaginary "mortgage" on all of Germany's agricultural and industrial wealth. One trillion of the inflated marks equaled one of the new. Simultaneously, rigorous economies were put into effect in every branch of the government, and taxes were increased. The public protested loudly, but the measures remained in force until they had the intended effect. The cure for inflation produced serious hardships, too. Prices fell, and overexpanded businesses collapsed. Unemployment rose sharply, wages stayed low, and workers labored long hours.

During 1924 the Allies at last helped end the crisis in Germany by formulating the Dawes Plan, named for Charles G. Dawes (1865–1951), an American financier and vice-president under Calvin Coolidge (1872–1933). The plan recommended the evacuation of the Ruhr by the French, the establishment of a special bank to receive reparations payments, a gradual increase in annual payments for the first five years, and an international loan to finance the German deliveries in the first year. This was followed by an extended series of loans from America that essentially funded reparations payments. The Nationalists attacked these proposals as a scheme to enslave Germany to foreign masters, and in the Reichstag elections of May 1924 they scored impressive gains, as did the Nazis and the Communists, while moderate parties suffered. But a coalition managed to win acceptance of the Dawes Plan in August by promising the Nationalists seats in the cabinet. When new elections were held in December, the Nazis and Communists sustained losses and the Social Democrats and moderates gained. Early in 1925 a Center—People's party—Nationalist coalition took office. Although Germany had moved appreciably to the right, foreign policy remained in the conciliatory hands of Stresemann, who was foreign minister through all governments between November 1923 and his death in October 1929.

During these less-troubled years, economic recovery proceeded steadily, until in 1929 German industrial output exceeded that of 1913. First-rate German equipment, coupled with superb technical skill and systematic adoption of American methods of mass production, created a highly efficient industrial machine. This "rationalization" of industry increased production, but led to overborrowing and some unemployment. *Vertical trusts*—which brought together in one great corporation all the parts of an industrial process from coal- and iron-mining to the output of the finished product—and *cartels*—associations of independent enterprises that controlled sales and prices for their own benefit—became characteristic of the German system. Emphasis was always on heavy industry, which meant that a big armaments program might assure continued prosperity. Throughout, reparations were paid with no damage to the German economy, because they essentially recycled money borrowed from the United States under the Dawes Plan.

In 1925, after President Ebert died, a presidential election was held in which three candidates competed. The Catholic Center, the Democrats, and the Social Democrats all supported the Center candidate. The Nationalists, People's party, and other right-wing groups supported Field Marshal von Hindenburg, then seventy-seven years old. The Communists ran their own candidate and thus contributed to the election of Hindenburg, who won by a small plurality. Until 1930 Hindenburg acted fully in accord with the constitution, to the distress of most of the nationalist groups. Although domestic issues of this period aroused great heat, they were settled by democratic process. In the elections of 1928 the Social Democrats were returned to power; prosperity had encouraged moderation and growing support for the republic.

In foreign affairs, this period saw a gradual increase in German participation in the system of collective security. In 1925 Germany signed the Locarno treaties with the former Allied powers, which took the French armies out of the Rhineland in return for a neutral zone and a frontier guaranteed by Britain and Italy, and set up machinery to arbitrate disputes between Germany and its neighbors. These treaties did not, however, guarantee Germany's frontiers with Poland and Czechoslovakia. In 1926 Germany was admitted to the League of Nations. In 1928 Germany accepted the Kellogg-Briand Pact, which outlawed aggressive war.

In 1929 a new reparations plan named after another American, Owen D. Young (1874–1962), chairman of the committee that drew it up, substantially reduced the total originally demanded by the Allies. The Young Plan also established lower rates of payments than those under the Dawes Plan and allowed the Germans a greater role in their collection. In June 1930 the Rhineland was evacuated by the Allies, four years ahead of the date set by the Treaty of Versailles.

Germany and World Depression, 1929–1933

But the economic depression had begun to knock the foundations out from under prosperity and moderation. An economic depression is a sharp and deep decline in trade and general prosperity. In the worldwide depression of 1873 to 1896, prices had fallen, agricultural distress had intensified—made worse in Europe by bad harvests followed by wet summers and by competition from Argentine and Australian meat and Canadian and American grain—and banks had collapsed, especially in Austria and France. While scholars do not agree on the long-range causes of the depression, it was apparent to all that the new "world slump" of 1929–1934, while short, was extremely intense and was particularly destructive of middle-class confidence in the United States, Germany, and Austria.

The depression had, in fact, already begun before the Wall Street stock market crash in October 1929, for agriculture had declined as overproduction and poor distribution brought prices down and as speculation on the stock market had led to general financial recklessness. American banks now withdrew their funds from Europe. The Austrian Kredit-Anstalt, the largest commercial bank in Austria, was made bankrupt in 1931 when the French, themselves in dire economic need, withdrew short-term credit. In Germany a shortage of capital and foreign credits quickly curtailed industrial production, leading to a decline in exports and a reduced need for transportation (especially shipping), which triggered further widespread unemployment.

The need for economic planning seemed evident, and since totalitarian movements of both left and right generally already had a commitment to such long-range planning, those most hurt by what quickly became known as the Great Depression turned increasingly toward these movements and away from a free-market economy. For capitalists, the Bolshevik solution was not acceptable; for nationalists, convinced that the depression had been caused by unsound economic practices in another country, one solution was tariffs. Since fascist movements advocated economic nationalism and centralized state planning for the economy, they quickly gained new adherents. In Germany unemployment insurance cushioned the first shock for the workers; the lower middle classes, painfully recovering from the period of inflation, had no such barrier between them and destitution. Their desperation helped Hitler, whose fortunes during the years of fulfillment had fallen low. Meanwhile, however, Hitler was preparing the instruments of force, especially by creating the *Schutzstaffel* (Defense Force, or SS), an elite, blackshirted guard of honor under the direction of Heinrich Himmler (1900–1945). The SS membership requirements emphasized "racial purity," and its members would become the nucleus for the *Gestapo*, or "secret police."

The government fell in 1930 over a disagreement on unemployment insurance benefits. Hindenburg appointed as chancellor Heinrich Brüning (1885–1970), a member of the Catholic Center party, and instructed him to shape an emergency cabinet not restricted by party allegiance. President Hindenburg, now eighty-two, had fallen under the influence of General Kurt von Schleicher (1882–1934), an ambitious and clever political soldier who had schemed his way into the president's favor. Hindenburg wanted to rule by decree, as the constitution authorized him to do in an emergency. By failing to pass Brüning's economic program, the Reichstag gave Hindenburg the opportunity he wanted.

A presidential decree proclaimed the new budget. When the Reichstag protested, Hindenburg dissolved it and called new elections for September 1930. Nazis and Communists fought in the streets and both gained greatly at the expense of the moderates. The Nazis' Reichstag representation rose from 12 to 107 and the Communists' from 54 to 77. Brüning had to carry on against the wishes of the electorate; supported only by Hindenburg, he, too, now turned authoritarian.

Political matters were now fueled almost exclusively by the deepening economic crisis. To avoid a new government in which Nazis would participate, the Social Democrats decided to support Brüning. When the Reichstag met, Nazis and Communists created disorder on the floor but voted together against government measures. These measures passed only because the Social Democrats voted for them. In 1931 Brüning tried to arrange an Austro-German customs union to coordinate the tariff policies of the two countries and help them fight the depression without affecting their political sovereignty. Whether such an arrangement between two countries that were both suffering from unemployment would actually have succeeded cannot be surmised; the impulse for Germany and Austria to unite politically might not have proved overpowering. In any case, the project raised in the minds of the Allies, especially the French, the specter of a "greater Germany," and the scheme was vetoed by the World Court.

Nazis, Nationalists, the veterans' organization of the Steel Helmets (*Stahlhelm*), the Junkers' Agrarian League, industrialists, and representatives of the former princely houses now formed a coalition against Brüning. This coalition had great financial resources, mass support, and private armies in the SA, the Stahlhelm, and other semi-military organizations. Because the left was split, nothing stood between this new right-wing coalition and political victory except Hindenburg, who controlled the army. Early in 1932 Hitler was invited to address a meeting of coal and steel magnates, whose financial support he won. Although some of Hitler's followers were now impatient for a new putsch, he curbed them, believing that the Nazis could come to power legally.

In the presidential elections of March 1932, Hitler ran as the candidate of the Nazis, and Hindenburg as the candidate of the Center, Social Democrats, and other moderate parties. Hitler polled 11,338,571 votes, and Hindenburg polled 18,661,736, four tenths of a percent short of the required majority. In the runoff election, the Nationalists backed Hitler, whose total rose to 13,400,000, as against Hindenburg's 19,360,000. The eighty-four-year-old marshal reelected as the candidate of the moderates was, however, no longer a moderate himself, but the tool of the Junkers and the military.

Responding to pressure from the state governments, Brüning and Hindenburg tried to ban the SA and SS, while Schleicher orchestrated protests against such a ban. Feeling he had been ill advised, Hindenburg told his chancellor he would not sign any further emergency decrees, and Brüning resigned. Schleicher persuaded Hindenburg to appoint Franz von Papen (1879–1969), a rich Catholic nobleman and a member of the extreme right wing of the Center, and he installed a cabinet composed of other noblemen.

The Center, however, disavowed Papen, who had the support of no political party or group. The Nazis temporarily tolerated him because he agreed to lift the ban on the SA and SS. But in foreign policy, Papen succeeded where

Brüning had failed, for the Allies scrapped the Young Plan and required Germany to pay only 3 billion gold marks into a fund earmarked for general European reconstruction.

On July 31, 1932, new elections for the Reichstag took place, called by Papen on the assumption that the Nazis had passed their peak, that their vote would decrease, and that they would then cooperate in the government. However, on July 20 Papen had dismissed the government of Prussia, where there had been over five hundred confrontations between storm troopers and those they saw as their enemies, on the grounds that it could not maintain public order. This played into the hands of the Nazis, who won 230 seats to become the biggest single party in the Reichstag; the Communists gained also, chiefly at the expense of the Social Democrats. The Democrats and the People's party almost disappeared.

Papen had failed. He now wanted to take some Nazis into the government, but the Nazis demanded the chancellorship, which Hindenburg was determined not to hand over to Hitler. Papen decided to dissolve the Reichstag and call new elections. By repeating this process, he hoped to wear down Hitler's strength each time, until he brought Hitler to support him and accept a subordinate place. Papen also put pressure on the industrialists who had been supporting Hitler, and Nazi funds began to dry up, leaving Hitler seriously embarrassed. The election of November 6, 1932, bore out Papen's expectations. The Nazis fell off from 230 seats to 196; and although the Communists gained substantially, Papen, too, won some support.

Thus emboldened, Papen designed a constitutional change that would have moved the Weimar Republic even closer to the policies of the corporative state: Power was to be returned to the hands of the propertied elite. Schleicher persuaded Hindenburg that the plan was naive and tried desperately to form a new majority. Failing, he stepped down, leaving the way clear for Hitler as the only person with a program and public support. Hitler demanded the chancellorship for himself. Papen consented, provided Hitler undertook to govern in strict accord with parliamentary procedure. Papen was to be vice-chancellor, and he still thought he could dominate the government, since only three of its eleven ministers would be Nazis. He therefore persuaded Hindenburg to accept Hitler as chancellor. But Papen underestimated Hitler. Although Hitler swore to Hindenburg that he would maintain the constitution, he did not keep his oath. The Weimar Republic was doomed from the moment Hitler became chancellor on January 30, 1933.

Germany Under Hitler, 1933–1939

Hitler's first weeks in power were devoted to transforming his chancellorship into a dictatorship. He dissolved the Reichstag and called for new elections. During the campaign, opponents of the Nazis were intimidated by violence and threats and were denied radio time and free use of the press. On the night of February 27, a fire mysteriously broke out in the Reichstag building. When he heard the news, Hitler exclaimed, "Now I have them," for he knew that the fire could be blamed on the communists. By the next morning, four thousand Communist party members were arrested, and by noon Hitler had persuaded Hindenburg to suspend the basic rights of the citizenry during the emergency. Arrest, indefinite detention, and terror were now embraced by the state. Germany was, in effect, a dictatorship.

Nonetheless, in the election of March 5 the Nazis won only 44 percent of the votes, which gave them 288 seats in the Reichstag. Using the SA as a constant threat, Hitler bullied the Reichstag. Except for 94 Social Democrats (the Communists were denied their seats), all members voted for an Enabling Act on March 23, suspending the Weimar constitution. Rather like Mussolini, Hitler had come to power within the letter of the law and used the legislature itself to create his dictatorship.

Dictatorship

Now Hitler could act as he chose, unimpeded by the laws. He instituted a ministry of propaganda under Josef Goebbels (1897–1945). He stripped the state governments of their powers and appointed governors from Berlin who could override the state legislatures. When Hindenburg died in August 1934, Hitler became president as well as chancellor, but he preferred to use the title *Der Führer*. This new move was approved by a plebiscite in which Hitler obtained 88 percent of the votes.

Political parties that opposed Hitler were forced to dissolve. The government banned Communists and Socialists (May 1933); the Nationalists dissolved themselves (June 1933); the government put an end to the Catholic parties (July 1933) and all monarchist groups (February 1934). The Stahlhelm was incorporated into the Nazi party. In July 1933 the Nazis were declared to be the only legal political party in Germany.

The appeal of the Nazis to a German people unused to democracy lay partly in their denunciation of the "disorderly" parliamentary system; a strong man who got things done struck a responsive chord in the public. In the elections of November 1933, there were no opposition candidates, 92 percent of the electorate voting Nazi, and there were only two non-Nazi deputies in a chamber of 661. As in fascist Italy and communist Russia, youth groups fed the party, which soon had a powerful regional organization all over Germany and among Germans abroad.

Within the Nazi party itself, however, a difficult situation was created by those who had believed Hitler's more radical pronouncements on social and economic questions. Many of these Nazis were concentrated in the SA, whose members, most of them from the lower classes, were also distressed by how Hitler had treated their organization. The SA had made possible his rise to power, but it was now an embarrassment to Hitler, no longer quite respectable, and certainly not in favor, as were the SS and especially the army.

On June 30, 1934, Hitler ordered and personally participated in a "blood purge," always remembered as the "night of the long knives." Ernst Röhm was shot, and so were as many as a thousand others, including the head of Catholic Action, and Schleicher and his wife. Hitler justified the murders, and house arrest for Papen, by declaring that the SA was planning a putsch and that the opposition and all who offended public morality (for Röhm was a homosexual) must be crushed. After June 1934 there was no effective opposition to Hitler left.

Racism and Political Theory in Practice

Soon after the passage of the enabling law, Hitler struck the first of his many blows against the Jews. In a country of approximately 60 million people, practicing Jews were less than 1 percent of the population. The Jews had become leading members of the professions and the arts and had made outstanding contributions to German culture. Since most Jews were patriotic Germans, many of them would probably have become Nazis if they had been permitted to. Instead, anti-Semitic doctrines required their ruthless elimination.

Racism now became part of state policy. The businesses and professions of the Jews were boycotted, and Jews were forbidden to hold office. In the "Nuremberg laws" of September 15, 1935, a Jew was defined as any person with one Jewish grandparent; all such persons were deprived of the rights of German citizenship. Intermarriage between Jews and non-Jews was forbidden as "racial pollution." Jews might not fly the national flag, write or publish, exhibit paintings or give concerts, act on stage or screen, teach in any educational institution, work in a bank or a hospital, enter any of the government's labor or professional bodies, or sell books or antiques. They were not eligible for unemployment insurance or charity. Many towns and villages refused to permit Jews to live inside their precincts.

In November 1938 a Jewish boy of seventeen, driven to desperation by the persecution of his parents, shot and killed a secretary of the German embassy in Paris. Two days later organized German mobs looted and pillaged Jewish shops all over Germany, burned and dynamited synagogues, and invaded Jewish homes to batter the occupants and steal their possessions. Known as the *Kristallnacht*, the "night of broken glass," this event made it quite clear even to foreign observers that Germany was officially pursuing anti-Semitism. The state then compelled the Jews to restore the damaged properties and pay a fine. Jews were forced to take special names, to wear yellow Stars of David, and to belong to a Reich "Union of Jews." Measures designed to drive the Jews into ghettos were but the prelude to their physical extermination in gas ovens during World War II.

Enthusiasm for "racial purity" led to the study of eugenics, to the promotion of widespread athleticism and the cult of physical health, and to the elevation of Hitler into a virtual messiah. Blond, blue-eyed, ideal "Nordic types" were urged to mate with each other early and to have many children. By the time the average woman was twenty-four years old she was expected to be a mother. To keep the race pure, sterilization was introduced, supposedly to prevent inherited disease. Medical experimentation of horrifying cruelty and of no scientific value was practiced during the war on human beings of "inferior" races—Jews, Poles and other Slavs, and gypsies. These practices were the direct outcome of Nazi "eugenic" legislation.

After less than three months in power in Germany, on April 1, 1933, the Nazis began a boycott of Jewish-owned businesses. The sign at the Jewish Tietz store in Berlin reads: "Germans defend yourselves, do not buy from Jews."   (National Archives)

In foreign affairs, German racism justified the conquest of all territory inhabited by Germans. In addition, the doctrine of *Lebensraum* ("living space" for the expanding "Nordic race") justified the incorporation of nonGerman areas. Hitler declared that what the Germans needed they were entitled to take, since they were a superior people.

Some German intellectuals had looked back with longing upon the Holy Roman Empire of the Middle Ages, the first Reich. Now that the war had ended the second Reich of William II, they hoped to create a third one, incorporating the old territories, no matter who now lived in them. This is the meaning of Hitler's use of the term "Third Reich" to describe the Nazi state, which he proclaimed would last a thousand years. A "scientific" basis for the Lebensraum theory was supplied by the teachers of "geopolitics," chief among whom was Karl Haushofer (1869–1946), who declared that Britain and France were decadent; that small powers must disappear; and that Germany must expand ruthlessly, occupying the "heartland" of Eurasia, and dominate the world. Another school of thought argued that Germany's future lay in an alliance with the Soviet Union, in which its inexhaustible work force would be joined with Germany's industrial output and military techniques.

Hitler revamped the German judicial system, abandoning traditional legal principles and substituting "folk" justice, which, Hitler said, totally subordinated the individual to the people (*volk*). People's courts, to which Hitler appointed the judges, were established (May 1934) to try all cases of treason, a crime that was now logically extended to include many lesser offenses against "the people." Concentration camps were established for enemies of the state, who could be executed without appeal. The Gestapo (*Geheime Staatspolizei*, Secret State Police), formally established in April 1933 in Prussia, was extended to all of Germany in 1934, with a free hand in opening private correspondence, tapping wires, and spying on citizens.

All economic life was brought under the regime. In agriculture, the Nazis aimed at self-sufficiency and at control of the peasantry. The Junkers were protected, and no effort was made to divide their vast estates. In 1933 a special law protected smaller farms against forced sale and attachment for debt, an act that won the small farmer to Hitler. But the government determined the production required of farms and fixed farm prices, wages, and fees for distributing farms products. Unused land was put under cultivation, and citizens had to grow vegetables in greenhouses in preparation for war.

In industry, Hitler proclaimed a four-year plan in 1933 and a second one in 1936. The first was aimed chiefly at economic recovery. Labor camps for men and women helped decrease unemployment, as did rearmament and public works. The second plan was designed to prepare for war. Output of raw materials was increased, and the materials were distributed first to armament and other war industries; labor was allocated in a similar way; prices and foreign exchange were controlled. The state also built strategic highways (*Autobahnen*), the first modern expressways, for the rapid movement of goods and troops.

The Nazis abolished all labor unions in 1933 and employers' associations in 1934. To replace them, a Labor Front was established to include all wage earners, salaried persons, professionals, and employers. Strikes and lockouts were forbidden. Workers were assured of jobs as long as they accepted the system. The Labor Front was also a spy organization, constantly on the alert for anti-Nazis in the factories; it could reduce their pay, fire them, or put them in jail.

As the second four-year plan went into effect, the workers became less mobile. They had work books detailing their past training and positions, and they could not get a new job unless the state decided it was more suitable. All graduates of secondary schools had to register with employment authorities, and men and women of working age could be conscripted for labor. Just before the outbreak of war, all agricultural and mining workers and certain industrial workers were frozen in their jobs. Meanwhile, the big cartel became the all-pervasive feature of German industrial organization—a system of profitable monopoly under state control. The minister of economics authorized controlled plant expansion, imports and exports, fixed prices and established costs, and allocated raw materials.

These processes of *Gleichschaltung* (coordination) were applied throughout German life, including education and the arts. Göring is said to have remarked, "When I hear anyone talk of culture, I reach for my revolver." Hitler's own artistic views were extremely simple: He denounced most modern art as non-Aryan. The school curriculum, especially history, had to be taught in accord with the Nazi doctrine of "blood and soil." Nazi racial doctrine, the great achievements of Germany's illustrious past, the military spirit, and physical fitness were the cornerstones of the new education.

The Christian churches, both Protestant and Catholic, were a problem for the Nazis. Extremists among Hitler's followers favored a return to a mystical paganism and the old German gods celebrated by Wagner's operas. Hitler himself, born a Catholic, had once declared that Germany was his only god. Yet power politics required him to come to terms with the churches, which still commanded the allegiance of most Germans. In the hope of avoiding state domination, the Lutheran ministry in 1933 organized a national synod, which the Nazis almost immediately took over by appointing their own bishop. The efforts of extremist Nazis to purge the Bible and to abandon the crucifix led to discontent.

In July 1933 Hitler and the Vatican reached a concordat, the Nazis' first international treaty, guaranteeing freedom of worship and permitting religious instruction in the schools. Catholics were to be allowed to form youth groups and to appoint professors of theology. But the Nazis did not live up to these terms. On the other hand, the Catholic church found much to oppose in the teachings to which Catholic children were exposed in the Hitler youth groups; in 1937 a papal encyclical attacked National Socialism. Still, Catholics supported Hitler's territorial ambitions, and the church took an ambiguous position on his treatment of the Jews. In general, Hitler carefully avoided a direct clash with the churches, and they remained silent.

A German woman cries as she hails Hitler during the Third Reich. In this powerful and undated image, it is unclear why she weeps. Is she overcome with emotion at the sight of the Führer? Or is this a reluctant salute by one who knows and perhaps has experienced the cruelty of the Nazi system? (Franklin D. Roosevelt Library)

Authoritarianism in Iberia

In the troubled years between the wars, nondemocratic authoritarian governments emerged not only in Italy and Germany but also in Spain, in Portugal, in the successor states to the Habsburg Empire (except Czechoslovakia), and in the other states of eastern and southeastern Europe.

Spain

In 1918 Spain was still a nation in which local loyalties contested with national sentiment. Catalonians and Basques continued to work toward separate states, and although the Catholic religion had united Spaniards against Muslims in the Middle Ages and against Protestants in the sixteenth and seventeenth centuries, the church was no longer so strong a force for unity. While Spain at times approached self-sufficiency in agriculture and industrial raw materials, its soil was poor and its farming antiquated, and rural areas were overpopulated. Poverty was commonplace, and the masses were increasingly discontented with their national leadership.

Spain had also suffered from a lowered sense of prestige. It had lost its empire to the United States in the short war of 1898, and in World War I it had remained neutral. The government had done little to improve agriculture, and farmers in Catalonia could not gain access to sufficient land to support themselves. There were many small landholdings and many large estates, but no middle ground for prosperous farmers. Spanish sheep, once prized, declined in competition against Australian and Argentine flocks, while Spanish grain from Castile cost more in Barcelona because of inadequate transport than did foreign grain from North America. By World War I Spain had no export market to itself in Europe except for cork, which was benefiting the area already best developed, intensifying the sense of disparity among the various regions.

Spanish industry was dominated by textiles. But production was largely confined to the home market, where the consumption of cotton was no higher than in eastern Europe. Although it was the most important part of Spain's industries, the cotton industry was unable to stimulate further stages of industrialization, as had occurred in France, Switzerland, and Belgium. Moreover, what small prosperity the textile industry brought to Spain was largely confined to Catalonia. Spain had little coal for heavier industry, and the iron industry in Bilbao used British coal until 1914. Spain also had to rely on British investments for its railroads, and both rails and rolling stock had been imported until the war curtailed them. In short, Spain had not achieved a breakthrough into modern industrialism, the level of agriculture remained low, the gap between the rich and the poor was very great, and there seemed little prospect of change.

When the Spaniards turned to revolutionary doctrine, it was chiefly to Bakunin's anarchist beliefs and later to Sorel's syndicalism. Anarchism (and anarcho-syndicalism) really took hold only in Spain. The industrial workers of Catalonia and the peasants of Andalusia who no longer attended Mass were anarchist; they wanted to destroy the state utterly rather than conquer and use it. Yet anarchism, which at its peak numbered a million to a million and a half adherents, could only harass governments, not overthrow them. The movement was deeply puritanical and anti-Catholic; its adherents burned churches and killed priests. A wave of assassinations put into office General Miguel Primo de Rivera (1870–1930), who proclaimed martial law, dissolved the Cortes (the Spanish parliament), imposed censorship, drove liberal critics into exile, and ruled from 1923 until 1930.

In the 1930s Spain also had a growing Marxist Socialist party with its own federation of trade unions. The socialists drew their first strength from the urban workers of Castile and from the mining and steel-producing centers of the north. When Spain became a republic in 1931, the socialists added many rural supporters, and the party numbered a million and a quarter in 1934. The socialists were moderates who had refused to adhere to the Comintern in 1920, but who had joined the revived Second International a few years later. Dissidents founded a small Communist party, and Catalonians had their own socialist organization.

On the extreme right was Carlism, founded in the nineteenth century as a movement supporting Don Carlos (1788–1855), a pretender to the throne. Carlism called for the restoration of the Inquisition, regarded the railroad and the telegraph as sources of evil, and rejected the Copernican theory of the universe. Carlism had its lower-class followers, too, especially among the rebellious farmers of Navarre in the north.

King Alfonso XIII (r. 1886–1931) ruled over Spain until 1931. Based on electoral corruption and intimidation, the "liberals" and "conservatives" in his governments took orderly turns at office, and the real power rested with the local political bosses. These alternating governments occupied the political center, which in fact was quite small. Once the prosperity brought by Spain's wartime neutrality was over, the clashes between the anarchists, the left, and the far right led many people to consider General Primo's rule necessary.

After Primo's resignation and death, King Alfonso restored the constitution. Municipal elections in April 1931 were viewed as a plebiscite on the monarchy. They resulted in a victory for the republicans, representing the lower middle classes of the towns, small traders, intellectuals, teachers, and journalists. The king left the country without abdicating. Elections to a constituent assembly in June 1931 brought in a republican-socialist majority, and in November the assembly forbade the king's return and confiscated his property. Spain was now a republic.

The assembly adopted a new constitution in December. This provided for a responsible ministry, a single-chamber parliament, and a president to be chosen by an electoral college consisting of parliament and an equal number of electors chosen by popular vote. It appeared clear that the army would rise against the republic whenever the opportunity presented itself and that the army would have the support of the church and the large landowners. Moreover, although the republic temporarily had socialist support, it did not have the support of the anarchists. Danger threatened from both the right and the left.

The first crisis arose over a new constitutional law defining the position of the church. The assembly rejected a moderate proposal that would have preserved the church as a special corporation with its own schools and might have proved acceptable to most Catholics. Instead, the assembly's law was more extreme; it closed church schools and ended state grants to the church after two years. This lost the republicans many supporters, especially among the lower clergy.

The anarchists expressed their dissatisfaction by major uprisings (1933), which the government put down by force. The jails were full, and unemployment was as high as ever. Repression of the anarchists lost the republic much support on the left but failed to gain it support from the right, which came back strongly in the elections of November 1933 as the largest party in parliament. Now the government helplessly swung to the right, and much of its previous legislation, especially laws affecting the church and the working classes, remained unenforced.

The socialists now competed with the anarchists for the loyalty of Spanish workers. Strikes and disorders multiplied. In October 1934 the socialists called a general strike to protest the inclusion of fascists in the government. Catalonia, declaring itself an independent republic, was deprived of its autonomy. The coal miners of the Asturias region in the north staged a revolt, backed by both anarchists and socialists, which was put down with the loss of more than three thousand lives. Intense hatred was directed at the new minister of war, General Francisco Franco (1892–1975).

Thus the right lost much public support; and now the left, under the impact of the Asturias uprising and influenced by the Comintern, united in a Popular Front for the elections of February 1936. For the first time anarcho-syndicalists went to the polls and voted for republicans, socialists, and communists. The left won a considerable victory, in part because it promised an amnesty for those involved in past outbreaks. Instead of entering the cabinet, Francisco Largo Caballero (1869–1946), leader of the left-wing socialists, now played at insurrection, acting as if he intended to seize power. Yet he had no forces of his own. The route to power for left-wing revolutionaries could open up only if the right attempted a military coup, if the government then armed the workers to fight it, and if the workers then won.

Simultaneously in 1936 the *Falange* (Phalanx) emerged on the right—a party founded in 1932 by the son of Primo de Rivera, José Antonia (1903–1936), a fascist who did not oppose agrarian reform or other socialist programs. The Falange used as its symbol a bunch of arrows and a yoke, and as its slogan *Arriba España* (Upward, Spain). Its program called for national expansion in Africa, the annexation of Portugal, and the building of an empire in South America. It established youth groups and a private army, as Hitler had done. Although the Falange polled relatively few votes in the election of 1936, it worked with army, monarchist, clerical, and Carlist groups for a counterrevolution. Everyone knew a military coup against the government was in the offing. In July it came, under the leadership of General Franco.

The Spanish Civil War (1936–1939) was the first act in the conflict that was to ripen into World War II. Fought with ferocity on both sides and amidst much talk of principle and ideology, it would come to divide many who observed it from the democracies with a passion not unlike that created by the Vietnam War thirty years later. The right-wing rebels made Franco chief of staff in November 1936. Decisively aided by Germany and Italy, Franco's forces pushed on to eventual victory, capturing the republican strongholds of Madrid and Barcelona in 1939. During the war the functions of the weak republican government were usurped by a series of workers' committees, and then a Popular Front regime under Largo Caballero came to office in September 1936. In government territory terror reigned, at first the work of anarchists, and after their suppression, of the communists, who—with the Soviet Union behind them—ruthlessly worked against their rival leftist parties in the regime.

For all its fascist trappings, the Franco regime still depended after the war upon the same classes that had supported the Spanish monarchy—the landowners, the army, and the church. The new regime was opposed by the poor in city and country, but the fear of a new civil war, which lay heavily on all classes, prevented open opposition. Franco ruled until his death in 1975.

Portugal

In the meantime, any Falangist designs on Portugal were blocked by the rise to power there of another dictator, Antonio de Oliveira Salazar (1889–1970). Portugal had participated in World War I, and the republican regime, which had driven King Manoel II (r. 1908–1910) from the country in 1910, governed until forced from office by a military coup in 1926. Two years later Salazar, a professor of economics at the University of Coimbra, became minister of finance on the condition that he be granted sweeping powers over the economy. Salazar's concern for sound finance during the world economic crisis won him many supporters, and in 1932 he became prime minister and progressively used his office to turn his party into the only legal option open to the Portuguese people. Salazar sought to remain neutral in the growing European conflict, and his authoritarian rule did not generate effective opposition from the political left. Not until 1968 did Salazar step down, Portugal's empire overseas still virtually intact but his dictatorship increasingly inert.

Successor States to the Habsburg Empire

The triumphs of the authoritarian right in eastern Europe are explained partly by the lack of a parliamentary tradition, partly by the failure to solve grievous economic problems, and partly by a popular fear of Bolshevism. Perhaps as important as all the other factors put together was the initial impression created by the successes of Mussolini and Hitler. The way to succeed, at least after 1935, seemed to be to put on a uniform, proclaim a doctrine of extreme nationalism, and launch a war of nerves against opponents and neighbors.

Austria

The Austria that was left at the end of World War I had a population of about 8 million, about 2 million of whom lived in Vienna, still a world capital, but no longer the center of a great state. Long the market for an enormous hinterland and the supplier of industrial finished goods to the agricultural provinces, Vienna was now cut off from its former territories by political boundaries and tariff walls. Between 1922 and 1925 Austrian finances were under direct League of Nations supervision. But one possible road to economic salvation—union of Austria with Germany—although voted by the assembly of the new Austrian republic in March 1919, was forbidden on political grounds by the Allies.

These two problems, economic survival and union with Germany, were complicated by the continuation of the political struggle between Social Democrats and Christian Socialists. The Social Democrats were a moderate Marxist party with strong urban support. The Christian Socialists were a conservative clerical party with a mass following in the countryside and among the urban lower middle classes and counted many priests among their leaders.

In the mid-twenties the two hostile parties organized private armies: the Christian Socialists, the *Heimwehr* (Home Guard), and the Social Democrats, the *Schutzbund* (Defense League). The Social Democrats governed Vienna, introducing measures for relief and for workers' housing, paid for by taxes on the rich. After 1930 Mussolini supported the Christian Socialists, who grew more fascistic in their outlook. The failure of Brüning's plan for a customs union with Germany and the related collapse of the Vienna Kredit-Anstalt bank increased tensions, and in September 1931 the Heimwehr tried its first coup, which failed. Efforts in 1932 to organize a Danubian economic cooperation scheme were rendered futile by Italian and German opposition. After Hitler came to power in early 1933, many Christian Socialists openly became Nazis.

The Christian Socialist chancellor, Engelbert Dollfuss (1892–1934), however, strove to curb the Nazis. To this end he suspended parliamentary government in March 1933. He forbade the wearing of uniforms by political groups and tried to expel Nazi agitators. In retaliation, Hitler made it prohibitively expensive for German tourists to visit Austria. In the face of Nazi-inspired disorder, Dollfuss banned the Nazi party. But he also attacked the Social Democrats, banning all parties except his own Fatherland Front, a union of all right-wing groups except the Nazis, and established a kind of clericalist corporative system. A raid on Social Democratic headquarters precipitated a workers' riot. The government then bombarded the workers' new apartment houses in which the Social Democratic leaders had taken refuge, breaking the Social Democratic party but alienating the workers and uniting them in opposition to the regime. Dollfuss had to depend on Italy to support him against the threat from Hitler.

Dollfuss' successor, Kurt von Schuschnigg (1897–1981), was committed to the same policies. But Mussolini now needed Hitler's support for Italian aggression in the Mediterranean. Schuschnigg tried to concentrate armed power in his own hands rather than those of the Heimwehr, and strove to come to an understanding with France and its allies to replace the tie with Italy. But he failed. To stave off violence he had to make concessions to Artur Seyss-Inquart (1892–1946), leader of the Austrian Nazis, and then humble himself by visiting Hitler at his Bavarian mountain retreat at Berchtesgaden. Hitler threatened full-scale invasion, and Schuschnigg agreed to bring the Nazi party into the Fatherland Front and to pursue the foreign policy goals dictated by Hitler. He also agreed to make Seyss-Inquart minister of the interior, the ideal position from which to direct a coup.

When Schuschnigg returned to Vienna, he realized that he had surrendered Austria, and he called for a sudden plebiscite, desperately hoping to win working-class support. This forced Hitler's hand. On March 2 he invaded Austria, even against the advice of Seyss-Inquart, and proclaimed his native land a province of Germany. In April a plebiscite on Austrian union with Germany—called *Anschluss*—resulted in a 99.75 percent yes vote, and the former Allied powers who had done nothing could content themselves that they had probably done the right thing.

Hungary

On October 31, 1918, eleven days before the armistice, Count Michael Károlyi (1895–1955) became prime minister of Hungary, after that country had severed its ties with Austria. One of the richest of the great landed nobles, Károlyi was also a democrat. He proved his sincerity as a social reformer by handing over the fifty thousand acres of his own estate to be divided among the peasants and by preparing a land-reform law. He made every effort to reach a compromise with the national minorities, but they were past the point where they would trust any Magyar. The French commander of the Allied armies demanded that the Hungarians withdraw from Slovakia. In March 1919 Károlyi resigned in protest over the loss of Transylvania.

Thwarted nationalism now combined with a growing radicalism. A left-wing government took over, dominated by Béla Kun, Lenin's agent. He put through revolutionary nationalization decrees and installed a soviet political system. The Allies could not tolerate a Bolshevik in Hungary. The Romanians invaded and drove Kun out; during 1919 and part of 1920 they occupied the country and stripped it of everything they could move. Meanwhile, under French protection, a counterrevolutionary government returned to Budapest, where Admiral Nicholas Horthy (1868–1957), a member of the gentry, became nominal regent for the absent and unwelcome Habsburg king and chief of state in March 1920.

The Treaty of Trianon (June 1920) confirmed Hungary's losses: a small strip of land to Austria, Transylvania to Romania, Slovakia to Czechoslovakia, and Croatia and other Serb and Croat territories to Yugoslavia. Thereafter, the most important political issue for the ruling groups in Hungary was *revisionism,* the effort to revise the treaty and get these lands back.

Most Hungarians, however, cared relatively little about revisionism. Hungary had no land reform; the great estates remained intact; nobles and gentry remained dominant. Behind a screen of parliamentary government, an authoritarian dictatorship governed the country. It was helped by a swollen bureaucracy, and it became more and more fascist in character as the years went by. In 1927 a treaty with Italy began a close association between Hungary and Mussolini.

While the Italians supplied arms to the Hungarians, Hitler favored Hungarian revisionism along with his own. After Austria had fallen to Hitler, he had Hungary in his pocket, and when he broke up Czechoslovakia in March 1939, the Hungarians seized the extreme eastern portion, Ruthenia, and a small part of Slovakia. To pursue revisionism, the Hungarians had to follow Hitler, since he alone offered the opportunity to redraw the map as they felt it should be drawn; so before war broke out, they had withdrawn from the League of Nations and had enacted anti-Semitic laws in the Nazi pattern. But because Hitler needed Romania, too, he would not give the Magyars all of Transylvania. Thus Hungary remained dependent on German foreign policy.

Yugoslavia

In the new kingdom of the Serbs, Croats, and Slovenes, proclaimed in December 1918, there came together for the first time in one state the former south-Slav subjects of Austria and Hungary with those of the former kingdom of Serbia. This was in most respects a satisfactory state from the territorial point of view; revisionism therefore was not a major issue. But the new state had to create a governmental system that would satisfy the aspirations of each of its nationality groups. Over this problem democracy broke down and a dictatorship was established.

Serbian political ambitions had helped to start World War I. The Serbs were more numerous than Croats and Slovenes together, and many Serbs felt that the new kingdom should be the "greater Serbia" of which they had so long dreamed. Orthodox in religion, using the Cyrillic alphabet, and having experienced and overthrown Ottoman domination, Serbs tended to look down on the Croats. Roman Catholic in religion, using the Latin alphabet, and having opposed Germans and Magyars for centuries, Croats tended to feel that the Serbs were crude Easterners who ought to give them a full measure of autonomy within the new state. The battle lines were drawn: Serb-sponsored centralism against Croat-sponsored federalism.

The Croats, under their peasant leader Stephen Radić (1871–1928), boycotted the constituent assembly of 1920, and the Serbs put through a constitution providing for a strongly centralized state. Both sides refused to compromise, and when Radić was murdered on the floor of parliament in June

1928, a crisis arose that ended only when King Alexander II (r. 1921–1934) proclaimed a royal dictatorship in January 1929. Alexander tried to settle the problem by erasing old provincial loyalties. There would be no more Serbia or Croatia but new administrative units named after the chief rivers that ran through them. The whole country was renamed Yugoslavia, as a sign that there were to be no more Serbs and Croats. But it was still a Serbian government, and the Croats would not forget it. Elections were rigged by the government, and all political parties were dissolved.

One result was to strengthen Croat extremists who had wanted an independent Croatia in the days of the Habsburgs, and who now combined this demand with terrorism, supported by the enemies of Yugoslavia–Italy and Hungary. The Croat extremists were called *Ustashi* (Rebels), and they were assisted by Mussolini. The Ustashi were deeply involved in the assassination of Alexander during a state visit to France in October 1934. Under the regency of Alexander's cousin, the dictatorship continued. In the summer of 1939 an agreement was reached with the Croats that established an autonomous Croatia. But by then it was too late, for war soon engulfed the Balkans.

Other Authoritarian Regimes in Europe

In Poland, the long-time champion of Polish independence Marshal Jósef Pilsudski led a military coup against the democratic government on May 11, 1926, and headed a military dictatorship that became ever more authoritarian. This coup was made possible largely because of the government's failure to grant concessions to national minorities and to deal with the economic problems left by the war and occupation. The violent hatreds that divided the political parties made Pilsudski's rule even easier. Once he had won power, he turned to the great landowners and big industrialists, building his government on their support and on that of his military clique.

In Romania entrenched corruption in political life coexisted with the parliamentary system. There was also widespread anti-Semitism, which was adopted as the chief program of the Iron Guard, a Romanian fascist party. Green-shirted and wearing small bags of Romanian soil around their necks, the Guard began to assassinate moderate politicians early in the 1930s. Economic dislocation and peasant misery, brought about by the worldwide agricultural depression, strengthened the Guard and other fascist groups. To head off a Guardist coup, King Carol II installed his own fascist dictatorship in 1938. Although the Guardist leaders were "shot while trying to escape," Romania could not avoid German pressure. After Hitler had acceded to the Soviet seizure of Romanian Bessarabia and northern Bukovina and had given Hungary northern Transylvania (August 1940), Carol had to abdicate, and Hitler's man took over with Iron Guard support.

In Bulgaria the threat of communism was a serious problem. Moreover, Bulgaria, like Hungary, was revisionist because of its failure to gain the Macedonian territory given by the peace treaties to Yugoslavia and Greece. The issue was made more intense by the presence of thousands of Macedonian refugees, who tended to join revolutionary terrorist societies. Bulgaria, which had no serious minorities problem, no rich landowners, no aristocracy, and no great industries, nonetheless produced political hostilities even more violent than those in countries where economic inequality prevailed. In 1920–1923 a peasant politician, Alexander Stambolisky (1879–1923), gave the country a period of reasonably popular government. But even he curbed the press as he fought both Macedonian terrorists and communists. His imposition of high income taxes alienated the bourgeoisie. In 1923 right-wingers murdered him and installed a strongly authoritarian regime. From then on communist plots, bombings, and Macedonian terrorist strife racked the country. After 1930 the Italian marriage of King Boris (r. 1918–1943) led to ties with Mussolini. In 1934 a military coup brought to power a group of army officers who installed a dictatorship of their own. But in 1936 King Boris imposed a royal dictatorship, which lasted until his death during World War II.

In Greece between the wars, the main issues were whether the country should be a monarchy or a republic and how to overcome the economic difficulties caused by the transfer of 1.25 million Greeks from Turkey. On the constitutional question, the Greeks wavered, voting for a monarchy in 1920, for a republic in 1924, and for a monarchy again in 1935. Economic dislocation strengthened communism among the refugees and in labor groups. Political instability was chronic, and the interwar period was punctuated by a series of coups, some by republican generals, some by monarchists, all more or less authoritarian. The last of these, General John Metaxas (1871–1941), was the most fascist. Metaxas, who became dictator in August 1936, abolished political parties, instituted censorship and political persecution of his opponents, and launched a program of public works.

The new states created during the Paris peace conference were forced to pledge fair and equal treatment of racial and ethnic minorities within their borders (a pledge the victorious powers did not make), and although there were degrees of difference, none lived up to their promises. In addition to systematic racism, all but Czechoslovakia soon reverted to dictatorial systems—most complete with their own versions of the pageantry, xenophobia, and authoritarianism of the fascist states. None of these regimes in eastern Europe was fascist in the truest sense of the term. In Italy and Germany the regimes rested on considerable popular support, at least initially, even though that support was kept alive by propaganda. In eastern Europe, on the other hand, the dictatorships rested on the police, the bureaucracy, and the army, and not on the support of the masses. Most dictators (Franco was an exception) developed the cult of self. In most, but not all, Jews were systematically persecuted. While the various fascist states had much in common, fascism never became the universalized international movement that communism explicitly aspired to become.

The Soviet Union

During the twenty-year crisis between the wars, an already authoritarian government in the Soviet Union became a totalitarian dictatorship, although one of the left rather than the right. From 1914 Russia had been in turmoil. By 1921, with the end of civil war, industry and agriculture were crippled, distribution was near a breakdown, and the communist regime was perilously near the loss of public support. When a large-scale anarchist revolt broke out early in 1921 and could not be suppressed until mid-1922, Lenin remarked that he was, at last, deeply frightened for the future of his nation. The mutiny of sailors at the Kronstadt naval base near Petrograd in March 1921 triggered a change in policy. The mutineers called for "soviets without communists," to be chosen by universal suffrage and secret ballot, for free speech and assembly, for the liberation of political prisoners, and for the abolition of grain requisitioning. Trotsky now realized that the proletariat itself was opposing the dictatorship of the proletariat and needed educating. Furthermore, revolution was not going to sweep Europe; Russia would be, for a time, an island of revolutionary socialism in a sea of capitalism. Trotsky therefore used the Red Army to crush the rebellion while Lenin embarked upon economic reform.

The Kronstadt mutiny led directly to the adoption of the New Economic Policy (always referred to by its initials as the NEP). But the underlying reason for the shift was the need for reconstruction, which seemed attainable only if militant communism were at least temporarily abandoned. It was also necessary to appease the peasants and to avert any further major uprisings. Finally, since the expected world revolution had not taken place, the resources of capitalist states were badly needed to assist Russian reconstruction.

Under NEP the government stopped requisitioning the peasants' entire crop, taking instead only what was needed to meet the minimum requirements of the army, urban workers, and other nonfarm groups. The peasants still had to pay a very heavy tax in kind, but they were allowed to sell the remainder of their crop. Peasant agriculture became in essence capitalist once more, and the profit motive reappeared. The whole system tended to help the rich peasant grow richer and to transform the poor peasant into a hired, landless laborer.

Elsewhere in the economy, under NEP the state retained what Lenin called "the commanding heights"—heavy industry, banking, transportation, and foreign trade. In domestic trade and in light industry, however, private enterprise was once more permitted. This was the so-called private capital sector of the economy, in which workers could be paid according to their output and factory managers could swap some of their products for raw materials.

Lenin himself described NEP as a partial return to capitalism and urged the communists to become good at business. Yet NEP was never intended as more than a temporary expedient. Lenin believed that it would take a couple of decades before the Russian peasant could be convinced that cooperative agriculture would be the more efficient. He also argued that a temporary relaxation of government intervention would increase industrial production and give the Russians a useful lesson in managerial skills.

Economic recovery was indeed achieved. By 1928 industrial and agricultural production was back at prewar levels. But NEP was bitterly disliked by leading communists, who were shocked at the reversal of all the doctrines they believed in. Those who took advantage of the opportunities presented by NEP were often persecuted in a petty way by hostile officials, who tried to limit their profits, tax them heavily, and drag them into court on charges of speculation. The Kulaks, prosperous land-owning peasants, had essentially the same experience. Thus the government often seemed to be encouraging private enterprise for economic reasons and simultaneously discouraging it for political reasons.

The Struggle for Power: Stalin against Trotsky, 1921–1927

Having survived an assassination attempt and, in December 1922, a paralytic stroke, Lenin died in January 1924. During the last two years of his life, he played an ever-lessening role. Involved in the controversy over NEP was also the question of succession to Lenin. Thus an answer to the questions of how to organize industry, what role to give organized labor, and what relations to maintain with the capitalist world depended not only upon an estimate of the actual situation but also upon a guess as to what answer was likely to be politically advantageous. From this maneuvering the secretary of the Communist party, Joseph Stalin, was to emerge victorious by 1928.

The years between 1921 and 1927, especially after Lenin's death, saw a desperate struggle for power between Stalin and Trotsky. Lenin foresaw this struggle with great anxiety. He considered Trotsky abler but feared that he was overconfident; he knew that Stalin had concentrated enormous power in his hands through his role as party secretary, and he feared that he did not know how to use it. When he learned that Stalin had disobeyed his orders in smashing the Menshevik Republic of Georgia instead of reaching an accommodation with its leaders, he wrote angrily that Stalin should be removed from his post as general secretary.

During these years Trotsky argued for a more highly trained managerial force in industry and for economic planning as an instrument that the state could use to control and direct social change. He favored the mechanization of agriculture and the weakening of peasant individualism by encouraging rural cooperatives. As Trotsky progressively lost power, he championed the right of individual communists to criticize the regime. He also concluded that only through the outbreak of revolutions in other countries could the Russian socialist revolution be carried to its proper conclusion. Only if the industrial output and technical skills of the advanced Western countries could be put at the disposal of communism could Russia hope to achieve its own socialist revolution; either world revolution must break out or Russian socialism was doomed to failure.

Trotsky's opponents found their chief spokesman in Nikolai Bukharin (1888–1938), the extremely influential editor of *Pravda*. A strong defender of NEP, Bukharin softened the rigorous Marxist doctrine of the class struggle by arguing that, since the proletarian state controlled the commanding heights of big capital, socialism was sure of success. This view was not unlike the gradualist position taken by western European Social Democrats. Bukharin did not believe in rapid industrialization; he favored cooperatives, but opposed collectives in which (in theory) groups of peasants owned everything collectively. In foreign affairs, he was eager to cooperate abroad with noncommunist groups who might be useful to Russia. Thus he sponsored Soviet collaboration with China and with the German Social Democrats.

In his rise to power Stalin used Bukharin's arguments to discredit Trotsky; then he adopted many of Trotsky's policies and eliminated Bukharin. He came to favor rapid industrialization and to understand that this meant an unprecedentedly heavy capital investment. At the end of 1927 he shifted from his previous position on the peasantry and openly sponsored collectivization, since agricultural production was not keeping pace with industry. He declared that agriculture, like industry, must be transformed into a series of large-scale unified enterprises.

Against Trotsky's argument that socialism in one country was impossible, Stalin maintained that an independent socialist state could exist. This view did not imply abandoning the goal of world revolution, for Stalin maintained that the one socialist state (Russia) would inspire and assist communist movements everywhere. But, in his view, during the interim before the communists won elsewhere, Greater Russia could still exist and expand regionally as the only socialist state. In international relations, this doctrine allowed the Soviet Union to pursue a policy of "peaceful coexistence" with capitalist states when that seemed most useful or a policy of militant support of communist revolution when that seemed desirable. Stalin's doctrine reflected his own Russian nationalism, rather than the more cosmopolitan and more Western views of Trotsky.

At the end of the civil war, Stalin was commissar of nationalities. In this post he dealt with the affairs of 65 million of the 140 million inhabitants of the new Russian Soviet Republic. He took charge of creating the new Asian "republics," which enjoyed a degree of local self-government, programs of economic and educational improvement, and a chance to use their local lan guages and develop their own cultural affairs, as long as these were communist-managed. In 1922 Stalin proposed the new Union of Socialist Soviet Republics as a substitute for the existing federation of republics. In the USSR, Moscow would control war, foreign policy, trade, and transport and would coordinate finance, economy, food, and labor. In theory, the republic would manage home affairs, justice, education, and agriculture. A Council of Nationalities, with an equal number of delegates from each ethnic group, would join the Supreme Soviet as a second chamber, thus forming the Central Executive Committee, which would appoint the Council of People's Commissars—the government.

Stalin was also commissar of the Workers' and Peasants' Inspectorate. Here his duties were to eliminate inefficiency and corruption from every branch of the civil service and to train a new corps of civil servants. His teams moved freely through all the offices of the government, observing and recommending changes. Although the inspectorate did not do what it was

Joseph Stalin, speaking to a Communist party congress in the 1930s. By this point the "man of steel" had eliminated all real or imagined rivals for power and was absolute master of the Soviet Union.   (Hulton Archive/Getty Images)

established to do, it did give Stalin control over thousands of bureaucrats and thus over the machinery of government.

Stalin was also a member of the *Politburo*—the tight little group of party bosses elected by the Central Committee, which included only five men throughout the civil war. Here his job was day-to-day management of the party. He was the only permanent liaison officer between the Politburo and the *Orgburo*, which assigned party personnel to their various duties in factory, office, or army units. Besides these posts, Stalin became general secretary of the party's Central Committee in 1922. Here he prepared the agenda for Politburo meetings, supplied the documentation for points under debate, and passed the decisions down to the lower levels. He controlled all party appointments, promotions, and demotions. He saw to it that local trade unions, cooperatives, and army units were under communists responsible to him. He had files on the loyalty and achievements of all managers of industry and other party members. In 1921 a Central Control Commission, which could expel party members for unsatisfactory conduct, was created; Stalin, as liaison between this commission and the Central Committee, now virtually controlled the purges, which were designed to keep the party pure.

In a centralized one-party state, a man of Stalin's ambitions who held so many key positions had an enormous advantage in the struggle for power. Yet the state was so new, the positions so much less conspicuous than the ministry of war, held by Trotsky, and Stalin's manner so often conciliatory that the likelihood of Stalin's success did not become evident until it was too late to stop him. Inside the Politburo he formed a three-man team with two other prominent Bolshevik leaders: the demagogue Gregory Zinoviev (1883–1936) and the expert on doctrine Leo Kamenev (1883–1936). Zinoviev was chairman of the Petrograd Soviet and boss of the Communist International; Kamenev was Lenin's deputy and president of the Moscow Soviet.

The combination of Stalin, Zinoviev, and Kamenev proved unbeatable. The three used the secret police to suppress all plots against them. They resisted Trotsky's demands for reform, which would have democratized the party to some degree and would have strengthened his position while weakening Stalin's. They initiated the cult of Lenin immediately before his death and kept it burning fiercely thereafter, so that any suggestion for change coming from Trotsky seemed an act of impiety. They dispersed Trotsky's followers by sending them to posts abroad.

Early in 1925 Stalin and his allies forced Trotsky to resign as minister of war. Soon thereafter the three-man team dissolved; Stalin allied himself with Bukharin and other right-wing members of the Politburo, to which he began to appoint his own followers. Using all his accumulated power, he beat his former allies on all questions of policy, and in 1926 they moved into a new but powerless alliance with Trotsky. Stalin now deposed Zinoviev from the Politburo, charging him with plotting in the army. Next, Trotsky was expelled from the Politburo, and Zinoviev was ousted as president of the Comintern. In December 1927 a Communist party congress expelled Trotsky from the party and exiled him. Ultimately all would die at Stalin's command—Bukharin, Kamenev, and Zinoviev were shot during the purges of the 1930s, and Trotsky was murdered in exile in Mexico in 1940. Stalin had won.

Mobilizing the Nation, 1928–1940

The Communist party congress also ended NEP and proclaimed that the new "socialist offensive" would begin in 1928. The twelve years between 1928 and 1940 were to see massive changes in Russian life—collectivized agriculture, rapid industrialization, forced labor, great purges, the extermination of all political opposition, the building of an authoritarian state apparatus, and a return of bourgeois standards in almost every aspect of social and intellectual life.

In 1928 the failure of the peasants to deliver as much grain to the cities as was required underlined the dangers inherent in the land divisions of 1917 and in the concessions of NEP. Farm productivity on the small individual holdings was not high enough to feed the city population. Food was expensive, yet the kulaks wanted more land. Grain was hoarded. The government economic plan issued during 1928 set a figure of 20 percent of Russian farms as the maximum to be collectivized by 1933. Yet during 1929 Stalin embarked on immediate full-scale collectivization.

The government did not have the money or the credit to import food and had no governmental machinery to force farmers to part with food that they were hoarding. Therefore, the government enlisted on its side the small peasants; in exchange for their assistance in locating and turning over the kulaks' crops, the peasants were promised a place on a collective farm to be made up of the kulaks' land and equipped with the kulaks' implements. The kulaks, Stalin declared in late 1929, were to be liquidated as a class. There were about 2 million households of them, perhaps as many as 10 million people in all. Their lands were now to be totally expropriated, and at the same time, they were to be barred from joining the new collectives. Since no provision was made for them, this move turned collectivization into an economic and social nightmare.

Peasants were machine-gunned into submission; kulaks were deported to forced labor camps or to desolate regions in Siberia. In desperate revolt the peasants burned crops, broke plows, killed and ate their cattle rather than turn them over to the state, and fled to the cities. More than half the horses in all the western Soviet Union, 45 percent of the cattle, and two thirds of the sheep and goats were slaughtered. Land lay uncultivated, and over the next few years millions died of famine. As early as March 1930 Stalin showed that he was aware of the incredible mistakes he had made, and he blamed local officials who, he said, had been too eager to rush through the program. Still, 50 percent of Russian farms had been hastily thrown together into collectives during that year. Only 10 percent more were added during the next three years, so that by 1933 a total of 60 percent had been collectivized. The number rose again, and by 1939 more than 96 percent of Russian farms had been collectivized.

Just as he stepped up the frantic pace of collectivizing agriculture, so at first gradually, then suddenly, Stalin shifted to forced draft in industry also. In 1928 the era of five-year plans began, each setting ambitious goals for production over the next five years. In 1929 and 1930 Stalin appropriated ever-higher sums for capital investment, and in June 1930 he declared that industrial production must rise by 50 percent in that year. Under the first five-year plan, adopted in 1928, annual pig-iron production was scheduled to rise from 3.5 million tons to 10 million tons by 1932, but in that year Stalin demanded 17 million tons instead. It was not produced, but Stalin's demand for it was symptomatic of the pace at which he was striving to transform Russia from an agricultural to an industrial country.

Part of the reason for this rapid pace lay in the collectivization drive itself. Large-scale farming must be mechanized farming. Yet there were only seven thousand tractors in all the western Soviet Union at the end of 1928. Stalin secured thirty thousand more during 1929, but industry had to produce millions of machines plus the gasoline to run them. Since the countryside had to be electrified, power stations were needed by the thousands. Millions of peasants had to be taught how to handle machinery. But there was no one to teach them and there were no factories to produce the machinery.

Another reason for the drive to industrialize lay in the tenets of Marxism itself. Russia had defied all Marx's predictions by staging a proletarian revolution in a country that lacked a proletariat. Yet despite the communists' initial political successes, Stalin felt that capitalism had a firmer basis than communism in the Soviet Union, as long as it remained a country of peasants. And so the communists were determined to create that massive urban proletariat which did not yet exist.

The goals of the first five-year plan were not attained, although fulfillment was announced anyway in 1932. Immediately, the second plan, prepared by the state planning commission, went into effect and ran until 1937; the third was interrupted by Hitler's invasion. Each plan emphasized the elements of heavy industry—steel, electric power, cement, coal, oil. Between 1928 and 1940 steel production was multiplied by four and one-half, electric power by eight, cement by more than two, coal by four, and oil by almost three. Similar developments took place in chemicals and in machine production. Railroad construction was greatly increased, and the volume of freight carried quadrupled with the production of the country's own rolling stock. By 1940 Soviet output was approaching that of Germany. What the rest of Europe had done in roughly seventy-five years, the Soviet Union had done in about twelve.

All this was achieved at the cost of dreadful hardship, yet eyewitnesses report that many workers were as enthusiastic as if they had been soldiers in battle. Valuable machinery was often damaged or destroyed by inexperienced workers. The problems of repair, of replacement, of achieving balance between the output and consumption of raw materials, and of housing workers in the new centers were unending and cost untold numbers of lives.

Administratively, the Soviet economy was run by the state. The *Gosplan* (State Planning Commission) drew up the five-year plans and supervised their fulfillment at the management level. The *Gosbank* (State Bank) regulated the investment of capital. An economic council administered the work of various agencies; its major divisions were metallurgy and chemistry, defense, machinery, fuel and power, agriculture and procurements, and consumer goods. Production trusts controlled the mines, blast furnaces, and rolling mills; these were the so-called *combinats*, or "great production complexes." In each plant the manager was responsible for producing the quota set within the maximum cost allowed.

The social effects of this economic program were dramatic. Urban population rose from about 18 percent in 1926 to about 33 percent in 1940. The relative freedom to choose one's job that had marked NEP disappeared. Individual industrial enterprises signed labor contracts with the collectives by which a given number of farm workers were obliged to go to the factories.

Peasants who resisted collectivization were drafted into labor camps. In the factories the trade unions became an organ of the state. The chief role of the unions was to achieve maximum production and efficiency. Trade unions could not strike or quarrel with management, although they could administer the social insurance laws and negotiate to improve workers' living conditions.

Thus, Stalin set himself against the old Bolshevik principles of equality. The Marxist slogan, "From each according to his capacity, to each according to his needs" was shelved in favor of a new one: "From each according to his capacity, to each according to his work." Where Lenin had allowed none of the members of the government to earn more than a skilled laborer, Stalin set up a new system of incentives. A small minority of bureaucrats, skilled laborers, factory managers, and successful collective bosses earned vastly more than the unskilled laborers and peasants. Together with the writers, artists, musicians, entertainers, and athletes who lent their talents to the service of the regime, these people—generally men—became a new elite. They had a vested interest in furthering a regime to which they owed everything. The old privileged class of noble landlords, already weakened at the time of the revolution, had ceased to exist. The industrial, commercial, and financial bourgeoisie, which was just coming into its own at the time of the revolution, was destroyed after 1928, despite the temporary reprieve it had experienced under NEP. Most of the old intelligentsia, who had favored a revolution, could not in the end accept Stalin's dictatorship, and many of them emigrated. Those who remained were expected to concentrate on technical advances and on new administrative devices for speeding the transformation of the country; that is, they were to be "social engineers," high-level bureaucrats, propagandists for the new society who did not question its basic tenets or its direction.

After 1928, therefore, the logic of Stalin's policies forced a systematic mobilization of thought that in time virtually became thought control. Marx had assumed that a radical change in human nature was possible by conditioning of the social environment. Lenin recognized, however, that the new socialist society presumed the existence of a "new man" and "new woman," who would have to be created as part of the revolution. Industrialization and the collectivizing of agriculture could work only if unproductive speculation gave way to applied thinking directed to the needs of the state; this was particularly so in economics, philosophy, and psychology, but history and literature must also be transformed. To transform them, they must be controlled.

The Soviet Union was noted for its economists, whose support was essential to give credibility to NEP. Some economists felt that the potential scope of state planning was severely limited; others thought total planning possible; some were optimistic about how fast industrialization could proceed; others were pessimistic. Those whose arguments were contrary to the political needs of Stalin were accused of trying to undermine the first five-year plan. Although Stalin had attacked only the economists for their failure to keep pace with successes, the philosophers quickly understood his message and turned to the practical application of philosophy to social problems.

In psychology, researchers such as Ivan Pavlov (1849–1936) emphasized how human behavior could be explained in terms of biological reflexes. Psychology also influenced education, and in time educators would argue that four factors determined behavior: heredity, environment, training, and self-training. Schools ceased trying to provide an environment in which the personality might develop and became institutions geared to turning out productive and loyal citizens.

But it was in literature and history—and in their explicit censorship—that the need to mobilize thought was most apparent. Literature was important because it influenced people, not because it was a path to truth. Declaring that neutral art was impossible, the Central Committee of the party gave its full support to peasant writers. A series of industrial novels sought to energize the people to higher productivity and pride. Maxim Gorky (1868–1936) became editor of a magazine on socialism, and he and others launched a series of histories of factories to focus attention on the nation's industrial triumphs.

History was to take communist partisanship as its guiding principle. At first non-Marxist historians were allowed to continue their work, but with the organization of the Institute of Red Professors (1921) and the Society of Marxist Historians (1925), Soviet historiography became increasingly intolerant of those who did not see history as a science or who continued to write of Peter as "the Great" or of Catherine II as other than a "dissolute and criminal woman." Nonetheless, as Stalin realized that world revolution was increasingly unlikely, and as the need for patriotism to meet Hitler's challenge became more evident, historians were able to return to writing of past figures who would give the Russian people a sense of pride.

Finally, to make thought control effective and thus change the environment, restrictions and ultimately censorship were necessary. In 1922 a review agency, the Chief Administration for the Preservation of State Secrets in the Press (or *Glavlit*, its Russian abbreviation), was established to censor the press, manuscripts, photographs, radio broadcasts, lectures, and exhibitions. A subsection, begun in 1923, dealt with theater, music, and other arts. Glavlit placed an official in each publishing house, broadcasting studio, customshouse, and so forth, to monitor how the law was being obeyed. Some publications, such as the official newspaper of the Soviet, *Isvestiya*, were exempt from Glavlit, and the autonomous republics could establish their own Glavlits.

In an increasingly literate society of the kind Stalin intended, control over the press would prove to be even more important. The government encouraged the establishment of newspapers as a means of informing and educating the people to revolutionary socialism; by 1927 there were 1,105 newspapers and 1,645 periodicals in the Soviet Union, and by 1965 the number had grown to 6,595 and 3,833, respectively, in sixty-five languages. To control this vast outpouring, a decree of 1935 established the Telegraphic Agency of the Soviet Union (or *Tass*) as the central organ for information in the USSR. Until 1961 Tass held a monopoly over the distribution of all foreign information within the USSR and over all information that moved from one Soviet republic to another.

The Written Record

THE DANGERS OF BACKWARDNESS

The strength of Stalin's motives is revealed in a speech he made in 1931.

To slacken the pace means to lag behind, and those who lag behind are beaten. We do not want to be beaten. No we don't want to. . . . Old Russia . . . was ceaselessly beaten for her backwardness. She was beaten by the Mongol Khans, she was beaten by Turkish Beys, she was beaten by Swedish feudal lords, she was beaten by Polish-Lithuanian gentry, she was beaten by Anglo-French capitalists she was beaten by Japanese barons; she was beaten by all— for her backwardness. For military backwardness, for cultural backwardness, for political backwardness, for industrial backwardness, for agricultural backwardness. She was beaten because to beat her was profitable and went unpunished. . . . We are fifty or a hundred years behind the advanced countries. We must make good this lag in ten years. Either we do it or they crush us.

Quoted in Isaac Deutscher, *Stalin* (New York: Mentor, 1950), p. 328.

The Stalinist State, 1931–1943

Stalin's program was not achieved without opposition. The crisis of 1931 and 1932, when industrial goals were not being met and starvation swept the countryside, created discontent inside the regime as well as outside. A few officials circulated memoranda advocating Stalin's removal as general secretary, an act that the party had the right to perform. Stalin jailed them for conspiracy, and one leading Bolshevik committed suicide. Stalin's second wife reproached him at this time for the ravages that the terror was working, and she, too, committed suicide in 1932. Then, in December 1934, Sergei Kirov (1888–1934), who was rumored to be heir to Stalin's position, was assassinated in Leningrad, probably on Stalin's orders. Using Kirov's death as an excuse, Stalin purged the party of his opponents, having hundreds shot for alleged complicity in the killings and bringing his old colleagues Zinoviev and Kamenev to public trial in 1936. They and fourteen others either admitted involvement in Kirov's death or signed confessions fabricated for them; they were executed. In a second trial (1937), seventeen other leading Bolsheviks declared that they had knowledge of a conspiracy between Trotsky and the German and Japanese intelligence services by which Soviet territory was to be transferred to Germany and Japan. All were executed. Then in June 1937 came the secret liquidation of the top commanders in the Red Army, who were accused of conspiring with "an unfriendly foreign power" (Germany) with a view to sabotage. All were executed after an announcement that they had confessed. The last of the public trials took place in March 1938, as twenty-one leading Bolsheviks, including Bukharin, confessed to similar charges and were executed.

But these public trials and the secret trial of the generals provide only a faint idea of the extent of the purge that was now transformed into the period known as the Terror. Every member of Lenin's Politburo except Stalin and Trotsky either was killed or committed suicide to avoid execution. Two vice-commissars of foreign affairs and most of the ambassadors in the Soviet diplomatic corps, fifty of the seventy-one members of the Central Committee of the Communist party, almost all the military judges who had sat in judgment and had condemned the generals, two successive heads of the secret police, themselves the leaders in the previous purges, the prime ministers and chief officials of all the non-Russian Soviet republics—all were killed or vanished.

Not since the days of the witchcraft trials or of the Inquisition—and then not on so grand a scale—had the test of political and ideological loyalty been applied to so many people, and not since the days of the French Revolution had so many died for failing the test. Arrests multiplied tenfold in 1936 and 1937. Anything was used as an excuse for an arrest: dancing too long with a Japanese diplomat, buying groceries from a former kulak, not reporting an Armenian nationalist neighbor. People simply went out to work one day and did not return—killed or sent to one of many huge anonymous prisons, or banished to Siberia. Most academicians and writers took for granted periods of exile and prison as natural parts of the rhythm of life. By 1938 at least 1 million Soviets were in prisons, some 8.5 million people had been arrested and most sent to prison camps and colonies, and perhaps 700,000 had been executed.

Stalin apparently wanted to destroy utterly all possibility of future conspiracies. So he trumped up charges against anyone who could conceivably become a member of a regime that might replace his own. Yet despite the purges the state did not break down. New Stalin-trained officials filled all top-level positions, and terror was enthroned as a principle of government, keeping all officials in constant fear for their lives and their jobs. In the end the purgers, too, were purged, used as scapegoats by Stalin for the Terror they had carried out at his command. Even Trotsky was pursued and killed. In August 1940 an assassin tracked Trotsky down to his refuge in Mexico and killed him with an ax.

In the midst of the Terror in 1936 Stalin proclaimed a new constitution. By its provisions no one was disenfranchised, as priests and members of the former nobility and bourgeoisie had previously been. Civil liberties were extended on paper, although they could be modified in the "interest of the toilers." Because the USSR was a one-party state, elections were an expression of unanimity. The right to nominate candidates for the Supreme Soviet belonged to Communist party organizations, trade unions, cooperatives, youth groups, and cultural societies; but all were completely dominated by the party. The party picked the candidates, and no more than one for each post was presented to the voters. The party controlled the soviets, and the party hierarchy and government hierarchy overlapped and interlocked.

Every citizen could apply for membership in the party to a local branch, which voted on the application after a year of trial. Communist children's organizations fed the youth groups, which in turn fed the party. The party was organized both territorially and functionally in pyramid form, with organizations at the bottom level in factory, farm, and government office. These were grouped together by rural or urban local units, and these in turn by regional and territorial conferences and congresses. The party organizations elected the All-Union party congress, which selected the Central Committee of the party. The Central Committee selected the Politburo. At each level of the party pyramid there were organizations for agitation and propaganda (or "agitprop"), for organization and instruction, for military and political training. The party exercised nearly full control over the government.

The highest organ of the government was the Supreme Soviet, made up of two houses—a Soviet of the Union, based on population, and a Soviet of Nationalities, elected according to national administrative divisions. In theory the Supreme Soviet was elected for a term of four years. The Supreme Soviet itself did little; it appointed a presidium, which issued the decrees and carried on the work of the Supreme Soviet between sessions. It also appointed the Council of Ministers (long called the Council of People's Commissars). This cabinet, rather than the Supreme Soviet or its presidium, enacted most of the legislation and was thus both the legislative and the executive organ of the state. Stalin was chairman of the Council of People's Commissars and of the Politburo, and general secretary of the Communist party. He was also commissar of defense, chief of the State Defense Council, which ran the country during wartime, and supreme military commander.

With the new constitution in place and Stalin's enemies dead or intimidated, the late 1930s brought a softening of revolutionary fervor. Simultaneously with the purges and the new constitution, the bread ration was raised; individual farmers could own their homesteads; new medals and titles were awarded to leading workers in plants and to scientists, engineers, and military officers. In the Red Army, the traditional czarist distinctions between officers and men were restored, and marshals were named for the first time. The standard of living went up as the production of consumer goods was encouraged; and workers were invited to spend their earnings on small luxuries previously unavailable.

The early Bolsheviks had destroyed the old school system, abolished homework and examinations, and allowed children to administer the schools collectively with their teachers. Attendance fell off, the schools became revolutionary clubs of youngsters, and the training of teachers was neglected. The universities deteriorated, since anyone could enroll in them at age sixteen. Degrees were abolished, and technical training was stressed, to the exclusion of other subjects. Under NEP this chaotic situation was modified, and the basic problem of increasing literacy was tackled seriously. But the ordinary school curricula were replaced by heavy emphasis on labor problems and Marxist theory. The Communist party itself took over the universities, purged the faculties, and compelled the students to spend one week in three at work in factories.

But now this system again changed drastically. Training of teachers improved, their salaries were raised, and they were admitted to the civil service. The prerevolutionary system of admissions and degrees in the universities was restored, as was the prerevolutionary school curriculum. Emphasis on political education was reduced, and coeducation was abandoned. Tuition fees were restored for secondary schools making higher education difficult to obtain, except for children of the new elite or unusually talented students who won state scholarships. Literacy rose to about 90 percent.

Very reluctantly Stalin came last of all to modify the traditional communist position on religion. Militant atheism had been the policy of the early Bolsheviks. Behind their attitude lay more than the standard Marxist feeling that religion was the opiate of the masses; in Russia the Orthodox church had always been a pillar of czarism. Many years of attacks on religion, however, had failed to eradicate Orthodoxy from among the people. When in 1937 Hitler built a Russian church in Berlin and took every occasion to speak kindly of the Orthodox church, Stalin had to respond. Declaring that Christianity had contributed to past Russian glory, the government abated its antireligious propaganda and permitted church attendance again. While the early revolutionaries had attacked the family as the backbone of the discredited social order, Stalin rehabilitated the sanctity of marriage and emphasized the family and its growth. The government lowered taxes on church property and appointed a new patriarch on whose subservience the regime could count.

Karl Marx, who had scorned and disliked Russia, would have been confounded had he lived to see that agricultural land, almost without a proletariat, produce the only major European communist revolution. Perhaps Marx was wrong, or perhaps what happened in Russia was not a Marxist revolution at all. It seems clear that Marx did not correctly estimate the revolutionary force latent in the Russian peasantry. Since Marx died in 1883, he could not foresee the ultimate inadequacy of the czarist regime, the start of effective Russian industrialization, the extent of the tensions created by World War I, or the feebleness of the provisional government of 1917. But it also seems clear that, to bring the Bolsheviks to power, it took Lenin's recognition of the importance of the peasantry, his grasp of the immediate situation, his willingness to risk everything, and his good fortune at being in the right place at the right time with the right weapons.

On the other hand, the revolution was not wholly Marxist. Once the Bolsheviks were in power, it was natural that the real situations they faced would modify their Marxist-Leninist theories. When civil war and foreign intervention brought chaos, NEP provided a necessary respite. Stalin combined Marxism, Russian nationalism, and ruthless politics in ways no one could have foreseen. Although it fell short of its goal, Stalin's program created an industrial state able to resist the blows that Hitler was to deal it. Servants of the state though they were, collectivized by force, industrialized by force, purged, terrorized, and struggling by the millions to exist in forced labor camps or to leave the country, the Soviets in World War II nonetheless, with the United States and other nations, defeated Hitler and his allies.

SUMMARY

The period from 1919 to 1939 was marked by the success of movements to the right. Although these movements were products of different societies, they had features in common: disillusionment with democracy for its failure to provide stability, aggressive nationalism, a sense of grievance, totalitarian government, and racism.

Fascism triumphed first in Italy after World War I. Mussolini, a socialist until the war, repudiated his old beliefs and shifted to militant nationalism. In a campaign of terror, Mussolini drove to power in the early 1920s. He established a fascist dictatorship, assuring his dominance by controlling the press and abolishing opposition parties.

Mussolini set up a corporative state in which the needs of labor and capital were subordinate to the interests of the state. Worker and producer syndicates had little real power or influence, which was held by the fascist bureaucracy. Mussolini pursued an aggressive foreign policy in the Mediterranean, Spain Ethiopia, and Albania.

After World War I, Germany experienced fifteen years of democratic government under the Weimar Republic. However, Weimar Germany went through three distinct phases: in the first, which lasted from 1918 to 1923, political threats arose from the left and right, and the nation was in economic chaos; in the second, which lasted from 1924 to 1929, Germany enjoyed political stability and relative economic prosperity; in the third, which lasted from 1929 to 1933, the right rose to power under Hitler, and economic depression cut the foundations from prosperity.

Hitler quickly established a dictatorship. He used the threat of a Bolshevik revolution to suspend constitutional government and build a strongly centralized state. He dissolved opposition political parties and crushed opponents within his own party. Once in power, Hitler embarked on a policy of eliminating Jews, and racism became a state policy. In foreign affairs, Nazi racist policies were extended to claiming lands inhabited by Germans.

In Spain, turmoil caused by divisions between left and right increased after the death of King Alfonso in 1931. During the Spanish Civil War (1936–1939), General Franco, aided by Italian and German forces, won a victory over the leftists. Franco established an authoritarian regime supported by landowners, the army, and the church.

In Portugal, another dictator, Antonio Salazar, rose to power. In eastern Europe, the successor states to the Habsburg Empire lacked parliamentary traditions. In the interwar period, authoritarian regimes were established in these nations.

After Lenin's death in 1924, a desperate power struggle unfolded in the Soviet Union between Stalin and Trotsky. Stalin used his strong base of support in the party to force Trotsky out of power. Under Stalin, an authoritarian regime of the left was intensified.

By 1928 Communists had rejected Lenin's New Economic Policy, which had aimed at reconstruction after the civil war. Between 1928 and 1941, Stalin imposed massive changes on Soviet life: collectivization, industrialization, elimination of opponents, and a return to bourgeois standards in social and intellectual life.

By the late 1930s Stalin had mobilized writers and historians to use Russia's past to increase Russian nationalism. For by then, the Soviet Union faced a coalition of authoritarian fascist regimes pledged to exterminate communism.

FIVE

The Democracies and the Non-Western World

∾

Idealists like President Wilson had expected that the collapse of the Romanov, Habsburg, and Hohenzollern empires would automatically ensure an increase in the number of democratic states. But, instead, much of Europe came under regimes that were hostile to liberal democracy. In the 1920s and 1930s the core of democracy remained the great North Atlantic powers—Britain, France, and the United States; the smaller states of Scandinavia; the Low Countries; Switzerland; and the inheritors of the British tradition—Canada, Australia, and New Zealand. Certainly the totalitarian aggressors bore great responsibility for the unleashing of a second world war. Yet a major factor in the deterioration of the twenty years' truce was the failure of the democracies to present a unified front against those who threatened world peace.

In the early 1930s Britain, France, and the United States were preoccupied with domestic problems. But this was the very time when international problems demanded equally urgent attention. International trade was steadily shrinking in response to the depression and mounting tariff barriers; the prospects for peace were steadily fading in response to resurgent and authoritarian nationalism. Nor was this all. During the twenty years' truce, the democracies faced a third set of problems. This third set involved the relations between the democracies and the non-Western peoples, many of whom were still under colonial rule. Particularly in Asia and the Middle East, non-Western peoples were beginning to assert their nationalism and to demand the loosening of imperial ties.

Thus, the discrete histories of the non-Western peoples, always part of "world history," as we customarily call it, now became an integral part of the history of "Western civilization" as well. Problems that would have been viewed as quite distinct two or three centuries earlier took on global significance.

Great Britain

Although on the winning side in World War I, Britain staggered from economic crisis to crisis. Immigration inward was steadily offset by emigration outward, especially to North America. Despite efforts to recover, the steam had left the British economy, which grew at half its prewar rate.

The Postwar Economic Crisis, to 1921

Besides tragic human losses from the war, Great Britain's economic losses were grave. The national debt after the war was ten times that of 1914. Many British investments abroad had been liquidated to purchase food and war materials. Forty percent of the great British merchant fleet had been destroyed by enemy action. The whole fabric of international trade on which Britain depended was torn in a thousand places in 1918 and could not be rapidly restored in the unsettled postwar world. To supplement British and French war production, the industrial plants of the United States, Canada, and India had been called on, and that stimulus made them more effective competitors of the British in peacetime. In addition, German industry, nourished in part by loans from America, once more took up the rivalry that had so alarmed the British before the war.

In short, the country that in Victorian days had been the "workshop of the world" could no longer provide full employment to its millions of workers. Those workers were in no mood to accept a lower standard of living, for they had fought the war and won it in the expectation of better things to come. They had been promised that the defeated enemy would pay the costs of the war, that Germany would be "squeezed until the pips squeak," and thereby give Britain a new start.

This hope was very early disappointed; no substantial reparations were paid to Britain. The return to peace caused a sudden boom in production to meet the postwar demand for goods that had been denied to civilians in wartime. This was accompanied by a sharp rise in prices and quickly followed by an equally abrupt collapse of the boom, leaving the nation in a severe postwar depression. By the summer of 1921 more than 2 million people were out of work, over one fifth of the labor force. Faced with the rising cost of living, the British government increased the very meager unemployment payments. However, large-scale unemployment was to be the plague of the interwar years in Britain; many never returned to work, and some young people did not find jobs until the eve of World War II.

The British economic decline was not yet catastrophic, although some gravely depressed areas, like the coal-mining regions of South Wales, began to show signs of permanent decay. What happened generally was a relative decline, the slowing down of an economy geared to dynamic growth, with a working population conditioned psychologically to a gradually rising standard of living and a middle class similarly conditioned to traditional comforts. Moreover, the tabloid newspaper, the movie, and the radio made the

British well aware that Americans and others enjoyed automobiles, radios, refrigerators, and telephones, while they did not.

Britain was suffering from those ills characteristic of postindustrial development, and it was the first nation to do so. There was still a lot of coal in Britain, for example, but much of it was costly to mine, since the most easily and cheaply worked seams were being exhausted. The industry was badly organized, with many small and inefficient mines running at a loss and with machinery and methods that were antiquated in comparison with the newer American and Continental mines. Productivity per work-hour was low. Worst of all, the 1920s saw the rapid rise of major competitors to coal—oil, and electricity based on water power—with a consequent decline of British coal exports. Since the British Isles had no petroleum and no very great potential in hydroelectric power, coal simply had to be mined. But the workers were unionized and in no mood to accept cuts in wages, while owners did not want to run their businesses at a loss. A strike in March 1921 focused national attention on this problem. The strike was settled in July by the government's consenting to pay subsidies to cover increased wages.

The Conservative and Labour Programs

Although the division of politics on the basis of class in Britain was perhaps neither as rigid nor as clear as in many other European nations, it is true that this was of major importance. The Conservatives, still often called Tories, tended to get the support of the propertied and the middle classes and others who believed that the way to attack new problems was with traditional "British" methods and with a minimum of government intervention. The Labour party had replaced the once all-conquering Liberals as the second party of the state, and they tended to get the support of trade unionists, left-leaning intellectuals, and others who came to believe that the scope of Britain's problems required more government involvement than had in the past been customary. In the struggle between Conservative and Labour, the old Liberal party was a sad casualty.

Although much challenged from many sides, the Liberals had won a massive victory in 1906 and held onto power through the political tumult of the prewar years. It had suffered a fatal split between its two greatest figures in December 1916, the issue being, understandably, how best to fight World War I. The majority of the party sided with the then Liberal prime minister, H. H. Asquith; a minority followed David Lloyd George into a coalition with the thoroughly united Conservatives, forming a new majority and a Lloyd George government, while driving Asquith and the orthodox Liberals from office forever. With the end of the war this Lloyd George–led coalition continued for several years until, realizing that the no longer popular wartime leader had become a liability, the Conservatives withdrew from it. When politics returned to coalition-free business as usual, the shattered Liberals could not reunite, and Labour replaced them as the alternative to Conservatism. After the fall of the coalition in 1922, the Conservative party won election and remained in power (either alone or in yet another coalition) for most of the period until 1945. The Labourites formed only two weak governments in these years, while the Liberals (despite their great history) sank to the status of a "third party" as, in a slightly different form, they remain today.

The state of world trade—as free trade Britain saw more and more nations turn to *autarky* (economic self-reliance, invariably bolstered with tariffs)—convinced many Conservatives in this period that the Tariff Reform plan introduced by Joseph Chamberlain in 1903 had more relevance than ever before; and their economic difficulties in the interwar years provided them a perfect rationale for defying a high-tariff world and uniting the British Empire through tariffs of their own. The problems with the scheme were as fascinating as the possibilities: While it might have created a tariff-girded secure market for Britain and her possessions, it had the same two flaws revealed a decade earlier. The biggest colonies, now called dominions, were striving to develop modern economies and had no wish only to be seen as sources of raw materials, markets for British-made manufactured goods and services, and recruiting grounds for the armed forces needed to support an imperial foreign policy. They were looking toward independent nationhood, and they wanted their own industries. The great domestic political difficulty of Chamberlain's vision remained the same as it was when it brought terrible defeat to the Conservatives in 1906: Tariffs meant a higher cost of living in the short run, and times to most voters were difficult enough without that added burden.

The Labour party's solution for Britain was one that had long appealed to socialists: nationalization, that is, government purchase and operation of key industries with fair compensation to their private owners (only the most radical minority suggested expropriation as in the Soviet Union). The key industries were transportation, utilities, coal, steel, and perhaps even textiles, cutlery, pottery, and machine tools—all the industries that seemed to thrive best on large-scale organization. But even nationalized industries would still face the fundamental problem of selling enough goods abroad to keep the economy going. Labourites argued, therefore, that nationalization would also enable British industries to produce more cheaply and efficiently by doing away with wasteful competition and inefficiency. Jobs would be secured and markets again exploited, and the increased efficiency in industry would produce new jobs. Removal of the need for profit would reduce prices and increase prosperity among the workers who would purchase more goods. It was a vision and a system that would have to wait until 1945 for a true test in Britain.

Politics Between the Wars, 1918–1936

Politics in these years came to be dominated by two figures who were quite unlike in almost all imaginable ways—Stanley Baldwin and James Ramsay MacDonald. Both were unlikely prime ministers. A product of a well-to-do business family and a Cambridge education, Baldwin (1867–1947) entered politics in middle age and languished in obscurity until the war, when his administrative and political skills showed themselves. He rose in the Lloyd George coalition and, after its chaotic breakup in 1922, became second only to the new Conservative prime minister, Andrew Bonar Law (1858–1923). When Bonar Law's health collapsed less than a year later, Baldwin succeeded him. He was deeply religious, thoughtful, and a believer in what he thought were the best elements of the British character—to his detractors he was indolent, unimaginative, and middle-of-the-road to the point of stasis. He was hugely popular because voters of all classes came to see him as like them— more drawn to his garden, his family, and his pipe than to precipitous action and dynamic solutions, which many associated with the disgraced Lloyd George style. He enjoyed much success in politics and yet made several great mistakes for which some party professionals found it hard to forgive him, yet the voters usually did and he always seemed to recover.

MacDonald (1866–1937) was quite another case. Born illegitimate and into poverty in a Scottish village, he was virtually self-educated and an early convert to socialism and pacifism. One of the founders of the Labour party, he entered Parliament in 1906, where he became the party's first leader. He opposed World War I on moral grounds and his reputation collapsed, but he painstakingly rebuilt it and again became a prominent figure in the political world of Labour.

Because of the electoral confusion resulting from the three-party contest in the 1924 election, for ten months MacDonald was able to form a minority government (with a plurality but not a majority of seats), supported for a time by the surviving Liberals. He returned under similar circumstances in 1929–1931, and once again his government failed—this time to be replaced by another coalition. MacDonald was tall, handsome, and eloquent. A gifted organizer and man of absolute moral principle, despite all the years of socialist rhetoric he turned out to be a reformer rather than a committed socialist and shrank from innovation in the depths of the world depression. He was much admired as the father of his party, yet he broke bitterly with it in the last years of his career and was never truly forgiven for what was seen as an act of party and class betrayal.

Neither the Conservatives nor the Labourites were able to carry out their full platforms. The Conservatives were frustrated by the refusal of the Commonwealth countries to go any further than to accept certain limited imperial preferences. The two Labour governments, obliged to rely on the Liberals for parliamentary support, were still too shaky to introduce measures as controversial as the nationalization of any industry.

For a few weeks in 1926 some 2.5 million trade union members attempted a general strike to support coal miners, who were striking to protest a cut in their wages. The general strike failed, but its brief course revealed fundamental British attitudes. Thousands of people from the middle and upper classes volunteered to keep essential services operating when a state of emergency was declared. Both sides remained calm and moderate, with neither side seeking all-out victory in a class war. When the general strike was called off, the miners eventually had to return to the pits on the owners' terms. In 1927 a Trade Disputes and Trade Union Act made all sympathetic strikes or strikes against the government illegal.

Meanwhile, two more steps were taken toward the political democratization of Britain that had begun in 1832. In 1918, in preparation for the election, the government had put through a reform bill that eliminated all the old exceptions to universal male suffrage and gave the vote to all males over twenty-one. Culminating the long campaign by women's suffragists, the bill also gave the vote to women. But it set the voting age for women at thirty years, thus ensuring that there would be more male than female voters. The distinction was too unsound to last, especially after experience demonstrated that women divided politically about the way men did. In 1928 a new bill gave women the vote at twenty-one.

Although signs of economic ill health persisted, Britain recovered somewhat in the late 1920s. But then came the Great Depression. Britain, already weakened, was one of the first nations to suffer; in eighteen months the number of unemployed jumped from slightly more than 1 million to 2.5 million. Faced by a serious government deficit and divided over how to meet it, by cutting social services or increasing revenue, the second Labour government of Ramsay MacDonald resigned in August 1931.

It gave way to a coalition of Conservatives, Liberals, and right-wing Labourites—headed by MacDonald. Many Labourites were dismayed by what seemed to them MacDonald's surrender to the forces of capitalism, and the deep split within the party crippled its effectiveness throughout the 1930s. For many Labour loyalists their own leader had committed the "great betrayal." The "National Government," as the coalition cabinet was called, reduced social services. Late in 1931, it took the decisive step of going off the gold standard and letting the pound fall in value. In 1932 it made the first firm move away from free trade by enacting protective tariffs, and it also ceased to pay its war debts to the United States. These measures did little to help the unemployed or get at the roots of British economic troubles. Nevertheless, partly because of Labour's disarray, two general elections, in October 1931 and in June 1935, returned a majority supporting the national government.

The National Government was dominated by Conservatives, and after the 1935 election the Conservative leader, Stanley Baldwin, became prime minister. Gradually the British economy pulled out of the worst of the depression, and Baldwin was able to balance the budget. In 1936, however, the great issue confronting Baldwin's cabinet was neither social nor economic but constitutional, as the cabinet forced the abdication of King Edward VIII (1894–1972) in the same year as his accession to the throne. Edward had fallen in love with a socially ambitious American divorcee and wanted to marry her. The royal family, the cabinet, and most of the British people opposed him, and he abdicated; he was succeeded by his brother, who became King George VI (r. 1936–1952).

The Irish Question, 1916–1949

The years between the wars finally seemed to bring a kind of solution to the Irish controversy. In 1916, as the nation struggled on the western front, the British put down the hopeless Dublin Easter rebellion with grim determination—and their unyielding severity created nearly a hundred martyrs to Irish independence and turned a quixotic insurrection into a national climacteric. While the Irish people seemed at first to have little sympathy for the rag-tag army of rebels, they soon embraced their memory and, with that, their cause—separatism, not the autonomy of the old dream of home rule. After Britain threatened to apply conscription to Ireland (which had been exempted from the national service laws) in April 1918, the Irish nationalists boycotted the British Parliament. The Irish crisis of 1914, postponed by World War I, was again at hand.

By 1919, however, home rule was no longer enough for many Irish nationalists. A new political party called *Sinn Fein* ("ourselves alone" in the Gaelic language) sought complete independence and was prepared to seize it by force. The years 1919–1921 were filled with violence, assassinations, arson, and guerilla warfare, as the secret Irish Republican Army and their increasing legion of sympathizers, who now supported their own illegal parliament, the *Dáil Eireann,* fought the police, the British army, and the irregular force that came to be called the "Black and Tans." It was a violent time during which atrocity often met atrocity: "A murder duel, fought in the dark," Winston Churchill called it. But public support in Britain could not be maintained for such a bloody policy, while in Ireland resolution and resistance seemed to grow stiffer every day.

The immediate result of the violent phase of the revolution was a compromise, for Sinn Fein split in two. The moderate wing was willing to accept a compromise in which Protestant Ulster would remain under direct British rule and the Catholic counties would be given dominion status under an independent assembly. The moderates negotiated with the British, and in 1921 obtained for the twenty-six counties of southern Ireland dominion status under the name of the Irish Free State. The Free State had its own parliament, the Dáil, and was completely self-governing, with its own army and its own diplomatic services. It did, however, accept the British Crown as symbolic head. The six predominantly Protestant counties of Ulster maintained their old relationship with Britain, including the right to send members to the Parliament at Westminster, but they also acquired their own parliament at Belfast and considerable local autonomy. Henceforth, Britain was officially known as the United Kingdom of Great Britain and Northern Ireland.

The radical wing, led by Eamon De Valera (1882–1975), insisted that the whole island, Protestant and Catholic, achieve complete independence as a unified republic. For the radicals, the compromise negotiated by the moderates was unacceptable. The Irish revolution now became a civil war between partisans of the Free State and those of a single republic, with a return to burning, ambush, and murder. But when the moderate leader Michael Collins

(1890–1922), once a ferocious revolutionary and by this time a supporter of the compromise, was assassinated, public opinion began to turn away from the extremists. De Valera, after refusing to sit in the Dáil because he would have had to take an oath of loyalty to the British king, attacked the civil war and ultimately decided to bring his party, the *Fianna Fáil*, into the national parliament in 1927.

De Valera's party won a plurality in the Dáil in 1932 and a majority in 1933; thereupon it abolished the oath of loyalty to the Crown and cut the threads that still tied the Free State to the United Kingdom. In 1938 De Valera became prime minister, and in 1939 the Free State showed that it was free from British domination by maintaining neutrality throughout World War II. In 1949 the final step was taken when Britain recognized the fully independent republic of Eire (Gaelic for "Ireland").

The Commonwealth, 1931–1939

Constitutional recognition of the essential independence of the dominions seemed to make them more loyal. The new status acquired by the dominions with the Statute of Westminster in 1931 was symbolized by a change in terminology. They were no longer to be considered parts of the British Empire, but free members of the British Commonwealth of Nations. In this new relationship, Britain would have to negotiate with the Commonwealth countries about tariffs, trade conditions, or immigration as with foreign countries.

Although Britain was unable to build a self-sufficient economic unity out of its dominions, still in 1939 the dominions all ultimately came into the war on Britain's side. They made this decision independently, however, for they had the legal right to follow the example of Ireland and remain neutral. Transfer of power to the major dominions was virtually complete.

France

In France both World War I and the postwar difficulties caused even more serious dislocation than they did in Britain. France had lost proportionately more in human lives and in material damage than had any other major belligerent. Two million Frenchmen in the prime of life were either killed or so seriously mutilated as to be incapable of normal living. In a land of only 39 million with an already low birth rate, this human loss affected all phases of activity. Three hundred thousand houses and twenty thousand factories or shops were destroyed. In a land of conservative economic organization where most work was done without large-scale machinery, this material setback would long be felt. Psychologically, victory did not compensate for the traumatic losses of the four years of struggle.

The Impact of the War, 1918–1928

France wanted revenge on Germany in every possible way. The French tried to extract reparations to the last possible sum, undeterred by the arguments of economists that Germany could not pay. But France insisted even more on keeping Germany isolated in international relations and without the physical means to wage war.

Meanwhile, France was experiencing an inflation that resulted in part from the cost of rebuilding the devastated areas—a cost that drained government finances and that was only partly covered by German payments. It resulted also from the high cost of maintaining armed forces (for the French dared not disarm), from the general disorder of international trade, and from the staggering debts piled up during the war by the French government, which, like the imperial German government, had preferred loans to taxes. By the mid-1920s the franc had slipped from its prewar value of twenty cents against the dollar to a dangerous low of about two cents. Premier Raymond Poincaré (1860–1934) initiated new taxes and stern economic measures which stemmed the decline of the franc. In 1928 it was officially revalued at 3.92 cents.

The French inflation, although mild compared with the German, nevertheless caused economic and social dislocation. Those French who had lent their government francs worth twenty cents were now repaid only one fifth of their loans. This very considerable loss fell with particular severity on the lower middle class, the *petite bourgeoisie*. The greatest sufferers were those living on their savings or on relatively fixed incomes. Inflation thus weakened a social class that had long been a mainstay of republicanism in France and added to the social tensions that formed the central theme of French domestic history between the two world wars.

Social and Political Tensions, 1928–1936

During World War I the French had temporarily put aside the great political and social conflict they had inherited from 1789. After the war the "sacred union" of political parties that had carried France through the struggle soon dissolved, and the traditional conflict was resumed. This is sometimes termed the conflict between the "two Frances"—the republican France of the left and the royalistic or authoritarian France of the right. The conflict was not a simple struggle between rich and poor. On the right the wealthier classes, many of them openly hostile to the existence of the parliamentary state, were reinforced by conservative peasants and by small business people and investors. Many of these petit bourgeois were not hostile to the Third Republic as such but were determined to resist any attempt to extend the social services of the welfare state.

On the left were the champions of the welfare state, the socialists and the communists, backed by the more radical workers; by many white-collar people, especially in the bureaucracy; and by some intellectuals. The postwar left was hampered by the split between the communists, who followed the Moscow line, and the socialists, who did not, and by a comparable schism within the major trade-union organization, the CGT (*Confédération Générale du Travail*, the General Confederation of Labor). Still nominally part of the left, but actually in the political middle and not anxious to extend the welfare state, was the Radical Socialist party, long the main party of the Third Republic. The Radicals were strong among the peasants of southern France and among white-collar and professional workers.

In the late 1920s, the Third Republic seemed to be getting the better of its internal difficulties. The world economic crisis that began in 1929 was late in striking France, and for a while it looked as though the French economy, less dependent on large-scale industry than that of the United States, Britain, or Germany, might weather the crisis much more easily. But France, too, depended on international trade, particularly on the export of luxuries. By 1932 the depression had struck, and the government was in serious economic and political difficulties.

The political crisis came to a head in February 1934 as a result of the Stavisky case, a financial scandal reminiscent of the Panama scandal of the 1890s. Serge Stavisky was a swindler with influential connections, particularly in Radical Socialist circles. He was finally exposed in December 1933 and escaped to an Alpine hideout, where he committed suicide—or, as many believed, was killed by the police lest he implicate important politicians. France was rocked by the event and also by the mysterious death of a judge who had been investigating the case. On the extreme right, royalists had long been organized in a pressure group known as the *Action Française* and were gaining recruits among upper-class youth. The *Camelots du Roi* (King's Henchmen), strong-arm squads of the Action Française, went about beating up communists, who responded with violence. Less fascist in character yet also supporting the right was a veterans' organization, the *Croix de Feu* (Cross of Fire). During the agitation following the Stavisky case, the Camelots du Roi, the Croix de Feu, and other right-wing groups took part in demonstrations against the government. The left countered with a brief general strike. Fourteen demonstrators were killed, and many feared that France again faced revolution.

The Popular Front, 1936–1937

Once more, however, as in the time of Dreyfus, the republican forces rallied to meet the threat, and once more, after the crisis had been surmounted, France moved to the left. Edouard Daladier (1884–1970), Radical premier, resigned, and a coalition of all parties except the royalists, socialists, and communists formed a national government, including all living former premiers. But the franc was again falling in value. In 1935 a ministry in which the dominant figure was Pierre Laval (1883–1945), a former socialist turned conservative, attempted to cut back government expenditures by measures similar to those that had worked a decade earlier under Poincaré; this time, however, they did not work. The forces of the left responded by forming a Popular Front, which for the first time linked together the Radical Socialist, Socialist, and Communist parties. It also had the backing of CGT, which had temporarily healed the schism between communist and noncommunist unions. In the elections of 1936 the Popular Front won, with the socialists at the top. The premiership was accordingly offered to a socialist, the Jewish intellectual Léon Blum (1872–1950).

The Popular Front came to power with a mandate from voters who wanted the government to distribute wealth more equitably. In June 1936 the government introduced an ambitious program of reform. Labor gained a forty-hour workweek, higher wages, vacations with pay, and provision for compulsory arbitration of labor disputes. The Bank of France, the railroads, and the munitions industry were all partially nationalized. Quasi-fascist groups like the Camelots du Roi and Croix de Feu were ordered to disband.

Impressive as this program was on paper, events, conspired to block its successful implementation. The communists, following orders from Moscow, did not really cooperate, for they refused to participate in the Blum cabinet and sniped at it in parliament and in the press. Business took fright at the growth of the CGT and at the effectiveness of sit-down strikes of French industrial workers in June 1936—the first widespread use of this formidable economic weapon through which struck plants were occupied by the striking workers, preventing the owners from using their weapon, the lockout.

The nation was soon bitterly divided between partisans and enemies of the Popular Front. Business and farming classes were traditionally reluctant to pay income taxes, which would have to be raised to meet the costs of social services; the economy was not geared to labor-saving devices; there were competing demands on the nation's money. Capital, however, was rapidly leaving the country to be invested or deposited abroad, and the monied class would not subscribe to the huge defense loans that were essential if the French armed forces were to prepare for the war that seemed to be approaching. Faced by mounting opposition, Blum was obliged to step down as premier in favor of a Radical in 1937. The Popular Front disintegrated.

The morale of the French sagged badly after the collapse of the Popular Front. Under the mounting international tensions of 1938 and 1939, the Radical Socialist premier, Daladier, kept France on the side of Britain in unsteady opposition to the Rome-Berlin Axis. Various measures of retrenchment—including virtual abandonment of the forty-hour week—kept the French economy from collapse. But the workers resented the failure of the Popular Front, and as late as November 1938 almost achieved a general strike, which the government combated by putting the railway workers under military orders. The "have" classes, on the other hand, were outraged by Blum's measures. Many of them were convinced that their salvation lay in a French totalitarian state. The France that was confronted with war in 1939 was not only inadequately armed; it was also psychologically and spiritually divided, uncertain of what it was to fight for or against.

Many in France had relied on their great empire to restore the flagging morale and material capabilities of the nation. Colonial troops, particularly from Senegal and North Africa, had helped to replenish the diminished ranks of the army during World War I and might do so again. Enthusiasts spoke of France as a nation of 100 million, which included the populations of the colonial territories. But the colonial populations were beginning to desire home rule or independence, especially in Algeria, Senegal, and French Indochina. Although some leaders of the French left urged concessions to such desires, little was conceded. In 1936 the Popular Front government negotiated treaties with Syria and Lebanon, granting them independence with many reservations, so as to safeguard the primacy of French interests. But this compromise was too much for the Chamber of Deputies, which refused to approve the treaties. Perhaps no policy pursued in the interwar years could have averted the disintegration of the French Empire that occurred during and after World War II, but the unimaginative policy that prevailed did nothing to reconcile the nationalists among the French colonial peoples.

The United States

Neither the human nor the material losses of the United States in World War I were at all comparable with those of Britain and France. American casualties were 115,000 dead and 206,000 wounded; the comparable French figures were 1,385,000 dead and 3,044,000 wounded in a population one third as large. Moreover, in purely material terms, the United States probably gained from the war. Yet in some ways the American postwar revulsion against the war was as marked as that in Britain, France, and defeated Germany. It helped to unseat the Democrats, who had controlled the federal government since 1913. The Republicans won the presidential elections of 1920 (in which women had the vote for the first time), 1924, and 1928.

Isolationism and Internationalism, 1920–1933

American revulsion against war also took the form of isolationism, the wish to withdraw from international politics outside the Western Hemisphere. The country was swept by a wave of desire to get back to "normalcy," as President Warren Harding phrased it. Many Americans felt that they had done all they needed to do in defeating the Germans, and that further participation in the complexities of European politics would simply involve American innocence and virtue even more disastrously in European sophistication and vice. As the months of negotiation went on in Europe with no final decisions, many Americans began to feel that withdrawal was the only effective action they could take. The Treaty of Versailles, containing the establishment of the League of Nations, was finally rejected in the Senate on March 19, 1920.

American isolationism was also expressed in concrete measures. Tariffs in 1922 and 1930 set successively higher duties on foreign goods and emphasized America's belief that its high wage scales needed to be protected from cheap foreign labor. The spirit of isolationism, as well as growing racist movements—this was the high point in American history of the Ku Klux Klan—also lay behind the immigration restrictions of the 1920s, which reversed the former policy of almost unlimited immigration. The reversal was hastened by widespread prejudice against the recent and largely Catholic and Jewish immigrations from southern and eastern Europe. The act of 1924 set an annual quota limit for each country of 2 percent of the number of nationals from that country resident in the United States in 1890. Since the heavy immigration from eastern and southern Europe had come after 1890, the choice of that date reduced the flow from these areas to a trickle. Northern countries like Britain, Germany, and the Scandinavian states, on the other hand, did not use up their quotas.

Isolationism did not apply to all matters, however. The United States continued all through the 1920s to insist that the debts owed to it by the Allied powers be repaid. Congress paid little heed to the argument, so convincing to most economists, that the European nations could not repay except with dollars gained by selling their goods in the American market, and that American tariffs continued to make such repayment impossible.

Yet the United States did not withdraw entirely from international politics. Rather, as an independent without formal alliances, it continued to pursue policies that seemed to most Americans traditional, but that in their totality gradually aligned them against the rising dictatorships. In 1928 the Republican secretary of state, Frank B. Kellogg (1856–1937), proposed that the major powers renounce war as an instrument of national policy. Incorporated with similar proposals by the French foreign minister, Aristide Briand (1862–1932), it was formally adopted that year as the Pact of Paris, commonly known as the Kellogg-Briand Pact, and was eventually signed by twenty-three nations. Although the pact proved ineffective, the fact that it arose in part from American initiative and that the United States was a signatory to it was clear indication that even if Americans did not wish to enter into any formal alliances, they were still concerned with the problems of worldwide stability and peace.

During the 1920s the United States was hard at work laying the foundations for the position of world leadership it reached after World War II. American businesses were everywhere; American loans were making possible the revival of German industry; American motors, refrigerators, typewriters, telephones, and other products were being sold the world over. In the Far East the United States led in negotiating the Nine-Power Treaty of 1922 that committed it and the other great powers, including Japan, to respect the sovereignty and integrity of China. When Democratic President Franklin D. Roosevelt resisted the Japanese attempt to absorb China and other Far Eastern territory a decade later, he was following a line laid down under his Republican predecessors.

Boom and Bust, 1923–1933

In domestic affairs, the 1920s were a time of frantic prosperity for the many who played the stock market. These were the years of Prohibition, of the speakeasy and the bootlegger, when the American media—newspapers, magazines, radio, and motion pictures—gave the impression that the entire nation was absorbed by short skirts, loosened sexual mores, new dances, and bathtub gin. Such activities occupied only a tiny minority of the people, of course, just as the "whipped cream" culture of turn-of-the-century Vienna had been unrepresentative of most Austrians. But by the 1920s there was a significant difference. Agricultural workers who had never recovered their sense of prosperity and people who still held to Victorian standards of conduct would be led to believe that boundless riches, social vacuity, and sin were typical of the upper classes.

The era was also a time of marked industrial progress, of solid advancement of the national plant and productive capabilities, vindicating President Calvin Coolidge's contention that "the business of America is business." It was an era of the steady expansion of standards of living heretofore limited to the relatively few, standards of living that seemed to some intellectuals vulgar, but that were nevertheless a new thing in the world. Unknown in Europe and envied there, the new lifestyle, vulgar or not, was much desired by nearly everyone. The United States became, in this era, the first true consumer society.

The era ended with the onset of the Great Depression. In 1928 Wall Street had enjoyed an unprecedented boom. Speculators by the millions were playing the market, buying stocks in hopes of quick resale at huge profits. They paid only a fraction of the cost in cash, borrowing the balance from their brokers, and often borrowing the cash investment as well. Not only stocks but houses, furnishings, automobiles, and many other purchases were financed on borrowed money. Credit swelled until it was no longer on a sound basis in a largely unregulated economy. Eventually, shrewd investors began to sell their holdings in the belief that the bubble would soon burst. The result was a self-fulfilling prophecy: a disastrous drop in stock values, beginning in October 1929 and continuing almost without letup to 1933. Both the speculators and the lenders were ruined.

The American stock market crash internationalized the depression, making certain almost no nation escaped it, but the causes of the economic sickness went well beyond this disaster. For a decade, agriculture in America and in Europe had lagged behind the relative or actual prosperity of industry and commerce—prices of farm produce were in 1929 little more than half of what they had been ten years before. Another fundamental element of the European economies, coal, had suffered—perhaps not as gravely but similarly. Competition from petroleum and hydroelectric power, as we have already seen, damaged the world market, while cheaply produced and transported coal undersold that of the traditional producers like Great Britain.

Also significant in understanding the onset and intensity of the depression was the use of credit in the Western economies. Farmers and manufacturers borrowed to finance expansion to meet the demands of wartime. Agriculture and mining were first to feel the result when supply exceeded demand; while industry continued more or less to prosper, farmers and mining companies strained and often failed to repay loans in the face of falling prices. Wage-earning workers in more prosperous sectors of the economy, even in America, gained comparatively slowly in increasing their buying power during the 1920s. Workers often did raise their standard of living by purchasing a house or a car, but they did it on credit, by assuming the burden of long-term installments.

To this should be added the effect of autarky among the great and small powers: Tariff walls were erected around the new nations like Yugoslavia and Poland and made higher among traditional high tariff nations such as the United States and France. Even Great Britain in 1931 began to move away from her customary free trade and toward Joseph Chamberlain's tariff reform vision, although not as fully as some other nations. The effect of this worldwide movement impeded both and, as a consequence, economic growth.

A further cause of the world depression was the interconnection of U.S. loans, reparations, and war indebtedness. The defeated powers, particularly Germany, were expected to pay huge sums to the victorious nations for damages caused by the war. No German government, whatever its affiliation, was enthusiastic to pay or even willing to make an effort to pay fully the enormous sums expected, especially by France and Belgium. The collapse of the German money system in the early 1920s was rectified through the receipt of regular loans from the United States under the Dawes Plan and from private American sources. This system paid for some reparations but also served otherwise to energize the German economy, for only one third of the more than 20 billion marks loaned was paid out in reparations. Hence, when the Dawes loans and private U.S. investments began to dry up in 1928 as American banks began to lose faith in the European economy, the entire financial system of Europe shook. Reparations as well as international war debts to America ceased to be paid, banks teetered and often collapsed, and the credit system of Europe began to sink.

By 1931, Britain abandoned the gold standard—that is, the pegging of the value of the British pound against gold and the willingness of the British government to exchange it for gold—and the value of the pound, the financial standard of the world throughout industrial times, sank. Other currencies followed suit, immediately or later. In fact, the financial crisis had, at least on paper, rendered the wealth of the world considerably smaller.

The New York stock market crash did not itself cause the Great Depression. The unevenness of prosperity, the falsity of the European recovery, the international tariff competition, and much more all came first. The unregulated credit system within the United States, too, had had a decade to do its damage. However, the collapse of the greatest stock exchange in the world, in the most attractive and hence most overheated economy in the world, the economy which was in many ways was the engine of European recovery, ensured that the greatest damage would be done to the greatest number of nations.

The Great Depression was very severe in many countries throughout the world, but nowhere was it worse over a sustained period than in the United States. Its effects may be measured by the figure of 16 million men unemployed at the low point in the early 1930s—something like one third of the national labor force. In terms of gross national product (GNP), one widely accepted statistic for calculating the health of an economy, the figure in 1929 had been cut nearly in half by 1933.

Yet this grave crisis in the American economy produced almost no organized movements of revolt, no threat of revolution. Some intellectuals of the 1930s did indeed turn to "social consciousness," and Marxism made converts among writers and artists. But the bulk of the population did not abandon their fundamental belief that the solution lay in the legal means provided by existing American institutions. Even before the election of President Franklin D. Roosevelt (1882–1945) in 1932, local authorities and private charities did much to soften the worst sufferings of the unemployed. They were helped by the Reconstruction Finance Corporation (RFC), which advanced government credits to release the frozen assets of financial institutions severely affected by the wave of bankruptcies and bank failures. President Herbert Hoover was generally committed to the philosophy of laissez faire, however, and aside from the RFC, his administration did little to cushion the effects of the depression. People who wanted a more vigorous attack on economic problems voted for the Democrats in 1932; significantly, very few voted for the socialist or communist candidates. In the crisis of the Great Depression, the two-party system continued to meet the basic political needs of most Americans.

The New Deal, 1933–1941

Victory seemed to give the Democrats a clear mandate to marshal the resources of the federal government against the depression. Franklin Roosevelt took office on March 4, 1933, during a financial crisis that had closed banks all over the country. He at once summoned Congress to an emergency session and declared a bank holiday. Gradually the sound banks reopened, and the first phase of the New Deal began. In the early months of 1933 the mere fact that a national administration was trying to do something about the situation was a powerful boost to national morale. The nation emerged from the bank holiday with a new confidence, repeating the phrase from Roosevelt's inaugural address that there was nothing to fear but "fear itself."

The New Deal was a series of measures aimed in part at immediate difficulties and in part at permanent changes in the structure of American society. It was the application to the United States, under the special pressures of the Great Depression, of measures that were being tried in European countries, measures often leading to the welfare state.

By releasing the dollar from its tie with gold, the short-term measures of the New Deal aimed to lower the price of American goods in a world that was abandoning the gold standard. They aimed to thaw out credit by extending the activities of the RFC and by creating such new governmental lending agencies as the Home Owners' Loan Corporation. They aimed to relieve unemployment by public works on a large scale, to safeguard bank deposits by the Federal Deposit Insurance Corporation, and to regulate speculation and other stock-market activities by the Securities and Exchange Commission. The National Recovery Act (NRA) of 1933 set up production codes in industry to regulate competition and to ensure labor's right to organize and carry on collective bargaining. The historical significance of many of these innovations rested in the fact that they were undertaken not by private business or by state or local authorities but by the federal government.

The long-term measures of the New Deal were, of course, more important. The Social Security Act of 1935 introduced to the United States on a national scale the unemployment insurance, old-age pensions, and other benefits of the kind that Lloyd George had brought to Britain. By extending and revising tax structures, including the income tax authorized by the Sixteenth Amendment to the Constitution in 1913, Congress in effect redistributed wealth to some degree. Congress also passed a series of acts on labor relations that strengthened and extended the role of organized labor. A series of acts on agriculture regulated crops and prices and provided subsidies on a large scale. And a great regional planning board, the Tennessee Valley Authority, used government power to make over the economic life of a relatively backward area by checking the erosion of farmlands, instituting flood control, and providing cheap electric power generated at government-built dams.

The presidential election of 1936 gave Roosevelt an emphatic popular endorsement. Yet the New Deal never regained the momentum it had in his first term. In retrospect it seems evident that the measures taken by the Roosevelt administration, combined with the resilience of American institutions and culture, pulled the United States at least part way out of the depression. Full recovery, however, did not come until the boom set off by the outbreak of World War II.

The spring and summer of 1939 found Americans anxious to remain neutral if Europe should persist in going to war. Roosevelt and his Republican opponents had been for some time exchanging insults. Yet in the pinch of the international crisis of 1939 it became clear that, although the nation was not completely united, it was not deeply divided. As so often in American history, the violence of verbal politics—in which language is often used with more vehemence than in Europe—masked a basic unity.

When, on September 1, the war came, the United States had already made many efforts to enlist the support of the Latin American states, so that the New World might once again redress the grievances of the Old. In 1930, before the so-called Roosevelt Revolution in American diplomacy, President Hoover's State Department issued a memorandum specifically stating that the Monroe Doctrine did not concern itself with inter-American relations, but was directed against *outside* intervention in the affairs of the Western Hemisphere. The United States was no longer to land Marines in a Central American republic; rather, American policy was to try to strengthen hemispheric solidarity. On these foundations, President Roosevelt built his celebrated Good Neighbor policy toward the other American nations, withdrawing the United States from Cuba and beginning the liquidation of formal American empire.

The old and the new, March 1933: Franklin D. Roosevelt and Herbert C. Hoover on the occasion of Roosevelt's inauguration as Hoover's successor as president of the United States. The outgoing president had seen his once-vast popularity disappear as the Great Depression worsened. Of Roosevelt's plans the nation knew little, other than that many wished for something, almost anything, to be done.   (Franklin D. Roosevelt Library)

The East Meets the West: Western History and World History

The interwar years were marked by a fundamental change in the relations between those nations associated with "Western civilization" and the nations and peoples of Asia and the Middle East, and to a lesser extent, of Africa. Although virtually the whole of the world had been brought into the European and American orbits during the age of imperialism, people in the West had not recognized that the societies of Asia and Africa had histories of their own. Even though the history of the West and that of other parts of the world had impinged upon each other through trade, cultural borrowing, the migration of peoples, and the setting up of empires, the histories of Japan or China, for instance, had not become significant as yet to an understanding of Western history. Now they would become so, and Western history and world history would be virtually indistinguishable.

Japan

Alone among non-Western peoples, the Japanese maintained full political independence during the golden age of imperialism. More than that, as the twentieth century opened, Japan was experiencing the industrial revolution and advancing to the status of a great power, a full (if unwelcome) participant in the struggle for imperial position. Since the Japanese made these impressive accomplishments without radically altering their traditional oligarchical and absolutist political structure, they remained fully "of the East," even as they became an integral part of Western history.

In the decade after World War I, it looked as though Japan might gradually liberalize its political institutions. The cabinets of the 1920s included many businessmen who favored vigorous expansion abroad but who also granted some measure of cautious liberalism at home. The suffrage was gradually extended, for example, and in 1925 all men received the right to vote; women were granted this right in only 1949. For the first time, Western-style political parties began to develop, especially in the cities, and seemed likely to give new vitality to the Diet, the relatively weak Japanese parliament. Trade unions also began to win a following.

However, interwar Japan did not evolve into a parliamentary democracy. By the early 1930s political power was falling into the hands of army and navy officers, many of whom were descended from the feudal samurai class. This officer clique hated the prospect of liberal civilian government and envied and mistrusted the business class. It found a potent political weapon in the institution of the emperor, who was supposed to possess the kind of political infallibility that Westerners had associated with a divine-right monarch. Putting their own words into the emperor's mouth, the admirals and generals used his pronouncements to further their own ends.

The consequence was a military dictatorship in Japan during the 1930s. Although popular elections continued to be held, their results were disregarded; businessmen supported the new regime out of fear or in anticipation of the profits to be secured from its adventures abroad. A cult of emperor worship grew, focusing popular loyalties on the divine mission of the emperor and ensuring popular submission to the will of those who ruled in his name. A corps of ruthless agents, named "thought police," hounded people suspected of harboring "dangerous thoughts." In short, Japan now had a government that exploited many uniquely Japanese traditions but in its operations also bore a striking resemblance to the totalitarian governments of Europe.

Nowhere was the parallel with European totalitarianism more marked than in the foreign policy of Japan between the two world wars. Like Hitler's Germany or Mussolini's Italy, Japan claimed to be a "have-not" nation. The Japanese, too, pointed to their steadily growing population and did all they could to encourage its further growth. Having experienced 125 years of zero growth before 1853—during which time they had improved their standard of living, consolidated their natural resources, and begun to urbanize and accumulate capital—the Japanese were well into a sustained period of economic and population growth. Between 1850 and 1950 (despite the intervening wars) the population soared from 32 million to 84 million. The Japanese, too, harped on the overcrowding of the homeland, its inadequate resources, and its restricted markets.

Behind these arguments lay real economic problems of sustaining the Japanese economy in the face of the depression and the worldwide disruption of international trade, problems of providing food and work for the population, which in 1930 numbered 60 million. In seeking to solve these problems by imperial expansion, the militarists of the 1930s were following a pattern that had already been set by the West. And they were also following the path marked out by the Japanese officers and politicians who had secured Formosa in 1895 and annexed Korea in 1910. During World War I Japan had tried in vain to subjugate China; by World War II it had apparently almost succeeded in doing so.

Korea, once so isolated as to be called the Hermit Kingdom, had first been united in A.D. 668. At various times it was associated with the Chinese empire. Now, from 1910 until 1945, it would be governed by Japan, which changed its name to Chosun. Racism grew in Japan in the 1920s and 1930s, toward Koreans, Chinese, and Westerners, and during the destructive earthquake that swept across the Kanto plain in Japan in 1923, leveling Yokohama and two thirds of Tokyo and claiming 140,000 lives, six thousand Koreans were killed by Japanese in frustration and rage.

China

China, meantime, was engaged in a great struggle to free itself from the hold of the Western colonial powers. The struggle was much more than a simple conflict between nationalists and imperialists. It was complicated by two additional elements in particular—the increasing threat to Chinese independence from an expansionist Japan and increasing communist intervention in Chinese politics. China faced the prospect of simply exchanging one set of imperial overlords for another.

By 1900 the Chinese Empire had lost much of its effective sovereignty through concessions of naval bases and economic and political privileges to the European powers and Japan. Following China's defeat by Japan in 1895, European imperialists had engaged in a hectic scramble for further concessions. A formidable reaction to this outburst of imperialist activity had erupted within China. The hard-pressed Manchu government had encouraged the formation of antiforeign nationalist secret societies, of which the most important was the Fists of Righteous Harmony. Missionaries called this group the *Boxers*, and when they revolted, the name was taken up by the Western press. The result of the Boxer Rebellion of 1900, in which more than two hundred foreigners were slain, was the use of troops by the foreign powers, including the United States, to protect their nationals and property against the Boxers. In 1901 they obliged the Manchu government to pay a large indemnity and to grant them rights that further impaired Chinese sovereignty.

The next Chinese rebellion, the revolution of 1911, was directed against the Manchu regime that had proved so incapable of resisting foreign imperialism. The movement was also directed against the West—against Westerners themselves or against local governors who seemed to be agents of the West.

Asia and the Pacific, about 1910–1926

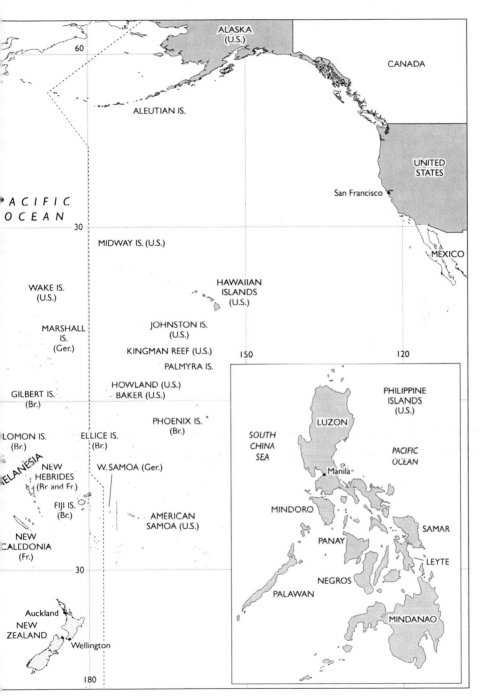

60

ALASKA
(U.S.)

CANADA

ALEUTIAN IS.

UNITED
STATES

San Francisco

PACIFIC
OCEAN

30

MIDWAY IS. (U.S.)

MEXICO

WAKE IS.
(U.S.)

HAWAIIAN
ISLANDS
(U.S.)

MARSHALL
IS.
(Ger.)

JOHNSTON IS.
(U.S.)

KINGMAN REEF (U.S.)

150

120

PALMYRA IS.

HOWLAND (U.S.)
BAKER (U.S.)

GILBERT IS.
(Br.)

PHILIPPINE
ISLANDS
(U.S.)

PHOENIX IS.
(Br.)

LUZON

LOMON IS.
(Br.)

ELLICE IS.
(Br.)

SOUTH
CHINA
SEA

PACIFIC
OCEAN

MELANESIA

NEW
HEBRIDES
(Br. and Fr.)

W. SAMOA (Ger.)

Manila

FIJI IS.
(Br.)

AMERICAN
SAMOA (U.S.)

MINDORO

SAMAR

NEW
CALEDONIA
(Fr.)

PANAY

LEYTE

30

NEGROS

PALAWAN

Auckland
NEW
ZEALAND

MINDANAO

Wellington

180

But it was a movement inspired at least in part by Western ideas and examples and often led by thoroughly "Westernized" Chinese.

From the start, two chief revolutionary groups displayed conflicting ideas about the nature of the new society that would replace the Manchus. One group formed the Nationalist party, the Kuomintang, led by Sun Yat-sen (1866–1925) and many young intellectuals who had studied and traveled in the West. Its leaders wanted a democratic parliamentary republic modeled on the Western political system, while preserving as much as possible the basic Chinese family and village structure, onto which Western industrial society was to be grafted. The other group, whose leader was Yüan Shih-k'ai (1859–1916), wanted a strong central government basically authoritarian in structure, with authority not in the hands of an emperor and the traditional and highly conservative mandarin bureaucracy but in the hands of strong men capable of modernizing China from above.

A struggle for power broke out between the assembly elected after 1911 and Yüan Shih-k'ai. The party of Sun Yat-sen was defeated, and by 1914, after a purge of the Kuomintang members of the assembly, Yüan Shih-k'ai issued a constitutional declaration that put him in the presidential office for ten years. Sun Yat-sen and his followers had failed to turn China into a parliamentary democracy. Yüan, however, died in 1916, leaving the new republic facing the prospect of the dissolution of all but the shadow of central control and the assumption of real power by regional strongmen. A new era of provincial warlords had begun.

In the same years, China also faced the aggressive attempts of Japan to take over the Far Eastern imperial interests of European powers now at war among themselves. Early in 1915 the Japanese secretly presented to the Chinese government the Twenty-One Demands, which amounted to a demand for something close to a protectorate over China. The Chinese republic, now at the lowest point of its strength, countered by declaring war against the Central Powers, thus securing at least the nominal protection of Britain and France. Unable to defy Western objections, the Japanese contented themselves with taking over the German concessions. At the end of the war the victorious Allies, with the United States in the lead, checked the ambitions of their recent military partner. In 1922 Japan was forced to sign a Nine-Power Treaty guaranteeing the independence of China. This rebuff to Japan was one of the first in a long chain of events that intensified the hostility of Japan toward the United States and ended, two decades later, in war.

After World War I, then, the main elements in the Chinese political situation were the Kuomintang, the communists, and the Japanese invaders. After the death of Sun Yat-sen, the Kuomintang came under the leadership of his brother-in-law, Chiang Kai-shek (1887–1975), an army officer trained in Japan. The nationalists of the Kuomintang were engaged in a constant and unsuccessful struggle to set up an effective central government against the provincial warlords. The Chinese communist movement began in the early 1920s. At first it was inspired by direct contacts with the Comintern in Moscow, guided by Soviet agents, and encouraged by leaders of the Kuomintang itself. For a time the Chinese communists were little more than the

Mao Tse Tung at the conclusion of the epic six-thousand-mile Long March from Jianxi to Shanxi between October 1934 and October 1935 to escape entrapment by nationalist forces. Setting out with eighty-six thousand followers (perhaps only a tenth of the original force reached their destination), the young communist revolutionary emerged from the trial as chairman of the Chinese communist party and commander of the Red army. The march marked the beginning of the end of dominance of the Chinese communist movement by European Marxists and also the beginning of the development of Maoist theory. (Franklin D. Roosevelt Library)

left wing of the Kuomintang, but a breach soon occurred between them and the more conservative elements led by Chiang Kai-shek.

The communists did badly in this early struggle for power. In 1926 Chiang's forces began a campaign of persecution and assassination against them; in 1927 they were expelled from the Kuomintang. An important reason for this setback was the failure of the Chinese communists to get effective support from Moscow, for these were the years of the Trotsky-Stalin feud. The conflict between the two Soviet titans was intensified by their differences over the "correct" Chinese policy for the Soviet Union to follow. Stalin, who was rapidly gaining the ascendancy, believed that China was not ripe for a proletarian revolution; therefore, he did nothing to help his Chinese comrades.

Nationalists and communists fought in word and deed for the allegiance, or the passive acceptance, of nearly 500 million Chinese, for the most part illiterate peasants. To transform China into a nation in the Western sense required more than building railroads and factories or promoting the study of modern science instead of the Chinese classics. It required getting the Chinese peasants to regard themselves as Chinese citizens. This indispensable process was beginning in the 1920s and 1930s.

The Japanese attack came in September 1931 in Manchuria, an outlying northern province of China that was a particularly tempting target for Japanese aggression. Manchuria had coal and iron; it adjoined Korea, already a Japanese possession; and it had never been fully integrated into China. Moreover, the Japanese regarded themselves as the natural successors of the Russians, whom they had driven from Manchuria in the Russo-Japanese war of 1904–1905. By 1932 the Japanese were strong enough to proclaim Manchuria the "independent" state of Manchukuo, under a puppet ruler, Henry Pu-yi (1905–1967), who as a child had been the last emperor of old China. The Chinese responded by boycotting Japanese goods; the Japanese countered by carrying the war to the Chinese port of Shanghai. Given the weakness of the Kuomintang government, effective Chinese resistance would have required full support from strong outside forces. Neither the Western powers nor the League of Nations gave China more than verbal support; the Chinese had to give up their boycott, and the Japanese remained in Manchuria. Tensions between China and Japan persisted, and the Japanese soon decided to absorb most of the rest of China. The invasion came in July 1937 without a formal declaration of war.

Militarily, the Japanese did very well. By October, when the key southern Chinese city of Canton fell, they had taken the strategic points along the coastal area and the thickly populated river valleys. Chiang Kai-shek took refuge in the interior province of Szechuan, where he set up his capital at Chungking on the upper Yangtze River. There, with Western aid, the nationalist government held out until the end of World War II and the collapse of Japanese imperialism.

Yet even at the height of their success, the Japanese had achieved no more than the stretching across China of a string of garrisons and the control of great cities like Shanghai and Peking. They held the railroads, subject to guerrilla attack, but away from the relatively sparse lines of modern communication they were helpless. Many Chinese villages in the area that were nominally Japanese never changed their ways during the occupation; nowhere did the Japanese win over the Chinese people.

The nationalists of the Kuomintang led the resistance to the Japanese from the beginning, but they, too, ultimately failed to win the full loyalty of the Chinese people. This was partly a military matter, for Chiang's armies were no match for the Japanese, who controlled the few industrial cities in China. During the long exile in Szechuan, moreover, the morale of the nationalists decayed. The ordeal, far from purifying and strengthening them, emphasized their alienation from the Chinese masses, their own corruption and intrigue, and their inability to live up to the early promise of Sun Yat-sen and the Kuomintang. It was the communists, not the nationalists, who succeeded in the end.

During the 1930s and the early 1940s the relative strength of communists and nationalists underwent a decisive shift. Both parties were in a sense totalitarian. Both were organized on the one-party pattern, which left no place for an opposition. The communists, pursued across much of China during the 1930s, ended up with a base in Yenan in the north; their strategic position somewhat resembled that of Chiang in Szechuan. But there was an important difference. In the long years of Japanese occupation, Chiang remained in Chungking with his army and his bureaucracy. The communists, on the other hand, managed to extend their network of organized armies and local councils in and around the Japanese in the north, and down to the sea and up through Manchuria. By 1945 the communists were ready for their successful conflict with the Kuomintang.

India

In India World War I had marked a crucial turning point. South Asians, growing in numbers and educated in the Western tradition, responded to Allied propaganda in favor of the war to save the world for democracy. Monetary inflation and other war dislocations fostered growing agitation for self-government. Already during the war the British viceroy and his experts were planning reforms. These plans were conditioned by tensions between Hindus and Muslims. About a quarter of the total population of British India was Muslim. In the Indus Basin and part of the Punjab in the northwest and in part of Bengal in the east, the Muslims were a majority; elsewhere they lived scattered among the Hindus and other non-Muslims.

While they might mix socially and in the civil service or the British bureaucracy, Hindu and Muslim felt strong antipathy toward each other, in part on deeply held religious grounds. Muslims opposed idolatry in all forms and felt that Hindu worship of many gods was unacceptable, and that the depiction of those gods in a variety of human, and often explicitly sexual, forms was sacrilegious. To the Hindu, much in the world was divine; the Hindu might worship the cow or other animals, which the Muslim might slaughter. The Hindu regarded Muslim practices as unclean, while the Muslim saw Hindu practices as unholy. It was not surprising, therefore, that after serious attempts to bring Hindu and Muslim into a unified resistance movement against the British, two separate bodies arose in the twentieth century—the Indian National Congress and All-India Muslim League.

Despite these difficulties, the Indian drive for self-government and independence went on steadily after World War I. For the Hindus, the Congress party was held together effectively and given extraordinary influence over the masses by one of the great leaders of the twentieth century, Mohandas K. Gandhi (1869–1948). Gandhi was a member of the *bania*, or shopkeeping caste. Educated at Oxford and therefore familiar with the West, trained in practical politics as a young lawyer serving the Indian minority in South Africa, Gandhi was admirably equipped to deal with both British and Hindus. He devised the technique of insurrection called *Satyagraha*, or nonviolent noncooperation, which appealed to the fundamental Hindu belief that force is illusory and therefore ineffective. A characteristic measure sponsored by Gandhi was the organized Indian boycott of British goods. The Mahatma,

Indian poet and politician Sarojini Naidu with Indian nationalist leader Mohandas Karam-
chand Gandhi—called the Mahatma, or Great Soul—during the Salt March of 1930. The
ostensible motive for the march was to protest the tax on salt levied by the British imperial
government, but the true goal was the end of British rule in the subcontinent, achieved at
last seventeen years later.   (Hulton Archive/Getty Images)

as Gandhi was known, also defied Hindu prejudice, directing some of his
hunger strikes not against the British but against the status of the untouch-
ables as pariahs outside the caste system.

Other Congress leaders, especially at the local level, were willing to imitate
Western methods of agitation, propaganda, and violence. Concession after
concession was wrung from the British, and as the Indians gained political
experience in provincial self-government and in civil service, dominion status was thought to be just around the corner. This was the situation at the outbreak of World War II. By the time the war was over, however, the mutual
antagonism of Hindus and Muslims seemed to require not a single unified

India, but two separate states, which would result in the partition of India in 1947.

The Middle East

The European powers had a long history of attempts to secure an imperial stake in the Middle East. Before 1914 the region was still poverty stricken. But by 1914 the first discoveries of petroleum had been made; today the Middle East contains the richest nations in the world. The whole area was not to share in this new wealth. The major fields were found in southwestern Persia, in the river valleys of Iraq, and along the Persian Gulf. These newfound riches heightened the interest of the European powers, and in the 1930s, as American experts began to worry about the depletion of oil reserves in the Western Hemisphere, American business entered the area to compete with well-established French and British interests.

Although the Westerners tried to maintain sufficient control of the Middle East to ensure the orderly exploitation of oil, they also tried to avoid the cruder sort of political imperialism. After World War I the Arab territories of the old Ottoman Empire were administered as Western mandates, not annexed as Western colonies. The French had received the mandates for Syria and for Syria's half-Christian neighbor, Lebanon. The British, who already held a protectorate over Egypt, were given the mandates for Palestine and Iraq. The only major Arab state enjoying anything like full independence was Saudi Arabia. It was an essentially medieval state, the personal creation of a tribal chieftain, Ibn Saud (1880–1953). The postwar mandates, which brought so much of the Arab world under imperial control, frustrated the aspirations of Arab nationalists. In these nationalist movements the usual ingredients—Western education, hatred of Westerners, desire to emulate Western technology—were mixed with adherence to Islam and a feeling of a common Arab identity.

Arab nationalism was already focused on the special problem of Palestine, for by the Balfour Declaration of 1917 the British had promised to open this largely Arab-populated territory as a "national home for the Jewish people." The immigration of Jews into Palestine, especially after the Nazis took power in Germany, raised their proportion of the population from about 10 percent to about 30 percent and caused repeated clashes between Arabs and Jews. Caught between Jewish nationalism (or Zionism) and Arab nationalism, the British tried in vain to placate both sides. On the eve of World War II, the British restricted Jewish immigration into Palestine and Jewish purchases of Arab lands in the mandate. The seeds were thus sown for the acute Palestine problem of the postwar period.

The French made few concessions to Arab nationalism, infuriating the Syrians by bombarding their capital of Damascus while quelling an insurrection in 1925 and 1926. A decade later the expectations aroused by the Popular Front's willingness to grant at least some independence to Syria and Lebanon were nullified when the French parliament rejected the draft treaties, intensifying the Arab sense of betrayal. Soon nationalist leaders in Algeria and later

The Written Record

DEMOCRACY AT THE VILLAGE LEVEL

Mohandas Gandhi was in pursuit of *Swaraj* (independence), and he wrote of it often. In 1921 he sought to explain "the secret of Swaraj."

The householder has to revise his or her ideas of fashion and, at least for the time being, suspend the use of fine garments which are not always worn to cover the body. He should train himself to see art and beauty in the spotlessly white *Khaddar* and to appreciate its soft unevenness. The householder must learn to use cloth as a miser uses his hoard.

And even when the householders have revised their tastes about dress, somebody will have to spin yarn for the weavers. This can only be done by everyone spinning during spare hours either for love or for money.

Under the pre-British economy of India, spinning was an honourable and leisurely occupation for the women of India. It was an art confined to the women of India, because the latter had more leisure. And being graceful, musical, and as it did not involve any great exertion, it had become the monopoly of women. But it is certainly as graceful for either sex as is music, for instance. In hand-spinning is hidden the protection of women's virtue, the insurance against famine, and the cheapening of prices. In it is hidden the secret of *Swaraj*. . . . The revival of hand-spinning is the least penance we must do for the sin of our forefathers in having succumbed to the Satanic influences of the foreign manufacturer.

Do I want to put back the hand of the clock of progress? Do I want to replace the mills by hand-spinning and hand-weaving? Do I want to replace the railway by the country cart? Do I want to destroy machinery altogether? These questions have been asked by some journalists and public men. My answer is: I would not weep over the disappearance of machinery or consider it a calamity. But I have no design upon machinery as such. What I want to do at the present moment is to supplement the production of yarn and cloth through our mills, save the millions we send out of India, and distribute them in our cottages. . . .

Just as we cannot live without breathing and without eating, so is it impossible for us to attain economic independence and banish pauperism from this ancient land without reviving home-spinning. I hold the spinning wheel to be as much a necessity in every household as the hearth. No other scheme that can be devised will ever solve the problem of the deepening poverty of the people.

M. K. Gandhi, *The Village Reconstruction, by M. K. Gandhi*, ed. Anan T. Hingorani (Bombay: Bharatiya Vidya Bhavan, 1966), pp. 5–7.

| Doing History |

NAMING AND NATIONALISM

One aspect of both modernization and nationalism is to change names that have long been used in a way now regarded as derogatory, false, not properly indicative of the values of the new society, or simply out of date as new forms of transliteration replace old in the West. Instances abound throughout this chapter. The great capital city of China, long known as Peking (and so referred to here), is now Beijing (and will be so called in subsequent chapters) because of the modernization of methods for transliterating Chinese characters and their sounds into English. Persia is now officially Iran, although it is nonetheless still correct to refer to the citizens of Iran as Persians, for one is used as a noun and the other as an adjective.

Thus not only in changing place names, but in their pronunciation, in the creation of titles, in the translation of phrases, history shows its biases and is quickly dated. Even in so apparently simple a matter as the pronunciation of the former British East African colony of Kenya lurks the sound of historical transition, since before independence the colony was pronounced "keen-ya," while the independent nation was properly pronounced "ken-ya." Historians must observe these distinctions if they are to be true to the time they describe.

in Tunisia were discussing with the Arabs of Syria and Lebanon how to make common cause against the French.

The British attempted a more conciliatory policy by granting some of their dependencies nominal independence. In Egypt nationalist agitation after World War I led Britain to proclaim that country an independent monarchy under King Fuad I (1868–1936). The British, however, still retained the right to station troops there. They also insisted that Westerners resident there be under the jurisdiction not of regular Egyptian courts but of mixed courts, on which Western judges outnumbered Egyptians. In 1936 an Anglo-Egyptian agreement provided for the eventual end of the mixed courts and the eventual withdrawal of British troops from the country, except along the Suez Canal. Meanwhile, Egypt continued to be closely allied with Britain.

Turkey, too, was undergoing a political renaissance. World War I reduced its territory to a cohesive national unit, the largely Turkish-populated Anatolia. To defend this core against further losses to the Greeks and to the victorious Allies, the Turks launched an ardent nationalist revival, dramatically extending the reforms begun by the Young Turks before 1914. The leader of this new political revolution was the gifted army officer Mustafa Kemal (1880–1938), who drove the Greeks from Anatolia and negotiated more favorable terms with the Allies at Lausanne in 1923. Under his guidance, the republic of Turkey was proclaimed in 1922, with a constitution modeled on Western parliamentary lines, although with a one-party system.

Kemal also imposed rapid, wholesale, and sometimes ruthless measures of Westernization. Women received the vote, began to serve as deputies in the parliament, and were, at least in theory, emancipated from Muslim restraints, although even Kemal did not dare to sponsor legislation banning the wearing of the veil in public. He did, however, require men to wear Western garb. The sacred law of Islam was replaced by a European law code; polygamy was banned and civil marriage required; the Western calendar was introduced; and the building of new mosques and repair of old ones were discouraged. The Turkish language was reformed by the introduction of a Western alphabet—a measure of major importance, for only a fraction of the Turkish people had ever been able to master the old Ottoman Turkish, with its heavy content of Persian and Arabic words and its difficult Arabic script. All Turks were now required to take surnames in the Western manner, and Kemal himself took that of "Atatürk" (Father of the Turks). At his death in 1938 Atatürk had revolutionized his country. Moreover, he had established its independence of the West, as the neutrality of Turkey during World War II was soon to demonstrate.

The example of Turkey was followed by the other traditionally independent major state of the Middle East—Iran (Persia). The Iranian revolution began in 1905–1906 in response to imperialist encroachments by Britain and Russia. The political structure inherited from the Middle Ages was changed into a limited monarchy with an elected parliament. This revolution proved to be abortive, however. The country, with its powerful, wealthy landlords, its peasants, and its tribes, did not adapt itself readily to modern Western political institutions. The shah was unwilling to give up his traditional powers, and the British and Russians were unwilling to give up their spheres of influence. During World War I, therefore, they both stationed troops in an ostensibly neutral Persia.

The Russian Revolution eased the czarist threat to Persian sovereignty, and at the end of the war Persian nationalists forced their government to reject a British attempt to negotiate a treaty that would have made the country a virtual British protectorate. The leader of the nationalists was Reza Khan (1878–1944), an able army officer of little education who deeply distrusted the Russians. He used his military successes to become, first, minister of war and then, in 1923, prime minister. Thereafter he tried to manipulate the *Majles,* or parliament, to his purposes, and he won the support of the army and the cabinet. After conferring with the clergy in the holy city of Qum, the forces of Islam also fell into line behind him. In 1925 the Majles deposed the Qajar dynasty and proclaimed Reza to be Reza Shah Pahlavi. Reza Shah lacked familiarity with the West, and his erratic attempts to modernize his isolated country often failed. He ruled in increasingly arbitrary fashion, also demonstrating mounting sympathy for the Nazis. In 1941, after Hitler's invasion of the Soviet Union, the British and Soviets sent troops into Iran and forced Reza Shah's abdication in order to secure the important trans-Iranian supply route to the Soviet Union.

The fate of Reza Shah was a reminder that some of the seemingly sovereign states of the non-Western world were not yet strong enough to maintain their independence against great powers. By World War II imperial ties had been loosened but by no means severed or dissolved; the full revolution against imperialism was yet to come.

SUMMARY

Great Britain was the first nation to suffer from the ills of postindustrial development. In the postwar period Conservatives wanted to preserve private industry and advocated protective tariffs against foreign competition. Labour called for nationalization of key industries.

Political democratization continued in Britain with all men over age twenty-one receiving the vote. Women over age twenty-one finally gained equal voting rights in 1928. A slight economic recovery in the later 1920s was followed by the Great Depression.

By 1919 Irish nationalists were demanding complete independence from Britain rather than home rule. In 1921 the twenty-six southern countries became the Irish Free State, while the six Ulster counties remained tied to Britain. Although Britain recognized the full independence of the Republic of Ireland in 1949, the problem of Northern Ireland remained.

France felt the impact of the war most heavily, both in terms of casualties and material damage. In the 1920s, as the rebuilding effort got under way, France suffered severe inflation as well as other economic and social dislocations. Political divisions inherited from the French Revolution resurfaced in postwar France.

Rocked by economic and political difficulties, French governments compromised with Hitler and Mussolini despite protests from the left. In 1939 France was poorly equipped militarily and psychologically to deal with the threat of war.

People in the French colonies of Algeria, Senegal, and Indochina demanded home rule or independence. The French mandates of Syria and Lebanon were given constitutions but not independence.

In the postwar period, the isolationist mood of the United States was reflected in its tariffs and in the policy of imposing quotas to limit immigration. Nevertheless, the United States was still involved in European and world affairs in the 1920s.

At home, the uneven prosperity of the Coolidge years and the unprecedented speculation on Wall Street ended with the stock market crash of 1929. The Great Depression was worse and lasted longer in the United States than elsewhere. Franklin D. Roosevelt introduced the New Deal to ameliorate conditions. Yet full recovery did not occur until the outbreak of World War II.

A liberalizing trend that occurred in Japan after World War I ended in the 1930s when the military acquired political power and imposed a military dictatorship. As in Italy and Germany, the Japanese regime embarked on an expansionist policy, claiming the need for living space, resources, and new markets.

In 1911 a revolution toppled the Manchu regime in China. China struggled to free itself from Western imperialist powers but was distracted by an internal conflict between nationalist and communist forces and by the threat of Japanese expansion. In 1931 Japan attacked Manchuria and in 1937 invaded China proper.

Indians agitated for self-government in the 1920s and 1930s, but irreconcilable differences between Hindus and Muslims prevented a united front. Gandhi, leader of the Congress party, advocated nonviolent noncooperation, which appealed to many Hindus.

In the Middle East, European powers were anxious to protect access to petroleum deposits. The mandate system that continued European control in the region frustrated the hopes of Arab nationalists. Although Egypt became independent, Britain had the right to keep troops there. In Turkey, Mustafa Kemal imposed wholesale Westernization. In Iran, Reza Shah's attempt to modernize rapidly met with only limited success.

SIX

The Second World War and Its Aftermath

In history nothing of consequence "just begins." Many developments are causes, and most are also effects—and so it is with the Second World War. This second conflagration of the twentieth century was in many ways a result of the unsuccessful peace settlement at the end of World War I, but it was also brought about by the economic dislocation of the interwar years and by the Great Depression itself. It was also made possible—even probable—by centuries of racism and xenophobia, by frustrated militarism in the totalitarian states, and even by well-meaning empathy among the democracies. So troubled were international relations for the twenty years after 1919, and so closely in time did the World War II follow on the first, that the interval between the two is sometimes called the "twenty years' truce." It is likely that historians in the distant future will consider the two wars really as one conflict, as they now consider the wars of the French Revolution and Napoleon essentially one war; but for the present, most historians continue to deal with them as a First and a Second World War—as World War I (1914–1918) and World War II (1939–1945).

International Politics Between the Wars

During the first part of the twenty years' truce, international leadership of the democratic world rested with Britain and France. Although supported in principle and at times in practice by the United States, they were increasingly unable to stem the rise of powers hostile to their preferred form of government—Italy, Germany, the Soviet Union, Japan. In the end, Germany once more waged aggressive warfare against the major Allies of 1918, although this time it was allied with two former enemies, Italy and Japan, each disappointed with its share of the spoils of 1918.

Nazi Germany maintained that the second war was the direct result of what its leaders called the "dictated peace" of Versailles. Supported by many sympathizers, the Nazis claimed that Germany was humiliated by the "war-guilt"

clause, stripped of territories and colonies, saddled with an unpayable reparations bill, and denied the normal rights of a sovereign state in armaments.
The settlement of Versailles did saddle the new German republic with a heavy
burden—a burden that was dictated in part by revenge and fear. With hindsight, a wiser Allied policy would perhaps have been to start the new government off without too great a burden. But hindsight is not history.

The West

The great hope for peace in Europe in this period was what came to be known
as "collective security," the belief that tranquility could be guaranteed
through the commitment of the many to come to the aid of any victim of
aggression. This faith lay behind the language of the League Covenant and
virtually all of the many international conferences of the 1920s—the series of
treaties signed at Locarno in Switzerland in 1925 being a textbook example.
Inspired by the German foreign minister Gustav Stresemann (1878–1929) and
embraced by his British and French counterparts, Austen Chamberlain
(1863–1937, eldest son of Joseph Chamberlain) and Aristide Briand
(1862–1932), the Locarno agreements were the crowning glory of this so-
called "era of fulfilment". They were meant to demonstrate German trust-
worthiness and acceptance of the borders on her western frontier with France
and Belgium created at Versailles. Along with these three, Britain and also
Mussolini's Italy signed as guarantors, promising to send military aid in any
defense against aggression by any other signatory. Germany assured the
French and Belgians that they had nothing to worry about, the French
affirmed a new moderation in their policy toward Germany since the fiasco
of the Ruhr occupation, and Britain and Italy seemed to pledge their commitment to peace among their neighbors. Collective security appeared to be
an achievable goal, and for several years people spoke of the "spirit of
Locarno" while statesmen hoped (fruitlessly, as it turned out) that Germany
might be induced to accept a similar agreement to guarantee her borders with
Poland and Czechoslovakia.

Ostensibly, the Locarno settlement endured for several years. It was nourished by the general prosperity of the French and the Germans and by the
policies of their respective foreign ministers. In 1926 Germany was admitted
to the League of Nations, an event that seemed to signify not only its restoration to international respectability but also its acceptance of the peaceful purposes of League membership. These hopeful impressions appeared to receive
confirmation when Germany signed the high-minded but impractical
Kellogg-Briand Peace Pact to outlaw war of 1928. In 1929 the French consented to withdraw the last of their occupation troops from the Rhineland by
1930, thus ending the Allied occupation of Germany at a date considerably in
advance of the one stipulated in the Versailles Treaty.

Although not a member of the League, the United States took a leading
part in furthering one of the League's chief objectives—disarmament. Meeting in Washington during the winter of 1921–1922, a naval conference of the

major sea powers achieved an agreement establishing a ten-year "holiday" in the construction of capital ships (defined as battleships and heavy cruisers). A conference at London in 1930 had less success in limiting noncapital ships, including submarines. The partial failure of the London naval conference was a portent. Two years later, after long preparation, the League itself convoked a meeting to address the problem of limiting military armaments. Not only League members but also the United States and the Soviet Union sent representatives to Geneva. This World Disarmament Conference of 1932, however, accomplished nothing.

By 1932 the Locarno spirit was dead, and the era of fulfillment had ended. One obvious explanation was the worldwide depression that had begun in 1929. In Germany the depression was decisive in putting Hitler in power. In the democracies, too, it had serious consequences for the peace of the world, since the depression sapped their morale and made them less confident. In any case, even when the era of fulfillment was most successful, there had been clear warnings that appearances and reality did not fully coincide. Despite all hopes to the contrary, the Germans remained unwilling to accept a Locarno-style settlement of their eastern frontiers, for no German politician of any party would ever acquiesce publicly to the Polish corridor that cut through East Prussia. Hopes of European collective security for the French had been replaced by reliance on a renewed alliance system and on a massive system of defensive fortifications, the so-called Maginot line (named for André Maginot, the war minister under whose leadership it was begun), on their frontier with Germany. The Germans, for their part, had begun a secret collaboration with the Soviet government to bypass the Versailles restriction on armaments.

Another unsettling factor was Soviet Russia. The West regarded it as a revolutionary power that could not be fully integrated into the international state system. The Soviet Union was the center of a revolutionary faith hated by Western politicians. Westerners simply could not trust a government that was based on the Marxist belief that all Western capitalist democracies were destined to collapse and become communist after a violent class war.

Yet another factor that led to World War II was the continuing failure of the three major Western democracies—Britain, France, and the United States—to present a united front. Although each was a capitalist and a democratic state, the nature of their governments differed. The United States had widely diverse ethnic communities that traced their origins to Europe and took different positions on the problems emerging there. Britain and France were often at cross-purposes within the League of Nations, and the United States, not being a member, could exercise only modest influence in bringing them together.

France, exhausted and suffering a decline in population, was trying to play the part of a first-rate power with only second-rate resources, and it lived in growing fear of a revived Germany. The French sought not only to apply in full the economic and political measures of the Versailles Treaty that aimed at keeping Germany weak but also to make up for Russia's defection as its eastern ally against Germany. Beginning in 1921 France did this by making alliances with the smaller states to the east of Germany—Poland, Czechoslovakia, Romania, and Yugoslavia. All except Poland were informally linked together as the Little Entente. To British politicians who remembered the long story of Anglo-French conflicts from the Hundred Years' War to Napoleon, the France of the 1920s seemed once more to be aiming at a dominant place in Europe.

Some advocates of "splendid isolation" had survived the war and made the British unwilling to commit themselves to intervene with force in Continental Europe. Although Britain did accept Locarno and its commitment to punish any violator, in the previous year the dominions had played a large part in British rejection of the more sweeping Geneva protocol, which would have committed its signatories to compulsory arbitration of international disputes. Pacifist sentiment in Britain and the dominions further strengthened the German perception that Britain would not resist limited aggression on the Continent.

The difficulties of the Anglo-French partnership partly explain the weakness of the League of Nations. One example of how the grand purposes of the League suffered from Anglo-French friction was the rejection of the Geneva protocol—which London worried would in the end depend entirely on British enforcement—supported by the French and killed by the British. Another occurred in 1923, when Mussolini, in a dispute with Greece, attacked and for a time occupied the Ionian island of Corfu in defiance of the League. In addition, the League had no means to enforce its decisions, and it was top-heavy, since the fully representative Assembly counted for less than the smaller Council, which Britain and France dominated. When these two powers disagreed, the League scarcely operated at all. During the Corfu crisis the League was crippled by Anglo-French discord over the Ruhr policy of France. After 1935 Germany was engaged in what some historians have called a "unilateral armaments race," while two of the greatest nations in the world, the United States and the Soviet Union, were generally absent from the overall balance of power.

Soviet Foreign Policy

In 1919 Lenin founded the Third International, known thereafter as the Comintern. It summoned communists all over the world to unite against the "bourgeois cannibals" of capitalism. Gregory Zinoviev was put in charge, and his chief assistants were mainly Russians. Labor, socialist, and anarchist parties in Bulgaria, Norway, Italy, and Spain began to adhere to the new organization, although some idealists withdrew in disgust when it became clear that the Bolsheviks were establishing a dictatorship in Russia through their secret police and army. Yet the Comintern continued to operate side by side with the Soviet foreign office, and during the next few years often in apparent contradiction to it. This duality gave Soviet foreign policy a unique and at times unpredictable character.

Treaties were concluded between the Soviet Union and Poland, the Baltic states, Scandinavia, Germany, and Italy, exchanging trade for a promise not to interfere in the domestic affairs of these states. While binding on the Soviet foreign office, these agreements did not, in reality, affect the Comintern. In 1922 the Soviets were invited to an international economic conference at Genoa. The British and French assumed that NEP meant a return to capitalism, and they worked out a scheme for investment in Russia. Not only did the Soviets reject this plan, but they signed the Treaty of Rapallo (April 1922) with defeated Germany, which provided for the renunciation of all claims for reparations and implied a German willingness to recognize Bolshevik nationalizations of industry. The other powers, especially France, were unwilling to grant such recognition because of the large investments they had in Russia before the revolution.

In 1923 at Lausanne Russia lost a dispute with Britain over international regulation of the Straits, and further friction with Britain arose over Afghanistan. But Britain recognized the Soviet regime in 1924. Many members of the Labour party, while aware of the bloodshed in Russia, had great admiration for the rapidity with which Lenin was modernizing Russian society. Later in 1924 the so-called Zinoviev letter was published in England, which purported to instruct the British Communist party in the techniques of revolution. It was probably a forgery, but the Zinoviev letter influenced the British voters to turn MacDonald's Labour party out of office and elect Baldwin's Conservative government. In 1927 a raid on the offices of a Soviet firm doing business in London produced further evidence of communist agitation in England, and the British government broke relations with the Soviet Union altogether. The United States, meantime, had no diplomatic relations with the Soviet regime and did not recognize it until Roosevelt became president in 1933.

During 1918–1927 the Comintern compiled a record of failure. First, the Soviet Union failed to restrain the Italian left in 1921 and thus contributed to the success of Mussolini in the next year. Next, its failure in Bulgaria to collaborate with a liberal agrarian regime allowed a right-wing group to triumph in 1923. Most important, it failed in Germany, where a revolution actually threatened in 1923 as a result of French occupation of the Ruhr.

The Soviets also failed in Poland, where they helped Pilsudski gain dictatorial power in 1926, after which he turned against them. They failed in the Muslim and colonial world. But their greatest failure came in China, where in 1923 the Chinese nationalist revolutionary leader, Sun Yat-sen, agreed to take communist advice and received one of the Comintern's best men, Michael Borodin (1884–1953). Borodin helped Sun reorganize the Kuomintang and admit communists to it. In March 1926, Sun having died, Chiang Kai-shek led a coup against the government and began to arrest communists. Stalin now fell back on a theory that the Bolsheviks had not espoused since Lenin's return to Russia in April 1917–that a bourgeois revolution must precede a socialist revolution, and that all the communists could do in China was to help Chiang achieve this first revolution. The eventual result was the massacre of Chinese communists by Chiang and a loss of prestige for the Soviet Union.

Stalin had apparently never really believed in the effectiveness of the Comintern as an instrument of world revolution. When he came to power he could not abandon it, however, because of the criticism he would have aroused and because he sought to dilute and eventually to eradicate the Trotskyite sentiments of some communists in other countries. He therefore applied to the Comintern the same techniques he had used against the party at home, and used the Soviet delegation to establish full control over it. The Comintern was thus influenced to denounce the enemies of Stalin: Trotsky and the left in 1924, Bukharin and the right in 1928. Thereafter, there was no divergence between the Comintern and the foreign office.

Stalin then directed the Comintern into a new period of militant revolutionary activity. The Social Democrats of Western countries were now denounced as "social fascists" and the most dangerous enemies of communism. Yet Stalin's personal belief in the possibility of worldwide revolution seems always to have been slight. This lack of interest in the behavior of communists abroad led directly to the triumph of Hitler in Germany in 1933. The communists in Germany, who had been instructed by the Comintern that the Social Democrats and not the Nazis were their worst enemies, fought the Nazis in the streets but allied themselves with them in the Reichstag. They believed that a Nazi triumph would very soon be followed by a communist revolution. Thus even after Hitler came to power, the Soviets renewed their nonaggression pact with Germany.

The shock of realization that Hitler had meant precisely what he said about liquidating communists and the fear that the Soviet Union itself might be in danger soon led Stalin to support collective security. After Hitler had refused to guarantee the Baltic states jointly with Stalin, the Soviet Union entered the League of Nations in September 1934. The Soviet delegate, Litvinov, became an eloquent defender of universal disarmament and of punishment for aggressors. Soon afterward, the Soviets began to negotiate for an "eastern Locarno" security pact to balance the agreement reached by the western European nations. Although no such structure could be created because of Polish and German hostility to the USSR, the Soviet Union did sign pacts with France and Czechoslovakia in 1935 providing for consultation under the terms of the League and for mutual aid in the event of aggression. However, Soviet aid to Czechoslovakia, if the Czechs became victims of aggression, was to be delivered only if the French, who were bound to the Czechs by an alliance, honored their obligations first.

With the shift in Soviet foreign policy, the Comintern also shifted its line. In 1935 the communists' recent enemies, the Social Democrats and bourgeois liberals of the West, were embraced as allies against the fascist menace. Communists were to join popular fronts against fascism and might welcome anyone, no matter how conservative, who would stand with them on this principle. Revolutionary propaganda and anticapitalist agitation were to be softened.

The Soviet Union and the western European bloc each assumed that the chief purpose of the other was to turn the full force of Hitler's forthcoming attack away from itself and in the opposite direction. That Hitler intended to attack, few doubted. On September 12, 1936, he specifically declared:

> If I had the Ural mountains with their incalculable store of treasures in raw materials, Siberia with its vast forests, and the Ukraine with its tremendous wheatfields, Germany under National Socialist leadership would swim in plenty.[*]

There was, then, much reason for the West to hope that the attack would be directed against the Soviets; this Stalin was determined to avert.

Soviet intervention in the Spanish Civil War demonstrated Stalin's real position. General Francisco Franco had obtained aid from Mussolini and Hitler. The Soviets, although reluctant to intervene in Spain because of their anxiety to prove their respectability to the Western powers, realized that a failure to help the Spanish republic would cost them support all over the world. But their aid of "volunteers," money, and arms came too late. The Soviets hoped that the Western powers would also intervene, but Western neutrality in Spain helped convince Stalin that a Western alliance could not be counted on.

Still more important was the Western appeasement of Hitler, which reached its climax in the Munich agreement among Britain, France, Germany, and Italy in September 1938. From the Soviet point of view, Munich's grant of Czech lands to Hitler and the French failure to support Czechoslovakia and thus make operative the Russo-Czech alliance could have only one purpose—to drive Hitler east. Stalin was apparently ready to support the Czechs if the French did; when they did not, he apparently decided that he had better sound out Hitler for an understanding. Thus a truly effective alliance between Stalin and the West proved impossible between 1935 and 1939.

When the British and French realized that appeasement had failed to stop Hitler, they reluctantly sought a firmer alliance with the Soviets. From March to August 1939, Stalin kept open both his negotiations with the West and his slowly ripening negotiations with the Germans. The British and French mission, when it finally arrived in Moscow, was not composed of sufficiently high-ranking men to inspire Soviet confidence. Moreover, the Western powers would not agree to turn over to Stalin the territories that he wanted as a bulwark against Germany—Finland and the Baltic republics.

The growing eagerness of the Germans to secure a nonaggression pact gave Stalin his opportunity to divert war from the Soviet Union. In May 1939 Litvinov was dismissed as foreign minister because he was Jewish and therefore could not negotiate with the Germans; he was replaced by Vyacheslav Molotov (1890–1986). In the pact that Molotov eventually reached with Hitler on August 23, 1939, each power undertook to remain neutral toward the

---

[*]Adolf Hitler, *My New Order*, ed. Raoul de Roussy de Sales (New York: Reynal and Hitchcock, 1941), p. 400.

other in the event of war. A secret additional protocol provided for a division between Germany and the Soviet Union of Poland, which Hitler was about to attack; this put the Soviet Union's frontier farther west in the event of a subsequent German attack.

The publication of the Hitler-Stalin pact necessitated an abrupt shift in the world communist line. Now it was once more necessary for communists to denounce liberals and Social Democrats as enemies and to call the war that Hitler launched against Poland within a few days an "imperialist war," in which there was no difference between the two sides in which communists should not get involved. Thus Soviet foreign policy, especially under Stalin, was one major avenue in the road to the war that erupted in September 1939.

The Road to War, 1931–1939

By the mid-1930s, many commentators believed that a second world war was inevitable. A series of interconnected events, in China and Ethiopia, in Germany, Austria, and Spain, and sometimes faltering responses by Britain, France, the United States, and other nations, brought full-scale war ever closer. Between 1931 and 1939, these events precipitated the world once again into war.

A First Step: Manchuria, 1931

The first decisive step along the road to World War II was the Japanese seizure of Manchuria in 1931. Henry L. Stimson (1867–1950), President Hoover's secretary of state, responded to the seizure by announcing that the United States would recognize no gains made by armed force. Stimson hoped that Britain and the other democracies might follow this American lead, but his hopes were largely disappointed. The League of Nations did send a commission headed by the earl of Lytton (1876–1947); the Lytton Report of 1932 condemned the Japanese act as aggression. Neither the United States nor the League, however, fortified its verbal protests by effective action. Japan, refusing to accept the report, withdrew from the League of Nations in March 1933. One useful result of the crisis was that it caused the British to give up their "ten-year" rule, in place since 1919 and mandating that no major war need be anticipated for ten years from the current date.

A Second Step: German Rearmament, 1935–1936

The next breach in the League's structure was made by Germany; in October 1933 Hitler revealed his self-confidence and his willingness to take risks. First, he withdrew from the League. In March 1935, much more happened: Britain reversed her long-time policy of trusting to diplomacy to guarantee security and published a *White Paper on Defense*, revealing plans for rearmaments. Hitler, throwing aside his Versailles obligations, announced first the existence of the air force Germany was not supposed to have (but had been planning and building since the Weimar years) and, a week later, revealed legislation to raise a large conscript army.

The response to these illegal acts by the *Führer* set the pattern for the next few years. On 17 April the League condemned Germany's repudiation of treaty obligations—which in no way deterred German rearmament; and a few days earlier the former Allied powers, Britain, France, Italy, and Belgium, met at Stresa in Italy to discuss the situation. They agreed in what the press called the "Stresa Front" to cooperate and remain in watchful and close communication, although each lacked faith and confidence in the others. Such suspicion seemed to some observers to be borne out when in May the French signed a unilateral alliance with the Soviet Union against German aggression—and still the Germans continued to rearm. In June the British signed a naval agreement with Germany limiting the German navy to one third the total size of the British and the German submarine force to 60 percent of that of Britain (Hitler could not hope to build a surface fleet of that size and meant to build as many submarines as he wished, when he wished). The Stresa Front was riven with distrust: The British and French exchanged suspicious glances, an anxious Belgium began to edge again toward official neutrality (a step taken in 1937), and Mussolini reconsidered his options.

The next risk Hitler ventured was even more provocative: the "reoccupation" by German troops in March 1936 of the demilitarized Rhineland on the French border—in violation once again of the Versailles pact. Many of his generals thought the *Führer* had gone too far this time and waited for the crash. It never came, as the still essentially pacific democracies did nothing.

A Third Step: Ethiopia, 1935

A subject that was much on the minds of the British and French ministers at Stresa was the small and isolated state of Ethiopia (then called Abyssinia). Ethiopia had remained independent largely because its imperial neighbors—Britain, France, and Italy—would neither agree to divide it nor let any one of the three swallow it whole. Technologically, politically, and economically it was *in* but hardly *of* the twentieth century at all: It was an absolute monarchy without real suffrage or parliament, emperors often came to power through intrigue and assassination, and slavery was still common while literacy was not. Yet, it had threatened no other nation, and, very importantly, it was a member of the League of Nations. Ethiopia was under threat from the ambitions of Mussolini, master of neighboring Italian Somaliland—and the British and French saw no reason to antagonize him as they tried at Stresa to tie him to their cause (and keep him divided from his fellow fascist, Hitler).

In 1934 a frontier incident occurred at a desert post in Italian Somaliland—or in Ethiopia, for both sides claimed the site. France and Britain were ready to appease Italy, partly because they hoped to align Mussolini with them against Hitler. In October 1935, the *Duce*'s troops invaded Ethiopia. Over the protests of the Ethiopian emperor, Haile Selassie (1892–1975), in December they secretly offered Mussolini what came to be called the Hoare-Laval pact (named for the British and French foreign ministers at the time), which would have given the dictator much Ethiopian territory and control over the rest.

The semblance of a technically independent kingdom had to be maintained as it remained a member of the League. Mussolini was prepared to accept, but news of the draft treaty leaked to the Paris and London press and spawned widespread righteous indignation in Britain and a more mixed reception in France. To save face, Mussolini denied the entire episode and continued the military operation; in early 1936 the king of Italy acquired the coveted title of emperor of Ethiopia. Only Germany among the great states dared express public approval—within a year Mussolini would take Italy out of the League and would announce the formation of the Rome-Berlin Axis.

The League of Nations had already formally condemned the Japanese aggression in Manchuria and the German denunciation of the disarmament clauses of the Treaty of Versailles. In 1935 it promptly declared that, by invading Ethiopia, a League member, Italy had violated its obligations under the Covenant of the League. Now the League made the momentous decision to move from words to deeds. This decision was supported by most of its members and was urged on by the British, the French, and most movingly in a speech delivered to the League in Geneva by Haile Selassie, speaking in Amharic, the language of Ethiopia, while Italian fascists hissed and booed. On October 11, 1935, fifty-one member nations of the League voted to invoke Article 16 of the League Covenant, which provided for economic sanctions against a member resorting to war in disregard of its commitments.

But the sanctions against Italy failed. There were loop-holes; oil, for instance, was not included in the list of articles barred from commerce with Italy, which had only meager stockpiles of this vital war material. There was much recrimination among members of the League over what articles should be placed on the prohibited list and over the British and French failure to check Italian movements of troops and munitions through the Suez Canal, which Britain then controlled. Germany was no longer in the League and was wholly unaffected by its decisions. No major power applied sanctions rigorously, so that the effectiveness of economic sanctions was not really tested. The League was hardly a factor in the increasing tensions, and no one was surprised when Italy, like Japan and Germany, withdrew from the League in December 1937.

A Fourth Step: The Spanish Civil War, 1936–1939

The Spanish Civil War, which broke out in July 1936, was the emotional catalyst that aroused millions of men and women all over the Western world. The war pitted fascists, monarchists, and conservatives of the right against socialists, communists, anarchists, and a few liberals of the left. As in most great civil wars, there was really no center. It was a quasi-religious war, waged with the great violence that marks wars of principle. Almost from the very start it engaged the emotions of the West through individual foreign enlistments and the active though covert intervention of other nations.

The Spanish Civil War proved to be a rehearsal for the larger war that was approaching, as the fascist nations tested their weapons. One of the first deliberate aerial bombardments of a civilian population took place in April 1937, when low-flying planes, apparently German, devastated the Basque town of Guernica. Intervention by Italy and Germany was decisive and effective; it was less determined and effective by communist Russia; and it was feeblest of all by Britain and France. Early in 1939, with the fall of Barcelona, the civil war was over, and once more a fascist-leaning group had won.

A Fifth Step: The Marco Polo Bridge, 1937

The war between China and Japan had fallen into a lull when, on the night of July 7, 1937, a skirmish between troops of the two nations at the Marco Polo Bridge near Peking led to full-scale war once again. Later it would be claimed by both parties that the other had instigated the renewed conflict, although only the Japanese had reason to do so. A united anti-Japanese front had taken shape in China. An incident between Japanese and Russian forces on the Amur River the month before had made it clear that the Soviet Far Eastern army need not be feared, and a wave of nationalism in both China and Japan escalated mutual hatreds beyond the capacity of politicians to control them.

As first Peking and then Shanghai fell to the Japanese, the Chinese government appealed to the League of Nations. Sanctions would work only if the United States joined in them, but the American secretary of state suggested "parallel" rather than "joint" action with Britain, and President Roosevelt, although clearly opposed to Japanese advances in the Far East, called for a "quarantine" of aggressor states. But following a Japanese attack on the American gunboat *Panay* on the Yangtse River, the Americans appeared ready to discuss joint Anglo-American economic action. However, by then Britain wanted a political and military agreement that went further than the United States was prepared to go.

A Sixth Step: Anschluss, 1938

The immediate origins of World War II lay, however, in a mounting series of German aggressions. Hitler had begun openly rebuilding his armed forces in 1935, and in a secret meeting with his commanders on November 5, 1937, he revealed his plans. He made clear that his two greatest potential enemies, Britain and France, eventually would have to be dealt with. More immediately, he meant to have Austria and Czechoslovakia, and, regardless of what he considered the timidity of some of his generals, he was quite willing to face the great democracies in war to accomplish this end.

Ever since 1918 there had been a strong movement in Austria for some sort of union, or *Anschluss*, with Germany. Union of any sort was expressly forbidden by the 1919 peace treaties, and this movement had been particularly opposed by Italy and France. In 1934 Austrian Nazis had attempted a clumsy *putsch*, and Mussolini had shown his displeasure by dispatching troops to the Brenner Pass. The Stresa Front had come to nothing, but the remilitarization of the Rhineland, German support of the invasion of Abyssinia, and the Rome-Berlin Axis of 1936 were hard facts that made it easier for Mussolini to accept Anschluss.

Early in 1938 the Austrian-born Hitler was ready to act: He began a violent propaganda campaign by press, radio, and platform against the alleged misdeeds of the Austrian government. In February 1938 he summoned Austrian chancellor Kurt von Schuschnigg (1897–1977) to Berchtesgaden to make his threats, and in March Hitler moved his troops into Austria without meaningful resistance. Austria lost its independence and its name, becoming the Reich province of Östmark.

A Seventh Step: Czechoslovakia Dismembered, 1938–1939

The Czechoslovak republic was the only state in central or eastern Europe where parliamentary democracy had succeeded after World War I. It had inherited some of the most highly developed industrial regions of the old Habsburg Empire; consequently, its economy was far better balanced between industry and agriculture than were those of the other states of eastern Europe. This healthy economy was mirrored in the social structure, where a working balance was maintained among peasants, middle classes, and industrial workers. But the Czech government could not keep the country from ultimately being destroyed by outside pressures working on its sensitive minorities. The Sudeten German minority of 3.25 million looked down on the Slavic Czechs and resisted the new republic. From 1933 on, Nazi agitation became increasingly serious in Czechoslovakia.

Early in 1938, having secured Austria, Hitler made demands on the Prague government for what amounted to complete Sudeten autonomy. On September 12 he made a violent speech at Nuremberg, insisting on self-determination for the Sudeten Germans. This was the signal for widespread disorders in Czechoslovakia, followed by the proclamation of martial law by the government of Czech president Eduard Beneš (1887–1948). The successor to Baldwin, Neville Chamberlain (1869–1940), the second son of Joseph Chamberlain and brother of Austen Chamberlain, was convinced that only he could save the peace. In September 1938 he proposed to Hitler that he personally visit Germany to settle the Czech controversy. This the sixty-nine-year-old prime minister did twice, with, he thought, mixed success. Hitler became agitated and adamant, insisting that the Reich must have the Sudetenland; Chamberlain was equally adamant that the breakup of Czechoslovakia was preferable to European war but that Hitler must accept that it had to be done by peaceful means. Finally, Chamberlain was allowed (with the help of Mussolini, who was in Hitler's confidence) to "convince" the *Führer* to agree to a four-power conference to settle the matter. On September 29, 1938, Hitler, Mussolini, Chamberlain, and Édouard Daladier (1884–1970) of France met in Munich. No Czech representative was present at the meeting.

Munich was a sweeping victory for Hitler. Czechoslovakia was partially dismembered; its Sudeten borderlands were turned over to Germany; the Czechs were obliged to hand over Teschen and other areas to the Poles; their entire economy and transportation system were weakened; the defense of their frontiers was made impossible by the loss of the border mountains and their fortifications. Slovakia was given autonomy within a federal state, emphasized by the official change in spelling from Czechoslovakia to Czecho-Slovakia.

The Czech leaders had found it impossible to resist the Germans without French and British aid, and their people acquiesced bitterly in the settlement of Munich. The Germans had played skillfully on the differences between the more industrialized Czechs and the still largely agricultural Slovaks. But even had the country been strongly united, Munich would have ruined its morale. Hitler acted quickly. In March 1939 Hitler sent his army into Prague and took over the remaining Czech lands, meeting no real resistance. Hungary, anxious to reclaim some of its lost territory, occupied Ruthenia, the eastern most province of Czechoslovakia, with German consent.

The best defense that can be made for Munich and appeasement is that the West was either genuinely trying to avoid war or that it was buying time to prepare for a war that it knew to be inevitable but for which it was not yet ready. In September 1938 the democracies were in a stronger military position relative to that of Germany than they would be in September 1939. It is also true that Chamberlain, unlike Daladier, believed that German demands were based on not unreasonable complaints that could be traced back to the flawed peace of 1919; even worse, he proposed to negotiate with Hitler as he would with any statesman—a grotesque mistake. The British and French prime ministers were in agreement, and millions all over the world apparently agreed, in hoping that the acquisition of the Sudetenland would satisfy Hitler and Germany. Some Westerners even hoped that Hitler might join with them against communist Russia, or get himself so entangled in eastern Europe that he would bring on a Russo-German war. Hitler's words and deeds, however, had given no real basis for such hopes. As early as November 1937 he had announced to his close advisers his unalterable intention of destroying Czechoslovakia and moving on into Poland and the Ukraine.

The actual destruction of Czechoslovakia in March 1939 seems not to have surprised anyone. But the mixture of resignation, condemnation, and resolution with which this action was greeted in the West marks a turning point. The days of appeasement were over, as Britain and France made clear their intentions to guarantee the borders of Poland, and Britain started a peacetime draft. Nazi leaders made no secret of their feeling that the British and French were decadent, inefficient, and too cowardly to resist an inspired and rejuvenated Germany. Yet there is evidence that Hitler expected at least a local war with Poland, and that he was quite prepared to confront the French and the British if need be. Hitler had strengthened his system on May 22 by concluding an offensive-defensive "Pact of Steel" with Mussolini, who only six weeks before had conquered Albania. Both nations obviously intended further aggression.

The Final Step: Poland, 1939

Poland was clearly going to be Hitler's next victim. The Germans regarded the Polish Corridor dividing East Prussia from the rest of Germany as an affront; so, too, was the separation from Germany of the free city of Danzig, German in language and tradition, on the edge of the Polish Corridor. On March 23, 1939, Hitler took the port town of Memel from Poland's northern neighbor, Lithuania. At the end of the month, the British and French responded by assuring Poland of aid in the event of a German attack. It is unlikely that Hitler believed that they would live up to such a pledge.

The critical issue in the tense half year that led up to the outbreak of war on September 1, 1939, was whether Poland would undergo the same fate as Czechoslovakia and receive no support from the Western democracies. The British government made it clear that it would back away no longer. The critical issue now was the attitude of the Soviet Union. Hitler had an understandable fear of a war against major powers on two fronts. But the Soviets deeply distrusted the British Tories under Chamberlain. This mistrust was not dispelled by a diplomatic mission that Britain and France sent to the Soviet Union in the summer of 1939. The Western powers proposed a mutual assistance pact, but the negotiations were inept and halfhearted and the British negotiators lacked high rank. Hitler, who was also negotiating with the Soviet Union, put Foreign Minister Ribbentrop himself on the job. The Anglo-French overture to Moscow came to nothing; the Soviet leaders had apparently concluded that if they did not come to terms with Hitler, he would attack them.

To the horror of the West, on August 23, 1939, Stalin signed a nonaggression pact with Hitler. On September 1 the German army marched into Poland. On September 3 Britain and France honored their obligations and declared war on Germany. The democracies had not been able to halt a dedicated, ruthless, organized state. Since the Great Depression the Western democracies had been committed to helping their citizens attain minimum standards of material comfort; normally they would produce butter before guns. Their totalitarian opponents, on the other hand, were able to convince or intimidate their people to agree that butter was to be attained in the future by making use of the guns if need be. They had persuaded their citizens to go without for the sake of military preparations; democratic states would find it difficult to get such sacrifices from their people until the war had actually begun.

World War II, 1939–1942

Since military experts tend to prepare for the last war in planning for the next, both France and Germany in the 1930s built confronting lines of fortifications on their common frontier. The Maginot line on the French side and the

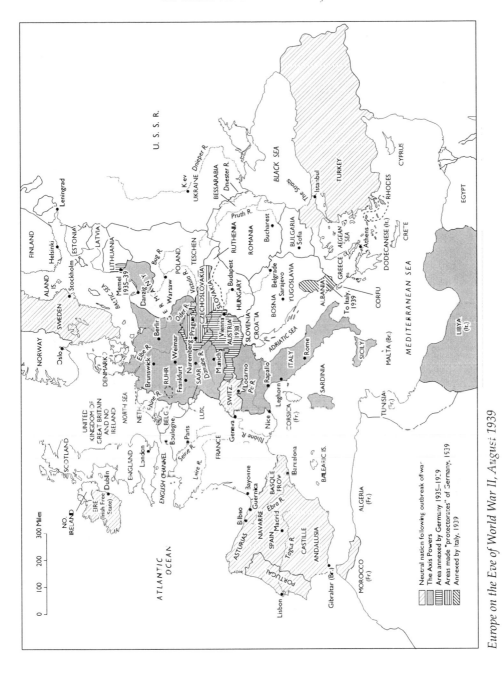

Europe on the Eve of World War II, August 1939

Neutral nation following outbreak of war
The Axis Powers
Area annexed by Germany 1935–1939
Areas made "protectorates" of Germany, 1939
Annexed by Italy, 1939

Hitler and Mussolini appear in an open car before cheering crowds in Munich on September 29, 1938. This follows the signing of the accords with Britain and France that ended the existence of the Republic of Czechoslovakia and yet failed to guarantee what British Prime Minister Neville Chamberlain called "peace in our time." (National Archives)

Siegfried line on the German were far more formidable than were the trenches of 1914 to 1918. With the outbreak of hostilities, most people expected that the war would be decided primarily in the area between France and Germany, and that it would be a closely confined war, perhaps quite brief with at most only diversionary activity in other parts of the world.

But as Germany was joined by its Axis partners, Italy and Japan, and as the United States entered on the Allied side, World War II became much more fully a world war than World War I had been.

In 1939 Germany was ready for war, but neither France nor Britain was fully prepared. Moreover, Germany did not need to fight on two major fronts, since the pact with Stalin had neutralized the Soviet Union. However, France, which had held only one front in World War I, now had to maintain troops along the Spanish and Italian borders to guard against an attack by those nations. Still, German success was predicated on a quick victory; otherwise, the United States might once again be drawn into the war, the British would gain time to supply their troops and resources from their dominions, and the obviously superior British navy would begin to close off German food supplies.

On land, the German forces were undoubtedly superior. They were better equipped than either the French or British. Still, the French army's reputation was excellent, and the German leaders saw the defeat of France as their essential first task. Because the French were known to be especially weak in tanks and antiaircraft defense, the Germans turned to the ideal combination—massive use of tanks in close cooperation with aircraft, especially the Stuka bomber, which could divebomb enemy positions.

German plans all focused on moving rapidly by means of the *blitzkrieg*, or "lightning war." This became even more true when Mussolini declared himself to be a "nonbelligerent." No one doubted that he stood behind Germany, but it was thought that he would not actively commit his troops to the war. For Britain and France, ultimate victory rested on delay, forestalling a quick German victory until their lack of preparation could be offset by control of the seas, superior industrial production, and the support of world opinion, which, they felt, would be in their favor. The Soviet Union remained unpredictable and might be turned around. If Hitler did have to fight a real war on two fronts, the *Wehrmacht* (armed forces) might be bled deeply and long enough to weaken its western thrust. While this did not seem probable in 1939, this is what did, in fact, happen; as the Soviet, or eastern, front wore down Germany's forces, a successful invasion of occupied France became possible by 1944.

On all fronts aerial bombardment—toward the end of the war carried on by German pilotless aircraft and rocket missiles—brought the horrors of warfare to urban civilians. Military experts had been inclined to believe that civilians could not possibly stand aerial bombardment and that any country whose cities were subject to sustained bombardment would be obliged to sue for peace. Yet European and Asian civilian populations endured months of attack; German civilian deaths from air bombardment alone have been estimated at about 500,000. Organized systems of shelter and partial dispersal of populations enabled the people of heavily bombed cities like London, Berlin, and Tokyo to endure what were in effect front-line conditions.

At the very end of the war, a technical innovation was introduced that radically altered the character of war. This was the atom bomb, developed in secrecy by American, Canadian, and British experts, with scientific support from German and Italian refugees. It was first used by the United States on the Japanese city of Hiroshima on August 6, 1945; one single bomb destroyed something over half that city. Somewhat less damage was done by a second and different bomb dropped on Nagasaki three days later. More than 100,000 people were killed in the two cities by the two bombs.

Early Successes of the Axis

The first campaign of World War II reached its expected conclusion. No one had seriously expected isolated Poland to stand up for long against the German and Soviet armed forces or expected Britain and France to act rapidly enough to help their Polish ally decisively. Yet the speed of the German con-

The Written Record

WINSTON CHURCHILL'S LEADERSHIP

One skill of the highest value to leadership is the ability to inspire others with one's own example, and with one's oratory. Winston Churchill was a superb writer and public speaker. On May 13, 1940, he gave the House of Commons his fearsome prescription for victory.

I would say to the House, as I said to those who have joined this Government: "I have nothing to offer but blood toil, tears and sweat," We have before us an ordeal of the most grievous kind. We have before us many, many long months of struggle and of suffering. You ask, what is our policy? I will say: It is to wage war, by sea, land and air, with all our might and with all the strength that God can give us; to make war against a monstrous tyranny, never surpassed in the dark, lamentable catalogue of human crime. That is our policy.

You ask, what is our aim? I can answer in one word: It is victory, victory at all costs, victory in spite of all terror, victory, however long and hard the road may be; for without victory there is no survival.

In Britain's darkest hour, when Hitler's troops had reached the English Channel and Britain's last continental ally, France, had collapsed, Churchill rallied the British people to a remarkable and united war effort.

We shall fight on the beaches, we shall fight on the landing grounds, we shall fight in the hills; we shall never surrender, and even if, which I do not for a moment believe, this island or a large part of it were subjugated and starving, then our Empire beyond the seas, armed and guarded by the British Fleet, would carry on the struggle, until, in God's good time, the New World, with all its power and might, steps forth to the rescue and liberation of the Old.

From Hansard, *British Parliamentary Debates*, House of Commons, June 4, May 13, 1940.

quest surprised almost everyone. The Luftwaffe (air force) soon gained absolute command of the air and used it to disrupt Polish communications and to spread terror with its dive bombers. Special fully motorized German task forces swept through the less mobile Poles.

Hitler's collaborator, Stalin, hastened to invade Poland from the east; he also occupied and then annexed the Baltic republics of Estonia, Latvia, and Lithuania. Fear of Germany and an imperialistic desire to expand also drove the Soviets into a war with neighboring Finland in November 1939. The Soviets, who had perhaps miscalculated the strength of the Finns, did rather badly at first. For a time the British and French considered massive aid to the Finns. By March 1940, however, Soviet forces had worn down the Finns; they secured bases and annexed Finnish lands that were close to Leningrad. This "winter war" with Finland helped push Hitler toward the fateful decision in 1941 to make war on the Soviet Union, for German military experts concluded from Soviet difficulties that an easy victory would be possible.

In April 1940 the Germans secured their northern flank. Without declaring war, they invaded neutral Denmark and Norway by sea and air. Denmark, totally unprepared, was occupied almost without resistance. Norway, also unprepared but favored by rugged terrain, put up determined opposition. Neither the British nor the French could help with more than token forces, and by the end of April Norwegian resistance had been broken. A puppet government was installed under the Norwegian fascist Vidkun Quisling (1887–1945), thus introducing into the English language a synonym for *traitor*. The Germans now had excellent bases for air and submarine action against the British.

For eight months following the declaration of war, the great democracies did not directly and fully engage the Wehrmacht—there appeared to be much sitting and waiting, while Hitler and Stalin gobbled up the periphery. This inactivity was nicknamed the "Phony War" by the British, wondering anxiously when the real war would begin. The great blow was struck without warning on May 10, 1940. The German armies invaded the Low Countries and thus bypassed the Maginot line. Both the Belgians and the Dutch had been anxious in the 1930s to avoid compromising themselves by planning for joint resistance with Britain and France against a possible German attack. They were now to suffer the full consequences.

Through the Ardennes hills on the Franco-Belgian border, the Germans poured their best motorized troops into France. In a blitzkrieg that once more capitalized on the lessons of 1914, the Germans resisted the temptation to drive at once for Paris, but instead pushed straight through northern France to the English Channel, where the port of Boulogne fell on May 26, a little more than two weeks after the start of the campaign. By this stroke the Germans separated the British, Belgian, and a large part of the French troops from the main French armies to the south.

Meanwhile, in Britain Chamberlain had resigned. He was succeeded as prime minister by Winston Churchill (1874–1965). Chamberlain was neither a man of action nor an appealing or heroic figure; Churchill was to prove himself all this and more.

In despair, the British and French attempted to pinch off the German motorized thrust by a concerted attack from north and south. But the Belgians, badly disorganized, decided to surrender, and neither the French nor the British could rally themselves to carry out the movement. In the last days of May, when the German army failed to finish them off when they had the British bottled up, the British withdrew by sea to England from the beaches around Dunkirk at the northern tip of France. With protection from the Royal Air Force, an extraordinary flotilla of all sorts of vessels, including private yachts and motorboats, got the men out, although most of their equipment had to be abandoned.

The explanation of why German forces did not press their advantage at Dunkirk remains unclear. There is some reason to believe, as some historians do, that Hitler himself favored sparing the British forces trapped on the coast because he believed that Britain was no longer a real threat—perhaps even that the island nation might be induced to withdraw from the war. However, a respite in the attack seems to have been ordered first not by the *Führer* but by the German field commanders, and when the assault was pressed after two days, the British perimeter was secured and the "miracle of Dunkirk" of May 26–27 was accomplished: the evacuation to Britain of more than 224,000 British and 110,000 Allied troops—although all heavy equipment had to be abandoned. This all concerned the Germans relatively little, as Belgium surrendered on May 28, and the Wehrmacht began their great push toward Paris. The French army was unable to mount a defense, and the Germans marched southward almost unopposed. On June 13 the French government fled the capital, declaring Paris an open city. It fell to the Germans on the following day.

The battle of France was thus decided by mid-June 1940. But the French might still have tried to defend the south or, failing that, used their navy and merchant marine to get as many troops as possible across the Mediterranean into French North Africa, where they might have continued the fight against the Germans with British aid. Some French leaders, of whom General Charles de Gaulle (1890–1970) was the most vocal, wished to do this. To persuade them to do so, Churchill made France the extraordinary offer of a complete governmental union of the two countries to continue the struggle. But his offer was not accepted.

It continues to be difficult to define how and why France fell so easily. The German armed forces were formidable, but France, too, had a great army and a large air force. Much of the collapse had to do with the poor quality of the French high command, political as well as military, particularly when contrasted with the careful planning and execution of battle by the German commander, Karl Gerd von Runstedt (1875–1953). Much of Germany and all of her army had for twenty years been focused on one goal—expunging the shame of 1918. France, however, had the burden of three generations of political, moral, social, and class division in the Third Republic; seventy years of frequent scandal, chronic instability, and bureaucratic ennui; and (like all of Europe) a decade of economic dislocation—all in the republic that since 1871 had satisfied neither the right nor left. The fall also had to do with the fact that many in France feared and hated Bolshevism more than they did Nazism—with the fact that some in France believed that perhaps Hitler was essentially right. Perhaps most of all it had to do with the horrible sacrifices of 1914–1918, with the horrible devastation of their country and with the millions dead and wounded in the last war against the Germans. Many Frenchmen had been haunted for twenty years by the telling phrase of 1917: "Never again." Whatever the reasons, France had been defeated in a month.

On June 16 French premier Paul Reynaud (1878–1966) was supplanted by the eighty-four-year-old hero of the last war, Marshal Henri Pétain

(1856–1951). Pétain and his colleagues were determined on peace at any price, and on June 22, 1940, an armistice was signed at Compiègne. By this armistice the French withdrew from the war, handed over three fifths of France, including the whole Atlantic and Channel coasts, to German occupation, and retained only the central and Mediterranean regions under strict German supervision. "Unoccupied France" was ruled from the little resort city of Vichy, where Pétain set up an authoritarian, antidemocratic state of which he was chief. His government was known simply as Vichy France.

Some of Pétain's supporters were pro-German. But most of them were sure that Hitler had won the war and were coming to terms with what they regarded as the inevitable German total victory. They did not believe that Britain could successfully resist the German war machine that had defeated France. Their army was demobilized, and their navy either immobilized in France or scattered among North African ports. The situation of Vichy France was extremely delicate and ambiguous, and the problem of who collaborated and who resisted the Germans would plague the French nation for years after the war was over.

Even in the dark days of June 1940, a few French patriots led by Charles de Gaulle refused to give up the fight. With British aid, de Gaulle set up a French National Committee with headquarters in London. A nucleus of French soldiers taken off the beach at Dunkirk, plus a stream of refugees who left France in the next few years, made up the Free French, or Fighting French. Back in France, a secret Resistance movement gradually formed to prepare for eventual liberation. While North Africa, strongest of the French colonial areas, was controlled by Vichy, some of the colonies rallied to the Free French from the start. Although weak, the Fighting French were at least a rallying point. They set up an effective radio center in England from which they conducted a propaganda campaign against Vichy and the Germans, beamed across the Channel to the homeland.

On June 10, 1940, Mussolini brought the Italians into the war against France and Britain, too late to affect the outcome of the battle of France. This "stab in the back," as Franklin Roosevelt called it, further outraged American opinion. Italy was anxious to secure some kind of success that would offset the great gains of its German ally. The war, up to this time confined to northern and western Europe, would soon spread to the Mediterranean.

The Battle of Britain

The Germans had not really worked out a plan for dealing with Britain. Hitler seems to have believed that with France out of the war, Britain would make a separate, compromise peace in which Germany would dominate the Continent of Europe and Britain would retain its overseas empire. Mixed with his hatred for England was a misleading idea that Germany and England were natural allies. Unlike France, there were no natural allies available to him in Britain, however. Britain had interned all German subjects in the country (including Jewish refugees) and had locked up nearly eight hundred

members of the British Union of Fascists, including their leader, Sir Oswald
Mosley (1896–1981). For more than four centuries Britain had gone to war
rather than accept one-power domination over western and central Europe
or a hostile occupation of the Low Countries.

Hitler was counting heavily on the possibility that German submarines
could eventually cut off British supplies of food and raw materials from overseas and thus starve it into submission. But this would take a long time, and
Hitler was impatient. The obvious thing to do was to attempt a landing in
England; however, the Germans had made no real preparation for amphibious warfare and had no specially designed landing craft. A hastily assembled
flotilla of miscellaneous vessels was badly damaged by British aircraft, and
early in August 1940 Hitler and Göring, his air marshal, made the fateful
decision to try to do the job solely with air power.

The Battle of Britain that followed had two main phases. First, in August
and early September, the Luftwaffe attempted in daylight raids to wipe out
merchant ship convoys, Royal Air Force bases, and aircraft on the ground.
The Germans shortsightedly mounted only a few attacks against the installations of the new early warning *radar* (from "radio detection and ranging")
system. Then in early September the Germans changed their tactics to wide-
ranging bombing of the city of London itself: This was the "Blitz," meant both
to terrorize the civilian population and to punish British resistance. On September 17 Hitler postponed indefinitely "Operation Sea-Lion," his invasion
plan. Germany still had enormous air-strike capacity, but his air force had
sustained huge losses and failed to win air superiority. This was the "nation's
finest hour," as described by Churchill, that exceptionally effective wartime
leader and master at stirring national pride. Although air attacks would continue against Britain until 1942, the aerial Battle of Britain was over. Night
bombings continued throughout 1940, but even in the especially hard-hit
industrial city of Coventry, where the historic cathedral was targeted and
destroyed, industrial production capacity was not seriously diminished. Nor
did civilian morale break in the cities. Rather, if anything, the night bombings
strengthened the British will to resist.

Equally crucial during the battle of Britain was the battle of the Atlantic,
since it was essential that convoys from North America bringing needed supplies get through to Britain. The British navy proved equal to the task, shep-
herding convoys across the ocean, sweeping harbors of mines floated in by
the Germans, and seeking out the highly effective German submarines.
Shipping losses for the British rose alarmingly through 1940 and into 1941.
Unable to destroy the German submarines by aerial bombing, the British
began to hunt them down at sea using radar. The German surface navy initially operated along the French coast and in the Indian Ocean, but it was
beaten back from the Atlantic when the heavy battleship *Bismarck* was sunk
in May 1941 by a combined air and cruiser attack. Thereafter the British controlled the surface of the sea, while the Germans still prowled beneath the
waters. Although Allied and neutral shipping losses ran to 23 million tons

during the war, radar, sonar, escort carriers, and destroyer groups effectively neutralized the German submarine advantage.

The Mediterranean and Soviet Campaigns

Hitler now faced the possibility of a long stalemate. He turned at first to the strategy of getting at Britain through its Mediterranean lifeline to India and the East. His ally Mussolini invaded Greece from Albania in October 1940 without informing Hitler. The Greeks pushed the Italians back halfway across Albania, but the Germans rescued Mussolini.

Just how far Hitler himself wanted to invest in the Mediterranean is not clear. Certainly he toyed with the idea of a campaign against the British fortress of Gibraltar through Spain. But Franco wanted too high a price from the French for his consent to a German march through Spain, and Hitler was unwilling to risk driving Vichy France, which still controlled French North Africa, too far. The Germans had to be content with backing up Mussolini in Greece and attacking Egypt from the Italian colony of Libya. Their efforts to organize local action against the British and French in the Middle East were suppressed without grave difficulty by British and Free French troops in Syria.

The German commitment to help the Italians in Greece took valuable German divisions away from another task in the spring of 1941. Although Hitler forced on the frightened government of what remained of Yugoslavia a treaty allowing German forces free passage across Yugoslavia to Greece, a Serbian uprising overthrew the Yugoslav regime, and thereafter the Germans had to combat guerrilla resistance and to dismember Yugoslavia. The British did their best to back up their Greek allies, but once more they were not strong enough. German air power crippled British naval power in the Mediterranean, and by May the Axis had conquered the Greek mainland. The British defeat appeared total, but in fact the Germans had invested far too much armament in the Balkan campaign.

The other task for which the German forces were needed in the spring of 1941 was the conquest of the Soviet Union. Hitler had firmly resolved not to engage in a war on two fronts. Yet by his invasion of the Soviet Union on June 22, 1941, he committed himself to just such a war. The Soviet Union was indeed a tempting goal. The Nazi plan had always looked to the fertile areas of Poland and southern Russia as the natural goal of German expansion. After the successful blitzkriegs in Poland, western Europe, and now Greece, Hitler and his military experts believed that they could beat the Soviets in a single campaign before winter set in, a view British and American military advisers privately shared. Once the Soviet Union was conquered, the Germans would have little trouble disposing of Britain.

In addition, Stalin had engaged in the brief "Winter War" with Finland between November 1939 and March 1940. Although ultimately victorious, neither the Soviet armies nor their commanders had performed well in seizing and holding territory from the small and underpopulated Finland. This did not go unnoticed in Berlin, which suggested to the *Führer* that a quick defeat of the Russian colossus might be relatively easy.

Furthermore, Hitler had returned to his old suspicion of Bolshevism. He knew that Stalin had agreed to the pact with Germany for opportunistic reasons, and that the Soviet Union might well change sides in any event. The pact had destroyed Poland, the natural wall between the two enemies. And the Soviet Union had already been expanding in ways that reinforced Hitler's distrust. In June 1940 Stalin had demanded of Romania the province of Bessarabia, and also northern Bukovina. The Germans had expected the Soviet seizure of Bessarabia, but not of northern Bukovina; they permitted the seizure, however, telling the Romanians that they could expect no help from Hitler. But that was as far as Hitler's cooperation with Stalin in eastern Europe went. The reannexation of Bessarabia had given the Soviets the mouth of the Danube, controlling an important artery. The Soviets seemed to be moving into southeastern Europe, a region in which the Germans were not prepared to let them operate alone.

Only a few weeks after the Soviet seizure of Romanian territory, Hitler asserted his own southeastern interests by forcing the Romanians to cede territory to Hungary and then guaranteeing the new Romanian frontiers, a guarantee that could apply only against the Soviets. Soon afterward German troops appeared in Finland, "to reinforce the German armies in Norway," Hitler explained. And in the autumn of 1940 German troops entered Romania proper "to guard the Romanian oilfields against British sabotage." These maneuvers on his new frontiers deeply disquieted Stalin. Then in October 1940 Italy attacked Greece, and the war spread to the Balkans; German troops moved into Bulgaria, which the Soviet Union regarded as essential to its own defense. With Germany established in Yugoslavia and victorious in Greece by May 1941, Stalin knew that an invasion of the Soviet Union was logically next.

The Soviet Union was not conquered, but Hitler's plan, "Operation Barbarossa," almost worked. There was a successful blitzkrieg; within two months the Germans were at the gates of Leningrad, and by the end of October they had conquered the Ukraine. Soviet losses rose into the millions of killed or captured. In sheer distance, the German armies had pushed more than twice as far as they had in France. Yet as the Russian winter closed in, the Germans had taken neither Moscow nor Leningrad. Much Soviet heavy industry had been transferred to the remote Urals, and existing plants there and in Siberia had been strengthened. The vast resources of the Soviet Union were still adequate for Soviet needs. The government had not collapsed, and national spirit was high. Moreover, the Germans had shown once more, as they had in the battle of Britain, that their planning was far from perfect. Their troops were not sufficiently equipped to withstand the rigors of a Russian winter. Confident that the summer and autumn would be sufficient to finish the campaign, the German planners had left the winter to take care of

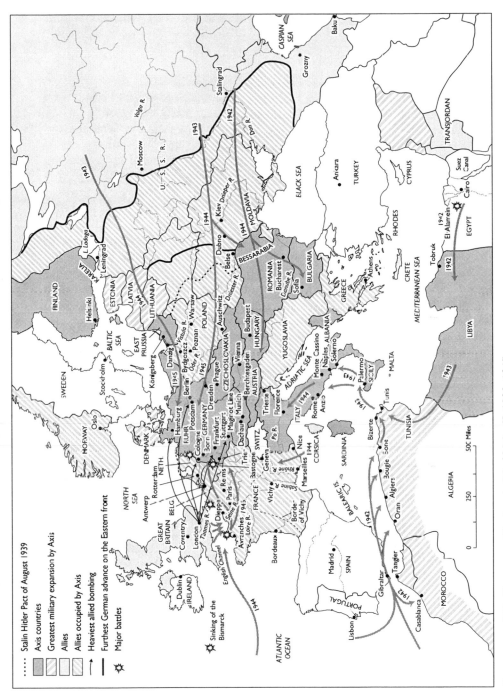

European and Mediterranean Theaters in World War II, 1939–1945

itself. In winter fighting between December 1941 and May 1942, the Soviets regained much useful ground.

The United States Enters the War

Although the United States had a strong isolationist element and some Nazi sympathizers, American opinion had, from the very beginning of the attack on Poland in 1939, been far more nearly unanimous against the Germans and Italians than it had been against the Central Powers in 1914. With the fall of France in 1940, anti-Axis sentiment grew stronger, reinforced by a growing belief that if Hitler won in Europe, the United States would be his next victim. It was also true that very few Americans favored U.S. entry into the war. Still, by the end of 1940, Americans accepted the nation's first peacetime military draft.

Between June 1940 and December 1941, the Roosevelt administration, with the consent of Congress and with the general backing of American public opinion, took a series of steps "short of war" to aid Britain and later the Soviet Union. The American government transferred fifty "overage" destroyers to the British in exchange for Atlantic naval bases in British colonies, supplied the British with arms, and used the American navy to help get these supplies across the Atlantic. Above all, in March 1941 by the Lend-Lease Act, the United States agreed to supply materials needed for defense, including food, to "any country whose defense the President deems vital to the defense of the United States." Supplies at once began flowing into Britain and later to other anti-Axis powers. Also in early 1941 U.S. and British military staffs were engaged in secret talks over coordination, should the United States enter the conflict.

In 1936 Germany and Japan had concluded an Anti-Comintern Pact, agreeing to assist each other in case of aggression by the Soviet Union. In March 1939, as he prepared for European war, Hitler had pressed the Japanese emperor, Hirohito (1901–1989), to join a tripartite alliance with Germany and Italy, but the Japanese estimated that they would not be ready for a Pacific war before 1942. Hirohito agreed to a military alliance with Hitler, provided that Japan need not enter a general war until it felt strong enough to do so. Hitler rejected the latter provision. In September 1940 the two nations agreed that if the United States attacked Germany, Japan would come into the war. But the three-nation Axis would not be truly formed until Japan moved its timetable forward and struck at the United States in December 1941.

Meanwhile, the Japanese took advantage of the fall of France and the Netherlands and of the weakness of Britain. They penetrated into French Indochina (Vietnam) by agreement with Vichy France, even as they continued to press their campaign on the mainland of China. The American government continued to oppose what it considered Japanese aggression. The Japanese government fell increasingly into the hands of military leaders who felt that war with the United States was inevitable and who preferred to strike before the American democracy could fully prepare itself. Had the

Bomb damage at Hickham Field in Hawaii on December 7, 1941, in President Roosevelt's words a "day of infamy."   *(Franklin D. Roosevelt Library)*

United States been willing to back away from its persistent opposition to Japanese expansion, the war in the Pacific could perhaps have been avoided, but the Americans remained adamant.

In the summer and autumn of 1941 the American government took steps to freeze Japanese credits in the United States, to halt Japanese access to raw materials, and to get the Japanese to withdraw from China and Indochina. Negotiations toward these ends were going on between the Japanese and Americans when on December 7, 1941, the Japanese struck the American naval base at Pearl Harbor in Hawaii. Grave damage was inflicted on ships and installations, but American power in the Pacific was by no means destroyed. Moreover, the "day of infamy" produced almost unanimous support in the United States for the immediate declaration of war against Japan. Germany and Italy honored their obligations to their Axis partner by declaring war against the United States on December 11. As 1942 began, the war was literally a world war.

It has been asserted that Roosevelt and his political advisers had deduced the Japanese plan and essentially allowed the attack to go forward in order to ensure American entry into war against Japan as well as Germany. It is true that American cryptographers in an operation code-named *Magic* had begun to break the cipher of the Japanese diplomatic service, but this was in its early stages and there had been no hint that Pearl Harbor was a target, nor December 7 the appointed day. Although it is true that America was not as prepared at this vulnerable point as was prudent—the military commanders in Hawaii, for example, were not kept fully informed of Magic decoding conclusions, and word that the Japanese meant to break diplomatic relations did not reach Pearl Harbor until after the attack—there is no credible reason to believe that the Roosevelt administration engaged in any such conspiracy.

War with Japan was officially declared the day following the attack on Pearl Harbor. The understandable confusion of those who wondered how these events effected the European war was soon cleared away, as three days later Germany and Italy declared war on the United States in support of their Japanese ally. A notorious breaker of treaty obligations, Hitler chose to honor the German-Japanese-Italian Tripartite Pact of 1940, and it proved to be a mistake of incalculable proportions equaled only by his decision to attack the Soviet Union.

Although the United States was far better prepared now than in 1917, it was still at a disadvantage. Against Germany, it could do no more than increase its aid to Britain and the Soviet Union and take part in the struggle against German submarines. Against Japan, the United States was almost as powerless. Its Pacific outposts of Guam, Wake Island, and the Philippines fell in rapid succession. Nor could the British and the exiled Dutch governments protect their colonies in Southeast Asia, which the Japanese had also attacked. By the spring of 1942, with the fall of Singapore, the Japanese had forced the largest surrender of a British army in history. They had acquired Indonesia from the Dutch, possessed the oil of Borneo and the rubber of the Malay States, and had virtual control of Siam (Thailand) and Burma.

The Japanese attack on Pearl Harbor had been made possible only by close coordination of air and sea forces. They had attack bombers close to Australian shores, and they had dramatically demonstrated during their rapid conquest of the Malay peninsula that they dominated the seas at least to the mid-Pacific. Public opinion was particularly shaken when the only British capital ships east of Suez, the battleship *Prince of Wales* and the cruiser *Repulse*, were destroyed in the Gulf of Siam by Japanese air attack. The Americans, who understood that they were to carry the primary responsibility for the Pacific war, realized that they must turn the Japanese navy back if their own aerial strike forces were to be able to enter Far Eastern waters.

Victory for the United Nations

There were several turning points in the struggle thereafter. The earliest was a series of naval actions in which Japanese expansion was stopped. In these actions, carrier-based American airplanes played a decisive role. On May 7, 1942, in the battle of the Coral Sea in the southwest Pacific, Allied sea and air power halted a possible Japanese invasion of Australia and its protecting islands. In June American sea and air power dispersed a Japanese fleet that was seeking to conquer Midway Island. Although the Japanese landed on

American territory at Attu and Kiska in the Aleutian Islands of Alaska, they never seriously threatened Hawaii or the mainland.

In Europe the Americans and the British were not yet able to respond to Soviet pressure for a second front on the Continent. But in November 1942 they did land in French North Africa and were rapidly established in force in Morocco and Algeria. The Libyan segment of the long North African coast had been held by the Germans and their Italian allies since the beginning of the war in the Mediterranean. At the time of the North African landings, the British, under General Sir Bernard Montgomery (1887–1976), were holding a defensive line inside the Egyptian frontier near El Alamein. But on October 23, 1942, the British started on a westward offensive, which was planned to coordinate with an eastward offensive by the American General Dwight D. Eisenhower (1890–1969), commander of the Allied forces in French North Africa. The vise closed slowly, but in May 1943 Free French, British, and American troops took the last Axis strongholds of Tunis and Bizerte and accepted the surrender of some 300,000 Axis troops.

The North African campaign had clearly been a turning point. The Allies had successfully made large-scale amphibious landings, and they had annihilated one of the most renowned of Axis forces, commanded by Erwin Rommel (1891–1944), "the Desert Fox." North Africa was by no means the main battleground, but it was nevertheless a major campaign in which the Allies gained confidence and prestige.

The great turning point on land was the successful Soviet defense of Stalingrad (now known as Volgograd). After their stalemate in the Soviet Union in the winter of 1941–1942, the Germans turned their summer offensive of 1942 away from Leningrad and Moscow and toward the oil-rich regions to the southeast. This push toward the Soviet oil fields carried the Germans deep inside the Soviet Union, but it fell just short of the rich oil fields of Grozny and Baku. Russian distance, weather, manpower, and ability to take punishment were too much for the overextended Germans. Their armies were thrown back at Stalingrad, and early in 1943 the Soviets started the long march westward that was to take them to Berlin two years later.

A much less spectacular turning point was the Allied victory in the battle of supply, yet this victory was of the greatest importance. Even for the Soviets, an important source of supplies was the United States. But the United States was separated from its allies by vast distances of water, and the precious supplies had to move across the seas. If the Germans could stop this movement or reduce it greatly, they might still win. They made important improvements in their submarines, but there were simply not enough of them, and the countermeasures of the Allies—radar, coordination of naval vessels and aircraft, the convoy system—slowly reduced the number of sinkings.

The Axis on the Defensive

In the last two years of the war the Axis powers were on the defensive. Both in Europe and in Asia the Allies attacked with land forces along definite lines of march—campaigns of the traditional kind. But the way for these armies was made easier by two new factors in warfare: air power and modern propaganda, or psychological warfare. Air bombardment, at least until the atom bomb at Hiroshima, was never the perfect weapon that the prophets of air power had predicted. But as the superior Allied air power grew and was used systematically to destroy enemy capabilities in critical materials like ball bearings, machine tools, locomotives, and oil—and as American airplanes dropped incendiary bombs on the relatively flimsy Japanese cities—air power did much to destroy the Axis will to resist.

Intelligence achievements were also important: Beginning in 1940 and building on early work done by Polish intelligence, the British had collected an assembly of scholars, puzzle enthusiasts, and technicians and had begun to solve the "unbreakable" German *Enigma* military cipher. This code system required the use of highly secret machines that created codes out of seemingly random sets of numbers, and breaking it was a monumental exercise that remained a well-kept secret until many years after the war. The successful operation and the secrets learned from it were code-named *Ultra*. By 1943, Ultra, American-conducted Magic, and related operations meant that the British were systematically reading most high-level German communications and the American were decoding Japanese military and diplomatic messages.

The attack by land on Germany and Italy was pressed in three directions—by the Soviets from the east, and by the British, French, Americans, and other Allies from the south and west. In the south the Allies crossed from North Africa to Sicily in a successful amphibious operation (July 1943) within two months of their final victory in Tunisia. From Sicily they moved in another six weeks to the mainland of Italy at Salerno and Anzio. These landings were costly, and troops were pinned down for weeks. German forces kept the Italian campaign going for longer than the Allies anticipated, but the Allied victories of the summer of 1943 were sufficient to put Italy out of the war. Top officers of the Italian army and others close to the king, helped by dissident fascist leaders, engineered a coup in July that brought about the fall and imprisonment of Mussolini and resulted in some negotiations between the Allies and the new government headed by Marshal Pietro Badoglio (1871–1956).

But the Germans were unwilling to abandon their Italian defensive line. In a rare show of facist loyalty, Hitler sent a detachment of German troops to rescue Mussolini in September 1943 and set him up as the head of a "fascist republic" in the North—a post in which he continued until he was executed by partisans in April 1945. In June 1944 the Allies succeeded, after particularly severe fighting around Monte Cassino, in breaking through to Rome, which was declared an open city, and by August they were in Florence. They could not effectively move further north, however, until the final collapse of the Germans in their heartland early in 1945.

At a conference of Churchill, Roosevelt, and Stalin in Teheran in December 1943, the decision was made to open the long-delayed second front. The landings in France began on "D-Day," June 6, 1944, under the command of Gen-

Adolf Hitler, accompanied by German officials, grimly inspects bomb damage in 1944 in this German photograph captured by the U.S. Army Signal Corps at the close of World War II. This is a rare image, for unlike the British king and queen or Prime Minister Churchill, the fascist dictators seldom appeared in public to empathize with their citizens for their war losses. (National Archives)

eral Eisenhower. The Allies' choice of the Normandy coast surprised the German high command, who believed the landings would come farther north and east along the English Channel. In the greatest combined operation and amphibious invasion in history, supported by 4,000 naval vessels and 10,000 aircraft, more than 100,000 Allied troops were landed on a massively fortified enemy coast in the first two days. Within three months another 2 million men joined them. In their four years of occupation the Germans had fortified the French coastline, but the Allies had also used those four years to study, invent, and plan. Allied landing craft, amphibious trucks, naval and air support, artificial harbors, and a well-organized supply system gained a beachhead for the allied land forces. From this beachhead, a little over a month after D-Day, they were able to break out at Avranches and sweep the Germans back across the Seine in a great flanking movement led by the American general George S. Patton (1885–1945).

A long-planned auxiliary landing on the French Mediterranean coast, to be followed by a march north up the Rhône-Saône valleys, was launched on August 15, 1944, and met very little opposition. Everywhere the French Resistance movement welcomed the liberating forces, some of whom were heirs of the Free French of 1940. Paris, a symbol as well as a place, was liberated toward the end of August.

The Germans were beaten back but not disorganized. In July 1944 conservative elements, both military and civilian, attempted to assassinate Hitler to pave the way for negotiations. But Hitler survived the bomb intended for him, executed the plotters, and retained a firm grip on the German state by killing five thousand people suspected of complicity. The Allies were encouraged by their rapid successes in July and August to try to destroy the German armies before winter or cut them off from their homeland; however, Patton's mechanized troops ran out of fuel. The new German pilotless planes and rocket-propelled missiles limited Allied use of Antwerp as a port of supply, and by late autumn the Germans had retired in good order to their own Siegfried line.

Although falling back, the Germans hoped, as in World War I, to prevent an assault on Germany itself. They still had an army of 10 million in the field. Hitler was pressing the development of the jet plane, which he hoped could still save Germany. To buy another winter, in late September 1944 he called up the last reserves, ordering all able-bodied males between sixteen and sixty into the service. Not wishing to give Hitler the winter, Eisenhower ordered an airborne assault to leap over German defensive lines on the lower Rhine, but plans for a linked ground-air attack went badly, and the airborne army had to be rescued. The Allied offensive, having overreached its supplies, was now bogged down, and Hitler ordered a final counteroffensive sweep through the Ardennes forest on Antwerp, the Allies' supply port. A German armored attack on December 16, with the advantage of fog, snow, systematic infiltration, and complete surprise, threatened to throw the Allies back in the Battle of the Bulge, just short of the German border, and completely surrounded an American airborne division at Bastogne. As the weather cleared,

Normandy, D-Day 1944: the view from a landing craft as American troops wade ashore under German gunfire. In the greatest sea-borne invasion in history, supported by more than 4,000 ships and boats and 10,000 aircraft, more than 100,000 men were landed in the first two days.   (Franklin D. Roosevelt Library)

Allied air strikes and German fuel shortages stopped the German counter-advance.

Germany now had no more men or supplies to throw into the battle. German oil production had been given a deathblow, and tanks had to be hauled to the front by oxen. The catastrophic technique of firebombing was being used. The British put Dresden to the torch in a massive incendiary raid on February 13–14, 1945, with the loss of 135,000 lives, many of them refugees pouring in from the east, running from the Soviet advance.

The Soviets had been pushing on relentlessly ever since Stalingrad. In the campaign of 1943, while the Western Allies were busy in Italy, the Soviets won back most of their own territories that had been lost in 1941 and 1942. They kept up the pressure during the winter and started an early spring campaign in the south. By the autumn of 1944 the Soviets had been able to sweep across Romania and Bulgaria to a juncture with the Yugoslav communist guerrillas under their leader Marshal Josip Broz, called Tito (1892–1980), and were ready for the attack on Hungary. In the center and north, they had recovered all their own territory and were ready to attack Germany across

Poland from the east. Poland, caught between the advancing Soviets and the retreating Germans, was devastated. In August the provisional government of Poland in London ordered a mass uprising in Warsaw. The battle within Warsaw continued until October, when the Germans at last succeeded in crushing it, at the cost of more than 200,000 Polish casualties. The Soviets, on the outskirts of the city, did not intervene, waiting for the Polish Resistance to be destroyed so that they might create their own collaborators. This was the last German victory.

The rapid conclusion of the battle of Germany followed. The Soviets had not stopped for winter but had pressed on through Poland to menace Berlin early in March. The Western Allies broke through the Siegfried line in February, crossed the Rhine, and entered the heart of Germany. Early in February 1945, Stalin, Churchill, and Roosevelt held another summit conference, this time at Yalta in the Crimea, and confirmed final plans for the conquest of Germany. It was plain that the Germans could not hold out for long. The Allied planners wanted to settle peacefully which areas of Germany each of them would occupy and govern after the German defeat. The decision was reached to give the Soviets the honor of taking Berlin, a decision that, in effect, confirmed their hold on Poland as well. At the time this view seemed to recognize the fact that during the two years of successful offensive against the Germans, the Soviets had pinned down many more German divisions than had the Western Allies. Stalin further demanded that Germany pay $20 billion in reparations, with half the sum to go to the wartorn Soviet Union. The Soviets fought their way into a Berlin already pulverized by the air power of the Western Allies. Hitler and his former mistress shot themselves in his bunker suite, and their bodies were covered with gasoline and burned.

The war Hitler had unleashed in Europe killed 17 million soldiers and 18 million civilians at the lowest extreme. No European war in history had been so destructive, so corrosive to the doctrine of progress and to the concept of human beings as rational. As fuller details of the war, suppressed by censors during the heat of battle, became known to the public, the sense of elation in victory was also seriously compromised by the awareness of how unpredictable and how devastating war had become.

Committed from the outset to ridding Germany of the resident Jewish population, the Nazis from their earliest days employed brutal intimidation to try to force Jews to leave the country. Once in power, they made it national policy, and by 1938 almost a third of Germany's half million Jews had emigrated. Even though the 1938 Anschluss had added the former Austria's 200,000 Jews to the German total, by September 1939 there remained but 350,000 in the enlarged Reich. With the coming of war emigration slowed dramatically, and the Nazis turned to deportation. They even toyed with the idea of creating a kind of Nazi-controlled Jewish reservation on the French island of Madagascar, although the bizarre scheme came to nothing. Ultimately the plan on which the Nazis agreed was the concentration (the Nazis were already expert at the use of "concentration camps") of the Jewish population under Nazi control—grown much larger as the east European conquests increased. In charge of execution of the plan were SS officials Reinhard Heydrich (1904–1942), called "the hangman," and Adolf Eichmann (1906–1962). Murder came to be a favored method of dealing with the large captive population, and even before official policy resolved to set up the death camps, more than a million Jews had been killed.

By 1942 the "final solution" to the Jewish problem was revealed as six death camps were established in Germany and occupied Poland. Before the end of the year the firm policy was in place that all Jews within reach of the Reich, regardless of their location, were to be killed. The Jewish race, in Nazi parlance, was to be extinguished. The favored process was asphyxiation through the use of cyanide gas, although millions were simply shot; the crematoria where the bodies of victims were to be destroyed are now infamous, although in the end they proved to be overwhelmed by the magnitude of the task of disposing of the evidence. Hence, the executioners resorted to the age-old device of mass graves. The magnitude of the evil was and remains staggering, but so does the massive logistic commitment. In the midst of a great war, thousands of men, a large part of the rail system, massive amounts of munitions, and, of course, great sums of money were invested in the highly organized effort to murder millions of noncombatants. The murderous plan was pursued without relent throughout the remainder of the war, and even as the tide of war turned against the Germans the death camps continued in their cruel work. This was *genocide*—literally the murder of a people—and had the war continued, all of continental European Jewry would most likely have been wiped out. The result was nothing less than a Holocaust: six million violent deaths and the near extinction of the Jews and their culture in Germany, Austria, Poland, Romania, Lithuania, and Ukraine.

The Allied advance into Germany fully revealed for the first time the horror of Nazi treatment of all others styled "inferior" in their ideology: Gypsies, homosexuals, Slavs of all nationalities, and especially Poles. Treated similarly were, of course, political opponents, intellectuals, many clergymen, and virtually anyone thought to be in any way resistant to the Third Reich. During 1945 one after another of the concentration camps and death camps were liberated in Germany, Austria, and Poland, and the names of Auschwitz (the most notorious death camp, where 2 million died), Belsen, Buchenwald, Dachau, Nordhausen, Mauthausen, and others came to be associated with the savage war of oppression and genocide. Untold thousands died of starvation and brutality and in bizarre medical experiments.

The effects of the Holocaust were devastating. Efforts to cover up, account for, or explain away such monstrous behavior would corrode political and social life for generations. The nations that received Jewish immigrants—Britain, the United States, Canada, and others—benefited enormously. Displaced Jews, and Zionists who had long dreamed of a homeland in Palestine, would create a new Jewish state, Israel, leading to a state of almost constant undeclared war in the Near and Middle East. The diaspora of the Jews would enrich new societies in ways the racist theories of Hitler could never have imagined.

Slave laborers who survived the German concentration camp at Buchenwald, near Jena. German policy called for Jews and other "undesirables" who were physically able to be worked until no longer useful, at which time they were exterminated. This photograph was taken as these men were liberated by the United States Army 80th Division on the eve of the German collapse in 1945. (National Archives)

After the war many people would ask why Germans who knew of the systematic killing of Jews had not protested it; why the Soviets, as they moved into Poland, had not stopped it; why the Western Allies had not made them early targets of liberation; why the pope had not spoken out; or why the Jews themselves had not organized more systematic resistance within the camps. There is little agreement on these questions, although there is little disagreement about the magnitude of the deaths and the importance of the questions those deaths give rise to.

On May 8, 1945, Churchill and Harry S. Truman (1884–1972)—who had become the American president on Roosevelt's death that April—announced the end of German resistance, the day of victory in Europe, V-E Day. It was symbolic of difficulties to come that Stalin was offended because the Western Allies had accepted a formal surrender at Reims in France. He chose to announce separately, on the Soviet Union's part, the final victory over Germany, and not until the next day.

The War in the Pacific

V-J Day, the day of victory over Japan, was now the all-out goal of Allied effort. The Soviet Union had refrained from adding Japan to its formal enemies as long as Germany was still a threat. Britain and the United States, on the other hand, were anxious for the Soviets to enter the war against the Japanese. This desire was responsible for many of the concessions made to Stalin in the last months of the German war.

The attack on Japan had been pressed in three main directions. First, in a process that the American press soon called "island-hopping," the American navy drove straight toward Japan from the central Pacific. One after another, the small island bases that stood in the way were reduced by American naval forces, which used both air support and amphibious methods. Each island required an intense beach assault and pitched battle: Tarawa, Eniwetok, Kwajalein, Iwo Jima, Okinawa, Saipan, and Guam.

Second, the Americans and Australians, with help from other Commonwealth elements, worked their way up the southwest Pacific through the much larger islands of the Solomons, New Guinea, and the Philippines. The base for this campaign—which was under the command of the American general Douglas MacArthur (1880–1964)—was Australia and such outlying islands as New Caledonia and the New Hebrides. By October 1944 the sea forces had won the battle of the Philippine Sea and had made possible the successful landing of MacArthur's troops on Leyte and the reconquest of the Philippine Islands from the Japanese.

The third attack came from the south in the China-Burma-India theater. The main effort of the Allies was to get material support to Chiang Kai-shek and the Chinese Nationalists at Chungking and, if possible, to weaken the Japanese position in Burma, Thailand, and Indochina. After Pearl Harbor, when the Japanese seized and shut the "Burma Road," the only way for the Allies to communicate with Chiang's Nationalists was by air. Although the Western Allies did not invest an overwhelming proportion of their resources in the China-Burma-India theater, they did help keep the Chinese formally in the fight. And as the final campaign of 1945 drew on, the British, with Chinese and American aid, were holding down three Japanese field armies in this theater.

The end in Japan came with a suddenness that was hardly expected. From Pacific island bases, American airplanes had inflicted crippling damage on Japanese industry in the spring and summer of 1945. The Japanese fleet had been almost destroyed, submarine warfare had almost strangled the Japanese economy, and the morale of Japanese troops was declining. Nonetheless, American leaders were convinced that only the use of their recently invented atom bomb could avert the very heavy casualties expected from the proposed amphibious invasion of the Japanese home islands. Some commentators believe that racism also played a role in the decision to use the bomb on the Japanese rather than on any European people, although the bomb was not, in fact, ready for use in time to affect the European war. An additional motive for its use was a desire to demonstrate to the Soviet Union, which many feared would turn upon the Allies at the end of the war, just how powerful America's new weapon was. The result was the dropping of the first atom bomb on Hiroshima on August 6, 1945.

On August 8 the Soviets, who had agreed to come into the war against Japan once Germany was beaten, invaded Manchuria in full force. Faced with what they felt was certain defeat after the dropping of a second atom bomb on Nagasaki, the Japanese government decided not to make a last-ditch stand in their own country. On September 2 the Japanese formally surrendered in Tokyo Bay. Japan gave up its conquests abroad and submitted to American military occupation. Purged of most of its militarists, the Japanese government continued to rule under nominal Allied (actually American) supervision.

The Allied Coalition

The Grand Alliance, as Churchill liked to call it, known in its last years as the United Nations, had mustered overpowering strength against Germany, Japan, Italy, and such collaborators as the Axis powers could secure in the Balkans, Southeast Asia, and western Europe. Britain and the Commonwealth, the Soviet Union, and the United States were the heart of the Allied coalition. Nationalist China, for all its inefficiencies, had tied down hundreds of thousands of Japanese soldiers, and the resources of the French Empire and the French Resistance movements at home and abroad had been valuable. The Allies had been able to count on the resources of many Latin American nations, and Brazil had been an active member of the alliance. In this truly global war, Brazilian troops had fought in Italy along with American (including Japanese-American), French imperial, British imperial, pro-Allied Italian, Polish, and other troops. At the very end of the European war, Argentina, too, declared war on Germany and Japan, even though its fascist leader, General Juan Perón (1895–1974), had hoped for a German victory.

The instruments of Allied union were the summit conferences of the Big Three—Roosevelt, Churchill, and Stalin—with the political and military advisers and experts, plus the more frequent Anglo-American conferences. Even before the United States entered the war, Roosevelt and Churchill met off Newfoundland and issued the Atlantic Charter (August 14, 1941), in which they declared support for the freedom of the seas, equality of access to economic opportunity, abandonment of aggression, and the restoration of rights to conquered peoples. Formal conferences—between Roosevelt and Churchill at Casablanca (January 1943) and Quebec (August 1943), and among the Big Three at Teheran and Yalta—concluded agreements that had been steadily carried on at lower political and military levels. From July 17 to August 17, 1945, a final conference at Potsdam (near conquered Berlin) brought together the United States, Britain, and the Soviet Union. With two new figures attending, President Truman and Prime Minister Clement Attlee (1883–1967), they met to confirm the Yalta decisions.

Churchill (soon to be voted out of office), Roosevelt (fatally ill), and Stalin meet at Yalta in the Crimea, February 4–11, 1945. The conference marked the high point of Allied coopera-tion, and agreement seemed to be reached on the destruction of German militarism, the encouragement of democratic governments in the liberated territories, and the creation of a more effective international body to replace the League of Nations. The Promise of Yalta never became reality, however, and the world soon experienced forty-five years of cold war. (National Archives)

But there were grave military and political matters to be ironed out. For the actual direction of operations in the field, the British and Americans had decided to set up a complete intermeshing of staffs. All down the line, an American in command always had a Briton as his second, and a Briton in command always had an American as his second. Even the intelligence-gathering apparatus of the two nations was meshed. At the highest level, the combined chiefs of staff, in close touch with top American and British gov-ernment officials, did the overall planning. The Soviets could not be brought into such close military cooperation, and Soviet troops in the field always fought on their own.

During the war the Allies had agreed that the Axis powers were to be forced into "unconditional surrender." The Germans must be beaten unmis-takably, and Allied troops must enter Berlin as conquerors. There must be no political negotiation at all, simply unconditional military surrender. In

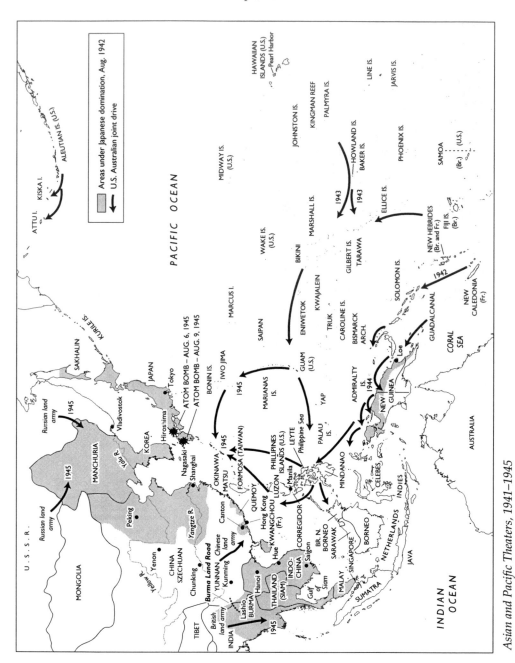

Asian and Pacific Theaters, 1941–1945

Britain and the United States there was some opposition to this policy during the war, partly on humanitarian grounds, but also because people feared that the prospect of unconditional surrender would stiffen the German will to resist and would unite the nation behind Hitler. In retrospect, it seems unlikely that Hitler would ever have negotiated with the Allies; and after the failure of the attempt to kill him in 1944, there was little chance that the Germans themselves would overthrow the Nazi government.

Another political problem created a much clearer rift between the British and the Americans. The underlying issue was just how far anti-German elements in France, Italy, and other occupied lands had to go to prove that they were democratic enough to secure the backing of the Western powers. Here the difference in the underlying tone of American and British policies was evident in the views of Roosevelt and Churchill. Roosevelt was convinced that if the Allies did not interfere to support conservatives and reactionaries in the occupied lands, but instead allowed these peoples to choose their form of government freely, they would choose democracy. Churchill was less idealistic. He was eager to use any elements that were hostile to the Germans, even if their hostility was quite recent. Furthermore, Roosevelt began to press Churchill for a commitment to decolonization, especially of India, at the end of the war, while Churchill responded that he would not preside over the dissolution of the British Empire.

In French politics the issue was further complicated by Roosevelt's suspicions of de Gaulle, the chosen leader of the French liberation movement. To Churchill, de Gaulle was a difficult but indispensable ally. As it turned out, the Gaullists, in collaboration with the organized French Resistance in the homeland, did take over the civilian administration of French territory as it was liberated, and France by free popular vote restored a democratic form of government. In 1946 the Italians also narrowly voted for a republic. What had threatened at one time to be a serious difficulty between American policy and British policy was resolved by the liberated people themselves.

But the political issue that bulked largest after World War II was the problem of potential Soviet domination in eastern and southeastern Europe. At Yalta the Western powers had allowed Stalin to push his armies westward and had relied on his promises to permit free elections in Poland, Hungary, Czechoslovakia, and the Balkans. Most of the smaller eastern European countries had moved toward fascist totalitarianism before World War II, and a transition to communist totalitarianism would not be difficult. Churchill, who never trusted Stalin, did not dare risk losing Soviet manpower and material resources during the war. Appeasement of Stalin seemed absolutely essential. At the end of the war, the western European states, although victorious, were so near impoverishment that they could play no major role in the balance-of-power politics that would follow, so that the Soviets and Americans soon became the only superpowers. Contrary to its hopes and public expectations, the United States was drawn deeply into European and Asian matters.

With the end of hostilities came the reckoning of costs, and they were beyond anything that had come before them. The Soviet Union lost at least 7.5 million military and another 10 million civilian dead; Japan lost a total of 2 million; Germany suffered losses of 3.5 million military and a million civilians; Britain, France, and Italy each lost a total of 400,000; and the United States lost 290,000 military personnel. Estimates for China are impossible to verify, but experts agree that the vast country sustained at least 2.5 million total casualties and perhaps as many as five times that number. These are but examples. As noted earlier, more than 6 million Jews and other victims of Nazi fanaticism died in the hands of their captors. Monetary costs may have been as much as $4 trillion. The physical destruction resulting from the war was virtually incalculable: Cities like Dresden and Hiroshima all but ceased to exist; ancient sites and monuments were obliterated; art treasures disappeared; and entire environments were contaminated, possibly forever. The industrial, health care, and transportation infrastructures of the most technically advanced continent were destroyed. Millions were barely alive and at the edge of starvation.

When the war ended, there was no peace. The defeat of Germany and Japan was almost immediately followed by the rise of a new aggressor, the Soviet Union, which had already given clear warning of its intentions. The long shooting war was followed quickly by sharp antagonisms between the Soviet Union and its former allies, a degree of hostility so intense it was soon called the *cold war.*

Aftermath

The devastation wrought by the years of war in Europe and the Pacific exceeded that even of World War I, resulting in a total of at least 50 million dead—more than half of them civilians. None of the important cities of the major belligerent nations outside of the United States was undamaged. Despite a sharply rising postwar birth rate and vast programs of economic reconstruction, such losses could never be fully repaired. Moreover, new and terrifying problems faced the world: While the end of the war in Europe came in April 1945 with the collapse of the Third Reich under the weight of Allied invasions from the east and west, the war against Japan ended only in August after the explosion over the cities of Hiroshima and Nagasaki of the world's first atom bombs. The display before the world of a weapon of such power made real the fear that another general war of great powers might result in the extermination of all life on this planet. The United States and then the Soviet Union were at first the only powers able to initiate or pursue nuclear warfare. Likewise, they were far larger in area, resources, and population than the other great nations (China was at this time on the verge of her own drive toward industrial modernization) and became the ideological and technical leaders, as well as the bankers, of a newly reorganized bipolar world. In their mutual distrust and competition over the half-century that followed lay what came universally to be called the Cold War.

The Postwar Settlement

Enemy attack and occupation had caused incalculable devastation inside the Soviet Union and left millions of survivors destitute; but the nation's capitalist ally, the United States, had remained unattacked in its heartland and had invented and used atomic weapons. It took Stalin four years (1945–1949) to catch up by making his own atom bomb. Scientific information provided by Soviet sympathizers within the United States and obtained through the Soviet espionage network in the West made significant contributions to this achievement, but only the high level of Russian science and technology and the absolute authority of the Stalinist dictatorship to concentrate resources to this end made it possible at all.

Although the Soviet Union and its former Western allies agreed on peace treaties with Italy, Hungary, Romania, and Bulgaria, no such treaty could be concluded with Germany or Japan. The Soviet Union also concluded a peace treaty with Finland in which it took a portion of Karelia. From Romania, the Soviet Union again took Bessarabia and northern Bukovina, and it annexed part of former East Prussia and the easternmost part of Czechoslovakia.

The chief surviving Nazi leaders were tried at Nuremberg in 1946, and twelve were sentenced to death for war crimes. Defeated Germany was divided into four occupied sections—American, British, French, and Soviet. The Soviet sector extended from eastern Germany to west of Berlin, which, as the former capital, was also divided into four occupation zones, one for each of the Allies. This arrangement was designed for temporary military occupation, but it continued because no treaty could be reached. The failure to reach any settlement over Germany left the most serious problem in Europe unresolved.

In 1949 the three Western powers promoted the union of their respective sectors as the Federal Republic of Germany—West Germany—with its capital at Bonn. The Soviets responded by creating the communist German Democratic Republic—East Germany—with its capital at Pankow outside Berlin. Many West Germans were eager for reunion with their fellow Germans in the Soviet zone. Yet a reunification of Germany under Western capitalist auspices was what the Soviets feared most, believing that it would mean a revival of aggression. An all-communist Germany was equally intolerable to the Western powers.

In Asia the most grievous problem remained that of China. The Chinese communists, who had challenged Chiang Kai-shek's ruling Kuomintang party for power, kept their forces active during the Japanese occupation. By 1949 the communists had defeated Chiang Kai-shek, who took refuge on the island of Formosa (Taiwan), where the communists could not follow because they had no fleet. In the last years of the struggle, Chiang had lost his hold over the Chinese people; the morale of his own forces was low, and an ever-mounting inflation ravaged the economy. By 1950 mainland China had gone communist and formed part of the Soviet bloc, while Chiang's government in Taiwan remained part of the American bloc. American foreign policy had suffered a major defeat.

Elsewhere, the Soviet Union pursued its goal of world communism through the agencies of individual Communist parties. Communist parties existed in virtually every country, often varying in the degree of subservience to the Communist party of the Soviet Union (CPSU) and the Soviet government. The United States, by contrast, had no ideologically disciplined supporters in most of the world.

The two superpowers each became the leader of a great coalition whose members were attached by bonds of self-interest. The members of the loose American coalition in 1945 included the Western Hemisphere nations, Great Britain, the British Commonwealth, western Europe, Japan, and the Philippines. The Soviet coalition included the countries of eastern Europe and, by 1949, China. The border between the two coalitions ultimately ran along an irregular north-south line through the European Continent, with Scandinavia, West Germany, France, Austria, Italy, and Greece to the west and the Baltic states, East Germany, Czechoslovakia, Hungary, Yugoslavia, and Albania to the east. In a speech delivered on March 5, 1946, while receiving an honorary academic degree at Westminster College in Fulton, Missouri, Winston Churchill spoke of an "Iron Curtain" being drawn across the continent. From this moment the line and the division that it symbolized had both a vivid name and an almost spiritual meaning in the West.

Turkey belonged to the Western coalition, and portions of the Middle East and of southeast Asia were linked to it by a network of pacts. The dividing line between North and South Korea—with the Soviet Union occupying the north and the United States the south—represented a kind of Asian extension of the long frontier between the two coalitions. Over this long frontier came aggressive Soviet probing operations that led to crises and in several cases to wars.

Repeatedly, the West made gestures toward easing relations between the two coalitions. In 1946 Stalin refused to join in a United Nations atomic energy commission. In 1947 the United States proposed an international plan of massive American economic aid to accelerate European recovery from the ruin of the war—the Marshall Plan, named for General George C. Marshall, American secretary of state (1880–1959). The Soviet Union refused to accept the aid for itself and would not let its satellites participate in the Marshall Plan. The former Western allies subsequently formed the nucleus of the North Atlantic Treaty Organization (NATO) in 1949. The Soviet coalition founded the Cominform (Communist Information Bureau) in 1947 as a successor to the former Comintern, and created the Warsaw Pact (1955), binding eastern Europe together, as a reply to NATO. The United States and Britain sought in the 1950s and 1960s to prevent the spread of atomic weapons. Their plan called for a joint multilateral (nuclear) force (MLF). Because the Germans would

A Closer Look

SOVIET-AMERICAN RIVALRY AND THE COLD WAR

In 1947, at the outset of the cold war, as the Soviet Union continued to expand its influence throughout Europe, a leading American policy analyst, George Kennan (1904–   ), published a highly influential article in the American journal *Foreign Affairs*. In it he discussed what the United States should do to offset Soviet influence. He wrote under the pseudonym "X," although he had, in March 1946, sent the text of his argument, called "The Sources of Soviet Conduct," as a cable directly to the U.S. Department of State. At the time Kennan was the second-highest ranking American diplomatic officer in Moscow. The Foreign Affairs article is reprinted here:

In actuality the possibilities for American policy are by no means limited to holding the line and hoping for the best. It is entirely possible for the United States to influence by its actions the internal developments, both within Russia and throughout the international Communist movement, by which Russian policy is largely determined. This is not only a question of the modest measure of informational activity which this government can conduct in the Soviet Union and elsewhere, although that, too, is important. It is rather a question of the degree to which the United States can create among the peoples of the world generally the impression of a country which knows what it wants, which is coping successfully with the problems of its internal life and with the responsibilities of a world power, and which has a spiritual vitality capable of holding its own among the major ideological currents of the time. To the extent that such an impression can be created and maintained, the aims of Russian Communism must appear sterile and quixotic, the hopes and enthusiasm of Moscow's supporters must wane, and added strain must be imposed on the Kremlin's foreign policies. For the palsied decrepitude of the capitalist world is the keystone of Communist philosophy. Even the failure of the United States to experience the early economic depression which the ravens of the Red Square have been predicting with such complacent confidence since hostilities ceased would have deep and important repercussions throughout the Communist world.

By the same token, exhibitions of indecision, disunity and internal disintegration within this country have an exhilarating effect on the whole Communist movement. At each evidence of these tendencies, a thrill of hope and excitement goes through the Communist world; a new jauntiness can be noted in the Moscow tread; new groups of foreign supporters climb on to what they can only view as the bandwagon of international politics; and Russian pressure increases all along the line in international affairs.

It would be an exaggeration to say that American behavior unassisted and alone could exercise a power of life and death over the Communist movement and bring about the early fall of Soviet power in Russia. But the United States has it in its power to increase enormously the strains under which Soviet policy must operate, to force upon the Kremlin a far greater degree of moderation and circumspection than it has had to observe in recent years, and in this way to promote tendencies which must eventually find their outlet in either the breakup or the gradual mellowing of Soviet power. For no mystical, messianic movement—and particularly not that of the Kremlin—can face frustration indefinitely without eventually adjusting itself in one way or another to the logic of that state of affairs.

Thus the decision will really fall in large measure on this country itself. The issue of Soviet-American relations is in essence a test of the overall worth of the United States as a nation among nations. To avoid destruction the United States need only measure up to its own best traditions and prove itself worthy of preservation as a great nation.

George F. Kennan, "The Sources of Soviet Conduct," *Foreign Affairs*, XXV (July 1947), pp. 581–82.

participate, the French rejected MLF and in 1966 withdrew their military forces from NATO and forced NATO headquarters to be moved out of France.

In the Middle East, the Baghdad Pact and its successor, the Central Treaty Organization (CENTO), proved to be no more than a series of unstable agreements among the United States, Britain, Turkey, Iran, and Pakistan. With the withdrawal of Iraq from the Baghdad Pact in 1959, no direct alliances linked the Arab world with the West. The neutral nations remained outside the coalitions. Some, like Switzerland or Sweden, were simply maintaining their traditional policies of not aligning themselves with any grouping of powers. But most were newly independent nations. Of these India was the most influential, taking much-needed economic assistance from both coalitions. As economic aid became an instrument in the cold war, neutral nations tried, often with success, to play one side off against the other, while, in turn the two great powers sought to turn the newly independent nations into client states.

The decade that followed World War II, then, witnessed the creation of what was often termed a bipolar world, dominated by the two blocs of nations, each led by a rival superpower. The generation that inherited all of this had little choice but to grow accustomed to it and to the Cold War, that unrelenting competition between the two sides in the political, military, intellectual, and economic spheres. Although there was to be no nuclear confrontation between the two superpowers and their allies, many in the world became used to living under the shadow of the idea that such a holocaust was a real possibility. Although statesmen and diplomats on both sides often negotiated and even compromised in private, neither power bloc could appear in public to give way to the other. It was against such a backdrop that the second half of the twentieth century was to be played out.

SUMMARY

Some historians today consider the time between the two world wars as simply a twenty-year truce. Yet the 1920s had offered hope for peace, as shown by the Locarno spirit. This hope was dashed by the Great Depression that helped put Hitler in power.

Between 1918 and 1938 Soviet leaders shifted their view on the likelihood of a world communist revolution. Hitler's successful rise to power in Germany posed a threat to the Soviet Union. Stalin tried to counter this threat by negotiation. Both the West and the Soviet Union sought to turn Hitler's aggression against the other.

The period from 1931 to 1939 was marked by various international crises, each of which moved the world closer to war. The major crises included Japan's seizure of Manchuria (1931); German rearmament (1935–1936); Italian invasion of Ethiopia (1935); German and Italian intervention in the Spanish Civil War (1936–1939); Japanese invasion of China (1937); the Anschluss with Germany (1938); the dismemberment of Czechoslovakia (1938–1939); and the German invasion of Poland (1939)—the final crisis that forced Britain and France to abandon the policy of appeasement.

In September 1939 Germany was ready for war. Hitler had reached an accord with Stalin that gave Germany security from war on two fronts. In the opening stages of the war, the German blitzkreig resulted in a string of victories that gave the Axis powers control of much of western Europe. The use of aerial bombardment brought civilians into the front line of war.

Germany was drawn into the Balkans and the eastern Mediterranean in an effort to weaken Britain by cutting its route to India. In 1941 Hitler also attacked the Soviet Union. The Japanese attack on Pearl Harbor brought the United States into the war. By the spring of 1942 Japanese expansion in Asia and the Pacific had reached its height.

The turning point in the war came in 1942. In the Pacific, the battle of the Coral Sea prevented the Japanese invasion of Australia. The successful North African campaign (1942–1943), the Soviet defense of Stalingrad, and the Allied success in maintaining its supply lines forced the Axis powers on the defensive in 1943. The end of the war in Europe in 1945 revealed the full horrors of extermination camps and opened the controversy over how the Holocaust had been allowed to happen.

In the Pacific, American and Allied forces moved against Japan on several fronts. Finally, the Americans decided to use the newly developed atom bomb to prevent the heavy casualties that would be involved in an attack on the Japanese home islands.

Chronology

1883–1885	Friedrich Nietzsche, *Thus Spake Zarathustra*
1888–1918	r. Emperor William II of Germany
1888	Social Democratic party founded in Austria
1889	Eiffel Tower built in Paris
1889	Vincent van Gogh, *Starry Night*
1890	Invention of the Maxim gun
1890	Alfred T. Mahan, *The Influence of Sea Power in History*
1891	Motion picture camera patented
1892	General Francisco Franco
1892	Claude Debussy, *Afternoon of a Faun*
1892	Paul Gauguin, *Spirit of the Dead Watching*
1893	Karl Benz builds first motor car
1893	Herbert Spencer, *System of Synthetic Philosophy*
1894–1917	Franco-Russian Alliance
1894–1895	Sino-Japanese War
1894–1906	Dreyfus Affair
1894–1917	r. Czar Nicholas II of Russia
1896	First modern Olympic Games held (Athens, Greece)
1896	Battle of Adowa
1896	Nobel prizes established
1896	Theodore Herzl, *The Jewish State*
1898	Fashoda Crisis
1898	Pierre and Marie Curie discover radium
1898	Russian Social Democratic party founded
1898	Spanish-American War
1898	First German navy law
1899–1902	Boer War

1900–1946	r. King Victor Emmanuel III of Italy
1900	Thomas Mann, *Buddenbrooks*
1900	Boxer Rebellion
1900	Sigmund Freud, *The Interpretation of Dreams*
1901–1908	Theodore Roosevelt president of the United States
1901	Guglielmo Marconi sends first radio transmission across the Atlantic
1902–1910	r. King Edward VII of Great Britain
1902	V. I. Lenin, *What Is to Be Done?*
1902	John A. Hobson, *Imperialism: A Study*
1902	Anglo-Japanese Alliance
1903	Joseph Chamberlain proposes tariff reform
1903	Ford Motor Company founded
1903	Bolsheviks gain control of Russian Social Democratic party
1904	Anglo-French Entente
1905–1906	First Moroccan Crisis
1905–1907	Antonio Gaudi, Casa Mila apartment house, Barcelona
1905	Revolution in Russia
1905	Russian duma formed
1905	Claude Debussy, *La Mer*
1905	Albert Einstein, special theory of relativity
1906	British Labour party founded
1906	Introduction of the Dreadnought class battleship
1906	Women in Finland gain the vote
1906	Liberal party victory in British elections
1907	Anglo-Russian Entente
1907	Arnold Schönberg, *First Chamber Symphony*
1907	Pablo Picasso, *Les Demoiselles d'Avignon*
1908	Young Turk revolution
1908	Bosnia and Herzegovina annexed by Austria-Hungary
1908	Georges Sorel, *Reflections on Violence*
1909	Robert E. Peary reaches the North Pole
1909	Frank Lloyd Wright, Robie House, Chicago
1910–1936	r. King George V of Great Britain
1911–1912	Chinese Revolution

1911	Parliament Act
1911	Second Moroccan Crisis
1911	Roald Amundsen reaches the South Pole
1911	Chinese Revolution
1912–1913	Balkan Wars
1912–1921	Woodrow Wilson president of the United States
1912	Vassily Kandinsky, *Improvisation 28*
1912	*H.M.S. Titanic* sinks on its maiden voyage
1913	Igor Stravinsky, *The Rites of Spring*
1913	Women in Norway gain the vote
1913	New York Armory Art show
1914–1918	World War I
1914	Panama Canal opens
1914	10.5 million immigrants enter the United States
1914	Battle of the Marne
1914	Battles of Tannenberg and the Masurian Lakes
1914	First use of poison gas in warfare
1915	Sinking of the *Lusitania*
1915	D. W. Griffith, *The Birth of a Nation*
1916	Easter Rebellion in Ireland
1916	Introduction of the tank in warfare
1916	Battle of Jutland
1916	Lloyd George becomes British prime minister
1917	March Revolution in Russia
1917	United States joins the Allies
1917	Third Battle of Ypres (Passchendaele)
1917	Balfour Declaration
1917	November Revolution in Russia
1918–1919	Influenza pandemic kills 20 million
1918–1921	Russian Civil War
1918	Treaty of Brest-Litovsk
1918	Woodrow Wilson issues the Fourteen Points
1918	Oswald Spengler, *The Decline of the West*
1918–1919	Sparticist uprisings in Germany

1918	Allies intervene in Russia
1918	Women in Britain gain the vote
1919–1922	Irish Revolution and Civil War
1919–1922	German Nazi party organized
1919	Opening of the Versailles Peace Conference
1919	League of Nations established
1919	Comintern founded
1919	Amritsar Massacre
1919	Robert Wiene, *The Cabinet of Dr. Caligari*
1920s	Modern environmental movement begins
1920	Women in the United States gain the vote
1920	Carl Jung, *Psychological Types*
1920	U.S. Senate rejects the Versailles Treaty
1920s–1930s	Rise of independence movement in India
1921–1928	The Soviet New Economic Policy
1921–1927	Stalin and Trotsky struggle for power
1921–1923	Arnold Schönberg develops twelve-tone music
1921–1922	Washington Naval Conference
1922	Treaty of Rapallo
1922	James Joyce, *Ulysses*
1922	T. S. Eliot, *The Wasteland*
1922–1943	Mussolini rules Italy
1922–1923	German economic collapse
1923–1925	French occupy the Ruhr
1923	Marcel Proust, *Remembrance of Things Past*
1923	First birth control clinic (New York)
1923	George Gershwin, "Rhapsody in Blue"
1924	Dawes Plan
1924	Giacomo Matteotti, "The Fascists Exposed"
1925	Locarno Treaties
1925	Adolf Hitler, *Mein Kampf*
1925	Werner Heisenberg and Max Born formulate quantum mechanics
1925–1926	Walter Gropius, The Bauhaus, Dessau, Germany

1925–1940	Rapid urbanization of the Soviet Union
1927	Hermann Hesse, *Steppenwolf*
1927	Charles Lindbergh flies nonstop across the Atlantic
1927	Alan Crosland, *The Jazz Singer*
1928	First television broadcast
1928	D. H. Lawrence, *Lady Chatterley's Lover*
1928	Alexander Fleming discovers penicillin
1928	First Soviet Five-Year Plan
1928	Kellogg-Briand Treaty
1929–1930	Le Corbusier, Savoye House, Poissy-sur-Seine, France
1929–1939	Forced collectivization in the Soviet Union
1929	Lateran Treaty
1929	E. M. Remarque, *All Quiet on the Western Front*
1929	Virginia Woolf, *A Room of One's Own*
1929	Collapse of the New York Stock Exchange
1929–1934	The Great Depression
1931	Statute of Westminster
1931	Henri Matisse, *The Dance*
1931	Japan seizes Manchuria
1932–1933	Mass famine in the Soviet Union
1932	Britain enacts protective tariffs
1932	World disarmament conference
1933–1945	Administration of Franklin D. Roosevelt
1933–1945	Adolf Hitler rules Germany
1933–1934	*Gleichschaltung* and the creation of the Nazi dictatorship
1934–1936	The Long March
1934	Stavisky case in France
1934–1938	The Terror in the Soviet Union
1935–1936	German rearmament begins
1935	Nuremberg Laws in Germany
1935	Social Security enacted in the United States
1935	Italy invades Ethiopia
1936	r. King Edward VIII of Great Britain

1936–1937	Premier Leon Blum leads French Popular Front
1936–1939	Spanish Civil War
1936–1952	r. King George VI of Great Britain
1936	J. M. Keynes, *General Theory of Employment, Interest and Money*
1937	Japan invades China
1937	Pablo Picasso, *Guernica*
1937	Papal encyclical attacks Nazism
1938–1940	King Carol II of Romania installs fascist dictatorship
1938	Germany annexes Austria
1938	Munich Conference
1938	Germany occupies Czechoslovakia and Memel
1939–1945	World War II
1939	New York World's Fair
1940	Fall of France
1940	Churchill becomes British prime minister
1940	Battle of Britain
1941	Orson Welles, *Citizen Kane*
1941	Germany invades the Soviet Union
1941	Japan attacks Pearl Harbor, Hawaii
1943	Italy surrenders to the Allies
1944	D-Day invasion of France
1945	Germany surrenders
1945	Attlee becomes British prime minister
1945	Atomic bombs dropped on Hiroshima and Nagasaki
1945	Japan surrenders
1945	Yalta conference
1945	United Nations established
1946	Churchill's "Iron Curtain" speech
1946	Nuremberg war crimes trials
1947	India and Pakistan gain independence
1947	Discovery of the Dead Sea scrolls
1948	Berlin airlift
1949	Soviet Union tests atom bomb

1949	North Atlantic Treaty Organization (NATO) founded
1949	East and West Germany created
1949	Communists victorious in Chinese civil war
1949	George Orwell, *1984*
1949	Simone de Beauvoir, *The Second Sex*

Suggestions for Further Reading

CHAPTER ONE: The New Age

General Accounts

Oron J. Hale, *The Great Illusion, 1900–1914* (New York: Harper & Row, 1971). Still perhaps the most helpful survey of European society in the fourteen years before the First World War. Of similar vintage but perceptive and readable is Peter Gay and R. K. Webb, *Modern Europe Since 1815* (New York: Harper and Row, 1973).

Alan S. Milward and S. B. Saul, *The Development of the Economies of Continental Europe, 1850–1914* (London: Allen & Unwin, 1977). Thorough survey of the emergence of the twentieth-century industrial economies.

Charles Tilly, Louise Tilly, and Richard Tilly, *The Rebellious Century, 1830–1930* (Cambridge, Mass.: Harvard University Press, 1980). Enlightening essays comparing American and European developments.

Victor F. Weisskopf, *Physics in the Twentieth Century* (Cambridge, Mass.: MIT Press, 1972). A survey of the profound changes in the fundamental science of the century.

Arts and Ideas

Malcolm Bradbury and James MacFarlane, eds., *Modernism, 1890–1930* (New York: Penguin, 1976). An introduction to the directions taken by modern literature.

Peter Gay, *Freud: A Life for Our Time* (New York: Norton, 1988). A well-balanced interpretation of the life and work of the pioneer psychoanalyst.

George Heard Hamilton, *Painting and Sculpture in Europe, 1880–1940*, 2nd ed. (Baltimore: Penguin, 1967). An accessible survey of the field. Also useful are Henry-Russell Hitchcock, *Architecture: Nineteenth and Twentieth Centuries*, 4th ed. (Harmondsworth, England: Penguin, 1977) and Herbert Read, *A Concise History of Modern Painting*, 3rd ed. (New York: Penguin, 1974).

H. Stuart Hughes, *Consciousness and Society* (New York: Vintage, 1958). A classic study of the evolution of the dominant trends of social thought of the early twentieth century.

Steven Kern, *The Culture of Space and Time, 1880–1918* (Cambridge, Mass.: Harvard University Press, 1993). Fascinating study of the impact on society of how time is perceived in modern society.

J. Moore, *The Post-Darwinism Controversies: A Study of the Protestant Struggle to Come to Terms with Darwin in Great Britain and America* (Cambridge, England: Cambridge University Press, 1979). Excellent examination of the modern difficulty of rationalizing religion and science.

Abraham Pais, *Subtle Is the Lord: The Science and Life of Albert Einstein* (Oxford: Oxford University Press, 1982). Thoughtful biography of the great physicist, sensitive to making his ideas accessible to the layman.

Nicholas Pevsner, *Pioneers of Modern Design: From William Morris to Walter Gropius,* reprint ed. (New York: Viking Penguin, 1986). Excellent study of the nature of how things came to look as they did in the period.

Charles Rosen, *Schoenberg,* rev. ed. (Chicago: University of Chicago Press, 1996). Insightful study of the revolutionary composer. Also useful in understanding the revolution in modern music is Eric Salzman, *Twentieth-Century Music: An Introduction,* 2nd ed. (Englewood Cliffs, N.J.: Prentice-Hall, 1974).

Theda Shapiro, *Painters and Politics: The European Avantgarde and Society, 1900–1925* (New York: Elsevier, 1976). Study of the interaction between political and aesthetic ideas in a volatile era.

R. Hinton Thomas, *Nietzsche in German Politics and Society, 1890–1918* (Dover, N.H.: Manchester University Press, 1983). Rather than a biography of the philosopher, a study of the impact of his thought on the intellectual and political ideas of the Germany of William II.

Robert Wohl, *The Generation of 1914* (Cambridge, Mass.: Harvard University Press, 1979). Fascinating analysis of the ambitions and desires of the younger generation of Europe before they were called on to fight the First World War.

Society

T. B. Bottomore, *Classes in Modern Society* (New York: Pantheon, 1965). Clear explanation of the meaning and place of social class in modern times. Equally useful, and by the same author, is *Elites in Modern Society* (New York: Basic Books, 1964).

Gary S. Cross, *A Social History of Leisure Since 1600* (State College, Pa.: Venture Publishing, 1990). Broad survey of how Europeans and others have spent nonworking time.

T. H. Hollingsworth, *Historical Demography* (Ithaca, NY: Cornell University Press, 1969). Still a standard work in understanding the impact of population on social development. Certain of the essays in D. V. Glass and Roger Revelle, eds., *Population and Social Change* (New York: Crane, Russack, 1972), are also enlightening for this period.

Jacques Kornberg, *Theodor Herzl: From Assimilation to Zionism* (Bloomington: Indiana University Press, 1993). Sensitive biography of the intellectual development of the father of Zionism.

Neil McMaster, *Racism in Europe, 1870–2000* (New York: Palgrave, 2001). The most recent study of the phenomenon. Particularly helpful for an understanding of the nature of anti-Semitism is George L. Mosse, *Toward the Final Solution: A History of European Racism* (New York: Howard Fertig, 1978).

B. R. Mitchell, *European Historical Statistics, 1750–1970,* abridged ed. (New York: Columbia University Press, 1978). Invaluable collection of data.

Leslie Page Moch, *Moving Europeans: Migration in Western Europe Since 1659* (Bloomington: Indiana University Press, 1963). Explanation of patterns of migration within the European continent throughout modern times.

Jane Rendall, *The Origins of Modern Feminism: Women in Britain, France and the United States* (New York: Schocken Books, 1984). Comparative study of the roots of the modern feminist movement in the West. An enduring standard survey in this field is Richard J. Evans, *The Feminists: Women's Emancipation Movements in Europe, America and Australasia, 1840–1920* (London: Croom Helm, 1977).

Louise A. Tilly and Joan W. Scott, *Women, Work and Family* (New York: Holt, Rinehart, Winston, 1978). Painstaking analysis of the work women did.

Raymond Williams, *The Country and the City* (New York: Oxford University Press, 1973). Inquiry into the impact of the urban experience on artists and intellectuals.

C. Vann Woodward, *The Strange Career of Jim Crow,* 3rd ed. (New York: Oxford University Press, 1974). The most enduring study of the persistence in America of institutionalized racism into the twentieth century.

CHAPTER TWO: The Modernization of Nations

General Accounts

Guido DeRuggiero, *The History of European Liberalism,* trans. R. G. Collingwood (Boston: Beacon Press, 1959). A classic study of the development of the political idea, translated from the Italian by the philosopher-historian.

Matthew Fforde, *Conservatism and Collectivism, 1886–1914* (Edinburgh: Edinburgh University Press, 1990). Although concerned with Great Britain, this study reflects the concern of modern conservatism in the democracies with discovering a suitable response to the popular call for social reform.

Liah Greenfield, *Nationalism: Five Roads to Modernity* (Cambridge, Mass.: Harvard University Press, 1992). Provocative comparative study of the character of nationalism in France, Germany, Russia, Britain, and the United States.

Elie Kedourie, *Nationalism,* 4th ed. (Oxford, England: Blackwell, 1969); Hans Kohn, *Nationalism: Its Meaning and History* (Princeton, N.J.: Van Nostrand, 1965); and Boyd C. Shafer, *Faces of Nationalism: New Realities and Old Myths* (New York: Harcourt Brace Jovanovich, 1972). These volumes continue to be excellent introductions to the question.

Albert S. Lindemann, *A History of European Socialism* (New Haven, Conn.: Yale University Press, 1983). Clear analysis of the development of the socialist movement.

Michael Mason, *The Making of Victorian Sexual Attitudes* (New York: Oxford University Press, 1995). Excellent survey of the development of modernity.

T. Smith, *The Pattern of Imperialism* (Cambridge: Cambridge University Press, 1981); Daniel R. Headrick, *The Tools of Empire: Technology and European Imperialism in the Nineteenth Century* (New York: Oxford University Press, 1981). Useful works in understanding the background, theory, and practice of imperialism at its flood tide.

A. J. P. Taylor, *The Struggle for Mastery in Europe, 1848–1919* (Oxford: Oxford University Press, 1954). After a half-century of use, this provocative analysis by the most controversial historian of his generation remains crisp, informative, and innovative.

J. A. Thompson and Arthur Mejia, *Edwardian Conservatism: Five Studies in Adaptation* (London: Croom Helm, 1988). Essays on significant makers of British conservative opinion in the years before the First World War.

C. Vann Woodward, *The Comparative Approach to American* History (New York: Basic Books, 1968). Enlightening essays comparing American and European Developments.

France

Michael Burns, *Dreyfus: A Family Affair* (New York: Harper Collins, 1992) and Eric Cahm, *The Dreyfus Affair in French Society and Politics* (New York: Longman, 1996). Recent insightful appraisals of the Dreyfus case and its impact on France.

Albert Guérard, *France: A Modern History,* rev. ed. (Ann Arbor: University of Michigan Press, 1969). Sympathetic study by an American of French background. A richly detailed social and intellectual history is Theodore Zeldin, *France, 1848–1945* (Oxford: Clarendon Press, 1979). Other enlightening surveys are Alfred Cobban, *History of Modern France*, rev. ed., Vol. III (1871–1962) (London: Penguin, 1966); and David Thomson, *Democracy in France Since 1970*, 5th ed. (Oxford: Oxford University Press, 1969).

John H. Jackson, *Clemenceau and the Third Republic* (Westport, Conn.: Hyperion, 1979); Geoffrey Bruun, *Clemenceau* (Hamden, Conn.: Shoe String Press, 1968). Succinct studies of a formidable politician and his time.

Charles Rearick, *Pleasures of the Belle Epoque: Entertainment and Festivity in Turn-of-the-Century France* (New Haven, Conn.: Yale University Press, 1985). Enlightening study of popular culture and leisure in the era.

Frederick Seager, *The Boulanger Affair* (Ithaca, N.Y.: Cornell University Press, 1969. A revisionist refutation of a myth.

Eugen Weber, *Peasants into Frenchmen: The Modernization of Rural France* (Palo Alto, Calif: Stanford University Press, 1976). A complex, rich, and very significant achievement. Most impressive also is the same author's *France: Fin de Siècle* (Cambridge, Mass.: Harvard University Press, 1976). Weber turns to the rekindling of national consciousness and fervor in *The Nationalist Revival in France, 1905–1914* (Berkeley, Calif.: University of California Press, 1959).

Great Britain

P. J. Cain and A. G. Hopkins, *British Imperialism: Crisis and Deconstruction, 1914–1990* (London: Longman, 1993). The second volume of a massive and brilliant study of the greatest of the classic European empires. An older but still important study is Ronald Robinson and John Gallagher, with Alice Denny, *Africa and the Victorians: The Climax of Imperialism* (Garden City, N.Y.: Anchor Books, 1968). Also useful is the excellent study of the burden of racism that was an integral part of empire, Robert A. Huttenback, *Racism and Empire: White Settlers and Colored Immigrants in the British Self-Governing Colonies, 1830–1910* (Ithaca, N.Y.: Cornell University Press, 1976).

David Cannadine, *Aspects of Aristocracy: Grandeur and Decline in Modern Britain* (New Haven, Conn.: Yale University Press, 1994); and *The Decline and Fall of the British Aristocracy* (New Haven, Conn.: Yale University Press, 1990). Valuable analyses of the old aristocracy and of societal change brought about by the economics and politics of modernization.

George Dangerfield, *The Strange Death of Liberal England*, reprint ed. (Stanford, Calif.: Stanford University Press, 1999). A true classic and controversial since its publication in 1935, this study of the prewar political crises in Britain remains both entertaining and illuminating.

Pauline Gregg, *A Social and Economic History of Britain, 1760–1980*, 8th ed. (London: Harrap, 1982). Helpful survey of the impact on British life of an industrial economy.

Samuel Hynes, *The Edwardian Turn of Mind* (Princeton, N.J.: Princeton University Press, 1968). Detailed study of Edwardian tastes and manners.

Paul Johnson, ed., *Twentieth Century Britain: Economic, Social and Cultural Change* (London: Allison-Wesley, Longmon, 1994). Excellent and clear analysis of the evolution of British society in the century of democracy.

William L. Langer, *The Diplomacy of Imperialism, 1890–1902*, 2nd ed. (New York: Knopf, 1951). Detailed case histories from a particularly complex period.

Trevor Lloyd, *Empire. Welfare State, Europe: English History 1906–2000,* 5th ed. (Oxford: Oxford University Press, 2002). The latest edition of a long-established standard survey. Also excellent are Peter Clarke, *Hope and Glory: Britain, 1900–1990* (New York: Penguin, 1996) and an older work, Alfred Havighurst, *Britain in Transition: The Twentieth Century,* rev. ed. (Chicago: University of Chicago Press, 1985), one of the few such volumes written for an American student audience.

Philip Mason, *Patterns of Dominance* (Oxford: Oxford University Press, 1970). Examples of the varieties of colonial rule.

Thoedore Mommsen, *Theories of Imperialism,* trans. P. S. Falla (Chicago: University of Chicago Press, 1982). Concise, short discussion of the range of theories—Marxist, anti-Marxist, and non-Marxist—on the causes of imperialism.

Alan O'Day, *Irish Home Rule, 1867–1921* (Dover, N.H.: Manchester University Press, 1998), and Oliver MacDonagh, *States of Mind: A Study of Anglo-Irish Conflict* (London, 1983), survey the Irish Home Rule struggle.

A. P. Thornton, *Doctrines of Imperialism* (New York: Wiley, 1965); and Tom Kemp, *Theories of Imperialism* (London: Dobson, 1968). Useful analyses of the ideological background of British imperialism.

Germany

Ann Taylor Allen, *Feminism and Motherhood in Germany, 1800–1914* (New Brunswick, N.J.: Rutgers University Press, 1991). Excellent exploration of motherhood in German thought.

David Blackbourne and Geoff Eley, *The Peculiarities of German History* (Oxford: Oxford University Press, 1984). Original work that revises many of the conclusions historians have long had about Hohenzollern Germany.

Lamar Cecil, *William II, Prince and Emperor* (Chapel Hill: University of North Carolina Press, 1989), and *William II, Emperor in Exile* (Chapel Hill: University of North Carolina Press, 1996). The latest and best study of the complex figure at the center of the pinnacle and collapse of German imperial power. I. V. Hull, *The Entourage of Kaiser William II* (Cambridge, Cambridge University Press, 1982), offers the best picture of the German aristocratic power elite in the late imperial period.

Gordon A. Craig, *Germany, 1866–1945* (Oxford, England: Oxford University Press, 1978). Still perhaps the best survey of the first half of the century. Also quite useful is Richard J. Evans, *Society and Politics in Wilhelmine Germany* (London: Croom Helm, 1978).

L. L. Farrar, Jr., *Arrogance and Anxiety: The Ambivalence of German Power, 1848–1914* (Iowa City: University of Iowa Press, 1981). A close look at the years immediately preceding the First World War.

David Clay Large, *Berlin* (New York: Basic Books, 2000). Most recent study of the significance and history of the German metropolis.

W. N. Medlicott, *Bismarck and Modern Germany* (London: Hodder and Stoughton, 1974). A short but acute biography of the state-maker. The study by Alan Palmer, *Bismarck* (London: Weidenfield and Nicolson, 1976), is lively and balanced; that by A. J. P. Taylor, *Bismarck: The Man and the Statesman* (New York: Random House, 1967), is provocative and often highly critical.

Frederich Meinecke, *The German Catastrophe* (Boston: Beacon, 1963). A useful antidote to Taylor by a German historian.

John C. G. Röhl, *The Kaiser and His Court: Wilhelm II and the Government of Germany,* trans. Terence F. Cole (Cambridge, England: Cambridge University Press, 1994).

A recent powerful study of the workings of imperial government under the last emperor.

James J. Sheehan, *German Liberalism in the Nineteenth Century* (Chicago: University of Chicago Press, 1978). Difficult, careful unraveling of the failure of German liberalism.

The Habsburg Empire

Robert A. Kann, *The Multinational Empire* (New York: Octagon, 1964). A monograph, arranged by nationality; discusses national sentiments and the government's efforts to deal with them.

C. A. Macartney, *The House of Austria: The Later Phase, 1790–1918* (Edinburgh: Edinburgh University Press, 1978), and Alan Sked, *The Decline and Fall of the Habsburg Empire, 1815–1918*, 2nd ed. (New York: Longman, 1989), are excellent surveys of the last century of the Austro-Hungarian monarchy.

A. J. May, *The Hapsburg Monarchy, 1867–1914* (Cambridge, Mass.: Harvard University Press, 1951). Concise, general account.

Robin Okey, *Eastern Europe, 1740–1980: Feudalism to Communism* (Minneapolis: University of Minnesota Press, 1982). Clear, short history for the beginner.

Carl Schorske, *Fin-de-Siècle Vienna: Politics and Culture* (New York: Vintage, 1981). Brilliant essays on the relationship between culture as politics and Vienna as power center.

A. J. P. Taylor, *The Hapsburg Monarchy, 1809–1918* (Chicago: University of Chicago Press, 1948). Although somewhat dated, a spirited, brief treatment, well worth reading.

Italy

Derek Beales, *The Risorgimento and the Unification of Italy* (London: Longman, Green, 1982). Useful, clear appraisal.

Benedetto Croce, *A History of Italy, 1871–1915*, trans. Cecilia M. Ady (Oxford: Clarendon Press, 1929). A classic analysis, still much worth modern attention, by the great philosopher-historian.

A. W. Salomone, ed., *Italy from the Risorgimento to Fascism* (Garden City, N.J.: Anchor, 1970). An informative survey of the background of totalitarianism.

Christopher Seton-Watson, *Italy from Liberation to Fascism, 1870–1925* (New York: Methuen, 1967); Denis Mack Smith, *Italy: A Modern History* (Ann Arbor: University of Michigan Press, 1959). Standard accounts by ranking experts.

Russia

James H. Billington, *The Icon and the Axe* (New York: Vintage, 1970). Markedly rich, controversial interpretation of Russian culture.

Peter Brock, *The Slovak National Awakening* (Toronto: University of Toronto Press, 1976). Short essay on the intellectual history of cultural nationalism.

Charles Jelavich and Barbara Jelavich, *The Establishment of the Balkan National States, 1804–1920* (Seattle: University of Washington Press, 1977). Balanced, full account.

James Joll, *The Anarchists* (Cambridge, Mass.: Harvard University Press, 1980). A fine study of the extremist revolutionary movement in Russia.

Lionel Kochan, *Russia in Revolution, 1890–1918* (New York: NAL, 1966), and W. Bruce Lincoln, *In War's Dark Shadow: The Russians Before the Great War* (New York: Simon and Schuster, 1986), survey the years preceding the First World War and the 1917 Revolution.

Nicholas V. Riasanovsky, *A History of Russia*, 4th ed. (New York: Oxford University Press, 1984). Thorough and full study.

Gerold T. Robinson, *Rural Russia Under the Old Regime* (Berkeley: University of California Press, 1967). A splendid monograph on the peasant question.

CHAPTER THREE: Great War, Great Revolution

The Background

J. J. Becker, *The Great War and the French People* (New York: St. Martin's, 1986). A perceptive exploration of the French home front.

V. R. Berghahn, *Germany and the Approach of War in 1914*, 2nd ed. (New York: St. Martin's, 1994); Richard Bosworth, *Italy and the Approach of the First World War* (London: Macmillan, 1983); F. V. Keiger, *France and the Origins of the First World War* (London: Macmillan, 1983); D. C. B. Lieven, *Russia and the Origins the First World War* (London: Macmillan, 1983); and Zara Steiner, *Britain and the Origins of the First World War* (London: Macmillan, 1977). An excellent series of works concentrating on the issues surrounding the coming of war as they related to each of the great powers.

Vladimir Dedijer, *The Road to Sarajevo* (London: MacGibbon and Kee, 1967). Study of the Sarajevo assassins and of the role played by the Serbian leadership in the final crisis that touched off the First World War.

Fritz Fischer, *Germany's Aims in the First World War* (New York: Norton, 1967); *World Power or Decline: The Controversy over Germany's Aims in the World War I* (New York: Norton, 1974); and *War of Illusions: German Policies from 1911 to 1914* (New York: Norton, 1975). Three principal works available in English by the most controversial German historian of his generation, which powerfully indict the leaders of imperial Germany as the major culprits in causing the war.

Paul Kennedy, *The Rise and Fall of British Naval Mastery* (Atlantic Highlands, N.J.: Ashfield Press, 1983); and *The Rise of the Anglo German Antagonism* (Boston: Allen & Unwin, 1980). Excellent studies of the deterioration of relations between Britain and Germany in the years before the First World War.

H. W. Koch, ed., *The Origins of the First World War*, 2nd ed. (London: Macmillan, 1984); Gordon Martel, *The Origins of the First World War* (New York: Longman, 1996); Joachim Remark, *The Origins of World War I* (New York: Holt, Rinehart, 1976); and L. C. F. Turner, *Origins of the First World War* (New York: Norton 1970). Good, readable short histories of the coming of the war.

William L. Langer, *European Alliances and Alignments, 1871–1890*, reprint ed. (Westport, Conn.: Greenwood, 1977), and *The Diplomacy of Imperialism, 1890–1902*, 2nd ed. (New York: Knopf, 1951). Detailed scholarly analyses, including valuable bibliographies.

Walter Laqueur, *Russia and Germany: A Century of Conflict* (Boston: Little, Brown, 1965). Yet another factor in the background scrutinized.

George Monger, *The End of Isolation* (Westport, Conn.: Greenwood, 1976). British foreign policy reviewed. For Anglo-American relations, it may be supplemented by Bradford Perkins, *The Great Rapproachment* (New York: Atheneum, 1968).

Karen A. Rasler and William R. Thompson, *The Great Powers and Global Struggle, 1490–1990* (Lexington: University of Kentucky Press, 1995). Places all modern wars in historical perspective.

Gerhard Ritter, *The Sword and the Scepter: The Problem of Militarism in Germany*, 2 vols. (Miami, Fla.: University of Miami Press, 1970). Volume II deals with the European Powers and William II's Germany from 1890 to 1914.

Raymond J. Sontag, *Germany and England: Background of Conflict, 1848–1894* (New York: Norton, 1969). Excellent study of Anglo-German tensions in the half-century before the First World War.

Barbara Tuchman, *The Proud Tower* (New York: Macmillan, 1966). Instructive and readable account of the European societies that produced the Great War.

Samuel L. Williamson, *The Politics of Grand Strategy* (Cambridge, Mass.: Harvard University Press, 1969). Excellent assessment of the Anglo-French rapprochement before 1914.

The War

Frank Chambers, *The War Behind the War* (New York: Arno, 1972). On the "home fronts."

Richard Collier, *The Plague of the Spanish Lady* (New York: Atheneum, 1974). The drama of the influenza pandemic that swept the world in 1918–1919.

Modris Eksteins, *Rites of Spring: The Great War and the Birth of the Modern Age* (Boston: Houghton, Mifflin, 1989); Paul Fussell, *The Great War and Modern Memory* (New York: Oxford University Press, 1977). Excellent studies of the power of the World War in shaping modern consciousness.

Howard Elcock, *Portrait of a Decision: The Council of Four and the Treaty of Versailles* (London: Eyre Methuen, 1972). Analysis of the diplomatic decisions of 1919. Still useful is the classic study by Paul Birdsall, *Versailles Treaty Twenty Years After* (New York: Raynal and Hitchcock, 1941).

Martin Gilbert, *The First World War: A Complete History* (New York: Henry Holt, 1995); John Keegan, *The First World War* (New York: Knopf, 1999); Bernadotte Schmidt and Harold C. Vedeler, *The World in the Crucible, 1914–1918* (New York: Harper and Row, 1984); Excellent single-volume studies of the war. Recent short histories are Ian F. W. Beckett, *The Great War, 1914–1918* (Harlow, England: Longman, 2001); and Michael J. Lyons, *World War I*, 3rd ed. (Upper Saddle River, N.J.: Prentice-Hall, 1999). Although originally published in 1930, Basil H. Liddell Hart, *The Real War, 1914–1918*, reprint ed. (Boston: Little, Brown, 1963), is a classic study by a noted British military thinker.

Ernest R. May, *World War and American Isolation, 1914–1917* (Cambridge, Mass.: Harvard University Press, 1959), and *The Coming of War, 1917* (Chicago: Rand McNally, 1963). Reliable and balanced treatments of the events that made the United States a belligerent.

Elizabeth Monroe, *Britain's Moment in the Middle East, 1914–1956*, rev. ed. (Baltimore: Johns Hopkins University Press, 1981). Persuasive explanation of the contradictions in Britain's policy toward Arabs and Jews, particularly during the First World War and the ensuing peace negotiations.

Alan Moorehead, *Gallipoli* (Annapolis: Nautical, 1982); Alistair Horne, *The Price of Glory: Verdun, 1916* (London: Penguin, 1979). Excellent accounts of two of the most hard-fought campaigns of the war.

Gerhard Ritter, *The Schlieffen Plan: Critique of a Myth* (Westport, Conn.: Greenwood, 1979). Scholarly reassessment of the German master plan for victory in the West in 1914.

A. J. P. Taylor, *The First World War* (London: Penguin, 1978); B. H. Liddell Hart, *The Real War, 1914–1918* (Boston: Little, Brown, 1964). Lively, opinionated brief surveys.

Barbara Tuchman, *The Guns of August* (New York: Macmillan, 1962). Well-written narrative of the first critical month of the war and the crisis preceding it.

Richard M. Watt, *Dare Call It Treason* (New York: Simon and Schuster, 1963). The story of the most concerted French attempt to break the deadlock of trench warfare and of the mutiny that resulted from it in 1917.

Denis Winter, *Death's Men* (London, Allen Lane, 1978). Intense evocation of the experience of battle.

J. M. Winter, *The Experience of World War I* (New York: Oxford University Press, 1989). Profusely illustrated study; covers both military and civilian life.

Zloynek Zeman, *The Gentlemen Negotiators* (New York: Macmillan, 1971). Study of diplomacy during the war.

The Peace

John Maynard Keynes, *The Economic Consequences of the Peace* (New York: Brace and Howe, 1920); Etienne Mantoux, *The Carthaginian Peace; or, the Economic Consequences of Mr. Keynes* (New York: Arno, 1979). Respectively, the most famous attack on the Versailles settlement and a thoughtful counterblast focusing on the results of that attack.

Arno J. Mayer, *The Political Origins of the New Diplomacy, 1917–1918* (New York: Random House, 1970), and *The Politics and Diplomacy of Peacemaking* (New York: Knopf, 1967). Two studies that stress the role played by the fear of Bolshevism in the western democracies. For another interpretation, see J. M. Thompson, *Russia, Bolshevism and the Versailles Peace* (Princeton, N.J.: Princeton University Press, 1966).

Harold Nicolson, *Peacemaking 1919,* reprint ed. (Boston: Peter Smith, n.d.). Informative study by a member of the British delegation at Paris.

Robert Skidelsky, *John Maynard Keynes: The Economist as Saviour* (New York: Penguin, 1994). Volume II of a three-volume biography.

The Russian Revolution: General

Robert V. Daniels, *The Nature of Communism* (New York: Random House, 1962); R. N. Carew Hunt, *The Theory and Practice of Communism* (New York: Macmillan, 1951). Excellent introductions to the subject.

Barrington Moore, Jr., *Soviet Politics: The Dilemma of Power* (Armonk, N.Y.: Sharpe, 1977). An illuminating analysis of the relationship between communist ideology and Soviet practice.

Richard Pipes, *The Russian Revolution* (New York: Knopf, 1991). The fullest and best account. An excellent brief survey is Sheila Fitzpatrick, *The Russian Revolution, 1917–1932*, 2nd ed. (Oxford: Oxford University Press, 1994).

The Russian Revolution: Special Studies

Charles L. Bertrand, ed., *Revolutionary Situations in Europe, 1917–22* (Montreal, Canada: Interuniversity Centre for European Studies, 1977). Studies of the ultimate failure to secure revolution in Austria-Hungary, Germany, and Italy.

Crane Brinton, *The Anatomy of Revolution* (New York: Random House, 1965). Comparison of the Russian Revolution with the French Revolution of 1789 and the English revolution of the mid-seventeenth century.

Robert Conquest, *Lenin* (London: Fontana, 1972). Standard biography in English. The latest study is Robert Service, *Lenin* (Cambridge, Mass.: Harvard University

Press, 2000). Also very good are M. C. Morgan, *Lenin* (London: Edward Arnold, 1971), and David Shub, *Lenin* (London: Penguin, 1977).

Isaac Deutscher, *The Prophet Armed, the Prophet Unarmed, the Prophet Outcast* (Oxford: Oxford University Press, 1980). Biography of Trotsky in three volumes.

Merle Fainsod, *Smolensk Under Soviet Rule* (Cambridge, Mass.: Harvard University Press, 1958). A unique study, based on a collection of captured documents of the actual workings of the communist system in Smolensk in the 1930s.

Marc Ferro, *The Russian Revolution of 1917*, trans. J. L. Richards (Englewood Cliffs, N.J.: Prentice-Hall, 1972). Close study of the fall of czarism and the defeat of the February Revolution. Also by the same author, *October 1917: A Social History of the Russian Revolution*, trans. Norman Stone (London: Routledge and Kegan Paul, 1980). Fine social history.

Sergei Petrovich Mel'gunov, *The Bolshevik Seizure of Power* (Santa Barbara, Calif.: ABC-Clio, 1972). Study of Lenin's triumph over his rivals.

Richard Pipes, *The Formation of the Soviet Union* (New York: Atheneum, 1968). Excellent monograph on the question of national minorities in Russia from 1917 to 1923.

Nicholas Timasheff, *The Great Retreat* (Salem, N.H.: Arno, 1972). Account of the "Russian Thermidor."

Donald W. Treadgold, *Lenin and His Rivals: The Struggle for Russia's Future, 1898–1906* (Westport, Conn.: Greenwood, 1976). Examines the alternatives to Lenin in the pre-Revolutionary period.

Adam B. Ulam, *The Bolsheviks: The Intellectual and Political History of the Triumph of Communism in Russia* (New York: Macmillan, 1968); *Stalin: The Man and His Era* (New York: Viking, 1974). Excellent detailed accounts. The first six chapters of the same author's *Expansion and Coexistence: The History of Soviet Foreign Policy, 1900–1930* (New York: Holt, Rinehart, 1974), deal with the period to 1941.

Theo H. Von Laue, *Why Lenin? Why Stalin? A Reappraisal of the Russian Revolution, 1900–1930* (Philadelphia: Lippincott, 1964). Thoughtful analysis of the causes of the communist victory in Russia.

Sources

Henri Barbusse, *Under Fire* (Totowa, N.J.: Biblio, 1975), and E. M. Remarque, *All Quiet on the Western Front* (New York: Fawcett, 1929). Two famous novels—by a Frenchman and German, written fifty years apart—reflect the horror aroused among intellectuals by trench warfare.

James Bunyan and H. H. Fisher, eds., *The Bolshevik Revolution, 1917–1918* (Palo Alto, Calif.: Stanford University Press, 1961). Substantial collection of documents and sources.

Robert V. Daniels, ed., *The Russian Revolution* (Englewood Cliffs, N.J., Prentice-Hall, 1972). A well-chosen and well-discussed selection of sources.

Leon Trotsky, *The History of the Russian Revolution* (New York: Pluto, 1980). Brilliant and biased study by the revolutionary and creator of the Red Army.

The Environment

Neville Brown, *History and Climate Change* (London and New York: Routledge, 2001). Covers a broad sweep from late antiquity to the present.

Susan Buckingham-Hatfield, *Gender and Environment* (London and New York: Routledge, 2000). Particularly useful for its lists of further reading.

J. Donald Hughes, *An Environmental History of the World* (London and New York: Routledge 2001). A survey based on case studies.

J. R. McNeill, *Something New Under the Sun* (New York and London: Norton, 2000). A comprehensive environmental history of the world in the twentieth century.

CHAPTER FOUR: Between the Wars: A Twenty-Year Crisis

The Roots of Fascism

Edward Hallett Carr, *The Twenty Years Crisis, 1919–1939* (New York: Harper and Row, 1964). Clear exposition of the relationship between fascism and foreign policy.

Alfred Cobban, *Dictatorship in History and Theory* (New York: Haskell, 1970). Highly suggestive survey reaching well back into history.

Roger Griffin, ed., *Fascism* (New York: Oxford University Press, 1995). Informative collection of essays on the theory, nature, and practice of fascism.

George Mosse, *The Crisis of German Ideology: Intellectual Origins of the Third Reich* (New York: Fertig, 1981); Fritz Stern, *The Politics of Cultural Despair* (Berkeley: University of California Press, 1965). Contrasting, solid studies of Hitler's forerunners.

Hans Rogger and Eugen Webers, eds., *The European Right: A Historical Profile* (Berkeley: University of California Press, 1965). Learned and stimulating collection of essays on right-wing movements in the various countries of Europe; includes good bibliographies.

Raymond Sontag, *A Broken World, 1919–1939* (New York: Harper and Row, 1971). Fine survey of the interwar years.

Henry A. Turner, Jr., *Reappraisals of Fascism* (New York: Franklin Watts, 1975). Review of interpretations of fascism, with emphasis on the arguments of the German scholar Ernest Nolte.

Russia

William L. Blackwell, *The Industrialization of Russia* (Arlington Heights, Ill.: Harlan Davidson, 1982). Full survey.

Edward H. Carr, *A History of Soviet Russia* (New York: Macmillan, 1951–1964). The only attempt at a complete history of the Soviet Union from original sources.

Robert Conquest, *The Politics of Ideas in the U.S.S.R.* (Westport, Conn.: Greenwood, 1976). Intriguing study of the mobilization of thought.

Robert Conquest, *The Great Terror: A Reassessment* (New York: Oxford University Press, 1990). Examination of how the Terror came about and of the heritage it established.

R. W. Davies, *The Socialist Offensive: The Collectivization of Soviet Agriculture, 1929–30* (Cambridge, Mass.: Harvard University Press, 1980). Thorough study of the theory, politics, and practices of Stalinist agriculture policy.

Merle Fainsod, *How Russia Is Ruled* (Cambridge, Mass.: Harvard University Press, 1963). Analysis of the Soviet system, firmly rooted in the historical background.

Loren R. Graham, *The Ghost of the Executed Engineer: Technology and the Fall of the Soviet Union* (Cambridge, Mass.: Harvard University Press, 1993). The subtitle tells all.

Naum Jasny, *Soviet Economists in the Twenties* (Cambridge: Cambridge University Press, 1972). On the NEP and post-NEP economic thought and the socialized agriculture of the USSR. Especially good on the *kolkhoz*.

Moshe Lewin, *Russia's Peasants and Soviet Power: A Study in Collectivization*, trans. Irene Nove (London: Allen and Unwin, 1968). Good study of the drive to collectivize.

Roy Medvedev, *Let History Judge: The Origins and Consequences of Stalinism*, trans. Colleen Taylor (New York: Knopf, 1971). Critical study of the dictator written by a dissident before the fall of the Soviet dictatorship.

Barrington Moore, *Soviet Politics: The Dilemma of Power* (New York: Sharpe, 1977). Illuminating analysis of the relationship between communist ideology and Soviet practice.

Christopher Reed, *Culture and Power in Revolutionary Russia* (London: Macmillan, 1990). Focuses on the intelligentsia.

Donald W. Treadgold, *Twentieth Century Russia* (Boston: Houghton Mifflin, 1981). Good basic text.

Robert C. Tucker, ed., *Stalinism: Essays in Historical Interpretation* (New York: Norton, 1977). Extremely useful collection for understanding the Stalinist dictatorship.

Adam Ulam, *Stalin: The Man and His Era* (New York: Viking, 1973). Excellent detailed account.

Italy

Victoria De Grazia, *How Fascism Ruled Women* (Berkeley: University of California Press, 1993). Recent enquiry into the role in theory and practice of women in the fascist state.

Charles F. Delzell, *Mussolini's Enemies: The Italian Anti-Fascist Resistance* (Princeton, N.J.: Princeton University Press, 1961). Remains the best study in English of this movement.

Herman Finer, *Mussolini's Italy* (Hamden, Conn.: Archon, 1964); H. A. Steiner, *Government in Fascist Italy* (New York: McGraw-Hill, 1938). Two solid studies by political scientists.

Jasper Ridley, *Mussolini* (New York: St. Martin's, 1998). Excellent recent biography of the dictator.

Gaetano Salvemini, *Under the Axe of Fascism* (New York: Howard Fertig, 1970). Lively work by an important antifascist Italian.

Denis Mack Smith, *Mussolini* (New York: Viking, 1982), and *Mussolini's Roman Empire* (New York: Viking, 1976). Recent appraisals that remain essentially hostile to Mussolini.

Elizabeth Wiskemann, *Fascism in Italy: Its Development and Influence* (London: Macmillan, 1970). Brief, clear analysis.

Germany

William Sheridan Allen, *The Nazi Seizure of Power* (New York: Franklin Watts, 1973). Close examination of how Nazism took over at the local level.

Karl D. Bracher, *The German Dictatorship* (New York: Holt, Rinehart, 1972). Excellent comprehensive study by a German scholar.

Michael Burleigh, *The Third Reich* (New York: Hill & Wang, 2000). A recent and useful survey of the world created by Nazism.

John S. Conway, *The Nazi Persecution of the Churches* (New York: Basic Books, 1968); Ernst C. Helmreich, *The German Churches Under Hitler* (Detroit: Wayne State University Press, 1979). Useful studies of the policy of the Nazi state toward organized religion.

Erich Eyck, *A History of the Weimar Republic* (New York: Atheneum, 1970). Superb, full examination.

Ruth Fischer, *Stalin and German Communism* (New Brunswick, N.J.: Transaction, 1982). Study of the role by the communist movement in the history of Germany between the wars.

Peter Gay, *Weimar Culture* (New York: Harper and Row, 1968). Excellent study of the cultural world of the interwar German republic.

Samuel W. Halperin, *Germany Tried Democracy* (New York: Crowell, 1946). Still useful survey of the Weimar Republic.

Ian Kershaw, *Hitler: Hubris, 1889–1936,* and *Hitler: Nemesis, 1936–1945* (New York: Norton, 1998, 2002). Most recent and acclaimed study of the dictator. Alan Bullock, *Hitler: A Study in Tyranny* (New York: Harper and Row, 1964), deserves the term classic; also excellent are Joachim Fest, *Hitler,* trans. Richard and Clara Winston (New York: Knopf, 1982), and Norman Stone, *Hitler* (New York: Knopf, 1982). Fascinating is Bullock's comparative study of the two dictators: *Hitler and Stalin: Parallel Lives* (New York: Knopf, 1992).

Franz L. Neumann, *Behemoth: The Structure and Practice of National Socialism* (New York: Octagon, 1963). Extremely useful analytical description.

David Schoenbaum, *Hitler's Social Revolution,* reprint ed. (New York: Norton, 1980). Examines the social and economic goals of the Third Reich and the policies implemented to achieve them.

Henry Turner, Jr., *Gustav Stresemann and the Politics of Weimar* (Westport, Conn.: Greenwood, 1979). Fine inquiry into a failed leader.

Robert G. Waite, *Vanguard of Nazism* (Cambridge, Mass.: Harvard University Press). Study of the Free Corps movement.

J. W. Wheeler-Bennett, *Wooden Titan* (New York: Morrow, 1936), and *Nemesis of Power* (New York: St. Martin's, 1954). Two first-rate and long-lived studies: the first a life of Hindenberg, the second a study of the role of the German army in politics, 1918–1945.

Elizabeth Wiskemann, *The Rome-Berlin Axis* (New York: Oxford University Press, 1949). Examination of the formation and history of the Hitler-Mussolini partnership.

Other Countries

Gerald Brenan, *The Spanish Labyrinth,* 2nd ed. (Cambridge: Cambridge University Press, 1960). Informative study of the Spanish Civil War against its historical and economic background.

Raymond Carr, *Spain, 1808–1939* (New York: Oxford University Press, 1982). Includes a careful examination of Franco in the light of earlier history.

Nicholas Nagy-Talvera, *The Green Shirts and the Others: A History of Fascism in Hungary and Rumania* (Stanford, Calif.: Hoover Institution, 1970). Full examination.

Stanley G. Payne, *Falange* (Palo Alto, Calif.: Stanford University Press, 1961). Good study of the Spanish Falangist movement.

Frederick B. Pike, *Hispanismo* (Notre Dame, Ind.: University of Notre Dame Press, 1971). Examination of the corporative state in Spain.

Paul Preston, *Franco: A Biography* (New York: Basic Books, 1994). Shrewd, balanced narrative.

Mary Louise Roberts, *Civilization Without Sexes: Reconstructing Gender in Postwar France, 1917–1927* (Chicago: University of Chicago Press, 1993). A stunning work of feminist theory.

Hugh Seton-Watson, *Eastern Europe between the Wars, 1918–1941,* 3rd ed. (Hamden, Conn.: 1993). Useful account dealing with all the eastern European countries except Greece and Albania.

Peter F. Sugar, ed., *Native Fascism in the Successor States* (Santa Barbara, Calif.: ABC-Clio, 1971). Helpful essays that examine the roots of fascism in the new states created by the Peace of Paris.

Hugh Thomas, *The Spanish Civil War,* rev. ed. (New York: Harper and Row, 1977). Best single work on the subject in English.

Bela Vago, *The Shadow of the Swastika: The Rise of Fascism and Anti-Semitism in the Danube Basin, 1936–1939* (Farnborough, England: Saxon House, 1975). Examination of the rise of the extreme right in the successor states years after the establishment and "legitimization" of fascism in Germany and Italy.

Sources

Adolf Hitler, *Mein Kampf* (London: Hurst and Blackett, 1939) Complete English translation of the Nazi bible; basic work to understanding the movement.

Adolf Hitler, *My New Order,* ed. R. de Sales (New York: Octagon, 1973). Speeches after the *Führer's* coming to power.

Jeremy Noakes and Geoffrey Pridham, *Nazism: A Documentary Reader,* 4 vols. (Exeter, England: University of Exeter Press, 1983–1998). Sources documenting the entire Nazi era.

Robert Payne, ed., *The Civil War in Spain* (Greenwich, Conn.: Fawcett, 1962). Original documents on the bloody conflict.

Albert Speer, *Inside the Third Reich: Memoirs,* trans. Richard and Clara Winston (New York: Macmillan, 1970). Memoirs of Hitler's architect, city planner, and munitions minister; invaluable picture of life among the Nazis.

Franz von Papen, *Memoirs* (New York: AMS Press, 1978). Apologetic autobiography by the right-wing politician.

Eugen Weber, *Varieties of Fascism* (Melbourne, Fla.: Krieger, 1982). Short history with selection of sources.

CHAPTER FIVE: The Democracies and the Non-Western World

The Political and Economic Climate

Eric Fischer, *The Passing of the European Age* (Cambridge, Mass.: Harvard University Press, 1943); Felix Gilbert and David Clay Large, *The End of the European Era: 1890 to the Present* (New York: Norton, 2002); Robert O. Paxton, *Europe in the Twentieth Century* (New York: Harcourt Brace Jovanovich, 1985). Reasoned and thorough surveys that place great emphasis on the importance of the First World War in understanding the decline of European power.

John Kenneth Galbraith, *The Great Crash* (New York: Avon, 1980); Charles P. Kindleberger, *The World Depression, 1929–39* (Berkeley: University of California Press, 1977); and David Landes, *The Unbound Prometheus* (Cambridge: Cambridge University Press, 1970). Valuable studies of the nature and context of the Great Depression.

Mark Mazower, *Dark Continent: Europe's Twentieth Century* (New York: Knopf, 1999); James Wilkinson and H. Stuart Hughes, *Contemporary Europe,* 9th ed. (Upper Saddle River, N.J.: Prentice Hall, 1998). Excellent surveys stressing intellectual history.

A. J. P. Taylor, *From Sarajevo to Potsdam* (New York: Harcourt Brace Jovanovich, n.d.). Useful survey of the period, stressing military-diplomatic developments.

Great Britain

Noreen Branson and Margot Heinemann, *Britain in the Nineteen Thirties* (New York: Praeger 1971). A study of the underclasses during the Great Depression.

George Dangerfield, *The Damnable Question: A Study in Anglo-Irish Relations* (Boston: Little, Brown, 1976). Balanced account of the Irish Question in British politics.

Martin Gilbert, *Churchill: A Life* (New York: Henry Holt, 1991). Perhaps the best, certainly one of the most complete, of the many one-volume studies of Churchill; by the author of most of the multivolume official biography.

Robert Graves and Alan Hodge, *The Long Week-End* (New York: Norton, 1963). Lively social history of Britain between the world wars.

Samuel Hynes, *The Auden Generation: Literature and Politics in England in the 1930s* (Princeton, N.J.: Princeton University Press, 1977). Survey of the attitudes and influence of writers of the interwar years.

Robert Rhodes James, *The British Revolution, 1880–1939* (New York: Knopf, 1977). Fine exploration of how Britain changed in fundamental ways.

Keith Middlemas and John Barnes, *Baldwin* (New York: Macmillan, 1970). Still the best full biography of Baldwin.

Henry Pelling, *Winston Churchill* (London: Macmillan, 1974). Balanced, full biography.

Stephen Roskill, *Naval Policy Between the Wars*, 2 vols. (New York: Walker, 1968). The first volume is especially good on the period of Anglo-American antagonism, from 1919 to 1929.

Robert Skidelsky, *Politicians and the Slump: The Labour Government of 1929–1931* (London: Penguin, 1970). Critical study of the failure of the second MacDonald cabinet.

Martin J. Weiner, *English Culture and the Decline of the Industrial Spirit, 1850–1980* (London: Cambridge University Press, 1985). Strong survey with an eye toward the interaction between cultural, economic, and political change.

France

René Albrecht-Carrie, *France, Europe and the Two World Wars* (Westport, Conn.: Greenwood, 1975). Illuminating study of French difficulties against their international background.

D. W. Brogan, *France Under the Republic* (Westport, Conn.: Greenwood, 1974). Stimulating survey.

Nathaniel Greene, *From Versailles to Vichy: The Third French Republic, 1919–1940* (Arlington Heights, Ill.: Harland Davidson, 1970). Lucid, brief survey of interwar France.

Stanley Hoffman et al., *In Search of France* (Cambridge, Mass.: Harvard University Press, 1963); James Joll, ed., *The Decline of the Third Republic* (London: Chatto and Windus, 1959). Insightful essays that remain valuable.

Julian Jackson, *The Politics of Depression in France* (Cambridge: Cambridge University Press, 1985). Study of the unhappy political climate in France in the years between the wars.

H. Stuart Hughes, *The Obstructed Path: French Social Thought in the Years of Desperation, 1930–1960* (New York: Harper & Row 1968). Meticulous analysis of French intellectuals in the interwar years and after.

Robert Soucy, *French Fascism: The First Wave: 1924–1933,* and *French Fascism: The Second Wave, 1933–1939* (New Haven, Conn.: Yale University Press, 1986, 1995). Two volumes that offer a detailed and fascinating examination of the makeup and impact on French society of the organizations of the extreme right.

The United States

Frederick Lewis Allen, *Only Yesterday* and *Since Yesterday* (New York: Harper and Row, 1972). Evocative firsthand social histories of the 1920s and 1930s, respectively.

James M. Burns, *Roosevelt: The Lion and the Fox* (New York: Harcourt Brace Jovanovich, 1970). Analysis of FDR as politician.

William Leuchtenberg, *Perils of Prosperity, 1914–1932* (Chicago: University of Chicago Press, n.d.), and *Franklin D. Roosevelt and the New Deal, 1932–1940* (New York: Harper and Row, 1963). Well-balanced and widely read surveys.

Arthur M. Schlesinger, Jr., *The Age of Roosevelt* (Boston: Houghton Mifflin, 1957). Detailed study by a sympathetic though not uncritical historian.

The Non-Western World

George Antonius, *The Arab Awakening* (New York: Capricorn, 1965). The classic sympathetic account stresses the rapid growth of Arab nationalism in the years during and immediately after World War I.

Erik Erikson, *Gandhi's Truth* (New York: Norton, 1969). Appraisal by a distinguished psychohistorian. May be supplemented by Robert Duncan, *Gandhi: Selected Writings* (New York: Colophon, n.d.).

John K. Fairbank, *The United States and China,* 4th ed. (Cambridge, Mass.: Harvard University Press, 1979); Edwin O. Reishauer, *The United States and Japan,* 2nd ed. (Cambridge, Mass.: Harvard University Press, 1965); W. Norman Brown, *The United States and India, Pakistan and Bangladesh,* 3rd ed. (Cambridge, Mass.: Harvard University Press, 1972); W. R. Polk, *The United States and the Arab World,* rev. ed. (Cambridge, Mass.: Harvard University Press, 1969); J. F. Gallagher, *The United States and North Africa* (Cambridge, Mass.: Harvard University Press, 1963). Volumes in the American Foreign Policy Library furnish scholarly appraisal of the recent history of the countries indicated.

Firuz Kazemazadeh, *Russia and Britain in Persia, 1864–1914* (New Haven, Conn.: Yale University Press, 1968). Excellent background for understanding the persistence of Iranian fears of Russia and the West.

Jean Lacouture and S. Lacouture, *Egypt in Transition* (New York: Methuen, 1958); Stephen H. Longrigg, *Syria and Lebanon Under French Mandate* (New York: Octagon, 1972); Joseph M. Upton, *The History of Modern Iran: An Interpretation* (Cambridge, Mass.: Harvard University Press, 1960). Perceptive studies of individual Middle Eastern states.

Gordon Lewis, *Turkey,* 3rd ed. (New York: Praeger, 1965), and Lord Kinross (Patrick Balfour), *Ataturk* (London: Weidenfeld and Nicolson, 1964). Respectively, a lively survey of the Turkish revolution and a clear biography of its chief architect.

Sources

F. Scott Fitzgerald, *The Great Gatsby* (New York: Scribner's, 1982). The famous novel that defined the jazz age in its time.

Frank Friedel, ed., *The New Deal and the American People* (Englewood, Cliffs, N.J.: Prentice-Hall, 1964). Sampling of different views.

André Gide, *The Counterfeiters* (New York: Random House, 1982). French middle-class values put under the microscope by a talented novelist.

Ernest Hemingway, *The Sun Also Rises* (New York: Scribner's, 1982). Widely considered the classic novel about the "lost generation" of disillusioned American idealists after World War I, by one of its key members.

Aldous Huxley, *Point Counterpoint* (New York: Doubleday, 1928) and *Brave New World* (New York: Harper & Row, 1946). Mordant novels written in the 1920s appraising contemporary mores in England and forecasting their future, respectively.

André Malraux, *Man's Fate* (New York: Random House, 1969). Excellent novel about Chinese communism in the 1920s.

Frances Perkins, *The Roosevelt I Knew* (New York: Viking, 1946). Perceptive appraisal by the secretary of labor in the Roosevelt years.

Howard Spring, *Fame Is the Spur* (New York: Viking, 1940). The career of the fictional hero, who is corrupted by political ambition, has many parallels to that of Ramsay MacDonald.

John Steinbeck, *The Grapes of Wrath* (New York: Viking, 1939). American classic novel of the "Okies" journeying from Oklahoma to California in the wake of drought and depression.

Evellyn Waugh, *Decline and Fall* and *A Handful of Dust* (Boston: Little, Brown, 1977). Two corrosive short novels, published in one volume, on English society in the interwar years.

CHAPTER SIX: The Second World War and Its Aftermath

General Accounts

P. M. H. Bell, *The Origins of the Second World War* (London: Longmans, 1986). Fine, short inquiry.

Maurice Cowling, *The Impact of Hitler* (Chicago: University of Chicago Press). Original look at British policies from 1933 to 1940.

Martin Gilbert, *The Second World War*, rev. ed. (New York: Henry Holt, 1991); John Keegan, *The Second World War* (New York: Viking, 1990); Henri Michel, *The Second World War*, trans. Douglas Parmalee (New York: Praeger, 1975); and Peter Calvocoressi and Guy Wint, *Total War: Causes and Course of the Second World War* (London: Allen Lane, 1972). Four excellent and massive histories.

Eric Hobsbawm, *The Age of Extremes: A History of the World, 1914–1991* (New York: Pantheon, 1995). Sweeping history that knits together much of the twentieth century.

Akira Iriye, *The Origins of the Second World War in Asia and the Pacific* (London: Longmans, 1987). The author sets the Pacific war into the context of world history.

Donald Kagan, *On the Origins of War and the Preservation of Peace* (New York: Doubleday, 1965). Fine analysis from ancient to present time.

Jon Livingston, Joe Moore, and Felicia Oldfather, eds., *Imperial Japan, 1800–1945* (New York: Pantheon, 1973). Draws upon Japanese scholars to give their point of view.

Michael J. Lyons, *World War II: A Short History*, 3rd ed. (Upper Saddle River, N.J.: Prentice-Hall, 1999). Excellent brief survey.

Samuel Elliot Morrison, *History of United States Naval Operations in World War II*, 15 vols. (Boston: Little, Brown, 1947–1962). Official but detached professional history; pays full attention to political and diplomatic problems.

R. A. C. Parker, *Struggle for Survival* (Oxford: Oxford University Press, 1989). Superb on economic, diplomatic, and military history.

Gordon W. Prange, *At Dawn We Slept* (New York: Penguin, 1983). The most nearly definitive account of the entry of the United States into the war.

Albert Seaton, *The Battle for Moscow, 1941–1942* (London: Hart-Davis, 1971). Model study of a crucial battle.

Nikolai Sivach and Eugene Yazkov, *History of the USA Since World War I*, trans. A. B. Eklov (Moscow: Progress, 1976). The United States and the Second World War from the official Soviet point of view.

Christopher Thorne, *The Approach of War, 1938–1939* (New York: Macmillan, 1969). Good short examination of the critical months leading up to the outbreak of war.

D. W. Urwin, *Western Europe Since 1945* (New York: Longmans, 1985). Crisp introduction. Gerhard Weinberg, *A World at Arms: A Global History of World War II* (New York: Cambridge University Press, 1993). Balanced, well reasoned, sweeping history.

Special Studies

R. J. Q. Adams, *British Politics and Foreign Policy in the Age of Appeasement, 1935–39* (Stanford, Calif.: Stanford University Press, 1993); R. A. C. Parker, *Chamberlain and Appeasement: British Policy and the Coming of the Second World War* (New York: St. Martin's Press, 1993). Two recent studies of the appeasement as a proactive, if ultimately disastrous, program. A recent highly readable defense of the Chamberlain policy is John Charmley, *Chamberlain and the Lost Peace* (London: Hodder and Stoughton, 1989).

David Bankier, ed., *Probing the Depths of Anti-Semitism: German Society and the Persecution of the Jews, 1933–1941* (New York: Berghan, 2000). Excellent collection of essays on the development of institutionalized anti-Semitism in the Third Reich.

Edward Bishop, *Their Finest Hour* (New York: Ballantine, 1968). Succinct illustrated history of the battle of Britain in 1940.

Larry Collins and Dominique LePierra, *Is Paris Burning?* (New York: Simon and Schuster, 1965). Deservedly popular account of the liberation of Paris.

Lucy Dawidowicz, *The War Against the Jews* (New York: Holt, Rinehart, Winston, 1975); Gerald Fleming, *Hitler and the Final Solution* (Berkeley: University of California Press, 1984). Two compelling, widely read essays on the planning and execution of the Holocaust. Also useful is Ronnie S. Landau, *The Nazi Holocaust* (Chicago: I.R. Dee, 1994). Largely differing views on the controversial questions of complicity and intent are explained in two of the latest and more controversial works on the "Final Solution": Christopher Browning, *Nazi Policy, Jewish Workers, German Killers* (Cambridge: Cambridge University Press, 2000); and Daniel Goldhagen, *Willing Executioners: Ordinary Germans and the Holocaust* (New York: Knopf, 1996).

Herbert Feis, *Churchill, Roosevelt, Stalin* (Princeton, N.J.: Princeton University Press, 1967). Fascinating and fair-minded account of their wartime relationship.

Otto Friedrich, *The End of the World: A History* (New York: Coward, MacCann and Geoghegan). Through a close examination of Auschwitz, places the Holocaust into perspective.

Felix Gilbert and G. A. Craig, *The Diplomats, 1929–1939* (Princeton, N.J.: Princeton University Press, 1953). Helpful symposium.

David L. Gordon and Royden Dangerfield, *The Hidden Weapon: The Story of Economic Warfare* (New York: Harper, 1947). Still useful popular account.

Stephen Hawes and Ralph T., White, eds., *Resistance in Europe, 1939–1945* (London: Allen Lane, 1975). Illustrative essays on the nature and effectiveness of the national resistance movements during the wartime occupations.

Gabriel Kolko, *The Politics of War: The United States and Foreign Policy, 1943–1945* (New York: Random House, 1968); Walter Lafeber, *America, Russia and the Cold War, 1945–1992*, 7th ed. (New York: McGraw-Hill, 1993). Two potent analyses of the origins of the Cold War and the bipolarization of world power: the first a more or less "new left" critique, the latter a more recent synthesis analysis.

William L. Langer and S. Everett Gleason, *The Challenge to Isolation, 1937–1940*, reprint ed. (Boston: Peter Smith, 1978), and *The Undeclared War, 1940–1941*, reprint ed. (Boston: Peter Smith, 1976). Solid long-lived studies of America's role.

Alan S. Milward, *War, Economy and Society, 1939–45* (London: Alan Lane, 1977). Necessary study of the economics of modern total warfare.

Charles L. Mowat, ed., *The Shifting Balance of World Forces, 1898–1945* (Cambridge: Cambridge University Press, 1968). Massive, synoptic history: Vol. XII of the *New Cambridge Modern History.*

Williamson Murray, *Lutwaffe* (London: Allen and Unwin, 1985). Best study in English of the German air force in the Second World War.

Richard Overy, *Interrogations: The Nazi Elite in Allied Hands, 1945* (New York: Viking, 2001). Fascinating study of the questioning of the captured Nazi leaders following their defeat.

Robert O. Paxton, *Vichy France: Old Guard and New Order, 1940–1944* (New York: Columbia University Press, 1982). The best explanation of the French collaborationist government, its supporters and opponents.

S. R. Smith, *The Manchurian Crisis, 1931–1932* (New York: Columbia University Press, 1948). On the watershed between prewar and postwar periods.

Charles C. Tansill, *Back Door to War: The Roosevelt Foreign Policy* (Westport, Conn.: Greenwood, 1975). Alleging that Roosevelt pushed America into war.

Telford Taylor, *Munich: The Price of Peace* (New York: Random House, 1979). Encyclopedic record of the policy, by the chief U.S. prosecutor at the postwar Nuremberg War Crimes Trials. The same author's personal recollection of these proceedings is also informative: *The Anatomy of the Nuremberg Trials* (New York: Knopf, 1992).

Neville Thompson, *The Anti-Appeasers* (Oxford: Clarendon Press, 1971). Discussion of the critics of the appeasement policy in 1930s British politics.

Donald Cameron Watt, *How War Came: The Immediate Origins of the Second World War, 1938–1939* (London: Heinemann, 1989). Imposing study of the year between Munich and the onset of war, by a distinguished diplomatic historian.

Barton Whaley, *Codeword Barbarossa* (Cambridge, Mass.: MIT Press, 1973). Discuses why Stalin did not believe Hitler would attack Russia; a study in psychological warfare and military and political intelligence.

Roberta Wohlstetter, *Pearl Harbor: Warning and Decision* (Palo Alto, Calif.: Stanford University Press, 1962). First-rate monograph.

Leni Yahil, *The Holocaust: The Fate of European Jewry, 1932–1945* (New York: Oxford University Press, 1990); Istvan Deak, Jan T. Gross, and Tony Judt, eds., *The Politics of Retribution: World War II and Its Aftermath* (Princeton, N.J.: Princeton University Press, 2000). Recent powerful works that concentrate on the effects of the Holocaust.

Sources

Noel Annan, *Changing Enemies: The Defeat and Regeneration of Germany* (New York: Harper Collins, 1995). Fascinating memoir of wartime spent in code-breaking, followed by service in the Occupation Government of Germany as the Bonn state was being created.

Hamilton Armstrong, *Chronology of Failure* (New York: Macmillan, 1940); "Pertinax" (André Géraud), *The Gravediggers of France* (Garden City, N.J.: Doubleday, 1944); Marc Bloch, *Strange Defeat*, reprint ed. (Darby, Pa.: Darby Books, 1981). Three perceptive studies of the French defeat of 1940.

Winston S. Churchill, *The Second World War*, 6 vols. (Boston: Houghton Mifflin, 1948–1953). Magisterial account of the war by a chief architect of Allied victory.

Charles de Gaulle, *The Complete War Memoirs* (New York: Simon and Schuster, 1940–1961). Beautifully written firsthand account of de Gaulle's own experiences.

Desmond Flower and James Reeves, eds., *The Taste of Courage: The War, 1939–1945* (New York: Harper and Row, 1960). Useful anthology of "war pieces."

Paul Fussell, *Wartime* (New York: Oxford University Press, 1990). Narrative, replete with quotations and extracts from sources.

Robert Gelletely, *The Gestapo and German Society* (New York: Oxford University Press, 1990). On racial policy and its implementation.

A. J. Liebling, ed., *The Republic of Silence* (New York: Harcourt, Brace, 1947). Excellent collection of materials pertaining to the French resistance movement.

Jeremy Noakes and Geoffrey Pridham, *Nazism: A Documentary Reader*, 4 vols. (Exeter, England: University of Exeter Press, 1983–98). Vols, 3 and 4 are particularly relevant to the Second World war period.

Esmonde M. Robertson, ed., *The Origins of the Second World War* (London: Macmillan, 1971). Documents and secondary sources on the controversial thesis of A. J. P. Taylor that Hitler was rational in his policy and had no "master plan" for war.

There are many additional memoirs of key figures in this great war. The following make a good beginning: Dwight D. Eisenhower, *Crusade in Europe*, reprint ed. (New York: Da Capo, 1977); Harry S. Truman, *Memoirs*, 2 vols. (Garden City, N.J.: Doubleday, 1958); Bernard Montgomery, *Memoirs*, reprint ed. (New York: Da Capo, 1982).

Index

CPSIA information can be obtained at www.ICGtesting.com
Printed in the USA
267613BV00003B/1/P